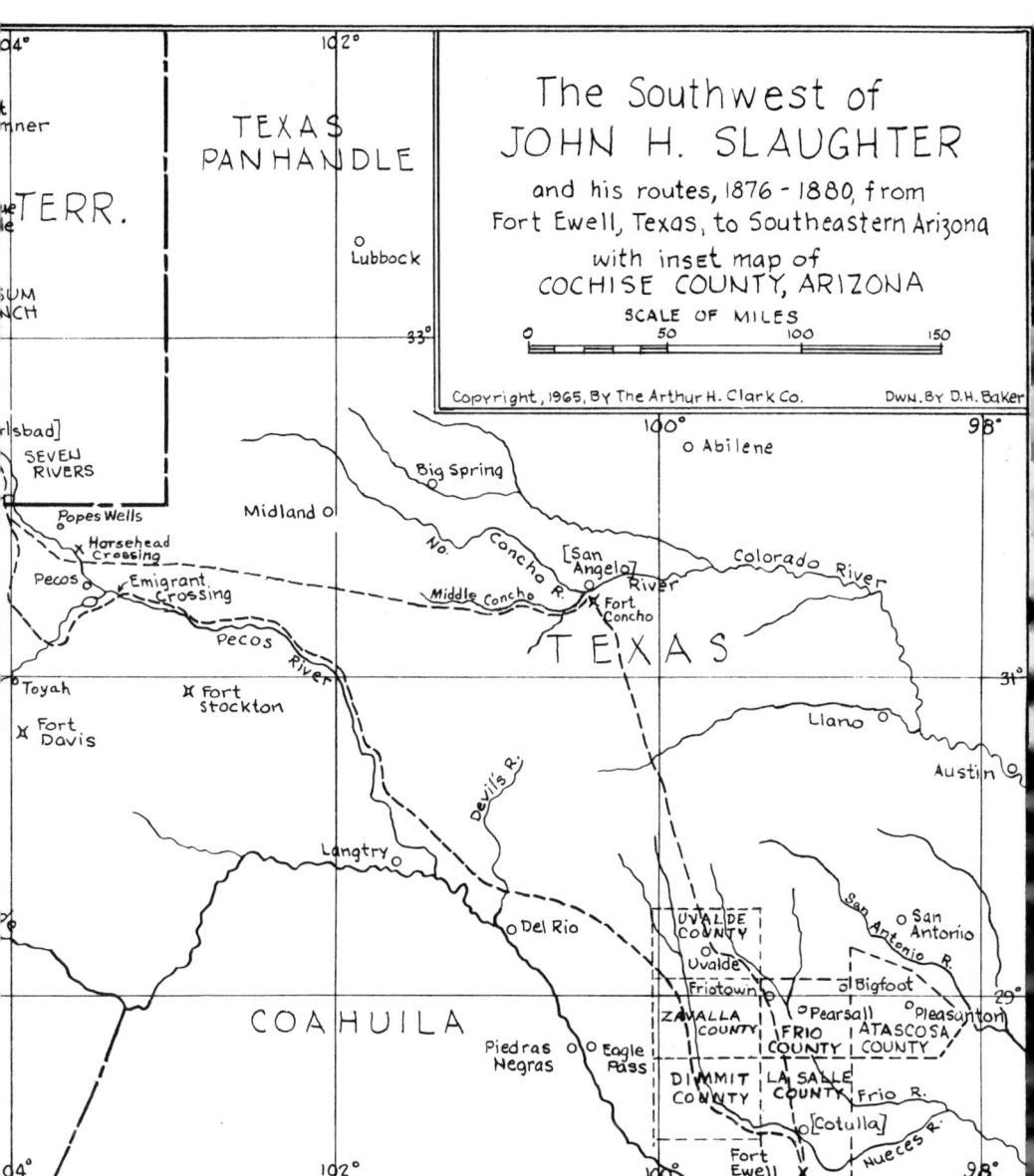

Western Frontiersmen Series
X

JOHN HORTON SLAUGHTER IN THE EARLY 1890s
A portrait in his duck-hunter's garb.

The Southwest of JOHN H. SLAUGHTER
1841-1922

Pioneer Cattleman and Trail-driver of Texas, the Pecos, and Arizona and Sheriff of Tombstone

by
Allen A. Erwin

THE ARTHUR H. CLARK COMPANY
Spokane, Washington
1997

COPYRIGHT © 1965, BY
THE ARTHUR H. CLARK COMPANY

All rights reserved, including the right to translate or reproduce this volume or parts thereof in any form or by any media

LIBRARY OF CONGRESS CATALOG CARD NUMBER 65-16512
ISBN 0-87062-278-1

Second printing, 1997

to
CAPTAIN BURTON C. MOSSMAN
of the Arizona Rangers –
last of the fine old-time Western lawmen
May his shadow never grow less

Contents

Foreword – the book, *by William McLeod Raine*	. . .	13
Foreword – the author, *by Ramon F. Adams*	. . .	15
Preface		21
1 Pioneer Heritage		27
2 Prelude to a Range Drama		35
3 Shaping a Cattle Empire		55
4 Beyond the Pecos		99
5 West of the Guadalupes		135
6 Territorial Apache Troubles		167
7 The Dutchman's Town		181
8 Bullets and Justice		213
9 Outlaws and Apaches		255
10 Business and Politics		269
11 Life on the San Bernardino		279
12 The Final Roundup		321
Bibliography		341
Epilogue		337
Index		349

Illustrations

John Horton Slaughter in the early 1890s	*frontispiece*
Ben Slaughter	51
Minerva Mabry Slaughter	51
William (Billy) Slaughter	52
Rock House of Charley Slaughter, near Friotown	69
Jim Speed	69
Wedding Certificate of John Slaughter and Eliza Harris	70
Jim East	103
McSween-Tunstall-Chisum Building	104
William James Chisum	121
Sheep Camp, Chavez Ranch in New Mexico	121
John H. Slaughter on "Nig," about 1919	122
Branding Time on the San Bernardino	155
John H. Slaughter at an Artesian Well	156
Cowboys who Worked for the CCC and for Slaughter	173
Captain Henry Ware Lawton	174
Jesse Fisher's Appointment as Special Deputy	223
Guns and Handcuffs used by Slaughter	224
Pancho Anderson and the Author	273
John H. Slaughter in 1907	273
Scene in Douglas, Arizona, 1903	274
Layout of the San Bernardino Ranch	278
John Slaughter Seated in his Favorite Rocker	291
John Slaughter and the Greene Boys	291
Adobe Schoolhouse on the San Bernardino Ranch	292
Cora Viola Slaughter and Addie	309
Eliza Merrill	309
Apache May	310
Clothing of Apache May	310
Re-recording of John Slaughter's Brand, 1919	327
John H. Slaughter at 80	328
John Slaughter in his Automobile	328
Map of the Southwest of John H. Slaughter	*endpapers*

Foreword — the book
by William MacLeod Raine

I have waited a long time for this book to be written, for John Slaughter, the famous little sheriff who cleaned the outlaws from Cochise County, Arizona, was not only one of the most fearless and efficient officers the Southwest has known, but also probably its most picturesque character. When he served notice to the bandits to "get out or be killed" he proved promptly that he meant it. He carried the law into the mesquite and drove the badmen from their nests in the hills.

It is fortunate that this story of John Slaughter has been assembled by devoting much time and money to gathering the facts of his life. This is an authentic biography of John Slaughter. Allen A. Erwin has researched for all the available material in books, manuscripts, newspapers, court records, libraries, and museums to present a complete picture of this audacious steely-eyed little man who tamed the wildest district in the West.

The book is much more than a tale of Slaughter's activities as a law officer. It shows how his life and that of his ancestors tie in with the histories of Texas, New Mexico and Arizona from the earliest days of American settlements in those regions. The Mexican and Civil Wars, the raids of the Kiowas, Comanches, and Apaches, cattle trail days, the land grants, in fact a picture of the development of this virgin terrain, all find a place in the book, because the Slaughters were so aggressively a part of the history of this region.

The book is appropriately dedicated to Burton C. Mossman, the old cattleman who organized and captained the

Arizona Rangers and did a remarkable job in doing much the same service for the territory as Slaughter had before him. "Cap" Mossman was the last of the fine old-time lawmen who put terror into the hearts of the outlaws.

No collector of western Americana can afford to miss this book.

Foreword — the author
by Ramon F. Adams

If ever a man who helped make our blazing western history deserves a published record of his life and deeds, it is John Slaughter. Since my late good friend William MacLeod Raine has written an introduction to this book — said to be his last piece of writing — I would like to say something about the author.

For many years I have wished some one would write this book, and now Allen Erwin, a conscientious student of western history, after many years of patient and exhaustive research, has put upon record the biography of this outstanding character.

I believe every reader would enjoy such a book more if he could learn something of the author, his background and the struggles he went through in gathering his material. So, laboring under this premise, I would like to let Mr. Raine tell you about the subject of the book while I tell you something about the man who wrote it.

I first met Allen Erwin in a bookstore in Dallas, Texas, during the early 1940s. At that time he had a radio program on Station WFAA of the Dallas Morning News. He was telling western stories and singing cowboy songs, and at the moment I met him in the bookstore he was searching for material. Suffering from kindred ailments, we became friends. After he left Dallas I did not see him again until the early 1950s when I ran across him in the lobby of the Santa Rita Hotel in Tucson, Arizona. I was there doing some research at the Arizona Pioneer Historical Society and he, with a lobbyful of other cowboys, was there to do some roughriding for the movies.

During our conversation he told me he was doing research on the life of John Slaughter between pictures, so you see he has spent many years at this task. Since I have learned how thorough he is, it is not surprising.

Allen was the youngest in a family of seven, born of French-Canadian ancestry. His father was a trapper, and Indian trader, later becoming a cowboy, making many trips down to Fort McLeod and Montana with cattle and horses. Then when news came of the gold strike in the Klondike he and another cowboy made a break for this excitement, but before getting there changed their minds. Mr. Erwin went to Winnipeg and there met the woman who was to become Allen's mother.

Later he moved to Saskatchewan before it became a province and there built a sod shanty, one with a partition in the center, one half being a horse stable, the other for family quarters. So you see Allen is somewhat of a pioneer himself. His early schooling was received in a one-room schoolhouse where he often had to spend the night because of sudden and severe blizzards and temperatures of forty below zero.

As a young horse wrangler he got his start as a cowboy, and being a fiddler of sorts, picked up some extra money playing for cowboy dances. During the years of his "growing up" period, he has followed such occupations as cowboy, trapper, prospector, country fiddler, section hand, railroad brakeman, hunter, farmer, sheepherder, wild horse catcher, dude wrangler, radio entertainer, song writer, recording artist, rodeo performer, watchman, policeman, motion picture cowboy, bellhop, elevator operator, agent, hobo, stable groom, horse trainer, treasure hunter, technical adviser, and others. Like many other writers, these varied modes of life have given him insight and experiences not obtained otherwise.

As a cowhand he has spent many years in Alberta, Saskatchewan, Oregon, Montana and Colorado working on such ranches as the 76, Bar U, CK, Circle, JHE, the Double O, Bell A, Lazy J, and many others. Like so many fiddle-footed cowboys he sometimes only spent a short time at each, that other side of the hill always calling.

During his travels throughout the West, especially in the Southwest, he heard so much about John Slaughter that he became more than just interested. He began searching out and reading every Arizona newspaper published between 1879 and 1922, and other newspapers which published articles about him after his death, such as the Bisbee *Review*. Articles and records concerning the Bank of Douglas, of which Slaughter was a member, were examined as well as the records of the Live Stock Board for the brands he had registered.

By now Allen's interest was so aroused he practically made it his one ambition to write a book about this fascinating character. He brought more tenacity into play now, for here was a work he loved. There was seemingly no end of research to be done as one lead directed him to another. Newspaper files of both Texas and New Mexico were examined; the court records of Cochise County, Arizona, such as deeds and inquests were delved into. The Lew Wallace Collection at Crawfordsville, Indiana, was where he found information of Slaughter's killing of Gallagher at South Springs, and other episodes of his life. Files of magazines such as the *Frontier Times, Arizona Highways* and others were studied, as well as old out-of-print books. The Witte Museum at Breakenridge Park, San Antonio, Texas, yielded records of some of Slaughter's cattle brands.

The General Administration Service in Washington and Senator Carl Hayden, of Arizona, were very helpful with such information, for instance, as the lieutenant's report to the adjutant, giving all details on the march after the Indians (said to be the Apache Kid's followers) who had the little Indian girl they called Apache May.

There was also a thorough examination of the records of the Texas counties of Bexar, Atascosa, La Salle, Frio, Live Oak, Dimmitt, Tom Green, Uvalde, Caldwell, Gonzales, Medina and McMullen as well as the newspaper files at Austin and San Antonio. He did not even pass up cemeteries where he thought some one was buried that he might find a date of death that might lead to an obituary notice in some newspaper which, in turn, would reveal some information. Books on geneology and family lineages were consulted, and members of the Slaughter family contributed all the information they could. Nothing was overlooked.

Numerous people were interviewed: nieces, nephews, and many others who knew John Slaughter. From Captain Henry Ware Lawton's daughter and grandson came the Lawton report when he was stationed at Fort Huachuca using the San Bernardino and Slaughter ranches during the campaign to bring about the surrender of Geronimo. These good people also supplied him with a marvelous collection of original photographs taken by Fly, the Tombstone photographer in 1886.

Much information was given him by the late Colonel Maurice Fulton, of Roswell, New Mexico, especially concerning Slaughter's arrest at Elk Springs by order of Lew Wallace, when Haskell Jones and his young son, John were arrested with Slaughter. Then followed interviews with the Jones brothers, and the information gathered from them was confirmed by newspaper reports. Mr. Erwin was fortunate enough to locate a sister of Slaughter's first wife in Texas as well as the family of Lease Harris, his father-in-law, also in Texas, from whom he gathered much material. In fact he interviewed people from all over Texas, New

Mexico, Arizona and California. If he heard of someone who had known Slaughter, he sought him out. A lead in Arizona might take him to Texas, and so he jumped from town to town, from state to state.

Like other researchers, he found that personal interviews were not always easy to get, nor dependable; that some were hostile and tried to set one upon the wrong track; and that others threatened a lawsuit if their names were mentioned. He ran into problems of people not wanting to give the information he sought for fear of something the family might not want to appear in print; some were leery about giving information which they thought might be of value, without them receiving compensation. Even some of the relatives gave him trouble, but these are dead now.

"I found that other writers doing research," he told me, "were not very cooperative. They seemed to feel that probably I was doing something they were contemplating doing themselves some day. However, I fixed my mind to the project, and it is not my nature to deviate come hell and high water. I knew what I was doing was preserving history, and there wasn't anything on the face of God's green earth that is more important.

"All my unpleasantness, however, was forgotten through the many fine folks I met. They made me feel that I was doing something worthwhile, and that there were still some fine folks in the world."

During his years of research he used every mode of transportation – horseback, bus, plane, train, even "by thumb," and when not so fortunate by "shank's mare." He went broke and borrowed, but never grew discouraged. Many were the times he went without food or shelter, a set ambition ever driving him on. Many times he became ill from exposure; he lost a 20-20 vision from eyestrain and suffered many other discouragements, but the greatest of all was the time when, while on another research trip, some one stole most of his material. This included volumes of photostats, memoirs, recordings, and other material which he had spent years gathering. All this would have made the average man give up, especially when some of it was material which could never be replaced.

The best way I can close this little foreword and express Allen's feeling for the handicaps and hardships he experienced in writing this bit of western history is in his own words when he told me:

"Now I'm sentimental and sensitive, and I feel it was these old-timers who suffered so that we could live in the fine style we do. They definitely should be commemorated. I do not feel the world owes me anything, but I do feel I have a duty to perform and that is to preserve the deeds of our forefathers, and I draw no line there, whether they be Eskimo, Indian or Pilgrim.

"This is a spiritual and religious obligation to our fellow man. So I feel my background gives me an understanding of what I am trying to accomplish. The contribution in dollars and cents is very small, but in respect to contributing something to having lived, I feel that this is one way of showing gratitude in some capacity that goes into understanding the reasons as to how we happen to have arrived upon the scene. My few talents are slanted toward preservation, construction, posterity and commemoration. John Slaughter is a mere small portion of that ambition. There is much to be done, much to be found and stored away for those to follow, so they might know the purpose for which we are here."

Nothing I might add could improve upon these sentiments.

Preface

John Slaughter was a man's man, in every sense of that word, strong, vigorous, with a high courage and quickness of wit to match his varied career, but with a gentleness and mischievous sense of humor that endeared him to women of character and loveliness. As a Civil War veteran, Texas Ranger, scout, pathfinder, trail-driver, cattleman, Sheriff, and member of the Arizona Legislature, his life spanned one of the toughest eras in the history of the American frontier West. He mingled with most of the well-known characters of the Wild West, from Big Foot Wallace, Sam Bass, Wild Bill Hickok, Ben Thompson, King Fisher, to Billy the Kid, and on down.

He was to know two happy marriages, one with a lady of beauty and kindness, and a courage almost unbelievable in one who was not physically robust. The other, with a lovely, high-spirited girl who gladly placed her life in his hands, traveling the high road of adventure with him, without a backward look. Both fought vigorously against strong parental objections to marry the man of her choice, and never did either regret that choice, though it meant facing hardships that would have caused weaker women to quail.

Quiet and unassuming, John Slaughter went about his affairs without outward emotion, whether the mission he was about to perform was coming to the rescue of a child or paying a visit to a dangerous enemy. Never was he too busy to stop and talk to a little tot, regardless of creed or color, and to buy it generous gifts. It would be very difficult for a stranger seeing him at one of these moments to recognize him as the man who sent terror into the hearts of the lawless. Whenever he heard of a destitute family or child in need, he was first to offer his assistance. On Sundays his ranch resembled a school yard as he entertained his young friends.

He appreciated his friends, and his loyalty was deep and true. He judged a man by what he was and what he could do; nothing less impressed John Slaughter. He had a large ranch table, specially made for guests, and hardly a Sunday passed without it being well filled. He never turned a hungry man from his door.

One of his most prized possessions was the horse "Buck Pius" which his friend, Captain Burton C. Mossman, to whom this book is dedicated, gave him when he retired as captain of the Arizona Rangers.

Erect as a cavalryman, Slaughter sat his horse, with feet forward in the stirrups, comfortably at ease. He kept three weapons on his saddle, a six-shooter, a repeating shotgun, and a Henry rifle. He was a man suited for the country in which he lived and looked a part of it: a man of the winds, the soil, the vast open country and the heavens above him.

He was always reluctant to tell of the trials and tribulations he had endured, or the good fortune which followed. Inscrutable, brilliant and witty, he accomplished his purpose with extraordinary effectiveness. Only an army ever prevented him from going about his regular duties. He lost three fortunes, and was grieved almost beyond endurance at the tragic passing of his beloved first wife, and two of their children; yet he rallied to amass a fourth fortune and find forty-three years of happiness with his second wife.

His Mexican cowboys called him "Don Juan," the Yaqui sharecroppers addressed him as "El Petron," and those who knew him well affectionately called him "Uncle John."

Though not a large man physically, his brilliance and ability to come quickly to the heart of a situation made him a man to reckon with. His footsteps on the sands of time were big and powerful, and a beacon to men who followed.

Prophetic indeed were his last wishes, and quite in keeping with a man whose whole being surged with life and who always wanted to be in the thick of things. He told his wife he did not wish to be buried in Tombstone, as it would become a ghost town; that he wished to be buried in Douglas, where the glory of the West would remain forever.

Satisfied was he that the Power that had guided him to safety so often in his life would now take him to pastures that are always green.

Much help and kind assistance was given in the assembling of the materials for this book – a task which could not have been accomplished without such aid. The bibliography lists many who granted interviews and contributed through correspondence. But a word of particular appreciation is due to:

Senator Carl Hayden of Arizona, for his efforts to supply needed material from the Library of Congress.

Mulford Winsor, director of the Arizona State Library and Archives, for allowing me to search through records and newspapers in that collection.

Eleanor B. Sloan, secretary, and her staff, as well as Mrs. George Kitt, past secretary, of the Arizona Pioneers Historical Society.

Mr. and Mrs. J. H. Macia of Tombstone, for their hospitality and all the leads they gave me to research.

Uncle Bill Hattich, of Los Angeles, California, for his stories on early Tombstone.

Mrs. Ella Robinson, librarian of the Southwest Museum, for use of the fine Arizona material in that collection.

Frank Cullen Brophy of the Bank of Douglas, for checking his collection for clues needed to continue my research.

Robert N. Mullin, my long-time friend, who has the finest material on Billy the Kid and on Tombstone.

The staff of the State Archives in Austin, for helping check points in Texas history.

Dr. Harold Cook of Agate, Nebraska, who vouched for his father's Texas frontier experiences.

My good friend William Keleher, who has authored the finest books on New Mexico local history.

Burton C. Mossman, of Roswell, New Mexico, for his long talks of his days with the Arizona Rangers.

Mike Cunningham of Bisbee, the last of its real oldtimers.

William J. Chisum, of Los Angeles, for helping to locate Barney Gallagher's grave on the old Chisum ranch.

Mrs. Lillian East Bouldin, of Douglas, sister of Jim East, for giving me a first-hand account of the Texas Panhandle.

Charles Lockling, of Bisbee, for singing me the song of Tombstone outlaws, so it can be preserved with early Arizona lore.

Pauline Garrett, of Las Cruces, New Mexico, daughter of the late sheriff, for her help.

Bill and Sam Jones and to George Coe, for first-hand details on phases of the Lincoln County War.

Nick Hughes, Jr., of Prescott, Arizona, for his boyhood remembrance of John Ringo and the Gayleyville crowd.

Ed Echols, of Tucson, for his fine stories of when he rode for the Jake Scheerer cow outfit.

George D. Stephens, of Douglas, for telling of his trail rides with John Slaughter.

Colonel Maurice Fulton of Roswell, for acquainting me more thoroughly with New Mexico history.

And to all the Slaughter relatives, and friends of the sheriff, for their many contributions and suggestions. The bibliography at the end of this volume indicates many who assisted with interviews and correspondence.

The Southwest of
John H. Slaughter

I

Pioneer Heritage

John Horton Slaughter saw the West grow from a scrawny infant to a robust giant. His cradle had been rocked in the midst of a lawless section of the country, where violence and hardship brought about a reign of terror which extended from Louisiana all the way to Arizona territory. Only a man with a firm understanding of human nature and with the will to stay alive could have endured it, and then be able to die with his boots off. John Slaughter was such a man.

A pioneering spirit in man may often be hereditary. Slaughters were adventurers, trail blazers and empire builders long before the first member bearing that name set foot in America. The burning desire to pioneer seems to have been natural for this hardy strain of people. To trace the origin of the Slaughter family in Germany and England is not the purpose here, but a bit about John Slaughter's American ancestry seems in order.

Branching out from the Old Dominion and leaning toward the South and later the West, we can say they were Southerners and Westerners to begin with. In the year 1620 the Slaughter ancestors came from England, to settle in Virginia.[1] Doctor Robert Slaughter was granted land near the banks of the James River that year. The coat of arms of the Slaughter family is found on a seal to a bond posted by William Slaughter, who had been made sheriff in 1685. The document showing this early family's heraldry had been

---

[1] A genealogy report on early families in America pertaining to the name of Slaughter, compiled by Dr. Rosalie Slaughter Morton, March 12, 1952. A copy in possession of George Slaughter, Roswell, N.Mex.

examined and confirmed in Essex County Courthouse in Virginia, as mentioned in Burke's "Landed Gentry," showing the location and place of origin of the Slaughter clan before coming to America. The family crest coincides with that of Slaughters living in counties Gloucester, Hereford and Worcester in England, thus showing that the colonists bearing the name were British.[2]

In the early deeds and records of Virginia we find the first mention of a John Slaughter when he took out a patent for land on May 30, 1635. Doctor Slaughter had married Frances Ann Jones, and they had three sons: Robert, Francis and Thomas. The latter, never too active in civic affairs, broke his family ties quite early and moved to Caroline County, and little is known about him or his descendants. His brothers gave momentum to the drive which put into motion their pioneering attributes. Francis was, however, the most prominent and active. The oldest manuscript on record in Culpeper County, Virginia, is the register of St. Mark's Parish. The parish was established by an act of the assembly in 1730, and had preceded Culpeper County which came into being in 1734. Up until 1734-35 the Parish had been in Spottsylvania County. Robert and Francis were the first church wardens of St. Mark's Parish, chosen by the vestry in 1731.[3]

From the family of Doctor Robert Slaughter, came a Revolutionary War soldier, Walter Slaughter, from whom we trace the direct lineage to John Horton Slaughter. From

[2] A genealogy on Slaughters of Culpeper County, Virginia, by C. B. Garrett, in possession of George Slaughter, Roswell, N.Mex., made from a copy of the original. Also a letter dated Feb. 5, 1901, to Col. C. C. Slaughter, Ft. Worth, Texas, from William Austin Slaughter, Mount Holly, New Jersey. Another letter with fine information on Slaughter families written by Janice Slaughter, June 10, 1940. A good account of Slaughter families has been written and compiled by Jane Griffith Keys.

[3] Probably the best thing done on early Slaughter families in America is found in a book, entitled *St. Mark's Parish,* by Reverend Philip Slaughter, a copy of which is in the Virginia State Library.

the very beginning it had become a custom for each of the families to name their children with the same given names as their predecessors, thus adding confusion. Several John Slaughters appeared in the family lineage research.

Walter Slaughter was farming in Anson County, North Carolina, when the Revolutionary War broke out. He had come there from Culpeper County, Virginia. He immediately enlisted in Captain Thomas Wade's company of light horsemen, as Wade had also been from Anson County. Walter's fighting was short – he was captured by the British. After the war he returned to North Carolina where he married Miss Margaret Webb. They gave issue to six children.[4]

During the 1790s, Walter and his family moved to Washington County, Georgia. He settled between the Ogeechee and Oconee Indians on a disputed strip long under bitter arbitration that had been ceded to the chief of the Creeks in August, 1790. The white man had not taken over complete ownership of the land when Walter settled there. In due time peace came, and Walter remained there to raise his family, spending the rest of his days in Georgia. It was now up to Walter's children to carry on in the Slaughter tradition.

With a good background in plantation operations, Walter's two sons, John and William, would seek a new horizon in search of prosperity. During the War of 1812, John was 27, the eldest of the two brothers. They set out for Mississippi, settling finally in Hinds County. John soon married a Miss Goodson, and William married Nancy Moore. This area had been close to the Natchez-Nashville road and had been settled quite rapidly. This had been a part of the Choctaw

---

[4] A genealogical report by correspondence from Minnie Slaughter Veal, a granddaughter of Rev. George Webb Slaughter, written to Allen A. Erwin in April 1950.

cession. John and William were hard-working and industrious. Their whole purpose in life seemed to be in raising a family, breeding fine livestock, and working in the fields. They were humble, simple, hardy people who loved adventure and pioneering.

John's marriage to Miss Goodson bore them five sons: Benjamin, Solomon, Reuben, Owen and Simeon.[5] Benjamin, the eldest, was born on Christmas Eve, 1813, in Hinds County. He was always called Ben, and in his later years "Uncle Ben." As customary, the oldest son shouldered much of the family responsibility, and therefore Ben had never seen the inside of a schoolroom, and had little knowledge of reading, writing or arithmetic. What he lacked in schooling had been made up in knowing livestock and the planting of crops. He was an excellent carpenter and handyman, with a thorough knowledge of the great outdoors. His manners were coarse, his language was rough, and his temper flared quickly. Though a small man in stature, he was well proportioned and could do the work of a man twice his size. Ben was largely responsible for the success of his brothers, and it was from these meager beginnings in Mississippi that the Slaughters of this branch of the family sprang to prominence. William's marriage to Nancy Moore bore them three sons, George Webb, Sam Moore, and William R. They followed in the same pursuits as Ben's family, and owned and operated a plantation in Hinds County, Mississippi.

The Slaughters remained quite content in Mississippi, and had in many respects flourished over their neighbors. They kept a large group of slaves to work the cotton and tobacco crops, and had enjoyed living the lives of successful planters. But Ben had always been restless and had been joshed about his Indian blood and his nomad inclinations.

---
[5] *Ibid.*

His lack of formal education and his rough mannerisms were a handicap to him on many an occasion. Nevertheless, his ambition overshadowed these handicaps, and drew the attention of Miss Minerva Mabry of Tuscaloosa, Alabama, who also lacked formal schooling but was well trained in gracious Southern manners. Her people were of Scotch-Irish extraction and were approximately on the same social level and prominence as the Slaughters.

If there were any differences between Ben and Minerva it had been lost in love. On February 19, 1834, they were married. For this occasion Ben had built a house on his father's land, and here they laid plans to raise their family. George Webb and Ben had been very close as first cousins and neighbors, but Ben had been envious when George left without him for Coahuila-Texas in 1829. Ben, having been obligated to his father at the time, could not leave and, despite word of George's exciting exploits in Texas, he settled down to work the plantation.

Stephen Austin's colonization of Texas by Americans provided a strong attraction to Ben, and many of his Southern friends had gone to the Mexican province to start anew. Though he was becoming well established in Mississippi, Ben yearned for an excuse to try his fortune in Texas.[6] The opportunity was provided when the call went out for volunteers to repel Santa Anna's threat to the security of the Americans in Texas.

Ben prepared a pack mule with supplies, and mounted on another, he set out for Texas in the spring of 1836. His route took him through Sabine Parish, Louisiana, past old Fort Jessup, traveling on the Natchitoches-San Antonio Road. Ben's trip was slow and circuitous, as he visited the sparsely inhabited settlements, all the while asking about the lands.

---

[6] J. Marvin Hunter, *Trail Drivers Of Texas*, (1925) pp. 200-202; also *Who's Who in America* 1909. C. C. Slaughter, Jr. (by interview) a letter to Wynona Jones, Lubbock, Tex. from Bob Slaughter, Dallas, April 25, 1928.

By the time he reached San Antonio the battle of the Alamo was over, and Ben went on to Gonzales and then to the San Jacinto battleground. He arrived in time for the last days of the celebrating of Houston's victory. Here he met a jubilant George Webb, who had played a major role in this drama.

George Webb had been selected as courier by Sam Houston, carrying messages back and forth through the enemy lines to William B. Travis at the Alamo. The message to abandon the Alamo had quickly changed to "Remember the Alamo," as a final stand was made against Santa Anna's forces at San Jacinto. Though Ben was disappointed at not being able to fight, he was pleased at what he had seen and heard from the American settlers. His decision was to go back home, and make arrangements to move to the new Republic. With the accomplishment of Texas independence, Ben remained for several weeks in Sabine County, then returned home with the same two mules he had used to make the journey to Coahuila-Texas.[7]

His son, William James, who had been born November 9, 1835, was now six months old, and Ben voiced his opinion the new babe looked more like his mother than his father. In fact, none of his children looked like him except his youngest son, John, whom Ben had named for his own father. It was four years before Ben finally was ready to move to Texas. Not until Charles Holmes, a second child, was born on June 17, 1839, did Ben finally have his way. By the time Ben had all his wagons loaded, his livestock gathered, and household supplies, seed, grain, and implements together, the oldest son was going on 6 years of age, Charles was 2 years old, and a third son was on the way.[8]

---

[7] Interviews with Artie Slaughter Roberts, daughter of Billy Slaughter, at Friotown, Texas, November-December 1950.

[8] Interviews with Fannie Slaughter Lucas and Sallie Slaughter, daughters of Charles Holmes Slaughter, at Carlsbad, 1950-1952.

Ben had made a two-wheeled conveyance on the order of a Red River ox-cart, with boards across for seats, big enough to accommodate Minerva, William (whom she called Billy), and Charles, with enough standing room for himself to drive a team of mules. The floor had been prepared with straw, covered with quilts, so his family could rest. The top was covered to keep out the rain and wind. It was fairly comfortable, and they averaged some fourteen miles a day.

The Slaughter party arrived in the early summer of 1841 in Sabine Parish, Louisiana. From nearby Fort Jessup had come the news of depredations being committed by the lawless element on both sides of the Sabine. Then, too, Minerva had taken ill over the long journey and Ben decided it best to stop until his wife gave birth to their third child.[9]

Stopping east of the Sabine River which had shaped the boundary line between the New Republic of Texas and French-American Louisiana, Ben persuaded a neighboring Mississippian, living near the village of Many, to allow Ben to share-crop with him. From here Ben took some of his hired help and crossed the ferry into Sabine County, Texas, where he built a log cabin and a shelter for his milk cows and chickens. On his previous trip, he had already taken up land along the waters of Huston Bayou, a tributary of the Sabine, where George Webb had suggested this to be a good location. In the meantime, a vegetable and grain crop had been planted in Louisiana by the slaves Ben had brought with him from Hinds County.

Minerva received the greatest birthday present of her life when the new baby arrived on October 2, 1841, just one day before Minerva's birthday. He was baptized by the Methodist minister and given the name of John Horton Slaughter. Ben had hoped for a son and gotten his wish. This trio

[9] *Ibid.*

of boys would be all the males born to Ben and Minerva, for all of the other children were girls. As the boys grew to manhood they would become known as the Slaughter brothers of Texas. They would comprise the Slaughter family of South Texas, and George Webb's boys would comprise the Slaughters of north and west Texas. The late Will Rogers simply had summed them up as "The Cattle Slaughters of Texas."

When young John was only three months old, the move to Texas, which Ben had long hoped for, was completed. John never boasted of Louisiana as his birthplace, and when he rose to become a prominent cattleman in Texas, he resented being joshed about having been born east of the Sabine. As he saw the beginning of the cow business, he felt it was a part of Texas and his position put him in the same category. However, John's older brother, Charley, later went back to Louisiana from Arizona and died near his younger brother's birthplace.

When John first began to walk he was playing on the biggest stage of broad plains in the land. The people who would lift him on their knees were the Daniel Boones and Davey Crocketts of that era. They were frontiersmen, Indian fighters, traders, plantation operators, scouts, mingled with thieves, rustlers, and border ruffians. His was to be the type of kindergarten schooling that would be appropriate in shaping his destiny. It would mold a character fitted to frontier needs, with an education of the great outdoors, and an understanding of human nature no schoolbook could teach him. This summation of knowledge would fall under the heading of an "Unwritten Code of the West," and would decide the difference between remaining alive or perhaps being buried on Boot Hill. The experiences of his later life would prove the value of the code to his longevity.

2

Prelude to a Ranch Drama

General William Henry Harrison, ninth president of the United States, had adopted a log cabin for the symbol of his party which was appropriate enough for the times. He had been born not too far from where the first Slaughters had settled in America along the James River in Virginia. He had spent much of his time in the West, having endured many hardships and physical labor. His was an understanding from experience, and this made him sympathetic with the situation that confronted the settlers of the new republic of Texas. His platform promised them a brighter day, and his wisdom and leadership was respected by the pioneer.

One month after taking oath of office, the new president died. In accordance with the provisions of the Constitution, the vice-president became his successor. On April 6, 1841, the oath of office was administered to John Tyler, also a Virginian. Under his administration a great deal of opposition was shown by northern states because of the issues of slavery extension, and the trend toward war with Mexico in the acquisition of Texas as a state in the Union.

On the last day of his official term as President, he finally saw his dream come true when on March 3, 1845, Congress passed a resolution setting the stage for the admission of Texas to the Union. This, then, would change the whole concept of what once was Mexico's most unpopulated possession. Ben Slaughter had calculated progress was on the way, and he had made his move at the right time.

George Webb Slaughter, now a Texas resident for 12 years, had come to Coahuila-Texas in 1829. He had become a successful freighter between Louisiana and the Mexican Province. He had acquired a knowledge of the era on both sides of the Sabine, and had known the river crossings. Ben had taken his advice and used Ryan's ferry crossing when he moved his family and wagons across. After Ben settled on Huston Bayou, he used Gaines' Ferry near present Pendleton. Nearby Sabinetown was also an important well-known port of entry.

The Sabine played an early part in Texas history, and the river not only drained the area of such tributaries as Boregas, Palo Goucho, Patroon, and Housing Creeks, but had become a commercial stream for river-boat navigation as well.[1] Barges had transported cotton, grain, lumber, household supplies, in addition to sheep, goats, cattle, hay, seed, hardware and other commodities to stock general stores and equip the settlers with their needs. Those who had light boats and skiffs visited one another along the stream, at the same time using them for fishing. Sabine County had many Mexican China trees, and a variety of foliage jutting out from its hilly red sandy soil. The pine-clad flats of the flood plains provided a shelter for the corn and cotton growers, whose land became a patchwork of small cleared-away sections.

It was a far cry from the well tilled soil of Ben's Hinds County home. He loved to hunt and fish, and work his plot of ground, but it was really not what he had wished for. Still it did provide the beginning of what appeared to be an opportunity to do well.

George Webb Slaughter had already begun to feel the wheels of progress turning. He had been a soldier, freighter, had carted Sam Houston's legal library from Nacodoches to Houston-town, had been active as an Indian fighter and stock raiser, and had been ordained a minister.[2] Ben was far

---
[1] Benjamin Lundy, *The Life, Travels and Opinions of Benjamin Lundy*, p. 115.

behind his cousin in activity and recognition in Texas. His time would come, however, and his son John would carry on in the Slaughter tradition and keep the name going in the pages of history.

George Webb had married Miss Sarah Mason of North Carolina and had begun raising a family. One of his sons was C. C. Slaughter, who would do for George Webb what John would do for his father, Ben. Both their names one day would be honored in the halls of the Trail Drivers' Association of Texas, while George Webb would be commemorated in the Alamo along with the names of Crockett, Bowie and Travis for his deeds during the siege.

It seemed wherever the Slaughters settled they were amongst Indians. Some were peaceful, but most of them hostile. That is what both Ben and George found when they came to Texas. George set out to do something about ridding the country of this menace, and had captained a ranger company to reinforce General Rusk and his men on the Neches to the west. In this campaign, the Cherokees under Chief Bowls had made a stand to discourage white settlement. These Texas pioneers had fought Indians before they crossed the waters of the Sabine, and the Indians were meeting with a stubborn foe accustomed to Indian warfare. The Cherokee, augmented by the fierce Comanche, would eventually bring every settler in the area to bear arms. But the Indians would remain for many moons, and a dozen presidents would have served the nation before peace would be achieved.

Of the earlier counties to see much unrest from trouble

---

[2] Mary Whatley Clarke, "Early Cattle King Headed Association," *The Cattleman.*

George Slaughter got the Rio Hondo Claim No. 127 covering the S ½ of SW ¼, Sect. 34 and SE ¼ Sect. 33, T. 6 N. R. 13 West and lying near the Sabine River in Sabine Parish, Louisiana. Application for confirmation of this claim was made April 13, 1823. State of Louisiana, State Land Office, Baton Rouge. Rio Hondo Claim 127.

within their borders were Sabine and Shelby. During the time Texas was under Mexican ownership, border ruffians along both sides of the Sabine carried on in a disgraceful manner against one another. When independence came Shelby had a mixture of smugglers, counterfeiters, promoters, gamblers, murderers, and highwaymen, and illicit practices of all sorts went on.

Lawlessness had had its roots deeply imbedded in the region when Slaughters came there. As far back as 1806 a Neutral Ground Agreement, a sort of "no man's land," had been under scrutiny by American and Spanish military officials, and both countries had recognized this area skirting the Sabine as a danger zone. Those who lived there or dared trespass, made their own laws. The slave trade and dishonesty in land disposal deals resulted in further lawlessness.

In 1842 two factions sprang up in Shelby County, both pretending their way of law enforcement was the most practical and just. They called themselves the "Regulators" and "Moderators." In reality they were made up of hot-tempered men, riding under the guise of vigilanteism. They now needed something to climax their intentions to carry out their reign of mob terror.

Then a criminal, Charles Jackson, murdered a respected citizen named Joseph Goodbread over sale of a slave. The factions took separate stands over this and trouble between them flared. But the main friction between the two factions was over fraudulent land traffic which went on in Harrison County as well as Shelby, the situation resulting from forgery of land certificates. It was necessary for the General Land Office to send out a traveling land board to investigate and examine all titles taken up in each county, in order to determine whether or not such titles could be legally patented. This investigation and the frustration it brought on, in addition to the curbing of the land shark, sparked a miniature civil war. Regulators and moderators came to grips and the feuds which developed in these two counties made it necessary for President Houston to send his militiamen to the troubled area to restore order.

Sabine County, with its two unruly neighbors of Harrison and Shelby to the north, could not help but feel the friction this had caused. People had developed a scowl of hatred, feeling insecure over the lands they had thought were rightfully theirs. But Texas was vast and land on the whole was dirt cheap. Its appraisal and worth had been judged by the length of settlement in a given area. Anglo-Americans were sprinkled between the Nueces and Sabine Rivers in a line with San Antonio and Austin, and northward toward Waco and the Red River. While in reality this was still wilderness, it was to the pioneer a margin between the untamed lands and civilization.[3] Therefore, settlement was attracted to this oblong region. The constitution promised all heads of families who had reached Texas before March 2, 1836, forty-six hundred and five acres of land, and an additional seventy-one acres above this amount for single men.

This attractive offer was extended to all who had reached Texas before August 1, 1836, and those who had received an honorable discharge from the army before December 14, 1837. George Slaughter qualified for any of these requirements. Ben, having returned to Mississippi, did not seek claim to any such land grants.

In 1839 the Texas Congress had passed a "homestead law," designed to stimulate the growth of settlement. It offered the settler protection by assuring him that none of his chattels could be confiscated to satisfy a debt. After Texas gained its independence, publicity extremely over-

---

[3] See William Ransom Hogan, *The Texas Republic: a social and economic history* for a good all-around picture of this period.

exaggerated the potential of Texas at this early date. Unhappy people who had experienced the panic of 1837 in the United States, and disturbances on the political scene in European countries, heard of this Utopia and were willing to take a gamble. Consequently, more settlements sprang up, pushing back the frontiers. An estimated seven thousand came to Texas using every means of transportation, between the late 1830s and the 1850s.

When Ben came to Texas, land was selling for as little as fifty cents per acre. The public domain seemed boundless and the horizon was the limit for a cow or horse to graze. An act of the Texas Congress, approved January 17, 1843, gave a sizable parcel of land to newcomers. Unconditional headrights comprising 320 acres had been granted. Ben's had been taken out on Huston Bayou, six miles southeast of Hemphill. In a speculative mood, Ben sold it to the man through whom the Bayou received its name. It was bought by A. Huston for $100, on March 26, 1844. Then Ben was granted an additional unconditional headright on June 1, 1846, under the same act, of another 320 acres.[4] The latter was located also in Sabine County ten miles distant from Milan. As a favor to his neighbor, James S. Ogden, he disposed of it for only $30. It was plain to see he had no intention of remaining in Sabine County.

Perhaps Sabine County offered a first step in the right direction for Southerners. Always where there are ports and navigable streams there is activity. Ben soon learned that this was not the location of his choice. He felt a certain priority and was trying to make up his mind which way to go. Minerva helped him make up his mind, as what she was most concerned about was a place to educate her children.

---

[4] By act of the Texas Congress, January 4, 1839, benefits of headrights were extended to all emigrants who should arrive in the Republic before January 1, 1840. On condition that he and his family would remain in Texas for three years, every household head was entitled to 640 acres.

Ben and his wife, Minerva, were not alone among the Texas pioneers who were illiterate. They did realize that a new era was blossoming on the frontier, and that it was a matter of good sense at least to have a minimum schooling. When Frederick L. Olmstead visited Texas in 1856 he observed that in the eastern part of Texas hardly once did he see a book or newspaper.[5]

Between the late 1850s and 1870s a vast change in education and learning swept the country. With the influx of various nationalities, several foreign tongues were being spoken. J. M. Morphis, an authority on Texas, heard quotations of such well-known writers as Moore, William Shakespeare, Robert Burns, and Byron soon after the Civil War. This was a sign of progress, but it also meant what once was a thinly populated area was diminishing rapidly in freedom of the public domain. Still there was ample space for the stockmen to graze their herds for a few more years, until the era of barbed wire fences would intervene. It would only then be necessary for cattlemen such as the Slaughters to cast an eye once again to the still unsettled parts of the territories of Arizona and New Mexico.

Matthew Caldwell was a Kentuckian and had reached Texas by way of Missouri. He had distinguished himself by participating in several Indian campaigns and was noted for his coolness and bravery. In 1833 he set out on horseback to Texas, crossing the Red River at Natchitoches, following the old Natchitoches-San Antonio Road which crossed Sabine County.

Here he became one of the leading figures in his section of the country. When a convention was called at Washington on the Brazos, March 1, 1836, he represented his district. He had joined Mr. Blount and Mr. Parmer, two other delegates to the conference. He then moved from Sabine County to Gonzales County.

---

[5] Frederick Law Olmstead, *Journey Through Texas* (New York, 1857) p. 365.

In 1838-1839 Caldwell commanded a company of rangers. In the next couple of years he had many a bloody encounter with the Indians. The historic "council house fight" would have an indirect bearing on what was to be John Slaughter's childhood playground. Appropriately enough, as if to condition him for his experiences with the Apaches in far away Arizona Territory, this had to do with Indians. The Council was held in San Antonio in March 1840, between Comanche and Texas Commissioners. Soldiers had captured some of the Indians and had them in custody as a retaliatory measure for white captives held prisoners by the Indians.

An exchange of prisoners was one of the reasons for the powwow. The Indians, many of them squaws, had concealed knives and tomahawks under their blankets. At a given signal they were to leap on their captives to conduct a surprise massacre. Twelve Chiefs, sixty-five of their warriors, and some squaws were killed in the melee. This set off one of the largest Indian attacks ever to have been sent against the white settlements. The Comanche joining with the Kiowa, numbering well over a thousand strong, bedecked in war paint and mounted on fiery ponies, swooped mercilessly down along the Guadalupe Valley, dealing out the most relentless of depredations. Screaming and waving their blood-stained tomahawks they sacked Linville, struck at Cuero and Victoria, plundering and killing as they rode, leaving a swath of destruction.

Then the Chiefs pointed in the direction of Lockhart, and once again the cry of revenge filled the lowlands, striking terror into the hearts of the defenseless people. At Linville a runner had been sent on ahead, passing the warning. By the time the Indians hit Plum Creek on the outskirts of Lockhart, they were met head-on by Captain Matthew Caldwell and Colonel Edward Burleson, commanding a crack group of seasoned fighters who had volunteered to strike back and put the redman to flight. In battle the Indians, superb horsemen as they were, held out for a while, but the deadly fire of these volunteers compelled them to retreat to the west.[6]

For years afterwards, Plum Creek area attracted hobby hunters gathering arrowheads and Indian weapons. This battle was staged where Ben Slaughter had decided to move. It had been a headright granted to Jeremiah Roberts. As a playground for Billy, Charley and John, it must have been a childhood inspiration to follow in the footsteps of Matthew Caldwell. And later the Slaughter boys would see plenty of Indian fighting.

Lockhart and the surrounding area were picturesque. Oak, walnut, live oak, and cedar covered about a third of the area. Rich prairie loam intermingled with sand on a slightly rolling plain, leveling off to a flat surface with a mixture of good grass ideal to meet the needs of farmer or stock raiser. This was enough to convince Ben that this was the ideal place.[7] In Sabine County the trouble over land titles, unpleasant neighbors, and with places elsewhere showing more progress, plus the war clouds brewing across the Mexican border, had helped prod Ben on to richer pastures. Moisture was always an asset, and the Lockhart area had it. Though beautiful as it was, it took on the name of "hog

---

[6] Matthew Caldwell, affectionately called "Old Paint," was born on March 8, 1798, moved with his parents from the Blue Grass State to Missouri Territory in 1818, fought Indians in Western Missouri, and went on horseback to Natchitoches in 1833. After Plum Creek, he commanded a company in the 1841 Santa Fe Expedition, was taken prisoner by the Mexicans, and released the next year to return to Gonzales. That September, he commanded 200 men against General Adrian Woll who had taken San Antonio. Too early this doughty warrior died at Gonzales, December 28, 1842. See Sam Houston Dixon, *The Men Who Made Texas Free*, pp. 81-84.

[7] A neighbor at Plum Creek, Joseph Barnett, had come from Ben's Mississippi in 1848 and the next year settled near Lockhart. For three years Barnett and his wife and 14 children lived in a small log cabin with no floor while he slowly prospered and finally built two log houses with floors of boards brought from La Grange. Like Ben, he dealt in cattle. *History of Southwest Texas*, (1907) p. 377.

wallow." A population count showed 4,088 whites and 1,381 negroes while Slaughters lived there. Livestock was estimated at 19,656 head of cattle, and 4,000 head of horses between 1846 and 1857 in Caldwell County. Unimproved lands were selling by 1857 for $2 to $5 per acre, and improved lands for $9 per acre.[8]

The town was well sheltered with fine specimens of live oaks, their branches laden with green moss. It was described as a small frontier hamlet with a sprinkling of log houses here and there, when Ben arrived. One of the town's most influential men, who deserves a great deal of recognition for its growth, was Edgar Huntley Rogan. No name is more respected and linked with the early development of Lockhart than his. He brought the first photographic equipment to Lockhart, and took the first daguerreotypes taken of the people and buildings, including family portraits of the Slaughter family. In later life he became a judge in Caldwell County. Lockhart was a great deal like the villages in Hinds County, and reminded the Slaughters of their origin. The open prairie, dotted with the mossy Longhorn, opened the dream of their future. Rolling gently, it stretched just to the west and south of the town, and nearby were the wells known as Lockhart Springs, forming a semi-circle in the surrounding hills. Twenty in number, these natural fountains supplied the settlers with good water. Soon a fair hotel with glass windows, but no heat, had risen.

These were the simple scenes that John Slaughter first remembered. Corn, cotton and cattle could make a people contented. The ancient Israelites may have yearned for milk and honey, but maize was the basic frontier food to Texans of Slaughter's youth, and they were as satisfied as if it had been manna. Corn might be toasted, boiled, or fried, grated into meal for sweet bread, popped, roasted or broiled. Corn-

---

[8] See *Texas Almanac*, 1857 (Galveston, 1856) p. 58.

meal mush was the children's chief dish, but hoecake and johnnycake were better treats for them. Milk and honey were as plentiful as in a Biblical paradise too, and were served with this ever-present maize.[9]

The Slaughters were probably dressed in homemade fabrics – poke bonnets and linsey homespun made from local cotton for Minerva and little Mary, Minnie, Martha, Delilah, and Elizabeth who soon arrived. Coats and pants were cut out for Ben and the three boys, all dyed with walnut brown from neighborhood trees. Luxuries were rare and had to be brought in by ox teams, for the village's main supply port was Lavaca, 130 miles away. Laundry was made clean by the creek with battle boards and biceps. Dancing, quilting bees, frolics, and house-raisings provided social contacts, and used up whatever excess energy that hard work might miraculously leave. Circuit riders solved most of the religious problems, and their missionary tasks were truly hard, as Cousin George well knew when he trekked the quagmires of early Texas and wished for real roads. He was a pioneer Baptist, representing a faith which, together with Methodism, was most successful in winning over converts there. Ben was a Methodist and a Mason.

Chills vied with hell's fire in frightening these otherwise brave people. They could fight Indians and border ruffians and battle badmen with pistol and musket while they won a wilderness with brain and muscle, but minister and doctor alone could defeat the invisible terrors. Unfortunately, medical help was always scarce in those days. Malaria, yellow fever, smallpox, and a dozen mysterious fevers came and went in south and east Texas during the 'forties. It seemed that pneumonia was as inevitable as December. Minerva Slaughter was often called upon to act as country doctor. Some trained physicians then specialized in one or

---

[9] Hogan, *op. cit.*, chapter II.

two treatments for all aches and pains, but John's busy mother had three mysterious medicines she always carried with her, and her trips were many over the countryside. She would travel sidesaddle, visiting her neighbors in any weather, and often stayed all night at a patient's house after having ridden twenty or thirty miles. Once Minerva made salve for the amputated leg stump of a man. The limb had been cut off with a meat saw. Its owner had been shot in the knee and got only a quart of whiskey as his anesthetic. Proving Minerva's medical abilities, he recovered and moved to Arizona. With common sense she raised a healthy family of seven to adulthood and brought up a girl named Lila MacDonald, and John's mother seldom lost any of her other "clients" either.[10]

Outside of the few real towns, schools were rare in central Texas, and these were not held in the winter months, for there was seldom any means for heating them. Ben Slaughter was not schooled in writing, but this had not deterred him from putting his "x" on many documents involving tens of thousands of dollars. Friends declared that he could read cattle brands as fast as an editor could go through a newspaper.[11] His "proof reading" was probably always more accurate than theirs, for he was extremely alert in both mind and memory. As are all parents, the Slaughters were proud of their enterprising young sons, and the boys got the best education that family means and primitive conditions could afford, even if that meant only a common school and its temporary teacher near Lockhart.

---

[10] Ed Roberts in an interview at Pearsall, Texas, 1950. Twins, born right after John, died in infancy. Elizabeth, the youngest, was born in 1859. Letter from Georgia Hiler Hays, John H. Slaughter's niece, Stayton, Oregon, January 31, 1952.

[11] Lockhart had no newspaper in those days, but Bastrop, about forty miles northeast, had a weekly. Olmstead, *op. cit.*, p. 10. Today Lockhart manufactures poultry mash and gains its prominence from surrounding rangelands, dairies and chicken production. Oil fields abound. It now has 18 schools. For years Lockhart has been known as the City of Oaks.

Truth is where one finds it, and education is certainly everywhere. The whole outdoors was John's school; people were his lessons, and ranch techniques his textbooks. John early learned Indian ways better than most savages. When he was about sixteen, Lockhart was still endangered by small Indian raids. The Comanches would hang around the wooded creeks watching the near-by San Antonio-Austin road. Whenever an opportunity was presented to attack a traveler, the Indians would suddenly sweep down, for most Comanches still used bows and arrows but coveted the white man's carbine, pistol and good mount. Although noted as the best horsemen of the Southern Plains Indians, the Comanches did not catch young John. He loved to seek them out and egg them on to chase him. There was many a thrill, but he was never caught, for on his best steed he outran them, and then suddenly would turn, riding through his pursuers and firing on either side. Even then he was a fine shot. At last the Indians learned his stratagem and refused to take chase!

One might think that he had no fear. That was almost wholly true, except for one thing. John feared lightning. It was the only ordinary menace that he could not cope with. Many a time he had seen it play along the horses' ears or out on the steers' horns, and dance about like a thousand glow-worms gone mad. Like devil serpents too, the fiery tentacles would streak through the black above and stampede a skittish herd. Gus Withers, a trail-boss friend, was struck once, knocked from his horse, and his tie pin melted and an eye burned out. Even in his later years John never got over this fright. All the ranch house shades were drawn, and he would often spend a restless night, tossing with each thunderous crash.

He learned much from his father, too, for in character and personality, as well as physically, he resembled the older man, probably more than did his two brothers. Like his son, Ben did not present an imposing appearance. But he fooled many a stranger! When one of his cowboys, a man named James H. Cook, first met him, the newcomer took Ben for an ancient Mexican cowhand, with the handle of a big butcher knife sticking out of one boot top, and his belt filled with Henry rifle cartridges. Ben was very dark all right. To some he looked like the Indians he had learned so well to fight. Ben was only five feet seven inches tall and as the years passed became more and more bent over. Even his speech was disarming. He talked seldom, and very, very slowly, in a voice which grew more shrill if he was excited. His words were also difficult to understand, especially for a Northerner, because he had a strong Southern accent. Ben always made his own corncob pipes and smoked all day long, a habit son John followed to his grave – though John's habit was with cigars. Matches were a new innovation and rare in early Texas, so old Ben used a flint rock to ignite a piece of punk for lighting his pipe. Like almost everything else he used, the elder Slaughter got these materials on his ranch. An oval steel ring slipped over the four fingers of his right hand was always used with the flint for lighting fires. In almost every article used, "Uncle" Ben and his family were self-sufficient. In character, they were just as self-dependent, always relying on their own resources and ready to adjust to any new situation.

Yet he never bent when he believed himself right. Hugh A. Taylor, who knew him well, declared, "Old Ben raised a great deal of Cain all the time." Caring little for clothes, he conveniently wore an Indian blanket, donned in Indian fashion as a coat. This kept him warm though it was never stylish outside a tepee. Even when at a fancy affair, he kept to his custom. One day, Ben went to a cattlemen's luncheon in the swank dining room of San Antonio's old Southern

Hotel at Military Plaza and Flores Street. Direct from freighting supplies, he stepped into the lobby. Other ranchers were there in broad-brimmed hats, Texas high-topped boots, cutaway coats and string bow ties. "Now, now," interrupted the unbending hotel manager, as he looked down a long cold nose at shabby old Ben, "you must not sit down at the table in a blanket. It is the rule of the hotel to wear a coat and tie in the dining room." Said Ben, "Wahl, ah ain't wearin' one, and ah'm still gonna sit in with mah neighborly boys." "Oh, no, no," insisted the fidgety manager, "here is a coat — wear this at the table." A little disgusted, but obligingly, Ben shed his Indian blanket and slipped into the fine Prince Albert, moving his six-shooter around in front to avoid a bulge. After the food, chatter and official comments, the assembly adjourned. As Ben started for the door in his elaborate new coat, he was pulled back by the same polished innkeeper. Demanding the return of the coat, the startled fellow only got in return, "No, you ——, you're an Injun giver, and ahm a takin' this home for keeps; you made me all embarrassed for wearin' it, and now she's mine." As his words were backed by a ready Remington revolver, eager to put in a word or two of its own, the manager made the motion unanimous, and "Uncle" Ben walked out to his bull team in the plaza and went home.[12]

Ben loved his land. Everything he valued was tied to it. By 1845 he was doing modestly well. Corn and cattle were his wealth. Yet he was always generous. His neighbors knew that whenever anyone got into trouble, "Uncle" Ben was the first out there to help him. He wanted no thanks and hated flattery. In fact, he never even celebrated a birthday, because as he dryly observed, he'd been born, and it was thus already celebrated.

---

[12] Hugh A. Taylor, interviewed by the author at San Antonio, 1950. Taylor was born west of Pearsall. His mother was Billy Slaughter's daughter, Amanda.

As indicated before, Ben had narrowly missed the Battle of San Jacinto, but he had helped his neighbors during the Mexican invasion of Texas in 1842, and for his trouble was made a prisoner. Along with his fellow-prisoner friend, Big Foot Wallace, he was forced to draw heavy loads of stone for construction. But like the legendary storyteller, Wallace, Ben Slaughter had a ready sense of humor. Knowing Spanish as well as any Coahuilan, he kept his Mexican guards in convulsions, and so gained their favor that he was one of the first prisoners exchanged. With a typical grin of remembrance, he often remarked, "We broke up many a cart and tore up lots of harness." Unlucky Big Foot spent twenty-two months on the Medina as a "guest" of the enemy.[13]

In 1846 the Mexican War came. Ben's favorite saying was "Ahm gwine down thar." Now it had an important meaning! He joined up at near-by San Antonio on April 14, 1847, and was mustered into service that day as a private in Company A, First Regiment, Texas Mounted Volunteers. Two months later, at Monterrey, Mexico, he became a soldier in Captain Baylor's company of Chevallie's Battalion, also of Texas Mounted Volunteers. Now, he had seen the Alamo paid for in full, and was stationed on the site of a great victory of that paying. He remained in the enemy's land until after peace was made, and then at Camargo was honorably discharged on June 30, 1848. A veteran without wounds, Ben made his way to San Antonio where he was enrolled as a private in Captain Hill's company of Texas Mounted Volunteers and thereafter served honorably against the Indians until he was discharged December 17.

After eighteen months, he was a civilian again. No wonder Ben later told one of his cowboys who had served

---

[13] Big Foot was much less lucky than Ben. During his captivity Mexican soldiers had staked him out for fourteen days; then a Mexican doctor rescued and nursed him. Crawford Laxson in the Pearsall *Frontier Times*, January, 1935, p. 167. Mrs. Frances Farris of Coronado, Calif., interview 1951.

BEN SLAUGHTER
Father of Billy, Charley and John.

MINERVA MABRY SLAUGHTER
Ben's wife, and mother of the boys.

WILLIAM "BILLY" SLAUGHTER
Eldest brother of John H. Slaughter.

PRELUDE TO A RANCH DRAMA 53

in the war but seven months, "Youse a shoat hoss." Among his war-time cronies was W. W. "Big Foot" Wallace, who often told stories on Ben. Both were colorful characters about whom legends could grow.[14] Ben returned to Lockhart, but in later years when he had settled in Frio County, he found his old friend on a farm not far away. Ben, Big Foot, Billy Armstrong, and M. H. Bramlette were long that county's only Mexican War veterans, and the tall lanky Big Foot more than made up for their small numbers by spinning yarns – big even for Texas!

---

[14] Wallace was one of Texas' best remembered characters. Born in Rockbridge County, Virginia, on April 3, 1817, he came to Texas in 1837, lived on the Colorado, and in 1838 was taken prisoner by the Lipan Indians, but in good Pocahontas fashion, a young squaw got him freed. In 1842 he served with Matthew Caldwell at the Battle of Salado. About this time he first met Ben Slaughter. Like him, he served in the Mexican War until its end. In 1850-1852 Wallace led Texas Rangers in Indian fighting. The latter year found him conducting U.S. mail from San Antonio to El Paso. Surviving Lipan and Comanche attacks, he moved to Medina County and later to Frio. The town of Big Foot, in the latter county, was named for him. Rather than join either side in the Civil War (about which he said, "Civil, hell, there never was a more uncivilized thing that ever befell any nation") he fought redskins. A bachelor all his life, he still loved all children. Although rough in looks and language, he was a kind, loyal gentleman. He died in poverty, but was buried on the grounds of the Texas capitol. Laxton, *op. cit.*, p. 167.

3

Shaping a Cattle Empire

It might be said that inasmuch as the Spaniards received the credit for creating a cattle industry, the distinction of adopting the cattle brand should go to Hernán Cortes, father of this transplanted industry. According to legend, three crosses resembling in shape the one in the Crucifixion made up the cattle brand of the first ancestors of the Texas Longhorn. It was a brand that must have reminded the forerunner of the American cowboy that this small herd was to be handled with special care.

For here was the beginning of what would one day be a lucrative business. This was the offspring of what once was a precious livestock cargo that had sailed from Spain to the Americas, over an uncharted course in the hull of a primitive sailing vessel. On the same small ship came the steed that would carry the vaquero over the plains and valleys to watch over these four-legged pilgrims. These cattle were intended to breed and accumulate, but not necessarily to stray and interbreed enough to become mavericks. But stray they did, and so did the Spanish cow pony. The latter, in time, furnished a mount for the Indian.

Destiny, it seemed, had planned a crossroads junction so that John Slaughter might begin a career. The meeting place for him and his contemporaries in the livestock raising business appropriately enough was this proving ground on the Texas plains. The terrain of the country in which the descendants of early Spanish cattle roamed, had many features. The brush, cactus, mesquite, muddy waters, hills, mountains and plains helped shape the methods of handling cattle. The disadvantage of having to saddle a wild horse out in the open, and break it in, and the method used in catching a critter for branding, or attending its ailments, had all contributed to the invention of certain range terms. Before the cowboys could thoroughly converse with one another, sign language and illustrations in the sand provided a means of explanation. The Spaniard brought terms only suited for his native land when handling livestock.

The new nomad operation created a whole new glossary of words. The cowboy put over his point usually with a flurry of words, emphasized in such a fashion that it sounded convincing, and more than that it carried with it certain cuss words. These, improperly used, were often interpreted as the exploding fuel to start a fight. Even the mixed-cooked dish of mulligan, because of the trouble it took and the ingredients that went into it, rated the name of "Sonofabitch Stew." One of the chief potencies that was thrown into it were the entrails of an animal, which these knights of the plains had so characteristically labeled as "mare guts." During the tending of the calf crop this stew was bolstered with a special delicacy known to every ranchman for its tender taste, made up of the male glands of a bull calf. Such names as lariat, lasso, corral, riata, rodeo, chaparejo, remuda, sombrero, had been coined. With an understanding of all this, the cowboy was molded into an individual type of character.

By the time John Slaughter came into the world, the Spanish-Mexican vaquero had been known for over three hundred years, but the American cowboy was just an infant. A change of custom and lingo were being readied for the transition when preacher-soldier George Slaughter joined in, to be followed by Ben and his sons.

Across the Rio Grande rode this vaquero in leather leggings, with huge rowel spurs, wearing the big sombrero, using a braided raw-hide riata and speaking Spanish. The change from his old customs would be adopted by the Americans. The Slaughters came to speak more in Spanish than they did in English. Most all their cowboys were Mexicans. The Indians conversed in Spanish part of the time, and the colored people that had come from the deep South adopted the language when helping their employers on the cow trails. The building of adobes, the growing of vegetables and pepper plants used in the Mexican foods, and the making of tortillas came from south of the Rio Grande. One of the specialized trades learned was the tanning of hides and the making of saddles. But the Americans also brought with them many of their customs and gradually a mixture of the two could be seen in the early way of life in Texas. Slaughters had been known for the development of a good strain of stock. From Mississippi they had imported sires and domestic bulls for this purpose. One of the very first of stock drovers was George Webb Slaughter. He was a pioneer trail blazer. Right after the Civil War he brought a herd through Sivell's Bend at Rock Crossing and followed Mud Creek divide to Rush Springs before other drivers used the more direct route.[1]

Ben's cattle needed good land, and so he was always concerned with land deals. On August 31, 1847, he bought for only $5.00, in his wife Minerva's name, a town lot in Lockhart, near the Springs. On October 2, 1848, John and Elizabeth Pittman sold Ben 82½ acres on historic Plum Creek. Land was becoming ever more valuable, so it cost him $175.[2] For $40 more Ben got an adjoining 20 acres from John M. Brite on the last day of 1850. But Ben, like his ancestors, saw other lands beyond the beckoning sunsets, and to a Texan of those times, sundowns looked bigger and more golden.

---
[1] See J. C. Richardson in *Frontier Times*, XVI, no. 12, September 1939, p. 546.
[2] This had been part of Jeremiah Roberts' headright, therefore the near-by stream was called Jerry's Creek. For the document, see Caldwell County, Records of Deeds, Book A, page 259.

On December 7, 1858, Ben Slaughter bought from H. C. Fountain for $400 a 320-acre tract southeast of Pleasanton in Atascosa County.[3] This was ideal cattle country, prairie throughout, with deep, dark, sandy loam, the heart of the cow paradise, and mostly well watered land, situated on La Parita Creek. Thus the family had moved a bit westward again. They were still pioneers, for the county had then only 1,136 whites and a scant 51 negroes — it was not cotton plantation country. Other figures prove that it was becoming ranching land, for already 8,805 head of cattle were grazing there. J. W. Murphy, a San Antonio resident, and Ben Slaughter's friend, Captain Fountain, had been Pleasanton's earliest settlers. Murphy's wife, an Oden, had come with her parents in 1856, locating near La Parita Creek. In 1860, Pleasanton was still merely a little village on the banks of Atascosa River. "Boggy" was the stream's English meaning, and its soft quicksand, looking firm to the tenderfoot, often carried down horses in a few minutes.[4] Also near La Parita dwelt Ben's old friends the Staytons, the Cook boys, the Toms and Jesse Lott. E. B. Thomas, the original settler in those parts, was also first to establish a general store, but dry goods didn't mean complete civilization.

In 1861 the Fountains, Ogdens, Slaughters and others gained lasting fame for their fight against the Comanches. Attacking in force, the savages killed settlers near town. One of these latter, Ed Lyons, sent Alex Anderson on a fast horse to rouse Pleasanton, but the Indians swept down on the would-be Paul Revere only a mile from his goal, shooting

---

[3] Hartwell Coleman Fountain had served in a regiment of his native South Carolina during the Mexican War, became a captain, and in 1847 remained in Texas. In 1856, he moved to Atascosa County and was elected one of its first officers. He died there in 1886. He had much cattle business with the Slaughters. See Clarence R. Wharton, *Texas under Many Flags*, IV, p. 311. See also County of Atascosa, Book of Deeds, A, no. 194. For a mention of the Fountain ranch, see R. J. Lauderdale and John M. Doak, *Life on the Range and on the Trail*, p. 117.

[4] Z. T. Fulmore, *History and Geography of Texas, as Told in County Names*, 17.

an arrow into his back. Unwarned, Eli O'Brien was out that morning and thought the horsemen he saw under some trees were fellow cowmen trying to scare him. When he discovered his error, the Indians were already stringing their bows and wheeling their ponies to give chase. O'Brien's steed was better than his caution, but when his foes caught up, Eli used a butcher knife on one of them and got a couple of arrows in his back. Though wounded, O'Brien escaped by leaping an arroyo, and the Indians turned back.[5] His life-and-death race rivaled John Slaughter's in legend.

At that time and place, the Slaughters' spacious home was made of elm poles and had a low roof of elm slabs or shakes, made with a type of splitting tool known as a froe. The structure lacked windows and had only a hard-packed earth floor, like the neighboring houses. Antelope, buffalo and steer hides served as floor covering.

As the children grew up here, Ben followed the custom of giving each son a cattle brand. Though hardened at a tender age, youngsters needed their parents' coaching, for the country was infested with bandits, lawless Mexicans and hostile Indians. So wild did the region seem that Ben's relative, James Mabry Neatherlin, ceased helping the elder Slaughter about 1860 and left the country with his family. Indians often passed through Uvalde, Sabinal and Frio canyons, stealing livestock and committing depredations.

Ben was not so easily routed as his kinsman. He remained. In those days a man was scarcely without his firearms. When he slept, Ben's were within easy reach. Muzzle loaders often adorned the walls, and a belt with the holster hung from a wooden peg. Yet more prosaic household items were near at hand, too. A cedar water pail with tin dipper or gourd hung by a hook on the wall; a towel, tables, Dutch oven,

[5] A. J. Sowell, *Early Settlers and Indian Fighters of Southwestern Texas*, pp. 253-254.

skillets, and a hard clay hearth helped prepare their victuals. Universal was the steaming coffee pot. At every Texas rancho this served better than a welcome mat and was a greeting to every passerby. All comers were welcome as guests, in accordance with the code of the West, for they brought the only outside news, telling the Slaughters and their friends of the lawless element, climatic disasters, cattle business, and the vague bigger world beyond Atascosa County. The beginning of the 'sixties brought a somber note to the news of the nation.

The 'fifties had been an important era. Texas was beginning to change into a great ranching state, a drama in which all Slaughters would play a prominent part. From now on they were destined to follow the dusty trails of the bovine. In spite of the herds of wild cattle in the west, the short-lived Republic of Texas had been a land of Southern crops rather than beef, and little of the Southwestern plains had been settled, though contemporary maps marked them as "Wild Cattle Country." There were few markets then for tough Longhorn meat, although by the 'fifties Texas cowhands had driven herds to New Orleans, Kansas City, St. Louis, and even Chicago. Then came the great American national crisis. For John Slaughter and his family, and for Texas, it was a decisive four years, as personally important to Slaughter as a later four years in Arizona which would make him immortal. From 1861 to 1865, Texas was transformed, but neither all for the good or the bad. John came through unharmed, if not in the best of health. Brother Billy, the oldest son, was married in July, 1858, and Charley, following what had almost become a wartime Slaughter custom, was wed at Lockhart in 1861 to Rebecca Wallen. Within a year father and sons went off to war.

Ben enlisted at San Antonio on November 2, 1861, serving as a captain of a company of Texas state troops until January 20, 1862. The next year he re-enlisted as a private under his neighbor, Captain John Files Tom of Atascosa County. Son John also enlisted in the same company. Captain Tom led his men against hostile Comanches at the head of San Miguel Creek. During the fight, both sides tried to reach a pile of rocks for protection. The Indians won the spot but not the battle. Within this organization the two Slaughters served in the Third Frontier District, defending Texas against other Indian threats. The redskin menace abated and Ben was mustered out February 20, 1864.[6]

His sons served at least as zealously, if not for so long. All three boys joined up at Pleasanton, mounting their own strong horses and riding off to serve the Confederacy. Billy had a roan horse and Charley a sorrel with a bald face. The steeds outlasted the Lost Cause, and Billy and John returned home with their same good mounts, though Charley came back riding a pack mule. Billy became a corporal in Company D under Captain John W. Stayton in Ragsdale's Battalion, Texas Cavalry, C.S.A.[7] He served from 1862 to 1864 and saw action at Sabine Pass, a significant battle of the war. Stayton later testified to young Slaughter's fine record. Charley was a private in the same battalion, which he and Billy had joined the same day, October 27, 1862, at Camp Wilson. An arm pass of that time laconically listed the

---

[6] John Files Tom, a Tennessean and son of an Indian fighter at Horseshoe Bend under Andrew Jackson, landed at the mouth of the Brazos in February, 1835. In March of the next year, he fought with Houston after some experience against Cos' army at San Antonio. When only 17, he was wounded, a hero and an officer. He limped for the rest of his life. In 1862, Tom moved to Atascosa County. In 1873, he represented his region in the Texas legislature. Finally, like Ben Slaughter, he moved to Frio County.

[7] John W. Stayton was born in Washington County, Kentucky, Christmas Day, 1830. Until 18 he remained on the farm, then became a student; at 26, he received his B.A. in law. That October, Stayton moved to Texas, settling in Atasocsa County in 1857. Before the Civil War he was twice elected district attorney. With secession, Stayton joined the Confederate army as a private, but soon rose to a captaincy. Prominent as a lawyer, he was appointed associate justice of the state supreme court in 1881. By 1888, he had become chief justice.

twenty-three-year-old as five feet five inches, 130 pounds, and a blue eyed, dark complexioned stock raiser. Years changed the total description but little. The next June, however, Charley was discharged from service due to ill health. Both he and John suffered from "cold chills" and malaria during their service. Soon afterward, Charley helped Captain Benavides in a local Atascosa County ranger company which was fighting bandits.

Apparently Billy was not as sick as his brothers, although he had the measles in camp. He fulfilled a family promise by returning home on his first furlough in almost unbelievable time, and riding his sturdy horse all the way from Louisiana.

John Slaughter's army career was somewhat more varied. Like most volunteers, he carried his own equipment, a good horse, valued at $130, camp equipment worth $20, and a $30 gun, plus a $5 knife. With this gear, he enlisted March 29, 1862, at San Antonio. What more appropriate captain could this young hunter of cattle strays have had than Lewis Antonio Maverick of San Antonio! Son of Samuel H. and Mary Maverick, Lewis was only two years older than his subordinate, but the family name had already become famous for the half-wild, unbranded cattle his kinsmen had owned and neglected.

John's Civil War record was made more against Indians than Yankees. As early as November, 1861, he had served 19 days in a company of Minute Men of Atascosa County, organized by his father. Later in 1864, after a sick leave, he served under Captain J. Bittick in the Third Frontier Division, Texas State Troops, in Burnett County. Such companies were organized under state acts to combat immediate frontier dangers. Slaughter served in them long after the War between the States had ended, and was known as the "boy lieutenant," a fearless fighter who was almost uncannily skillful with his firearms. In June, 1872, he enlisted as a private in a company of Minute Men of Texas Rangers, serving 42 days under Captain George Adams. Then in January, 1874, he again joined up, this time in the Brown and San Saba Company of Rangers, for a two-month term. John suffered no wounds in the Civil conflict, and his two brothers complained only of their minor illnesses. Sore and tired, Billy returned in late 1864 and for a time was sheriff of Atascosa County. Then in 1865 he moved from the family ranch to his own place between Dilley and Millet. As early as 1855 he had established a ranch in Atascosa County.

Warfare had not changed the boys much, except perhaps to temper their personalities a little. Sitting one day at his corral at Friotown and squinting yonder at his straggly corn field, old Ben philosophized to his neighbor-friend, James E. Roberts, "You know, Jim, ah axt the 'Ole Boss' (God) to send mah three boys home from the war – He did that. Then ah axt Him to make mah corn crop grow. He did that. Then ah axt 'The Ole Boss' to send some rain – but He plum ignored me, and ah'll ne'er axt for nothing any more – ah'll let mah corn go to hell." [8] Ben's faith was plain as a root and his wishes few and just as fundamental. Nevertheless, it seemed that Providence and the Civil War had worked together to provide a prosperous opportunity for the Slaughters. New circumstances were to build a cattle empire. Truly, Ben could let his corn go to hell!

Many a Texas veteran returning from the big fight had nothing more than the horse he rode. War had taken away all hard money, crops had been forgotten, and the State

---

[8] Much on the Slaughters during the Civil War was obtained in an interview with Ed Roberts at Pearsall in 1950. Thanks is rendered to Maj. Gen. William E. Bergin, Department of the Army, Office of the Adjutant General, Washington, D.C., for his kind help in obtaining photostats and records of the family during the Mexican and Civil wars.

government was hard up. The slaves had been freed. Much had gone to ruin, but one bit of neglect seemed a godsend. Texas cattle had been allowed to run wild and multiply. One day in 1863 in the Slaughters' own Atascosa County, a San Antonian found three women butchering a cow, for their husbands were in the army and there was no cowboy within miles.[9] Now the herds were tougher and bigger than ever.

The Civil War had other effects. For one, it had started railroad building in the Far West. The federal government had established as its policy the giving of land grants to spur peaceful national unity by rails. This meant fast communication, and quick transit spelled new markets for Texans. What now did the State have to sell to the wealthy and expanding Eastern city markets except cattle? As a result, there began the long drives to the Kansas railheads. Billy Slaughter made his first trail ride to Kansas with Jim Blackaller, a cowman neighbor. From the beginning, the family saw the riches in this new opportunity.

Charley Slaughter had sold his La Parita Creek land to Tom Vilbiss and moved over to Friotown, then the seat of Frio County. There he lived in a little wooden structure by the river while building a rock house half a mile east of the town-site.[10] This was still on the fringe of civilization, although Cabeza de Vaca had ambled through these parts as early as October, 1535. For Frio County, it was prophetic that the Spanish explorer who first saw Texas and New Mexico should be named "Cow's Head." A couple of centuries later the old San Antonio Road traced its dusty, nar-

---

[9] San Antonio *Semi-Weekly News*, March 5, 1863.
[10] Charley had bought a parcel of land from Calvin Musgrove on January 28, 1870. It cost him $600 and was the letter patent grant of John Neile, conveyed to Fountain on January 15, 1867. Originally, the ranch consisted of over 60,000 acres. After Charley's death, it was divided, sold, or given outright to his daughters and their husbands. The old stone house still stands, its rocks in fine condition. Dan J. Rheiner in correspondence from San Antonio, Texas, May 1952.

row way out across the northwestern part of the future county and forded the rushing Frio at Presidio Crossing, then to enter Old Mexico at San Juan Batista. Today, traces of the road exist, where passed churchmen, soldiers, adventurers, thieves – and cattlemen like the first Slaughters. St. Denis trod the road in 1714 when he went to San Juan Batista. Using the same trail, the Slaughters and their kind sold many of their beeves to San Antonio and Bastrop markets. Wily Santa Anna rode this route for his bloody enterprise at the Alamo. In 1844, the Alsatian settlement of Castroville was still the nearest town. Big Foot Wallace came a little later, and finally those dynasties of the plains: Frank, Grimes, Allen, Eastwood, Sheidly, Hays, Parks, Thompson, Oge, Burleson, Speed, Ward, Webb, Daugherty, Edwards, Crouch, Little, Blackaller, Berry, Bennett and Forrest families. In 1858 the first real government was set up, though for a time Frio remained under Bexar County, not to be a separate county until 1871.

For several years, more Indian arrowheads were to be seen than judges' gavels. In 1850 Bud English, Dean Oden and Dan Williams were killed by Comanches in a Fourth of July battle. George Daugherty and Levi English were seriously wounded.[11] Meeting almost spontaneously, one day in 1860, a few settlers sized up their unprotected situation and organized a ranger company, electing J. R. Burleson captain. Scalpings and murders were still aplenty. "Mustang" Moore was killed, but gave his name to a local town. James Winters, Frank Camp, Bud English, Dan Williams, Dean Oden, R. A. Sanders, Leonard Calvin Massey and William Rittenberg – these names were on the death roll before peace came. It was in the spring of 1873 that Massey died. His was probably the first grave in the new Friotown cemetery. A good fight was made, but forty-five savages

---

[11] Interview with Jake English, 1950.

escaped. Still that was a mild foray compared to the awful year 1876. The nation was celebrating its one hundredth birthday, but Frio had more on its mind to remember. At daybreak, the attack began. Billy Allen and Jim Berry were holding a herd near Indian Crossing on the Frio when Jim saw the Indians. They didn't molest him, but went up the creek six miles from town to Billy Slaughter's sheep camp where they came upon William Rittenberg, the foreman, and four Mexican herders. Down went Rittenberg and all his helpers. Next the Indians galloped up the Leona Valley where they killed a man named Butler, and Nick Briar, also hands of Billy and Charley Slaughter. Later that day, Rittenberg's red-haired scalp was found by his friends and interred with the body.

The same year, a locally noted murder took place. Jim Barnes, a man about 30, had come all the way from California on horseback, killing buffalo calves on the way for food. He took a job riding herd for old Captain Crouch, sidekick of Ben Slaughter. In performing his duties he witnessed a bit of local rustling — someone was hazing cattle across the Crouch pasture and going toward Loma Vista. Not long after that, this eyewitness was killed by the gun of John Rundles, in front of Babe Hand's saloon, which was right across the street from Friotown's rock courthouse.[12]

This was still not the end of badmen troubles for 1876, with which John Slaughter was well acquainted, adding to his training as a lawman. That spring, a man named Dancer who had killed a Mr. Greeley at the Concho ranch on the Frio, was taken to jail by the sheriff. This "hoosegow" was pretty poor, and Dancer escaped, later to be imprisoned at Castroville. He must have had a Western type of claustrophobia, for he got caught again, this time with a saw he had made for cutting through the double floor of his cell.

---

[12] Interview with Ed Roberts, Pearsall, Texas, 1950.

SHAPING A CATTLE EMPIRE 67

Just before the year was out, Billy Slaughter was over at the Frio Masonic Lodge. Probably he felt proud, for he was installed that day as lodge secretary. At 2:00 p.m. he had different emotions. "Indians, Indians," shouted a messenger from the town's outskirts. Like a stirred up beehive, the Frioites got busy. Forty able-bodied men, armed with rifles and six-shooters, mounted their horses and reported for action.

Early in the spring of 1877 the last attack came. Damage was minor — it was almost an anticlimax. The Indians stole 50 horses at Woodward's ranch but abandoned them when the rangers gave chase.

Indian raids had almost ceased, but twenty victims had been buried in 1876 in the little cemetery. The drama was played out, though the last act was even a little ridiculous. William Daugherty and a friend, Nolen, captured the last Indian chief found in that region. Nolen got a toe shot off, and the Indian escaped before they could reach the Friotown courthouse. However, a Mexican sheepherder killed the fugitive near Del Rio and sold his body for $10 to a physician who used the skeleton for scientific study![13]

The white villians were a lot harder to clean out. Still, Friotown was a comparatively quiet village. When the Slaughters came, it was still mostly a wilderness; one could look across the rolling plains and see open range for miles and miles. It was a stretch of wild land from San Antonio to the Rio Grande, kept burned off by Indian signal smokers, whose fires were often visible for fifty miles. Grass fires frequently resulted, and they were almost as much of a scare as Comanches. They were, however, not particularly disastrous for John's family. One might come upon unburned thickets of heavy brush with mesquite, blackbrush, guiajillo,

---

[13] Cotulla *Record*, January, 1932, XI, p. 165. This contains an article by O. W. Nolen entitled "J. C. B. Harkness."

catclaw, and brazil in the uplands, sometimes verging into live oak, elm, and persimmon on the bottom lands by the branching Frio.

In 1875, a small scale irrigation system was begun, but a flood swept away most of its canals. Even if this was true cow country, the Slaughters and their neighbors grew beans and potatoes in summer, turnips and mustard in the fall.

The town itself was growing slowly. In 1871, it had been laid out. At first the buildings were mostly of cypress from timber standing near the river. The lumber courthouse was a real community center. Around the square rose three general stores, two saloons, a couple of hotels, a restaurant, saddle and leather shop, two blacksmith shops, a Masonic Lodge, a church and a school. "Old Bib" opened the first store and kept a saloon in its cellar. "Aunt Jennie" Waldren and her spouse, Calvin, ran the main hotel, while "Doc" Neatherlin, friend of Ben Slaughter, was the town's saddlemaker. He made the saddle tree out of a forked green elm and covered it with rawhide. Always built extra large, his Mexican saddle horns were as big as plates. The Slaughters knew and admired them.

The jail was of course very practical, as it was used during the Indian attacks by the very best citizens. Texas prisons of those days were sometimes better for keeping Indians out than "whiteskins" in! This one could do both well. Its walls were a full yard thick, made of rock, and the lime came from a local quarry. Three heavy bars crossed the windows and a 3½ inch steel bar supported them. The ceiling was of mesquite logs about 18 inches wide and 14 feet long. This one-room, two-window jail saw many criminals, supposedly too tough to hold. Still, it had no lock, and men had to prop a twenty-foot-long cypress log against its door. It took six men to open it when court convened. When the wooden parts of the building burned in 1877, Billy

CHARLEY SLAUGHTER'S ROCK HOUSE NEAR FRIOTOWN, TEXAS
Built in 1871. Here Ben and Minerva spent their last years.

JIM SPEED
IN CONFEDERATE UNIFORM
Brother of Steve Speed, and close friend of John Slaughter in Frio and Atascosa counties. They were trail driving companions.

MARRIAGE CERTIFICATE OF JOHN SLAUGHTER AND ELIZA HARRIS Located in the Bexar County Courthouse, San Antonio.

Slaughter assumed full costs of restoring the building.[14] His brother, John, could have used as good a one later in Cochise County, Arizona.

The Slaughter children knew the school's interior much better. It also burned and was rebuilt, and experienced many changes of teachers. In the 'seventies, Amanda and Mary Slaughter, Billy's little daughters, learned their letters there. At a commencement, Amanda gave a brief essay, recited "Cock a Doodle Doo," and Mary, more seriously, rendered the "Psalm of Life."

In these calmer moments, basic religion gave inspiration. Occasionally, Andrew Jackson Potter, a famous fighting preacher, rode through this brush country on the Methodist circuit. Like Ben and his boys, the parson carried a six-shooter and a Spencer rifle, adding a Bible and two song books. Ben liked to sing, although he hardly had the voice for it. Neither did John. Ben's favorite was "When the Roll is Called Up Yonder, I'll be There." Potter's specialties were "Jesus, Lover of My Soul," and "The Old Church Yard." Other ministers came with the years, Reverends William C. Newton and John W. De Villis, among them. In June, 1880, the Rio Grande Baptist Association met at Friotown.

The Slaughter family had many a good time, much as they had enjoyed the rural social life at Lockhart. Fish fries, picnics, and Fourth of July outings were common.

The town stopped growing after Pearsall became the county seat in 1881, and many "newtimers" left. In later life, in 1920, John Slaughter returned to the Texas southland, for one more look. He drove in a horse carriage from Friotown to Uvalde and remarked that it was just about as

---

[14] The present Frio County courthouse at Pearsall bears the name of county commissioners, among them that of W. J. Slaughter. This granite building was erected in 1904.

he had left it 44 years ago, only the county seat had grown more dense with mesquite.[15]

In his Friotown days, Ben drank whiskey, but always could hold it. Probably he was often seen at the Lone Star. Tobe Eldridge remembers that his father fulfilled Ben's request to bring a bottle of whiskey from Uvalde. A little earlier, Ben sold whiskey himself – by the gallon. In the 1870's, he and his in-law ran a pioneer general store at Frio City, selling everything Texas could boast of![16] At the same time, Charley did business as a merchant, and was sued by G. W. Sanders for an agreement that went awry.[17]

"Cow talk" was a happier activity. This and cattle prices were the Slaughters' main interest. Billy's "T Diamond" and Ben's "BS" were as well known as the old stone courthouse. Billy knew well the possibilities of the region, and in 1878 he had sold his LaSalle County, Cibolo Ranch, and bought his brother's Frio lands. Ben had moved to LaSalle for a while near his son's place, where Ben himself had earlier secured rights and made some improvements. Then, in 1874, he too had gone on to Friotown. Now, all the Slaughters were in the cattle business.[18]

---

[15] Interviews with Ed Roberts and Artie Slaughter Roberts, 1950.

[16] C. J. Jones bought from the Slaughters 25 pounds of bacon at $3.85, a gallon of whiskey for $2.50 and assorted overalls, calico, velvet and "pain killer." Next day, June 8, 1877, Ben sold another half gallon of whiskey. See *Frio City Bulletin*, August 28, 1877.

[17] Ed Roberts interview.

[18] Ben was very active in cattle and land deals. On July 15, 1873, he let Muir A. McDonald, also of La Salle County, have his cattle branded RB for four years. The increase was all to be branded RB, and after the four year period, the stock would be divided, half to Ben, half to Muir. This was a fairly common practice. Next year, Ben borrowed $500 at 10% interest from R. M. Minus, a well-to-do Pleasanton publisher. As usual in that era, the sum was lent and repaid in gold. April 29, 1877, Ben bought for $800 a tract in Friotown (Lot 9, Block 1) from J. R. M. Harkness, the sheriff. Earlier, he had purchased Lot 1, Block 5 in the town from L. J. W. Edwards and sold it for $30 to Bernard McAffee on September 14, 1877. Sixteen days before that, he had sold for another $30 to his sons Billy and Charley (Lot 11, Block 7 in Friotown). See Book D, page 122, Frio County Deeds, 1877. Billy's and Charley's real estate was a 640 acre tract, situated on Live Oak tributary of Frio

John, however, liked to play a lone hand, but after serving in the Rangers, he went into partnership with his brothers, branding mavericks and selling and buying cattle. They bought the brand of the San Antonio Ranch Company when the northern markets opened in Abilene and later Dodge City, and other Kansas corrals and track junctions which attracted the cattlemen like magnets.[19] Like medieval escutcheons, brands and earmarks increased on the cattle estates. Along the old Chisholm Trail the Slaughters' cow symbols were as familiar as in other parts of Texas. Billy, Ben, Charley and John each had several brands now, including road brands. The herds that went on the trail generally were a combination of Billy's and Charley's; and John usually took his separately.

Ben's ranch activities were typical of family doings. In those days his cattle were all Texas Longhorns. Almost everything was still made on the ranch. Hobbles for horses were cut from fresh beef hide; and ropes, reins, quirts, and saddle rigging all came from Ben's rawhide. His sons had learned this lore when they learned the Texas drawl. Horsehair was also braided into ropes and bridles; rawhide and wooden pegs took the place of wire and nails. Those cattle not driven to Kansas were partly wasted, for there was little means of food preservation, and hot West Texas summers

River, six miles from Friotown. See Survey Book c, page 361, Frio County Deeds, Survey -1, August 28, 1887. Ben had also bought on September 5, 1877, a lot in town from Caven Woodward, cattleman and trail-driver friend of his sons.

[19] On September 22, 1871, John, Charley, and Billy Slaughter recorded in Friotown for their San Antonio Ranch Company the Brand CAV with earmark. After John Slaughter had left the company, Billy and Charley recorded on May 11, 1877, brands O and RB, and the next July 12 fixed on OO. On June 9, 1877, the San Antonio Ranch Company registered H3 on left side. November 22, 1889, they registered H3 on left side and H3 on left hip. On February 22-24, 1874, they had sold cattle bearing the following brands: CAV; LA; L7; HD; 5;11; O; HOX; OA; SUF; and TX. For $60,000 John L. Lytle and Thomas M. McDaniel of Medina County sold the San Antonio Ranch Company 4,000 head of mixed cattle in Frio County with road brand -6, and all other brands of that ranch. The sales also included 100 saddle horses.

meant that fresh meat would keep but a day or two. Just the best rib cuts were saved. The process of smoking meat was adopted by some for preserving. Meat was cooked by thrusting pointed sticks through it and putting one end of the poles in the ground. The meat was then broiled over a bed of mesquite or live oak coals. As a rule, the ranch's hogs got a feast from the poorer cuts.

As late as 1880, Glidden wire had not penetrated all of Texas. The first enclosures were called "cross" fences, simply of poles. Sam Hutchinson was the first man in Friotown to use them. Before the smooth and barbed wire eras, wild cattle were the general rule. The Slaughters prospered from hunting them. On one of these cow hazing expeditions, pack mules and ponies carried the cowhands' indispensable provisions – green-berry coffee, salt pork, corn meal, salt, pepper berry, and a couple of Dutch ovens, frying pans, a camp kettle, a coffee pot, and tin plates, knives and forks for the hands. They also took along a decoy herd of tame cows to lure the mavericks. Then, cowboys scattered into an indivisible circle about the wild ones, singing traditional "lullabies" all the while. It was the original chant known to the cowhand of that era, and John Slaughter knew it as no other sweet music. When tame and wild were well mingled, the men closed in, driving the herd away toward a special secure corral. Dangers, too were always present. Sometimes musk hogs would stampede the decoys; at other times the wild ones sought freedom and had to be necked to gentler beasts. Encircling the mavericks might have looked easy, but it was always perilous. "Brush poppers" risked their necks on moonlit nights by riding into the thick brush miles from camp and, with lightning motions, roping a wild steer.[20] The most successful way to gain

---

[20] Ed Roberts had eight accidents with horses. In 1891, a steer drove its horn through Ed's boot, and the resulting wound took three months to heal. Ed broke his collar bone twice. Yet, he was comparatively lucky. Besides cowboy ills, there was

control of a stampeding herd was to throw them into a mill, by circling the leaders. Sometimes, though, the effects of their crazy dash lasted for days. Never were they returned to the spot where they had become riled.[21] The crack of a twig of brush, the flash of lightning, or even the slightest noise, might throw the whole herd in a frenzy.

Even if one did not seek danger it was ever present. James Cook, one of Ben's hands, early noticed that everyone went armed at all times. No man would take off more than his jacket when on the trail, sleeping for hours without removing his boots. There was forever the chance of a brush with Comanches. The Civil War added still another factor — badmen.[22] Fugitives from justice roamed Texas, especially this western frontier, and turned to the logical temporary livelihood and cover-up of ranch work. The Slaughters met many an outlaw who came along the trail. It was the custom never to ask a stranger where he was from. Men who had ridden with William C. Quantrill back in Missouri, roamed about and were "plenty tough." However, most ranchers gave them warning of approaching lawmen. When two riders approached one another, they swung out in a semicircle, giving each ample berth to pass by. In some cases, it was because the cowman didn't want a desperado's vengeance. Another reason was lawmen on the beaten path. In

always the danger of cattle fever. For a while, Texas was shunned up north, due to it. One way the Slaughters and their hands could spot the disease was by the sick calves' habit of staying in the lake or creeks for hours.

[21] Eugene C. Barker, ed., *Readings in Texas History*, "Managing a Herd," pp. 612-617.

[22] Originally the term "rustler" meant a cowboy who received a fee from his boss for every maverick he found and branded. The cattle association paid five dollars for every head that a rancher found, or "rustled" up for it. As a region was setlted, big men combined against little ones, as in the New Mexican Lincoln County War. Thus the rustler became a criminal to the big dealers. Seldom, though, did these rustlers take a poor man's stock. During the decade 1876-1886, range vigilantes sprang up, took great powers upon themselves, and accused many, executed some. Jealousy for John Slaughter's success brought vigilante hatred against him.

many cases, though, the people would rather aid and even hire a colorful supposedly-wronged Robin Hood than the men who were out to get him. Sam Bass and Joel Collins attended now and then a dance held in Atascosa County in the '70s. During these outings, Bass, like many other frontiersman, occasionally stopped off at John Slaughter's ranch near Pleasanton.

A good many of the rowdies didn't seem to be bad at heart. Clay Allison, for instance, was a good-natured cowhand, the type that John Slaughter could always get along with and get a chuckle or two from. Six foot two and 175 pounds of practical jokes was this gay young fellow. Yet his humor was pretty dangerous too. He liked to ride through a cowtown backward in his saddle. As he went down the main street in this manner, he fired at lights and windows, clearing the way of unamused citizens. Sometimes he pulled a Lady Godiva stunt, racing through town clad only in hat and boots. At least this was quieter than his saloon antics. Maybe it was not original, but he got a great bit of fun out of making drinkers dance a jig to his symphony of bullets. Allison pulled four teeth from an unwilling dentist who had, by mistake, yanked a good one from Allison's head. Yet, Clay hated genuine desperadoes as much as Slaughter later did. Allison would shoot anyone who did not shoot for laughs. He killed several of them, and not in fun!

During Frio County's brief wild days, even "Uncle" Ben Slaughter almost got caught in the prickly meshes of fate. One November day in 1875, he was over at the Snodgrass store. M. D. Fortner, foreman of one of Billy's spreads, came in to buy some supplies. Fortner was on his way to Pleasanton, and Ben went along with him, chatting for a while in his peppery manner. At the river, Fortner dismounted to get a drink, and Slaughter went on ahead, telling his companion to catch up. Ben stayed overnight at

SHAPING A CATTLE EMPIRE

Waugh's ranch, but Fortner never showed up. Next morning some cowboys found his body on the road. It had a bullet in the head, another in the back, and his face had been beaten with a blunt instrument.[23]

About the same year, John Slaughter ran afoul of vigilantes. Things had become so hectic by about 1874, that for "good order" San Antonio had set up a vigilante committee, headed by Asa Minshul and Solomon Chiswell. It was a not uncommon occurrence for one or more men to be seen dangling from the limb of a tree, creating a ghastly sight. However, such powers are always bound to grow, nourished on the same evil they hoped to destroy. Many an innocent man fell victim to their crude practices. One day, they appeared at John's place near Pleasanton. It looked pretty bad for him, and the French cook, knowing that the self-made and suspiciously well-armed "lawmen" had been hanging around the place for some time, logically concluded that they were "out to get" his boss. The cook asked the newly-married Mrs. Slaughter if he might put some poison in their victuals. "Of course not," she refused, but it was perhaps fortunate for the self-appointed lawmen that little John did not meet them face to face. Certainly he had hired some men whose records he did not investigate. They did their work, and that was all that mattered. Legends have it, and they are probably correct, that by this time he had killed several human "sidewinders" whose evil shades had crossed his path. After this, John always hated vigilanteism.[24]

Most of the young men of bad name were of background like John Slaughter's, but had turned awry. Bitterness against Yankees, freed slaves, the defeat of the Confederacy and poverty had caused good marksmen to make the worst of a Western talent. "Wild Bill" Longley was one of this

[23] San Antonio *Weekly Express,* December 4, 1875.
[24] Interview with Nancy Slaughter Tubert, Tombstone, Arizona, 1950.

type. Like Slaughter, he relied on his luck, but optimism availed him not. He talked too much to the wrong people and was hanged in October, 1878, after having killed 32 men.[25] But for the grace of God, basic common sense, right rearing and balance, John Slaughter might have gone likewise. Instead he went forward to success in two honorable fields.

Slaughter fame and profits never were made easily. Before the big cattle drives to Kansas had begun, a few cattle buyers used to come to the Slaughter ranches and buy beeves gathered there, sometimes gathered for other owners. Then these herds were driven to some gulf port and shipped by boat to New Orleans or a northern market. Occasionally Mexican buyers came to Cibolo, Billy Slaughter's place, or to the Nueces, contracted for cattle, and had them delivered below the border. John made many trips to Mexico. Although profits were good, those markets were limited.

In later years, the long drives usually followed a pretty exact pattern. Ben and his boys gathered their herds about the last of March. Their range covered a tract of many square miles, and they worked this rich region from the forks of the Nueces and Frio rivers to their headwaters and south toward the Rio Grande, far beyond the old Cotulla ranch between San Antonio and Laredo. The cattle were next driven into great corrals, made expertly of sturdy mesquite timbers, and here road brands were put on the cattle so that other ranchers' cattle could be identified. Brand inspectors were forever present during trail drives. Records were kept, and the marketing expenses were deducted from sales proceeds, the remainder then turned over to the owners. Having an especially good business head, Charley was usually superintendent of marketing in Kansas.

---

[25] T. U. Taylor, *Bill Longley and his Wild Career,* (Bandera, Texas, 1925) is a good account of this badman's doings. He began his murders in 1866 and followed his "profession" until death on October 11, 1878, at Giddings, Texas.

Through the years, in Guadalupe, Atascosa, Frio, and La Salle Counties, cattle families were a close little group, making many business deals, often with only the unwritten contract of honor, talking each other's language as no outsider could, helping one another out, trading land, and often intermarrying. There was real comradeship in this prairie outpost. Among Ben's and his sons' friends and fellow stockmen were many whose names are now history. Col. B. L. Crouch, a real old-timer, had 67,000 acres in the '70s and raised red Durham cattle. He so prized his fine stock that he once bought a Durham bull and babied it to the point of having a man drive the beast overland for 125 miles to avoid the hazards of a wagon trip.

Jim and Steve Speed were also Slaughter friends. Their specialty was white-faced cattle. Joe Cotulla, though, was almost a legend. Born in Germany, he had come to Texas in 1856, then moved to Atascosa County. In 1862, Ben Slaughter paid Joe seven dollars per month in Confederate money for his work as a hand on La Parita Creek. That year he went with Ben, John, and other stockmen on a cattle selling trip to Mexico. After that expedition, Cotulla joined the United States Army, officially an enemy of his old friends. Later he returned to ranching, drove a herd to Abilene for L. B. Harris, in 1868, and on the way noted there were no towns and only three houses and one log cabin at the end of the trail. Harris and John Slaughter were to have far more important relations than these with Cotulla. After 1874, the German drove no more. Joe had spelled his last name with a K, but there was another fellow nearby named Ed Kotulla, and their mail and business contacts got mixed, so Ed and Joe met in San Antonio. They agreed to toss a coin. Joe lost and changed his initial. The railroad junction of Cotulla was named for Joe.[26]

---

[26] Interview with Simon and Paul Cotulla in Cotulla, Texas, 1951. Simon was Joe's son, and Paul his grandson.

Another Slaughter friend and business associate was J. C. B. Harkness who, after heroism in the Civil War, came to Friotown in 1874 and became a cowboy for Charley and Billy. In 1876, he went up the trail with Slaughter and Woodward. Joe Laxton, a Slaughter son-in-law, was one of the hands then.

In those days, the Nueces was called the "deadline" for sheriffs, and desperadoes hung out in remote ranches around there. The old Conchino Ranch was one of these hideaways. Friotown seemed to be "crawling" with cattle thieves in eventful 1876. The list of offenders tells the story better than an embroidered anecdote could. Henry Clay Johnson was charged with stealing six head of cattle; Wesley Walters, of three head; H. C. Johnson of the same; and William Dancer of a calf. John E. Gardner stole 50 horses, and Marion McBee was said to have made away with 16 head of cattle. Charley Slaughter was one of the jurors in the Frio District Court on the trial of Ben Stidham for cattle theft.[27]

Time was out of joint, and the moment was ripe to produce a man who could correct the situation. Harkness was just the one. In 1877, he was elected Frio's sheriff. Though rustlers and thieves in general marked him for death, he made the whole county safe and also cleaned up what are now Zavala and La Salle counties.[28] John Slaughter had a good example to follow right in his own backyard.

Still, basic honesty did live in that day. Old trailers have said that cowboy bullies were scarcer than desert water, and shirkers no more existed than a mirage. On the trail, valuables were left around freely and never taken. Charley Slaughter's word to a worker was better than the gold he always carried about his waist. The same could be said of his brothers. Joe McKinney, who worked for Charley for

---
[27] Interview with Nancy Slaughter Tubert, Tombstone, Arizona, 1950.
[28] O. W. Nolen, "J. C. B. Harkness of Frio County," *op. cit.*, p. 165.

three years at Frio, never collected any wages until he was through. Then Charley wrote him a check for $3,000 which he cashed in San Antonio.

Sam, Bob, Ben, and Bruce Neill were famous trail drivers who had known old Ben Slaughter in Lockhart and had moved to Atascosa County. Other old trailers Ben and his sons knew or hired were: John Little, W. A. Roberts, Harden Lawless, Billy Hinson, George Willcox, Jim Lowe, Jim Musgrave, Bob and Bill Jennings, and Ed Rutledge. Perhaps the largest operators south of San Antonio were Jim Lowe and John H. Slaughter.

In the Slaughters' day, it was natural to meet and know all the biggest and best of Texas cattlemen. When it came to these specialists, Frio County was not isolated or provincial, for all the trail drivers from Laredo, Corpus Christi, Brownsville and other important points brought their herds through Frio. There was hardly a cattleman in the whole Southwest whom John Slaughter hadn't seen or heard about. Some cattlemen drove through Pearsall itself, then went sixteen miles west to B. L. Crouch's ranch, and then turned north to Sabinal and on to Kansas via Bandera, taking the western trail to Dodge City. In 1886, there must have been much nostalgia when Bob Jennings made one of the last West Texas drives via Friotown with a two-thousand-head herd destined for the same place.[29]

Before the great days were gone, the Slaughter drives were typical. Nine to a dozen drivers accompanied the herd when it set out with the coming of April. Usually, the two most skilled men were "pointers." They fixed the trail and headed the herd. Wagon loads were cut to bare necessities, only a hot roll with a few extra clothes made up the hands' gear, which was placed in the hooligan wagon. Then, too,

---

[29] In July, 1876, when the Slaughter brothers' cattle were really paying, 312,048 head had reached Fort Worth so far that year. San Antonio *Express*, August 3, 1876.

there was no more shelter than a mere blanket roll for each man, and a wise fellow would keep himself in good health, if possible, as there was no medical aid at all. John Slaughter was never entirely well, as an occasional attack of asthma and tuberculosis slowed him up, but grit and wiry muscle carried him through. He succeeded so well at roughing it that a bed and a roof always seemed somewhat foreign to him. Cattle fever was more feared by him than human chills. The herds had to be coddled, while no cowman ever was. They moved up the trail at a slow pace, rarely exceeding twelve miles per day. They couldn't be rushed. Speed of the Slaughter herd was determined by the rear, and stronger cattle were kept forward out of the way of the weaker. The length and width of the herd was almost scientifically calculated, and kept fixed. The time of day meant nothing, although it could be fairly well told by the Big Dipper. Men ate on the trail whenever the cook found the place convenient. Water was the great determinant, but long stretches, even up to more than sixty miles, were trekked without it. When the bed ground was found, the riders closed in on all sides and crowded the animals together. Then, the cowhands rested a short distance away. The first night, two guards watched on about four-hour shifts, and then gave way to the next two.

The trek was lonely for everybody, and men had weeks or months of time to philosophize. This probably helped to make John as quiet and slow in speech as his dad. Along the dusty trail, made stifling by heat and dust from the ever moving hooves, not much talk was wasted anyway. As the rear was half a mile or more from the herd's head, most orders were given by fixed signal, not words.

By the seventies, buffalo were getting scarce and Indians had already learned to like beef. A wise trail boss would let them have a dozen or so of the poor sleepers trailing behind or crippled stock which probably would not live to finish the journey to Kansas. John and his family knew Indian ways and never had any real tragedies. Nevertheless, they were always on guard. Quannah Parker and his braves were a common sight. North of the Nueces River, Indian signs generally increased. Comanches had an annoying penchant for stampeding herds. They sometimes did this by running into the herd with their ponies, dragging a buffalo hide at the end of a rope. This stampeded both horses and stock, though the longhorn ordinarily chose the night to stampede. A brave might slip up, shoot a steer with an arrow and thus cause a stampede through the animal's mad dashes in pain. Often, too, the white man's horses became terrorized at an Indian's scent. John knew Indian tricks and trails, and had his own genius for finding new strategems and cattle paths. It was common to find an animal suffering from the effects of a broken arrow, the head still lodged in the flesh.

Mostly, the Slaughter herds after following the Western trail crossed the Red River at Doan's Crossing and reached Dodge City by midsummer; or they crossed the Eastern portal at Red River Crossing bound for Abilene. There the cattle were sold along with the unneeded cow ponies.[30] At this time, and later, Billy and Charley sometimes sent livestock as far north as Wyoming and Montana. Joe Roberts drove herds up there for them.

As the Slaughter sons prospered in cattle, their homes became centers of local hospitality. Ben and Minerva lived at first with Charley, one mile southeast of Friotown, and later at Billy's, another mile west. Meanwhile, their daughter, Delilah, or Lila, had married Bill McDonald, and afterwards, Walter Smith. Their daughter, Elizabeth, married Bill Hiler, a gay, fun-loving fellow, who had come to Texas as a boy and grew up in the cattle business. The six-

---
[30] For much of the above, see James H. Cook, *Fifty Years on the Old Frontier.*

foot, blue-eyed blond youth was a fine dancer and could play the fiddle like an expert. Besides, he spoke Spanish as well as his father-in-law, and knew Mexican psychology about as thoroughly. January 13, 1875, was their wedding day and the union took place at Charley's home. John saw his favorite baby sister wed. Later, when "Betty" had to go with her new husband into the wilderness, her sister, Mary Votaw, told her, "Betty, you can't take those three little children out there into that God-forsaken Indian country. You'll never live to tell the tale." Betty went to bed with many worries that night, but next morning was cheerful, and Bill's smile was even sunnier. Matching it with her own she told her sister that Hiler knew best. They went – crossing the Concho and continuing in the cattle tradition. No wonder John Slaughter almost worshipped such a sister!

Bill Hiler became range boss for M. Z. Smissen, a Swiss rancher holding a herd east of present Sterling City. After nine years, Hiler homesteaded, raised thoroughbred cattle and horses, and sent his children to school in China Valley.[31] Maybe the Slaughters could not boast three millionaires among their former cowhands, as the great Charles Goodnight did, but many a former employee did as well as Hiler. All were rich in spunk.

By the '70s, Charley Slaughter's children had all been born, and about half had died.[32] Charley was a good family man, as upright in this as he was in civic affairs. He never drank or swore, but the acceptable oaths he made were gilt-

---

[31] He died May 6, 1922. His widow moved to Hot Springs, New Mexico. See George Hays in *Frontier Times*, Pearsall, XIV, September, 1937, pp. 543-545. Georgia Hiler Hays says that the Slaughters resented her father. Their personalities definitely clashed with his, and they looked down upon him. Georgia Hiler Hayes, Stayton, Oregon, in letter January 31, 1952.

[32] They were: Sallie, who married W. H. Slaughter (no relation); Nancy, who wed Joe Hunt and later a Mr. Tubert; Nettie, wife of Dan Lucas; Laura, who married an Emerson; Benjamin; Whittey; John; Lou, who married John Lucas; Maude; and Jenny; and Fannie, who married George Lucas.

edged bonds. He was easy-going and thoughtful. His temper never got him into trouble, as John's often did. Evidently Charley was a patient man, too, because when a fellow once cheated him out of $7,000 through a worthless check, he did not take the theft too badly. Twenty-one years later he met that rancher on the street of Goldthwaite, Texas, and received the whole sum in cash! Another bit of waiting brought Charley $100 a month as a Confederate veteran.[33]

Billy was still different. Taller than John, he had blue eyes, and a fairer complexion than most Slaughters. Unlike the great sheriff, he had broad ability as a civil administrator, and was a budding politician. He was county commissioner in Frio for twenty-four years. After buying the La Parita ranch in 1855, he had purchased the old Triangle brand from J. H. Baldwin of California. In 1880 he bought his parents' Frio homestead for $1,500.[34] Billy seems to have shared John's Scotch-Irish temper. When something made him really mad, he never got over it. Yet, he had the family's courage, too. During the '60's he proved it.

In 1865, Billy and Charley, with Billy Votaw and the Neatherlins, their in-laws, had gone to the Nueces country with their families to ranch. There was almost no settlement there; ranches were fifty or more miles apart and Indians lurked in the brushy areas. Still the land seemed valuable to them, for during the war most of the livestock a bit farther east had been either driven off by frontier bandits or roving Comanches and had drifted to join the large herds of wild cattle in this challenging valley. In the 1830s maps of Mexican Texas had vaguely dubbed that area the land of "droves of wild cattle and horses." It was, if anything, a rare Texas understatement! The Slaughters had a good chance to recapture wild branded cattle and domes-

---

[33] Interview with Hugh A. Taylor, San Antonio, Texas, 1950.
[34] This was Pre-emption Survey 131.

ticate the unbranded ones. Their home was an old vacated ranch abandoned before the war. It was a communal project, for all were quartered, as a necessary protection against Indians, under the same spacious but low roof. All worked together, too, and used the same corrals. The women were often united feverishly but steadily melting lead and moulding bullets when menace approached. One such event was the breaking point for most. Indians had chased one of the colonists' small boys to the house, but retreated before the men returned from the day's roundup. Now, most of the men took their families back to civilization, but returned alone later to run cattle.

During those bloody days in La Salle County, Billy always cheered his brother and other relatives with, "When troubles multiply, sooner or later they get their worst, then they mend." [35]

His wife did not need much of a boost for her deep courage. About the same time, a Mexican rode up to the ranch house one afternoon, and told her that a raid would come that night. She faced him, cold and still as a branding iron in a snowdrift, and said in challenge that she would be ready. Then she sat up all night with a shotgun across her lap and her two little girls, Amanda and Mary, beside her. The Mexicans came on schedule, but did not attack the house. Like weasels in a henhouse, they rustled some beef and stole off.[36]

Billy had six daughters, Amanda, Mary, Fannie, Artie, Maggie and Ida.[37] Their careers of courage matched their parents'. Isaac Milton Taylor had been Charley's wagon boss. He went with his first bunch of cattle from Texas to Seven Rivers, New Mexico, and also made trips for John,

---

[35] J. Marvin Hunter, *The Trail Drivers of Texas* (1923), II, p. 610.
[36] Interview with William M. Higdon.
[37] All married local men: Fannie wed Daniel B. Little; Artie, William A. Roberts; Maggie, J. Newton Long; and Ida, Charles B. Woodward.

taking his herds to Dodge City and Abilene. Then, this six-foot-two-inch Texan saw Billy's oldest daughter, Amanda. Love came fast, but the next trail drive for Amanda's father must have been longer than usual for Milt. At last it ended, and he hurried back to Frio to marry her on August 4, 1880. Four years later he bought from his wife's Uncle Charley a tract on the Leona, fifteen miles southwest of Friotown. Their marriage was a long and happy one, producing eleven children of whom nine outlived their aged father.[38]

Joe Laxton, another of Billy's cowhands, married Mary Slaughter at Pearsall on January 12, 1886.

By the end of the 'sixties, John Slaughter had his own ranch in Atascosa and the eastern part of Frio County. It was fairly level land with a rolling surface and few hills and scattered oak, and much birch on the sandy soil. Luckily for Slaughter, he was almost always blessed with a region of abundant artesian wells. In time, the ranch flourished, and John had 2,500 to 3,000 head. Sometimes he began his drives with a mere 500, but gathered enough strays on the way to sell around 3,000 up north. Slaughter's road brands could be found west to the Devil's River, east to the Brazos, south to the Gulf of Mexico, and as far north as Concho.

In June, 1874, John, as assignee of the San Antonio Mexican Gulf Railroad Company, received from Texas 640 acres located in La Salle County, on the Nueces and twenty-four miles northwest of Fort Ewell. He later received an additional 640 acres in the same region. As in his father's case, free or cheap land was starting him off well.

John Slaughter had a ranching neighbor in Atascosa County about this time, and his rather strange name was Leasel "Bobo" Harris. John's place was about three miles

---

[38] Taylor died on November 8, 1927 at Pearsall. See Pearsall *Leader,* November 11, 1927. Interview with Hugh A. Taylor, San Antonio, 1950.

north of Harris', but their pastures joined. Now "Bobo" means fool in Spanish, but Harris should have chosen "Sabio" for most of his doings proved him shrewd and wise. John's neighbor had come from as old pioneering stock as the Slaughters. Born in Macon, Georgia, in 1825, he was brought with his family to De Witt's Colony in 1831. Leasel's father had died early, and his mother turned to running an inn at Gonzales, where Jim Bowie, Davy Crockett, William B. Travis and Sam Houston sometimes stayed. "Lease" knew them all and enjoyed an early boyhood which modern youths would have envied. Thrills were plentiful, for the boy and his mother became refugees with Houston's army at San Jacinto. Nevertheless, they all got a good view of the battle. His grandmother hadn't even time to put on her clothes. The little boy manfully drove the family wagon with its few rescued belongings. At San Jacinto, they saw Santa Anna after his capture. The Mexican general, like Granny, had been given no time to dress that April morn! At eighteen, young Harris joined the Texas Rangers and fought with Taylor's army at Monterrey long before Ben Slaughter got there. As early as 1850, he turned to the cattle business and drove his first herd to Abilene in 1867. By 1871 his was one of the largest herds belonging to any individual owner in that great cattle state. His main ranch was about fifty miles below San Antonio on the colorful old Laredo Road. His books showed at San Angelo a calf branding of 28,500 and total cattle of about 150,000.[39]

Now, John Slaughter must have been mightily impressed by these figures, but he was much more enthusiastic about Harris' daughter, Eliza Adeline. She was a five-foot-three, frail, fragile beauty with ash blonde hair, and lovely blue eyes, a graduate of Edmunds College in San Antonio. Although her health was very delicate, Eliza had as much

---
[39] Hunter, op. cit., II, 666.

courage and grit as any of John's sisters and often proved that she could be a real frontier matriarch. Now, John had been a bachelor quite a long time, some thought, although he was only thirty. Still, his two brothers had been happily married since the Civil War. At first, he thought of his old life, and probably wedded bliss didn't sound so sweet. Then, too, Mrs. Harris opposed any tendency of Eliza's and John's friendship becoming serious, but she was soon won over. John Slaughter was something of a lady's man, well built and with a trim, black beard, dark eyes and an olive complexion. His courage and bearing combined with self-assurance, outmeasured his brief five and a half feet. A full foot and a half short of Ben's friend, Big Foot Wallace, still it could be said of John that when he peeped over the sites of his equalizer he was the fiercest looking westerner ever to put a boot in a stirrup. Ferocity did not hide his gallantry, though. More and more often he popped up at the Harris ranch, supposedly to talk cattle. Now, John needed a little of a softer, gentler courage, the kind that goes with romance. Slowly he stored up his best fancy phrases, as he paid unusual attention to Lease's lovely daughter. Though he was not much of a talker, the courtship was surprisingly rapid. The wedding took place at the bride's parents' residence in San Antonio on August 4, 1871.[40] Within a year a daughter, Adeline or "Addie," was born in the same house, while the other members were born in the old rock house of Charley Slaughter near Friotown.

Two other children, a boy named Hugh, and a little girl, came later. Hugh died at John's ranch near Pleasanton. To make the tragedy worse, Lease Harris was in a buggy accident. He had his little grandson's casket in the carriage and was about to cross a creek enroute to the Pleasanton cemetery, but the horse was high spirited, a real racing trotter,

---

[40] Interview with Nancy Tubert.

and jumped suddenly, upsetting the buggy and throwing out the coffin and Harris, who had the reins so tightly about his hand that the wrist was broken. At the same time, Addie's little sister was being born. This third child died of pneumonia near San Angelo when she was about a year old. Later came another boy, Willie, who was never robust.[41]

Life was hard on the Nueces frontier, but the young mother could cope with almost anything. John was away on the range much of the time, and she had to deal with things alone. On one occasion, she was home with her ten-year old sister, Nancy, and the baby, Hugh, when a dozen Comanche bucks attacked the house. Eliza Adeline gave a negro hand a shotgun to guard the door, and with a gun of her own took her place by the window. Together, they held the attackers off until they gave up the siege and fled. The whole trouble was made more fearful by night.[42]

Life was not all rough, for Adeline spent much of her time in San Antonio where John owned a house on Gardner Street on the southwest outskirts.[43] To the east was Mission Concepcion Road. San Antonio was the "city" for them. Artificial gas lighting had arrived there in 1866, and while the young couple lived there, the telegraph came, and the Southern Pacific Railroad. The Menger Hotel was the social gathering place, and the Slaughters were much in it. Already the town had become a cotton mart for Mexico. Slaughter teams joined others coming to town, and corrals where stock could be secured were nearby. Adeline tended her household chores in a town of over 15,000, well provided now with schools, churches and newspapers, and even

---

[41] *Idem.*

[42] Interview with Nancy Isabelle Harris Cartledge, sister of Eliza Adeline Harris Slaughter, Austin, Texas, 1950.

[43] Jan. 23, 1875, Eliza Adeline and John sold their four acres on the east side of the San Antonio River (of Bennett Musgrave's grant) to Caroline Hindes. State of Texas, County of Bexar, Records Book 1, page 357.

more so with saloons. The dusty Mexican pueblo was fast giving way to an American city. Still living in town were 1,650 negroes, mostly ex-slaves. Near John's house, cattle grazed, and one needed to go only a few yards for good hunting. Many times John and Eliza Adeline went together on the plain, and her young sister Nancy helped gather the birds they had killed.[44]

Soon after John's and Eliza Adeline's union, Slaughter made another solemn contract with the Harris family. This affair was also close to the young man's heart – the cattle business. John became the partner of Lease Harris. In 1872, they were working together on the Nueces where Harris had a herd. Unfortunately, marauders from Mexico and a band of Comanches attacked and killed several of their cowboys. Never discouraged, in 1873, the two men took a reputed 65,000-head herd and trailed to Abilene, "following the North Star."[45] Often John worked as his own herd boss, taking part in every danger and hardship of these long drives. Like any hand, he put in fifteen hours a day and sometimes more when the weather was bad. It was nothing for him to be up all night, ready for Indian, rustler or hold-up man. Once a Mexican committed a crime against the partners, and John tracked him southward into several of the northern Mexican states which he had known so well through cattle buying and selling expeditions, and there he met the desperado and settled their differences in the usual custom. Slaughter and Harris made a good team.[46] The

---

[44] Nancy Harris Cartledge interview.

[45] Cook, *op. cit.*, p. 175.

[46] Harris, for $200, sold to Charley Slaughter, then living in Frio County, 505 acres lying on the south bank of the Frio. This was part of a "league and labor patented to R. J. Higginbotham." That was on April 24, 1874, as shown in the records of the County of Bexar. Harris and the Slaughters were always making some kind of cattle deal. For instance, on April 19, 1878, Lease sold Ben and Billy Votaw all his interest in some horses held by L. M. S. Pope, and some real estate in San Antonio, east of the river (Block 16). All this cost Old Ben and Young Votaw but $5.00.

older man was a good gambler in every sense. Owning cattle ranging from the Nueces to the Rio Grande, he was sure of losses. Mexican marauders once stole cattle worth an estimated $779,000. He also lost a large cargo of choice beeves in a ship disaster in the Gulf, yet he took it all in stride and went on to take other carefully calculated risks. He and John prospered from that most successful gamble of all, the Kansas market. Prices for steers had risen from a dull $1.00 to an active $20.00 a head as the Kansas Pacific's rails reached into the Sunflower State.

Lease Harris had other pretty daughters.[47] One of them, Mary, or "Molly" married Billy Childress whose relative, Polk Childress, had in 1871 for $600 purchased Charley Slaughter's La Parita Creek land. Billy had been born in Tuscaloosa, Alabama, in July, 1851, and came with his widowed mother to Pleasanton. It seems that love was often opposed in pioneer Texas, at least by Mr. and Mrs. Lease Harris! This time, it was Lease who did not favor the marriage of his little Molly to young Childress. It was not that Billy was poor, for his father was said to have left him $25,000, a great sum in that day. Lease was a man of unusual good judgment and he thought the boy irresponsible. Pretty Molly was only eighteen and Billy a dark-eyed

---

[47] Harris had married Martha Isabelle McKenzie in San Antonio in the home of Toliver and Martha Higginbotham, famous ranchers. Eliza Adeline was born in San Marcos, at her Grandmother McKenzie's. The other Harris children were Walter Clifton, Mary E. "Molly," Clara, William Wayne, Nancy Isabelle, Frank L., and Ralph Henry. Eliza Adeline died of smallpox, Walter of a throat ailment. Mary was never very well, but managed to reach 80. Clara died of the effects of a broken hip. William was killed when his horse stumbled, throwing him over a steer he was cutting out. Frank succumbed to liver trouble, and Ralph died from internal troubles and pneumonia. Lease had organized the Concho National Bank of San Angelo and was its first president. Son Ralph was first city treasurer of San Angelo. (Interview with Ralph H. Harris.) Ralph says that he and Frank once operated the Harris brothers ranch in parts of six West Texas counties, carrying the 7F brand. Today, they have 300 sections in Crockett, Upton, and Reagan Counties and 50 more in Coke County, all well stocked with cattle.

twenty-four-year-old when they won and were married by a Methodist minister at Harris' Atascosa ranch.⁴⁸

As a young frontier wife, Molly had as many scares as Adeline Slaughter, her sister. A year after her marriage, when enroute to Pleasanton from San Antonio, Mrs. Childress was carrying in her purse $500 of Billy's, left with her for safe keeping. The ride seemed long and warm that summer day, so Molly and her fourteen-year-old sister, Nancy, stopped the buggy to water their horse. Suddenly, a man on horseback came near and began to eye the purse. He gave his mount a drink, too. Molly got in the buggy as fast as she could and instead of driving to Pleasanton, turned off to flee to some kinfolk. The stranger followed for a while, then cut off – fortunately for the ladies, as the relatives were not at home.

Meanwhile, Billy Childress and John Slaughter became partners. Billy acted as John's agent, buying, selling and moving stock for the latter, who was usually far out on the range.⁴⁹ For instance, in November 1873, Childress bought for Slaughter all the range cattle of W. W. Perryman, T. M. McDaniel, R. S. Ragsdale, and John L. Lytle.⁵⁰

---
⁴⁸ Billy died of a stomach ailment on November 16, 1902. He had been a rancher all of his life and finally ended his days at Howard Wells, twenty-five miles southwest of Ozona, Texas. He and Molly had four sons, Pleas, who died in 1936, Walter, Hugh, and Lee, all three still living (1952). Their daughters were Eula and Pearl. The latter passed on in 1936. Their mother also died that year, on October 31, at the age of 79.

⁴⁹ On October 13, 1873, John Lytle, R. S. Ragsdale and F. M. McDaniel of Frio County sold to Childress and John Slaughter their interest in several brands: 5J; Y; ICU; ICJ; ICD; ICL; D; 16; L; XE; 116; TW; UD; IVY; O2; JLL; VX; XI. They cost $25,000, to be paid by the two parties in 1874. The rate of payment was: beeves, $12; 2-year olds, $6; calves, $9. They were also to give 25 saddle horses and a ranch on Block Creek, Frio County. See Frio County, Bill of Sales, Book A, page 445. During this partnership, Slaughter recorded several brands on December 3, 1874: RR; Slash S; SPD; JK; S; W; OE; -W; and six with various ear marks. Then Slaughter and Childress, on July 17, 1875, recorded "7".

⁵⁰ Frio County, State of Texas, Deed Records Book A, page 486, November 28, 1873.

In July, 1875, the partners sold to one Bennett Musgrave their stock and pasture in Atascosa and other counties west of the Colorado for $235,000.[51] John and Billy were partners on a Kansas drive. Childress drove the cattle part way and Slaughter took them the rest of the journey, giving Billy a $25,000 note for his share of the profits. In August 1874, Childress as Slaughter's agent bought from W. C. Daugherty certain stocks, a cavy yard of horses, two pastures on the Nueces, and four cattle pens, for which Childress gave Daugherty two promissory notes, one for $22,500 in gold to come due March 10, 1875, the other note for a like sum, to mature a year later. To secure their payment, Billy delivered to Daugherty a mortgage on twenty-eight brands, a cavy yard of horses branded UT, 7IN and 7 E, two pastures on the Nueces, and four cattle pens. John Slaughter signed the instrument on September 9, 1874. In September, 1877, Plaintiff Daugherty sued for payment in the Frio County court. John did not show up. Daugherty proved that very few, if any, of the described cattle were left, for nearly all of these mortgaged steers had been sold or driven off; only a scant number were even in the same state! Thus in January, 1879, the court decreed that Daugherty should recover from Slaughter $31,043 with interest at eight percent per annum.[52] The mortgages being foreclosed, Atascosa County's sheriff was ordered to sell the aforementioned property, the proceeds going toward paying the sum, its interest and court costs.[53] Some day Slaughter would see the positions reversed and he would be conducting such sales!

---

[51] This, however, excepted their useful Lagounias pasture, which was reserved. The pastures sold were those at Indian Bend Ranch and the Tula Ranch.

[52] Frio County Court, Record Book D, page 218, Judgment 9.

[53] On March 13, 1878, Leasel B. Harris gave David G. Portes power of attorney to sign his name to a deed of trust to Ben Slaughter to secure him as Harris' security in the attachment bond in which Daugherty was plaintiff and John H. Slaughter defendant. Lease Harris and W. C. Daugherty had had an upland ranch, according to Ed Roberts, when Harris lived at San Miguel Creek, 15 miles east of

In September, 1878, however, Slaughter and Childress found themselves in yet another lawsuit. This time, John E. Stanfield won by default the sum of $4,200 plus $560 interest at eight percent yearly from January 1, 1877, plus court costs.[54] Again, John did not appear.

Lone wolf as Slaughter was, the partnership and complicated trials must have become wearisome.[55] He and Childress, ten years his junior, wintered a bunch of cattle at Beaver Lake north of Del Rio in 1876 and then took them up the trail in the spring. They had made several such trips, but this was their last as partners. On May 12, 1876, he and Billy dissolved their partnership legally, the latter accepting the parting with good feelings and no little compensation. He got $10,000 "in hand paid," 1,800 head of cattle, and other considerations. John was also to pay all debts owed by their firm. After that John H. Slaughter made no more formal partnerships of that sort. He never even incorporated his later vast domain.

However, not all financial arrangements hurt Slaughter. In 1876 he and Jim Lowe were the largest owners in their region. Slaughter had James M. Neatherlin gather a herd and drive it up the trail that year. So large were his holdings that two other herds were rounded up and taken north by other trail bosses. Then John decided to sell out to Lowe, and it was arranged that Slaughter was to take his pay for

---

Pearsall. Daugherty sold him his brand and cattle, but took judgment for $20,000, which he collected. Later, Harris moved to San Angelo and became quite wealthy. Daugherty went far, too. At the same time that John H. Slaughter became sheriff of Cochise County, Arizona (1887), Daugherty became sheriff of Frio County, Texas, and remained so for many years. Afterwards, he went to West Texas and died there.

[54] John C. Stanfield *vs.* John H. Slaughter, State of Texas, County of Atascosa, December 27, 1878.

[55] On April 1, 1875, for $50,000, John Slaughter sold to his partner half interest in certain cattle, marks, and brands, on his ranges in Frio, Atascosa, McMullen, Live Oak, Bexar, and Medina Counties, and half interest in all saddle horses and ponies (geldings) with UT, 7IN, (Lazy HA), and 7E brands, and the same interest in pastures and pens on the Nueces, known as the Indian bend pasture.

all his interests in Lowe's cattle at a price previously agreed on. Slaughter was to take the cattle out of the county. Confusion and disagreement resulted, and Lowe was pretty much the loser.[56]

Billy did fine alone, too. In 1877 he and John's mutual father-in-law, Harris, bought some Coke County land and sent out a herd with Walter and Billy Childress in charge. Together they ran the spread for some years. In March, 1878, Billy was helping run Harris' La Conias Creek ranch in Atascosa County. Childress made a deal with Lewis and Buntzer for the ranch, receiving 500 head of cows and calves for it.[57]

In another way the Harris and Slaughter families were tied together. Billy Votaw, a big cattleman of those parts, was half-brother of Lease Harris. Votaw's father, serving as a cavalryman under Houston, had guarded the settlers who fled Gonzales after the Alamo's fall. On the trip he met Lease's widowed mother, let her ride behind him on his cavalry mount, and later married her. Later still, Lease Harris gave Billy Votaw a brand worth $10,000 and started his half-brother in the cattle business. This was a fine wedding present — Billy Votaw had just married John Slaughter's sister, Mary. His wedding suit had a rather unromantic adventure, though. Some Indians raided Votaw's ranch on the Nueces and stole it. After a time, Billy and his friends had a brush with an old Indian chief, whom they killed, and found him dressed in the bridegroom garb! Thus, like many another important clan, cattle dynasties had a way of uniting.

Of dynasties built on beef, the Slaughter clan has gained

---

[56] Ed Roberts interview. In order to secure Lowe in the payment of his four obligations (four notes) Slaughter made Lowe his lawful agent to sell any of his cattle at usual market prices. Bexar County Records, San Antonio, September 4, 1874.

[57] Hunter, *op. cit.*, II.

immortality. Christopher Columbus Slaughter, son of Ben's cousin George, was the founder of the most famous cattle raising branch of that family. He became president of the Texas and Southwestern Cattle Raisers Association in 1885. A full-fledged cowboy at 12 on his father's Sabine County ranch, "C.C." later settled and named Slaughter Valley on the Brazos. At one time his domain covered 200 miles square, or 25 million acres! Ben's boys never rivalled that. For a time, C.C. was Texas' largest individual taxpayer.[58]

At the Old Trail Drivers' Association barbecue of 1926, Will Rogers said it better, and included Old Ben's sons, too, when he mentioned the patricians of the range: "Their names were to me like you would look on presidents. I had heard all my life of such families as the Slaughters, the Pierces, the Pryns. . . Every business has its aristocracy."[59] To have gained such a tribute, the Slaughters' story rates its telling!

[58] Mary Whatley Clarke, "Early Cattle King Headed Association," *The Cattleman*.
[59] *Frontier Times*, April, 1940, XVII, no. 7, p. 317.

4

Beyond the Pecos

By the late 1870s, Texas was already too overcrowded to suit John Slaughter. The bulk of his cattle were being grazed in the region of the Devil's River in west Texas. To the north in the valley of the upper Pecos in New Mexico Territory there still was free range land, and a market for beef had long been made attractive to meet the needs of the various army camps and Indian reservations. The mining camps furthermore were active, and on the whole John Slaughter saw opportunity in making a change to improve himself as an important stock raiser.

Charles Goodnight and John Simpson Chisum had both pioneered the New Mexico area by the late 1860's. Chisum had by 1877 earned the name of "Cattle King of the Pecos," having come there with an estimated 100,000 cattle which he had driven from the head of the Concho in Texas. His headquarters had been at Bosque Grande, south of Fort Sumner. He had himself anticipated a change, and in November, 1875, sold his Bosque Grande ranch to a Mr. Hunter of St. Louis for something over $300,000, and moved farther down the Pecos to South Springs near the present Roswell.

In New Mexico again reigned the knights of infamy. Mexican rustlers, American cattle and horse thieves, and marauding Indians were still active. Even the highwayman was still enjoying a certain amount of freedom. This little incident, which had been experienced by the Pecos cattle king, was published in the Santa Fe *New Mexican* on January 21, 1876:

The stagecoach from Silver City to Santa Fe on their trip up, entered Cook's Canyon, with the confidence that the late peacefulness warranted.

No more Mr. Indian to stop and plunder, but the professional highwayman has come and did halt the coach of the Southern company, and did demand your money or your life from the passengers in the coach which was done.

John Chisum, the well known cattle owner of longhorns from Texas, and now a resident of the Hondo and Bonita, was one of the victims, and our friend, Conway of Santa Fe, another. Owing to the security of the times, and the lateness of the hour, these gentlemen were not prepared for an encounter (except what he slid into his boot, and his $600 gold watch and chain).

Mr. Conway lost his spare change and his repeater. The conductor was made to take the passage, tied to a wheel of his coach – and the driver had enough to do to hold on to his team, while the Roadsters went through coach and passengers, for the booty. They got the treasure boxes from Silver City in the shape of bullion being expressed through – amounting to some $4000 and got away with it.

Chisum is reported to have said to the robbers, "Now you have gone through us, Can't you give us a drink out of my own bottle of fine whiskey?" – And gentlemen of the road as they were, they did hand out the bottle with, "Take a drink all around, boys" – which the boys did, and goodbyes was exchanged, and the parties parted.

Chisum had always said that if he could get an antagonist down to a talk, he knew then he would win the argument. However, in this case he lost. The tempo had not changed much as Indians were still plundering as they left their reservations. But of all the plagues that hampered the cattleman, the rustler was the worst. John Chisum was usually the victim, because of the enormous area his cattle roamed, and the large herds he possessed. What looked good to Charley Slaughter, did not look sufficiently appealing to John. Chisum had been too deeply established, and had the cattle markets pretty much his own way. John Slaughter wanted to look at the Arizona Territory. He calculated that with Billy in Texas, Charley in New Mexico, and himself in Arizona, that together they would be in a position to carry out their operations quite successfully. John still had cattle in Texas, and this would mean that a drive to Arizona could be accomplished without hardship in three relays, each contributing to the trail drive.[1]

It was early in April of 1879 that Charley began moving stock and kinfolk to the new acres which he had bought on Seven Rivers from Thomas Gardner, an old hermit who lived in a Chosa near the Pecos.

The first herds into Lincoln County were wintered around Fort Stanton about 1863. It was three years later, though, that a couple of immortal ranchers made the occupation economically effective. After the Civil War, Oliver Loving, a cowman who had lived in the saddle and dared Indians for a score of years, became associated with his young friend, Charles Goodnight. The latter had planned the most daring trail-drive to go around the Comanche-ridden plains of West Texas to the south Concho rim, then cross the fearful waste lands to Horsehead Crossing on the fertile Pecos. The route would then follow this river to Fort Sumner, New Mexico, crossing the trails of the hostile Apache. Some might have thought the sixty-mile dry drive to the crossing as bad as any native, but Loving and Goodnight found it well worth the trouble. In 1866, with eighteen cowhands and two thousand head of cattle, they fixed the trail, conquering alkali sands and wastes, though the crossing took

---

[1] On June 1, 1880, for $32,000 Charley Slaughter sold to his brother Billy all his partnership interests in a section of land, 640 acres, situated in La Salle County, Texas, on the waters of Johan (Johnny) Creek, a tributary of the Frio; Surveys 7, 11, 9, 13, 15, 17, 19, 21, 23, and 27 were also included, as well as all other lands and real estate in La Salle County jointly owned with Billy, and one league in the name of Concepcion Carillo in Frio County, containing 13,121 acres. See State of Texas, Frio County Records, Book E, page 190. On July 31, Charley gave over to Billy all his rights to real estate, land certificates, notes, accounts, livestock, and brands in Frio, Atascosa, Medina, La Salle, Bandera, Uvalde, Kinney, Zavalla, Maverick, McMullen, Dimmit, and other counties. See State of Texas, Frio County, Book E, page 235. On April 21, 1881, Billy and Charley both conveyed 15 sections on Johnny Creek to Alonzo A. Millet of Dallas County.

three days and three nights. Despite the valiant hurry, to avoid loss through thirst, many poor stock never reached the Pecos. Loving's later trip was made bitter by Comanche-caused stampedes, and the trek cost him his life, after crawling for miles, wounded and suffering from thirst, only to die in spite of efforts to save him.

When he brought his more modest herd from Frio County, Charley Slaughter benefitted but little by going over the same route. He came through by way of Ft. Concho and Fort Stockton and headed for the Pecos, crossing it at Torres Ranch, about sixty miles below Horsehead Crossing. The river was higher than usual, and quite dangerous. Charley, however, had good men with him. Among them were Old Bat, John's negro servant he had hired in San Antonio, who now was ably acting as cook, Milt Taylor, Charley's young son-in-law, as wagon boss, Tom Hance, Bill Whitaker, and an aged, colorful Mexican driver called Old Said.

Taylor, making about ten trips in all, brought three herds for Charley, and John Slaughter eventually got most of them! The year before, John had driven Charley's cattle from Fort Ewell with his own bunch.[2] He had come this same route but crossed at Horsehead Crossing. Here he could see two lonely graves. Where the trail struck the Pecos, Goodnight had already noted an unlucky 13 resting places. Now Charley had made three trips himself to the new ranch site, returning to Texas each time for cattle, and finally bringing his family. Each trip took over a month.

As the family of five girls and two boys finally reached the Pecos, an Indian scrape offered them a more than thrill-

---

[2] Grace Miller White, "Goodnight-Loving Trail," in Pearsall *Frontier Times*, XIX, April, 1942; and H. J. Burton, "History of the J. A. Ranch," in *Southwestern Historical Quar.*, XXXI. J. Evetts Haley's great study Charles Goodnight, *Cowman and Plainsman* (Boston and New York, 1936) is unexcelled, and cannot be overlooked.

JAMES HENRY "JIM" EAST
AS CHIEF OF POLICE OF DOUGLAS, ARIZONA
An Oldham County, Texas, cowboy, and ex-sheriff of Tascosa
East was with the Frank Stewart posse when Billy the Kid
was captured at Stinking Springs.

MERCANTILE AND BANK BUILDING IN LINCOLN, NEW MEXICO
Operated by McSween, Tunstall, and Chisum. A landmark of the Lincoln County War.

ing welcome. Ahead of the three Slaughter wagons were a Mr. and Mrs. Graham who had taken the trail to their own new ranch, but as they reached Lancaster Hill Pass, savages swept down upon their little party, wounding Graham before he could fire, and killing his pretty wife with the first flying lead. Graham, falling under the wagon, escaped death but could not fight back. A companion named Murphy managed to get behind some rocks and there resisted for two hours, when the Indians rode off. Graham was tough enough to recover, but most of the caravan was not brave enough to remain. Again, Charley and his family viewed the charred bodies of the drivers of three government wagons at Howard's Well, but unlike their squeamish fellow travelers, did not turn back.[3] With three other families, they went on.

Arriving at Seven Rivers, the Slaughters lived in a house of two small adobe rooms with a large adjoining corral whose portholes might warn Indians that the horses inside would be defended. Apparently the Apaches read the warning poorly, for once three of them chased Charley all the way home from town, though he drew blood as poor compensation for a good scare.

In 1881, a band of Indians, led by a namesake of the Sioux Medicine man, Sitting Bull, stole some cattle and horses from Charley, and he and his cowboys took after them. The party consisted of Pete Corn, Marion Turner, Mark Fanning and Bill and John Jones. They overtook the Indians at Rocky Arroyo, about where Bill Jones' ranch was later established. Surprised at breakfast, the Indians fled, and the rancher got his stock back, only to lose it again when the thieves recaptured their loot. Upon sight of the Indians, Turner originated a timely saying, "Take to the toolies, boys."

[3] A letter from Fannie Slaughter Lucas, Carlsbad, New Mexico, Feb. 15, 1951.

Once, near Seven Rivers, Charley had a camp a couple of miles from where Carlsbad now stands. About sundown, when he was returning home, five Indians followed him. As he stood up in the stirrups, firing back, a bullet tore through the cantle of his saddle. Yet, though he had already ridden his stout horse forty miles that day, Charley outrode the hostiles and ever after called his pony "Telegraph." He retired it and treated the steed with great care. No wonder settlers were slow to come and make the land polite and peaceful!

Indeed, Indians were too plentiful, but white men continued scarce — at least the right kind did. Only a few families lived in the Seven Rivers area, and there were no schools. Charles B. Eddy, for whom Eddy County was later named, was a Slaughter neighbor. Within a three day ride was to be found Roswell, New Mexico, named for Roswell Smith, consisting of a couple of adobe buildings. Lincoln, the county seat, was the only real village. Among the few families there was warmth but lots of space. The nearest schools were at Anton Chico and Las Vegas, New Mexico, some three hundred miles by a rutted trail. Indians and loneliness were bad enough, but the Slaughters had the strange genius of moving into the territory at its bloodiest spot and time. The Lincoln County War had commenced, and a lad known as Billy the Kid was making his name known throughout the country. A conclave of economists, historians, and sociologists would bring forth many reasons for this particular frontier conflict, but strong and honest law enforcement would have been the best preventive medicine.

Typical of the cattle kings was John Simpson Chisum. Born in Tennessee in 1824, he moved to Texas at thirteen, entered politics at twenty-nine, and finally bought a herd of a thousand cattle which he trailed north to the Fort Worth-

Denton range. His herds had grown along with his beef profits during the Civil War. Chisum soon substantiated Goodnight's rosy prophecies. In 1866-67, Chisum moved a large herd from the Concho to Bosque Grande, his first settlement. Usually, he drove his herd across west Texas, and northward to Bosque Grande. By 1870 he had moved all his stock to the Pecos region. His "Long Rail" brand and the "Jingle-Bob" ear mark were seen far and wide by other cowmen.

In 1874, this bachelor cattleman was known as the "Pecos Valley Cattle King," and the next year had grown to be "Cow King of New Mexico." To back up the titles, he employed one hundred cowboys and ran eighty thousand head. Besides this, he had won a contract to furnish beef to Fort Sumner and various Indian agencies of Arizona Territory. To put it plainly, Lincoln County was the largest county in the United States, and Chisum was the biggest and most powerful man in it! Perhaps for a few years, he was the largest individual cattle owner in the world. His herds ranged up and down the Pecos and from Fort Sumner to well into Texas, a two-hundred-mile stretch.[4]

Chisum was a beloved character and got on well with Charley's family. John Slaughter's older brother was easy-going and not hard to get along with, anyway. His brood often went to parties at Chisum's ranch, and these affairs lasted four or five days. Mrs. Slaughter, who was having a hard time learning all the household chores since the slaves had been freed, usually attended in silken hoop skirts. Into the fine mansion came ladies of the latest fashions, though the men always wore cowboy clothes. No eastern dress was

[4] See Pearsall *Frontier Times*, xv, 1938, p. 99; and C. L. Douglas, *Cattle Kings of Texas*. John Chisum died in 1884. Later, the Hagerman estate sold the famous ranch to Cornell University for an experimental station. Interview with Mrs. Amelia Bolton Church, Roswell, New Mexico, 1950.

ever seen on a rancher. Among the excellent young dancers was Billy the Kid.[5]

John Chisum himself was a good mixer and loved music. He had established a strong alliance with Alexander Anderson McSween, of Lincoln, a successful lawyer and cattleman, and an English rancher named Tunstall who was in partnership with McSween. This group started the Lincoln County Bank. Across the street a few blocks west was the opposition party of Dolan and Riley. It was between the McSween faction and Dolan-Riley faction and their henchmen that a most disgraceful, one-sided affair resulted, known as the Lincoln County War. By this time Lawrence Murphy, another leader of the Dolan-Murphy faction, had died.

Now, as we know, Charley did not like trouble. As his scrapes with Indians show, however, he could always take care of himself. Yet, at any rate, he was neutral and had no white enemies, and even the outlaw element had to admit that here was a peaceful man. He had gathered his family about him and made them promise never to mention the Lincoln County War. Still, even he could not entirely escape the touch of the times. Vigilantes once came to his house, heavily armed. They stayed a few hours but did nothing.[6]

Into this tense scene came Billy the Kid. After a life of minor adventures, this young man reached the Pecos in the late '70s. Merely a youth, his mind was uncertain as to what faction he would finally take up with. With the meeting of young Tunstall, Billy quickly made a decision. After Tunstall's brutal murder, Billy adhered to McSween, a former Presbyterian minister. The Kid was certainly loyal to his friends. Although Billy the Kid did a little rustling, he

---

[5] Mrs. Nancy Tubert interview, 1950. In 1950, she was 90, yet able to read without glasses. Her wedding to Joe Hunt in the 1870's was the first wedding in Lincoln County. In 1889, this daughter of Charley Slaughter moved with her family to Sulphur Springs Valley, Arizona, and then in 1902 to Bisbee, where Joe died in 1904.
[6] *Ibid.*

seldom took from anyone who had but few stock. Pecos valley ranchers soon found that the only way they could make secure their beeves was to appoint a new sheriff. Billy was a jolly, friendly fellow and when he was near Seven Rivers would drop in on Charley Slaughter, and to a degree, the Slaughters must have sympathized with the lad. Charley had no reason to have "had it in" for the Kid. In fact, little Nancy Slaughter used to see him in a Fort Sumner store occasionally. There he stopped his pals from using profanity while ladies were present. Often on Sundays, Billy would attend religious services in McSween's parlor, though he and his friends never removed their gun belts. Little things revealing a gentler side made him locally popular.[7] Even Billy's pals' frequent pastime of opening other people's mail at the post office and adding a few romantic postscripts was looked upon with amused tolerance.

Strangely enough, and yet logically too, Billy's deadliest enemies were also frequent Slaughter guests. Big Bob Olinger, whom Billy killed in his famous escape, was often a guest at Charley Slaughter's house at Seven Rivers, and Pat Garrett used to come with his Mexican wife and spend the night. Mrs. Garrett was especially fond of Mrs. Slaughter's watermelon preserves, and they became fast friends. Once Garrett told Charley that there was talk among the people that Charley was suspected of being a United States Marshal, and therefore had left him strictly alone. This was because Governor Wallace had informers posted among the cowmen.

The Slaughter children, while visiting in Fort Sumner, saw the Kid, shortly after he killed Olinger and Bell, his two guards. They idolized Billy, as he always bought them candy, and they later scorned Garrett for waylaying their idol without giving him a fair chance for his life. Many

---
[7] Fannie Slaughter Lucas letter, Carlsbad, New Mexico, February 12, 1951.

adult neighbors thought the same. Knowing this, Garrett smiled at the youngsters, and his reply might have been made by John Slaughter regarding many a later brush with others who lived by the gun, farther west. Garrett explained sheepishly, "Well, it was his life or mine, and I felt mine was worth more." [8]

Though John Slaughter made fame as an Indian fighter, the spotlight had shifted for the time being, and Pat Garrett became the best known lawman of the Southwest. The killing of the Kid won him these many-times regrettable laurels, and Garrett was to meet fate one day in almost the same manner himself. Jim East, John Slaughter's friend, was an active member in the Frank Stewart-Garrett posse when Billy and his pals surrendered at Stinking Springs, on a bitter cold December morning in 1880. It was learned later that Billy was leaving the country for good and this capture prevented him from doing so. John Slaughter often remarked that Billy would have made him a good deputy had he lived. The Kid gave Jim East his Winchester, which eventually found its way to Beaver Smith, in Fort Sumner, for Smith claimed Billy still owed him for it.

John Slaughter was only another participant in this drama. He was yet only one member of a prominent ranching family, working hard, doing his best, and certainly minding his own business, yet he could speak with thunder when justly aroused. Perfectly fitted for his surroundings, he had fought Indians and rubbed shoulders with the worst type of western badmen. But a hard and colorful life in those early days was neither unusual nor noticeably spectacular. To survive beyond the Pecos, even the mediocre had to ride with vigor and shoot accurately. As little John began to range farther and farther adrift in gathering, buying and selling stock, he had to adjust himself to many new

---
[8] *Ibid.*

situations and varying people. No one could say that he wasn't changeable, but they could truthfully deny that he ever compromised. Slaughter was as swift to measure up a situation as he was fast to defend himself. In these attributes he surpassed the much overrated Pat Garrett who was now seeking political victory on his fame for having destroyed the prime nuisance of the panhandle cattlemen's association.

When John parted company and partnership with Billy Childress on the Devil's River in 1876, he followed on up the Pecos to South Springs, Bosque Grande, and then rode east to the Texas Panhandle. He rode into the cow camps of the LS, LX and XIT, and spoke with the range foremen. Before he left the panhandle, he bought some five hundred head. He drove these down to the Jingle Bob outfit run by John Chisum at South Springs, New Mexico. He would hold these cattle on the free range, until he could bring some other cattle he had with his Brother Billy in Atascosa County. His Fort Ewell headquarters in south Texas was usually the point he would drive from.

As he drove past the Chisum range, and picked up his "held" cattle from the free range, the herd seemed to grow larger than might be expected. If John Slaughter had any notion of convincing Chisum that Slaughter's five hundred head of steers would have offsprings, he was badly mistaken. Still Slaughter was never broken of the habit of starting out with a few and getting to his destination with twice as many. He just did not like to chase off those strays that got into his herd by accident. When cutting time came Slaughter was certain that the tally was short, and had claimed sixty head of unbranded yearlings. Finally Chisum showed a bill of sale corresponding with certain temporary paint brands, and Chisum, the humorist he was, invited Slaughter in for a drink. "You say they are yours," said the cow king, at the same time tearing up the bill of sale. But John Slaughter wanted to decide that over a game of poker. Chisum wasn't much of a poker player, but had so many cattle that he simply played bad poker just to win a friend, and Slaughter walked away chuckling to himself, knowing he would take with him some of Chisum's choice beeves.

From Dimmit County near the Slaughter trail out of Fort Ewell came a cowboy by the name of Barney Gallagher. He was now making his home around Fort Stockton, Texas. Here was a band of rustlers, and Gallagher was said to be one of them. His side-kick was a man remembered by some oldtimers as Boyd. Somewhere trouble had brewed between him and John Slaughter. He followed John's trail across the arroyos on up from Black River, leading past Seven Rivers up to South Springs, where Chisum was headquartering. On this occasion John Chisum was not home, but his brothers Jim and Pitser were present. Sometime before this Gallagher had killed a leader of a bunch of Mexican thieves and had taken his sombrero. It was a costly thing, mounted with silver and gold trimmings. All the rustler crowd were after Gallagher asking him to will it to them, if he should ever die. However this was far from Barney Gallagher's mind. He was brave and a good shot. His mission was to kill Slaughter, take his money belt and run off his cattle. He had brought his boys with him to do just that. There must have been some betting among the men, and Gallagher's wager was the valuable sombrero just in case he lost. Playing the role of a sure winner, Gallagher rode up to the tail end of the herd and spoke to one of the Slaughter cowboys. "You tell that little rat-headed-sonofabitch up front, I'm here to kill him." "Wait right here, I'll tell Mr. Slaughter what you said," was the reply, and the drag rider loped up to the pointers, and waved his boss down. Like vultures lined up a hundred yards off to one side sat Gallagher's men on horseback. They were not taking part, only joking about how the sombrero would look on them. Slaughter loped his horse at a good pace heading for the badman who had announced in such an unfriendly way that he had come to kill him. Gallagher was waiting for his man to come into range, holding a sawed-off shotgun in his hand. As Slaughter closed the gap, Gallagher spurred his horse to meet him and swerved to the side to make sure his buckshot would find it's mark. Since Slaughter's coat was flying in the breeze and his hands were on the rein, Gallagher must have thought it dead certain that his threat would be carried out. Then like a flash a pistol came as if out of nowhere. Slaughter kept his on the pommel of the saddle before him. One shot hit Gallagher in the heart, and he fell out of the saddle. Whether a second shot was fired is not known.

In 1876 Gus Gildea, a trail driver, stopped by the Chisum ranch on South Springs. He had known Gallagher in Dimmit County, describing him as a typical old-time cowboy of his day. He saw where Gallagher had fallen only shortly before.[9] Several accounts of this fight between Slaughter and Gallagher at South Springs have been published. But only the mention made by Gus Gildea and Raht, in his *Romance of the Davis Mountains,* give a reasonable clue. Fannie Slaughter, who lived on Black River when this happened, gave the account here mentioned. Will Chisum, who had arrived there a few months later, heard a somewhat similar account. However, when General Lew Wallace came into office as governor of New Mexico, he listed the killing as murder. This idea was conveyed to him by a man named Gilbert at Seven Rivers, and John Slaughter would hear more of this later.

It was learned that Slaughter had a misunderstanding

---

[9] J. Marvin Hunter in a letter, Bandera, Texas, April 27, 1952, and also, J. Marvin Hunter, ed., *The Trail Drivers of Texas,* (1923), II, p. 980.

with Gallagher and Boyd over a game of poker in San Antonio. It seems Slaughter was pointed out as being well fixed, and one who liked to play poker. Gallagher and Boyd decided to fleece him, as the story goes, by playing a game with marked cards. The game started on Commerce Street in a back room and went on for hours. Gold coin often appeared and the pots were raised to high stakes. Then when things looked good for Slaughter, he suddenly saw a crooked move involving a joker up the sleeve. Before Gallagher could rake in the pot, he found himself and Boyd staring down the muzzle of a six-shooter. Slaughter swept up the pot, stuffed it in his pocket, then made a quick exit into the dark, and got away. Now they were out to get the man who beat them at their own game. They saddled up and headed for Friotown, and after arriving with quite a mob, they rode up to Charley's rock house. When Charley answered the door they were certain this was John who was about the same size. In San Antonio all had been drinking, and they were in no condition to know whether Charley was John or vice versa. It took a lot of persuading that this was not John. Finally a little girl was given a message to call Billy Slaughter, as he was very much respected in the neighborhood. He came at once and saved Charley's life. By this time John had gone with Billy Childress to the Devil's River. Charley had told them John was in New Mexico, thinking probably the matter would be dropped. Charley's explanation must not have been clear, for they thought he said John was in Mexico, not New Mexico.

When William J. Chisum arrived at South Springs ranch to live with his Uncle John in December 1877, the grave of Barney Gallagher was still fresh. Gallagher was buried near an old irrigation ditch about a hundred yards from the old square adobe ranch house on the Chisum place near Roswell. His funeral was simple – he was stripped of his belongings, rolled in a saddle blanket and buried. After Slaughter had left, Boyd returned with a few of his henchmen and laid claim to Gallagher's expensive, embroidered and silver-mounted Mexican sombrero. He said Gallagher had promised it to him, should the latter die.

As William J. Chisum summed it all up, Gallagher was simply "Pecosed," which was the slang term used by the cowboys for anyone who met a similar fate along the banks of the Pecos River. Gallagher was only one of many who occupied an unmarked grave in that country.[10]

Down on Seven Rivers, a tributary of the Pecos, Charley had scouted a ranch location. Perhaps he didn't like the close call he had experienced in Texas from Gallagher's Fort Stockton rustlers. At first, Charley had a temporary camp at Seven Rivers. Along about 3:00 a.m., on the day after Gallagher was killed, a breathless messenger swiftly dismounted from his fleet-footed cow pony and found John's brother asleep. Rattling the wagon sheet that sheltered him, he brought the message that John had just killed a man at the Chisum ranch. Within a half-hour, Charley and his informant were headed for the Jingle-Bob headquarters, only to find that his younger brother had headed in the direction of the Casey Ranch, well out of danger of any of Gallagher's lurking henchmen.

While in New Mexico, John got a little relaxation racing horses with Charley. Charley owned a fine trotter and would give impromptu derbies on his layout. He claimed that brother John was a fine shot. Riding along the Pecos Valley, he could shoot a rabbit on the run with no special effort.

---

[10] *Ibid.* W. J. Chisum, nephew of John Chisum, located Gallagher's grave for the author in 1952. It is at the South Springs Ranch and remains completely unmarked. At the time of this killing, John Chisum was away on business. Governor Lew Wallace's list of wanted persons later listed the site of the killing as South Spring River Valley. See also Frank M. King, *Mavericks: The Salty Comments of an Old Cowpuncher*, pp. 74-75.

Recent events had proven that cottontails weren't his only prey.[11]

Such stunts made good practice, but the boss of the Underwood outfit was no rabbit. He seemed to want to follow John's new custom, and "reclaimed" more than 100 of John's cattle. With two friends, Underwood rode to the Texan's camp. Eyeing his unwelcome guest, John dismounted and made it clear no inspectors were welcome without the proper credentials. It is said a warrant was sworn out for Slaughter's arrest, but the deputy was unable to find John to serve the summons to appear.[12]

Long before 1880, John Slaughter had made his reputation in New Mexico, but he did not stay to make the land his home. Charley did – his branch of the family would keep on developing the territory. Late in 1883, Charley's restless habits led him to move farther south to the Black River – not that there was much there, as only antelope seemed to have been abundant. However, Charley and Milt Taylor camped in the area one noon, and before sundown had killed thirty-six rattlesnakes. The name Rattlesnake Spring has stuck. Charley was the first man to settle there. Slaughter Canyon, up in the Guadalupe Mountains, was also named for him. With his daughter, Fanny, Charley was hunting there one day and killed three bears and a mountain sheep. A ranch hand who had witnessed the hunt stated that "Mr. Slaughter had sure slaughtered them," and that the name was appropriate. The canyon, having numerous caves, is about as Charley first saw it.[13]

Black River and Seven Rivers country was a hang-out

---
[11] Interview with Mrs. Nancy Slaughter Tubert, Tombstone, 1950.
[12] Bechdolt, *When the West was Young*, p. 169; and Burns, *Tombstone*, p. 299. Burns tells of one John Richardson who swore out a warrant against Slaughter, but the deputy sheriff could not serve it. John Slaughter was a reasonable man. He went to Richardson's ranch, discussed the trouble, and the warrant was withdrawn, p. 300.
[13] A letter from Mrs. Fanny Lucas, Carlsbad, New Mexico, February 12, 1951.

for another dangerous nuisance, "the lawless." To help make New Mexico a good place to live, Charley entered politics. Thus, as brother John was taking a similar oath as sheriff out in Arizona, Charles H. Slaughter, on January 4, 1887, took his oath as assemblyman for Lincoln County in the 27th New Mexican Territorial Legislature, moving temporarily to Santa Fe.[14]

As a rancher, Charley will be better known. He enlarged his holdings by purchases and homesteading.[15] Perhaps of even greater distinction was the action of his one-time cowhand, Jim White. One glorious day while he was jogging along on his stock pony, he discovered a sight perhaps never before seen by white men. It was the world famous Carlsbad Caverns in the region where Charley Slaughter had once grazed his cattle.

In the 'nineties, Charley was on the move again. Wanting to be close to his brother John, he moved to Cochise County, Arizona, near Naco. Then, in 1902, he went to Oakdale, Louisiana. There, about 1917, he got malaria, and John's second wife went to nurse him at his Canyon Street home. Her help was effective. Charley recovered and was actively hunting and riding every day.[16]

John Horton Slaughter had something of the explorer, the crusader, and the gambler in him, as every pioneer must. He was a genius as a trailer, reader of nature-craft and

---

[14] State of New Mexico, Secretary of State's Office, Santa Fe, Misc. Records, Book 2, p. 26.

[15] On December 17, 1885, he bought from Adolph Mann 160 acres in Township 26, Lincoln County, for $500 – Book of Deeds II, Lincoln County, page 183. Charley got a homestead on public domain containing another 160 acres, as of November 3, 1891 – Certificate no. 886 deposited in the General Land Office, Las Cruces, shows he paid in full and got East ½ NW quarter of N-½ SW quarter of Section 35, Township 25, S of Range 24, East of N.M. Meridian.

[16] He had a horse which he fed at the same time early every morning, and when a neighbor named Tom Hogan found Charley's animal had jumped the fence, Hogan knew something was wrong. He found that Charley had had a stroke. He died at Oakdale, Louisiana.

signs. As an exponent of personal justice, he was a crusader. He was a professional gambler, even more in the cattle business than at cards. Ever since the Civil War, John Slaughter learned that taking a chance was more profitable than to remain still and economize. He was the equivalent of a modern day "Texas wildcatter," only his efforts were directed toward cattle and not oil. He would swap and horse trade with the best of them. Always a good listener, and a sly politician, he knew when and when not to engage in a cattle deal. Like most gamblers he had been faced with losses, and during his Texas career lost two large fortunes. Toward the end of his career he slowed down considerably, and invested his money wisely.

In 1877, while off to Arizona with Charley, a fourth child was born to John and Eliza. He was named after John's brother, William or Billy, but throughout his son's life he was always referred to as Willie Slaughter. He was slight, weighing the same as his father, and was never too strong. Willie was born in the old rock house that Charley built east of Friotown. It was from here that Eliza Adeline had gone to San Antonio to prepare for her trip west in 1878.

In Arizona, John and Charley had first run into Geronimo's followers. The Slaughters had been holding five hundred head of cattle in the vicinity of Pearce, Arizona, when a small party of Indians attacked some Mormon settlers. Hearing the shots, they spurred their horses and joined in the fight, managing to run the Indians off.

There were unpublicized events that had taken place between John Slaughter and Lease Harris, his father-in-law, and again with Billy Childress, his brother-in-law—always over cattle. Now another family encounter was shaping up, happening when John with his helpers set out with cattle, headed west toward Arizona. Another brother-in-law —Bill Hiler of Uvalde, husband of John's favorite sister,

Betty or "Tina" as John liked to call her — accompanied him in Texas as far as the Leona River, where Bill left his bride's small herd which had been given to her by Ben as a dowry. Then Bill went ahead to break a trail to Old Fort Ben Ficklin, to arrange for his herd and family until a home might be established. Upon returning to the Leona, Bill was surprised to find that John Slaughter had mistakenly taken some of Hiler's brand along with his own, an understandable occurrence when two herds are mixed and then one is cut out. Furious and disappointed, Bill returned to the Concho, bought land on Sterling Creek, and in 1882 moved his family to a four-room log cabin. A family feud had been established innocently, and when Bill was later Sterling City's first sheriff, John Slaughter, feeling that he had committed what appeared to be an injustice, did not come to see his favorite "Tina." [17]

Meanwhile, John returned and told his wife of his plans. As optimistic as he, she was ready to go. Charley's wife, who was looking forward none too comfortably to Pecos Valley privations, advised Eliza Adeline not to go. Her baby was but a few months old, and the young wife had never been strong. Arizona was even more empty than eastern New Mexico. There was no use talking, though, for her kind smile and gentle hand were needed to start anew. Thus it was that John went on ahead to Tucson to prepare the way, while Eliza Adeline with Willie and four-year-old Addie made the trip by stage and train. Their plans were all so careful, but few seemed to pay proper heed to the terrible epidemic that swept the Southwest.

In early April, while the Rio Grande was running high, Santa Fe, the colorful New Mexican capital, forgot politics for a while. Dreaded above all else in a land of abundant

---

[17] Letter from Georgia Hiler Hays, niece of John H. Slaughter, Stayton, Oregon, January 31, 1952.

superstition and lack of hygiene, was the cry "smallpox." Before the month was out, the cry had been heard at least ninety times. Dr. R. H. Longwill of the Board of County Commissioners worked himself to exhaustion vaccinating three hundred persons, most of them unwilling patients. Persuasion was hard, but at least it was possible. To root out the contagion was next to impossible. The natives, *pobres* and *ricos* alike, followed the age-old custom of leaving open the coffins of epidemic victims as the slow parade wound down the dusty streets from the adobe home to holy church, and then to the dustier grave. Many did not get the standard type of casket, as people died so rapidly that proper methods of burial could not meet the demand.[18]

Unfortunately, Slaughter's children and wife were not vaccinated. On the first lap of Adeline's trip in 1878, the stage made its usual stop for rest between Friotown and San Antonio. Following the old pioneer custom, she chatted freely about her trip with a woman who had sat at her dinner table. She was not aware that the stranger's face showed symptoms of smallpox. In San Antonio they stayed at the Menger Hotel, then, as now, one of the City's finest. There, nearby the Alamo, Adeline entertained her younger sister, Nancy Harris, and spoke of her stage trip to meet her husband John. In a few more days, Adeline became ill, but did not realize why. John met his wife at El Paso and took her on to Tucson, Arizona, where they stopped at a boarding house, and hired a Mexican lady to take care of their two children, Addie and Willie.

In a few days, John realized his wife had smallpox. A doctor was called, but it was too late. Just seventeen days after mother and babies had left Friotown, Eliza Adeline Slaughter was dead. It was the third real personal tragedy that John had suffered. Even at this terrible time he got

---

[18] Santa Fe *New Mexican*, July 30, 1877.

NEW MEXICO SHEEP CAMP
IN VALENCIA COUNTY
Owned by Amado Chavez. This was
Billy the Kid's hideout after shooting
Frank Cahill at Camp grant.

WILLIAM JAMES CHISUM
Nephew of John S. Chisum "Cattle King
of the Pecos"; brother of Sally Chisum.

JOHN SLAUGHTER ON HIS CUTTING HORSE "NIG" ABOUT 1919
Note his six shooter, handy on the pommel of his saddle.

little sympathy, for the boarders where they were stopping were furious that the little family had brought the epidemic there. Now, Addie and Willie were sick, too. Like a good father John did everything possible to pull his children through, using courage and common sense more than medicine.[19] His young wife Eliza Adeline died and was buried in Tucson. So deeply was Slaughter grieved that he could never bear to visit her grave again.

John Slaughter could not be at loose ends long – it just wasn't his nature. He could not revert to being a bachelor either. Loving children as he did, he hated to see his parents and brothers bringing up his little ones. Destiny seemed to intervene, and before he realized it, he was in love again.

Badly shaken but not defeated, Slaughter still had his dream of success in Arizona. In 1879 he was in New Mexico on his way to take over a herd of his cattle, the second one that brother Billy was trailing out from Texas. John met Amazon Howell, a small rancher living in a chosa on the banks of the Penasco and near the Pecos. The Howells made him so welcome he decided to wait right there until the herd reached Seven Rivers. The layover involved more than the Howells had anticipated, for Slaughter, always trusting to his guardian angel, must have foreseen his lucky romance with sixteen-year-old Cora Viola Howell. To meet, as will be seen, a second time on the wide windswept spaces of the West hardly seems a coincidence without fate having a hand in the game.

Slaughter backed his secret marriage preparations into closer ties by convincing the girl's father that he should throw in his hundred head of steers with the arriving herd and go to Arizona. Howell had not foreseen the motive behind these plans until it was too late. Slaughter, a great judge of human character, had had ample time to study his

---

[19] Letter from Artie Slaughter Roberts, Pearsall, Texas, November 15, 1950.

future mother-in-law and must have surmised that there would be strong opposition from her when it came to the time of asking for permission to marry the daughter. Very seldom wrong, it turned out that he had guessed correctly.

Born in St. Charles County, Missouri, Amazon "Cap" Howell gained his nickname as a Missouri River pilot. A Confederate soldier, he was imprisoned nine times before Appomattox and fought to that quiet end. The war took his meager savings, and like many other moneyless but not hopeless Southerners, he migrated to Montana with his growing brood. Howell found no gold, but still undaunted, he did odd jobs, then farmed in Galpin Valley, once ran a restaurant, and finally in 1869 moved to a farm eight miles from Hamilton, Nevada. There his son James was born. After another decade even confidence was about spent, but "Cap" set out for lusher grazing pastures with his small herd, and pointed them for Texas. Crossing into Arizona from Utah, they used historic Lee's Ferry to get their wagon across the Colorado, while their cattle swam the river. It was here that Cora Viola Howell first caught a glimpse of John Slaughter, who was returning from a trip up north by way of Lee's Ferry. No words were exchanged between the two; still, a romantic spark had ignited between a cowboy and a cowgirl.[20]

By the time the Howells reached the Pecos the cattle were trail jaded, and the family tired of the long trip. They decided to stop and farm while fattening their cattle. Years after the Howells vacated the old sheepherder's dugout, a pretty little town came to blossom on the New Mexico plain, called Artesia.

This was Billy the Kid's country and over these stretches of low rolling prairies galloped this fighting young demon of the West. He was Howell's first one-man welcoming

---

[20] Bernice Cosulich in *Arizona Daily Star*, Tucson, February 19, 1938.

committee. He, too, must have taken an interest in their beautiful daughter, for seldom did he make the ride from Seven Rivers to Lincoln, without stopping off for a visit.

Another visitor to Harrises was Tom Cochran, a sandy-haired, light-complexioned, sinewy fellow who had been involved in killing Billy's boss, the young Englishman named John H. Tunstall. To come to Howell's for protection against a posse of man-hunters was almost like walking into a trap, especially when the Kid might pop in any minute. He hid in Howell's corn crib with two of his men. When Rachael Howell's plucky daughter, Viola, tried to make Tom put on her dresses to disguise himself and flee down an arroyo, he refused. Whatever made him stay low was in his favor. For two others named Morton and Baker, who were mixed up in the murder of Tunstall, were not so lucky, and were taken prisoners at Howell's place, and escorted away by Dick Brewer's posse. On this occasion, Billy the Kid was a sworn deputy, acting on the side of the law. Had Tom Cochran been captured, he too might have met an earlier fate as did these prisoners. Later, Cochran became foreman of Slaughter's San Bernardino Ranch.

At Rocky Arroyo, near the Pecos, was the Howell place, a busy part of the country, for this was within the bounds of cattle baron John S. Chisum's free range. Now the Howells were soon to leave their New Mexico location and go in the opposite direction from which they originally had planned. Amazon accepted the challenge of Arizona, just as he had been lured by the promise of other frontiers. Taking his little family he threw in with John Slaughter, and followed westward along the Penasco through the Mescalero reservation, and through the Sacramento Mountains at Tularosa Canyon.

Slaughter had a way of taking the bad with the good, and seldom complained. Not much on oratory, but still a demon for action, Slaughter was well adapted to the surroundings he had chosen to live in. Things had gone too smoothly in the past weeks for the diminutive cowman. While he felt uneasy over some of his sick Texas cattle he obviously did not foresee the near future.

This time it was the law! General Lew Wallace, colorful author of the even more dramatic *Ben Hur* was, in 1878, appointed governor of New Mexico Territory by President Hayes. One of Wallace's assignments was to make a general cleanup of the lawless element in the southeastern part of the territory and restore peace.

Upon taking the reins of office, Wallace was informed by the United States Marshal that he had a large number of warrants that he dare not serve, and could not find deputies rash enough to attempt the service. The military commander at Fort Stanton prepared a list of killings that had been committed in his part of the country, naming those involved in the offenses. Wallace forwarded these statements to President Hayes and asked him to proclaim an insurrection in New Mexico. This was done, as the only way for Wallace to have the use of the troops for the purposes he desired. Wallace had use of four companies of cavalry for two months. John Slaughter had priority over the others on the wanted list, as his name appeared first, while Billy the Kid, who received the most publicity, was rated fourteenth on the list. They were as follows:

1. John Slaughter; 2. Andrew Boyle; 3. John Selman; 4. Selman, John's brother; 5. Gus Gildea; 6. Irvin; 7. Reese Gobles; 8. Rustling Bob; 9. Robert Speakes; 10. The Pilgrim; 11. John Beckwith; 12. Jim French; 13. Joe Scurlock; 14. The Kid (William Bonney); 15. Tom O'Folliard; 16. Charles Bowdre; 17. Henry Brown; 18. John Middleton; 19. Fred Waite; 20. Jacob B. Mathews; 21. Jesse Evans; 22. James J. Dolan; 23. George Davis, alias Tom Jones; 24. Rivers; 25. James Jones; 26. William Jones; 27. Marion Turner; 28. Caleb Hall (Collins); 29. Haskill Jones; 30. Buck Powell; 31. James Hyson (Hysaw); 32. Jake Owens; 33. Frank Wheeler; 34. Joe Hill (Olney).

In Slaughter's case, the killing of Barney Gallagher had been listed not as self-defense but as murder.[21] However, Wallace dropped the murder charge and concentrated upon Slaughter as another cattle drover who had to be stopped for cattle inspection. Reports of missing cattle on the XIT range in the panhandle of Texas, with warnings by cattle detectives Charles Siringo and John W. Poe to be on the lookout for illicit brands, was causing havoc among the trail-drivers. This gave Wallace a reason to stop Slaughter.

Why was John Slaughter so mentioned? Well, it was certainly true that he had "the toughest bunch of cowboys in his outfit." But Slaughter hired a man because of what he was worth to him, and not because of his past record, which did not carry much weight in that day and time. Some of Slaughter's men became outlaws after delivering his herd to Arizona. In some cases, the bad ones reformed. Cochran was one of these. Conversely it had been said that Slaughter killed a man named Tobin in Texas over a misunderstanding. Anyway, the death of Gallagher pointed the finger of suspicion at John Slaughter. "Birds of a feather flock together" must have been "Ben Hur" Wallace's maxim.

The governor stated his aim was to crush a number of cattle camps, such as those of Beckwith, Shedd, and Pat Coghlan, "King of Tulerosa," and "thoroughly cleanse the region about Seven Rivers.[22] These are the places from which the thieves and murderers issue to do their work, and to unload their plunder of whatever kind." On March 12, 1879, orders for a detachment of soldiers to inspect different corrals became public. Any owner unable to show a bill of sale was to be arrested and taken to Fort Stanton.[23]

---

[21] Lew Wallace MSS, Indiana Historical Society, Indianapolis.

[22] From R. M. Gilbert's "Account of Outlaws' Hiding Places in the Vicinity of Seven Rivers, to Governor Wallace," c. 1879, a microfilm of MS in the possession of Maurice G. Fulton, Roswell, New Mexico.

[23] Maurice G. Fulton, a student of Wallace materials, in a letter from Roswell, New Mexico, May 12, 1952.

At this moment, John Slaughter, with Howell, was resting his herd at the head of the Penasco, getting them in shape to make Tularosa Canyon and go out over the vast stretches of sage country to Arizona. A heavy snow had fallen and the weary, thin stock were kept on the bedground until it melted. Slaughter went into camp at Mahill, near Elk Springs where the mountain grass was suitable for grazing. Now these cattle had put Slaughter into a ticklish position. He had got more than he bargained for when he asked old "Cap" Howell to throw in with him, for among Howell's one hundred head were some he had bought from a widow on the Felix River, who probably got them from rustlers. Some of these were said to have belonged to Tunstall, and were stolen at the time of the young Englishman's death. John himself bought twenty-three head from Tom Cochran, who was sympathetic to the Dolan-Riley faction, which was accused of confiscating young Tunstall's stock. As far as Howell and his future in-law were concerned, they bought them and paid cash.

Being a shrewd man and one well informed of political doings, Slaughter had learned that Wallace was planning to screen out all the undesirables. This meant a general clean-up, taking the good with the bad. Hearing he was "number one" on the wanted list, Slaughter wrote directly to the Governor, pleading innocence, hoping it might have some effect:

> Head of the Penasco
> March 8, 1879
>
> DEAR SIR: I write you as I am under arrest according to your orders. I have a herd of cattle and order by Lieutenant Dawson to take them to Fort Stanton. But as I hear it is a very poor place to hold stock, I request (illegible) having to take them there as it is a great deal off the road and the stock is very poor. They are giving out and dying (illegible) the road. I want to ask you if you will do the

favor of letting them be stopped at Elk Springs, as there is good feed and water, as I think anybody who wish to see the stock could come out much easier than to drive them to Stanton. It would be considerable loss and expense to drive them down. If you could see the stock you could not insist (illegible) there being driven down. Governor, I don't know what you have against me. But I have not done a thing, I know of, to try to evade the law.

I hope you will not detain me long, as I have these cattle and no one in charge except myself. The men I have are boys and negroes. If I am detained long I am liable to lose them all. You have truly heard that the stock was stolen property but you will find out (illegible) the only trouble about the cattle is on account of the 23 head Tom Cochlin bought here of Mrs. Casey, and I have a Bill of Sale to them from Tom Cochlin with two witnesses, and Capt. A. Howell has the same thing, over one hundred head in the herd of his own. Whoever has to look over the cattle could come out, it would be a great accomodation. It is a considerable expense to have to stop long, and I hope you will do the best you can for me and oblige,

J. H. SLAUGHTER [24]

Altogether, the Governor caught up with 17 of the 30-odd men on the list, and a few of them were tried at the April term of the court at Lincoln. Governor Lew Wallace's meeting with Slaughter evidently was not too satisfactory in view of the following message to the commanding officer at Fort Stanton:

Lincoln, New Mexico
Captain Purington   March 25, 1879
Commanding Fort Stanton

DEAR SIR: I had a talk with Slaughter and think he had better for the time being be put under arrest and guard in the Trader's Store. Tomorrow I will be up and see you about his case and others.

Respectfully Your Friend,   LEW WALLACE
Governor of New Mexico

John Slaughter was taken into custody by a detachment of

[24] Fulton to Erwin, Roswell, New Mexico, April 22, 1952. See also Lew Wallace papers, above cited.

soldiers in charge of Lieutenant Byron Dawson and temporarily detained in the post trader's store at Fort Stanton.[25]

On March 29th, Wallace again wrote Captain Purington, stating he thought it well enough to take Slaughter's parole, on condition that he did not drive his herd away until they had been inspected by the probate judge and keeper, nor go away from his herd. Once Slaughter would have found these conditions hard to follow, and it is doubtful that he would have put up with any further annoyance from any cattle inspectors, but he kept his word that he would not move from the bedgrounds until every beef was inspected. For this waiting, Slaughter lost five hundred head of his best cattle.

The Mesilla *News* of May 17, 1879, gave Wallace a good thrashing in print for the way he was treating the cattle drovers. It accused him openly of stealing five hundred head of Slaughter's stock. A citizen of La Mesilla went to visit Slaughter to get his side of the story and Slaughter was quoted as saying:

> Yes, he went for me with a large body of armed men, took 500 of cattle from me, without any right, justice, or authority of law, and arrested me besides.

Asked what the Governor gave him for the cattle he took from him, Slaughter mischievously grinned, "Why, he gave me taffy, of course." [26]

With Slaughter minus five hundred head of steers he was in no mood to be caught cat-napping again. But this time

---

[25] Mesilla *Independent*, April 3, 1879, tells of the bringing in of "Messrs. Slaughter & Jones from Penasco, arrested by order of Gov. Wallace – what for not known." Jones and Marion Turner, whom John Slaughter knew and dealt with, were toughs who deserved the more permanent jailing they got.

[26] Mesilla *News*, May 17, 1879, attacked Wallace's "unwarranted way" of arresting citizens who were not even informed (as Slaughter had not been) of the accusations against them. The Las Cruces *Thirty Four* of May 28, 1879, also editorialized against Wallace's actions. The governor's life was threatened, and he travelled for a time under guard.

he had reason to be day-dreaming; he was in love with a pretty daughter of the wide-open spaces. Being put three weeks behind schedule, and having his herd trimmed of five hundred cattle, Slaughter was all the more determined to make Ariozna his home. A couple of weeks after he arrived in Tombstone, two Texans sheepishly arrived in town – the same two cattle detectives, John W. Poe and Charley Siringo – only to learn that Slaughter had sold his herd immediately on arrival. Slaughter looked at them through half-squinted eyes and chuckled. After that, he was left alone. There was more to this chuckle than appeared on the surface. The two detectives had learned that Slaughter's cowboys were reinforced with some pretty tough men at Tularosa. So the detectives had good reason to lag behind.

Now, with a song in his heart and the crack of his stock whip popping over his head, the herd strung out for Arizona. He was now master of the situation. A few miles from Tularosa he sent a man to find the justice of the peace, for a marriage was to be performed in all the dignity and tradition of the cow country. This bad experience of losing his cattle called for a celebration. However, his trouble was not over; he still had to have the consent of the girl's mother. The sixteen-year-old Viola atop a spirited mount rode beside the man who had won her heart. Even then she was an excellent equestrienne, and for this too Slaughter could be proud of her.

Now, John Slaughter seemed jinxed with disapproving would-be mothers-in-law. First, Mrs. Lease Harris had had her qualms about his wooing her daughter, then Mrs. Amazon Howell proved equally reluctant. Rachael Howell was a beautiful woman herself, a Dixie belle who had not been born to stand beside a pioneer champion and tame the wilderness. Southern to the core, through all her life she would dance and sing whenever she heard anyone play "Dixie." This high-strung, emotional person had her reverse side – a timid, strait-laced attitude unfitted for the West. Yet Viola's mother had been an uncomplaining wife to her quiet, hard-working spouse. She bore children without doctors and lost and buried them without flinching. Still, that did not make her any more prepared to lose her favorite daughter through marriage! When on one of those perfect spring days of 1879 Cora Viola said that she and John were in love, Old Amazon was delighted, but his wife was firmly opposed. She said that Viola hadn't known Slaughter long enough and that he was too old for her. They had met the previous August, but eight months before. Then too there were John's six-year-old daughter and nineteen-month-old baby son. Why should Viola be nursemaid and mother to them? Yet, in spite of everything, it was like mother, like daughter, and Viola had her own way in the end.

On April 16, 1879, John and Viola were married in the pretty little town of Tularosa, nestled at the base of the Sacramento Mountains.[27] A score of years earlier, the village had been founded by Spaniards and Mexicans. Now with about four hundred inhabitants, it was growing wealthy. Situated at an elevation of nine thousand feet, and protected from heat and cold, this shipping center boasted that it had never had a crop failure since 1862, and was already called the "Oasis of New Mexico." Still, only a couple of months later, Victorio, greatest general of the Apaches, camped in the basin, angry and looking for trouble. Right now, the weary travelers must have thought the area a miniature heaven. In spite of her own narrowness and John's nonconformity, Mrs. Howell came to respect and almost worship her determined but soft-hearted son-in-law.

---

[27] Letter of L. Edward Edgington, Alamagordo, New Mexico, May 5, 1952.

The folks didn't linger long. All Arizona and the next forty-three years were to be their honeymoon. Yet, there were to be hardships, too. John Slaughter was not a well man. He never was strong constitutionally, though his muscles were wiry and powerful, and his character had the strength of armor in compensation. Health as well as wealth were his reasons for this Arizona pilgrimage. For the next four years it was not certain whether or not he could gain the first goal in Arizona. Probably he had a mild case of tuberculosis. Medical knowledge of that day was scant, and a "weak chest" was the usual diagnosis for many lung troubles.

Desperate for health, in 1883 Slaughter sold all his Arizona cattle to William Lang, who drove the herd to his ranch in Animas Valley. Then John, his wife, and the two children started for Oregon, for a change in ranch locations and to gain good health. All the money he had possessed was around his waist in his familiar old money belt. By train they went through Colorado to Salt Lake City and Ogden; then to Boise. After that, they traveled by stage. At one station, the agent told the stage driver that some tough characters had been hanging around that day. Then he told John that if he had any money he had better turn it over to the driver for safe keeping. John replied acidly, "Well, I have no money with me, and if I did I am damn well able to care for it myself." Later he found that his suspicions were correct. The agent was in with a gang of stage robbers and was using a standard trick. In the coach John had Viola wear the treasure belt. Before long she was scared into hysterics! No one dozed that night. John stayed alert, holding a pistol in his lap, and his wife was well occupied contemplating her fears, and holding her eyes as wide open as the full moon above them.

When the stage reached the next town, Slaughter had a

severe lung hemorrhage. They decided right then to return to Arizona where he was convinced he belonged. At Silver City, New Mexico, Slaughter took a contract to supply beef for the Santa Fe Railroad.[28]

Now, destiny, which John Slaughter so thoroughly believed in, had used health to make sure that he would keep his date with history.

---
[28] Reminiscences of Mrs. Cora Viola Slaughter, February 5, 1939.

5

West of the Guadalupes

Arizona Territory was to the Texas ranchman a last frontier. It still had 35 more years until 1912 when it would become a State. In fact, when John Slaughter first saw it in 1877, Cochise had been dead just three years. His toll of human lives was eighty-seven persons slain.

Now with Cochise buried in his stronghold, John Slaughter would trail his cattle right before the shadow of the Dragoon Mountains. A few years before this would have been foolhardy. But the region was still not free from Indian attack. Arizona was still scarcely populated, and had not increased a great deal by the turn of the century. In 1880, the population was estimated in the main communities; beginning with Prescott having 2,074 people; Phoenix, 1800; Globe, 1400; Florence, 942; with Tucson, the heaviest population, numbering 9000. From these figures it was easy to visualize the few that were in the outlying areas. With Schieffelin's Tombstone, the fastest-growing town of all, having an estimated 6000 to 7000 people in a little more than a year, it only seemed logical that this area would attract a man such as John Slaughter.

Whenever there is a mining boom, prosperity is close at hand, but this was not all. From the Guadalupes in the east, beyond the Whetstones to the west, from the Mexican province of Sonora to the pine-clad regions of the San Francisco Mountains to the north, the area was suitable for grazing. John Slaughter liked what he saw in the San Pedro and Sulphur Springs valleys in the southeast corner of what was Pima County. Explorer Francisco Vasquez de Coronado had come there with a thousand mules and pack horses, and with a drove of wild cattle, as early as 1540. In 1805, far to the north, Lewis and Clark had seen wild horse descendants of those that strayed and multiplied. In 1806 Lieutenant Zebulon Pike was so annoyed over the presence of great numbers of wild horses, that it was necessary to send out an advance guard to frighten them away. Father Eusebio Francisco Kino on his mission to the land of the Pima Indians brought in the first domestic stock to Southern Arizona. He founded the first Spanish ranches on the Santa Cruz, Magdalena and Altar Rivers. He might well be accredited with being the first cattle king in the area.

California and Oregon, as well as the East, had contributed to building up a good grade of beef cattle in Arizona. John Slaughter had only a few years to wait until the railroad would have saved him the trouble of driving cattle overland. Although he and Charley were there in 1877, his Texas cattle herd was not thrown on the trail until the beginning of 1879. He had not too many left in Atascosa County, and had disposed of his biggest herd in 1876 on the Devil's River. These were the days when a drover started out with four thousand head and by the time he had reached his destination, the herd had grown double the amount. This method of "sweepin' in" while you go, was a headache to brand inspectors and detectives working for cattlemen's associations.

John Slaughter had some of the worst outlaws in the country on his trail drive; one of these had left the James gang to get a new start. Some of his good hands were Billy Grimes, Wake Benge, Jeff Lewis, Tad Roland, Billy Claiborne, and Tom Cochran. The latter had been involved in the Lincoln County War. It was a new venture for most of them and was their first trail drive to Arizona. Most beloved and loyal of all was John Swain, referred to as "Sweeney," a Negro about Slaughter's age who had been given to young

John years before. Being a small lad, Swain was called "Little John" in honor of his new master.[1]

Their first big problem was floating the wagons and swimming cattle across the Rio Grande during one of the worst floods in history. Later, cattle were caught in a snowstorm crossing a high New Mexican range. Four trips were made in all, each an adventure that would have inspired Dante. Crossing the Jornada del Muerto with little water would give anyone an accurate picture of the inferno. There was a ninety-mile drive with no waterhole for days. Finally, the stock was turned loose in Sulphur Springs Valley. In 1879, this region was a sea of grass. Too, it was near the San Carlos Indian reservation where John had received a beef contract from the government.

In 1881, Slaughter went to the Pecos River and traded his sheep for a third herd of cattle, being driven from Texas by Charley Slaughter. Viola and little Addie went along this time. They sent their light wagon and bedding ahead with the cowboys and then went themselves by train. It was quite a change from the earlier trips. When the party got off at Deming, New Mexico, they expected to meet the herd, but found nothing except a junction bolstered by one saloon and some railroad workers' house-cars. It was bitter cold and a gale was blowing. Fortunately, Viola's brother, Jimmy Howell, had brought along some double blankets and a quilt. A railroad worker's wife gave them some victuals, but they had to camp a couple of nights before the herd arrived. Another snowstorm west of Fort Bayard on the Mimbres engulfed them for three days more. Only daughter Addie, wrapped in a buffalo robe in the bottom of the wagon was not frostbitten. Slaughter's ear was frozen.

---

[1] Los Angeles *Times,* September 1, 1940. This interesting issue contains an article by Laurence Cardwell entitled "John Swain Interviewed." Much information along this line was also obtained in an interview with Mrs. Minnie Minus Fitzgerald, San Diego, August 21, 1949.

A stage driver offered to take Viola on to Fort Stanton, but she would not leave the rest. Next day, the driver and his three passengers were on their return trip. As they reached about the same spot where he had met the Slaughters, Indians attacked, killed them all and burned the coach. Only the fury of the blizzard had delayed the incident one night. Charred ashes remained snowed under. The area they traversed was overrun by Victorio and his pillaging Apaches. Viola was always afraid of Indians. Frequent scares never made her immune. When the Indians tried to stop the wagon to beg tobacco, she threw it out while the horses kept going. Nevertheless, she was always eager to go along with John.[2]

With such determination, they could hardly fail. Lucky circumstances, as John would have called them, helped the Slaughters succeed the sooner. Tombstone, the mining camp located by fabulous Ed Schieffelin, was born the year Slaughter first saw Sulphur Springs Valley. Hard-working miners have good appetites, and nothing satisfied them as well as beef. John Slaughter soon had enough cash to expand. By 1884, he was through with his Oregon wild goose chase and was "sold" for life on Arizona. Now he wanted a big place, a promising ranch.

For a time, Slaughter kept watching and inquiring about places. Finally, Tad Roland came to his boss and said that he knew of a wonderful piece of land. It was a land grant, and he had checked on it quite well and found that the place contained about 65,000 acres, mostly in Mexico, but partly in Arizona Territory. A man named G. Andrade, living in Guaymas on the Sonora shore of the Gulf of California, owned the layout. With the keen eye and genius of a bred-in-the-bone cowman, Slaughter gave the place a quick examination; then, before he had seen it all, decided def-

---

[2] Reminiscences of Viola Slaughter, February 5, 1939.

WEST OF THE GUADALUPES 139

initely on buying, and set off for Guaymas. At Fairbanks, a man got off the train and told John that Andrade was in Benson, Arizona, and would be there until 7:00 p.m. the next day. Slaughter wired Andrade, and next morning met him in Benson. He purchased the spread. Later, after long litigation, the Federal Government was to cut away some 2,300 acres, but John never lost an inch of his Mexican holdings.[3]

> I shall never forget the first sight of the ranch from Silver Creek – the valley stretching far out before us, down into Mexico, rimmed and bounded by mountains all around. Nor shall I forget the thrill of knowing that it was all ours, our future lay within it. It was beautiful. I shall look down over that valley several times before I am 105 and recall all the happiness our work, struggles and play gave us at the San Bernardino.

Thus reminisced Viola Slaughter fifty-four years after that first long look beside her proud husband. The mountains that inspired her were the Pedregosa, Chiricahua, Peloncillo, and Guadalupe ranges which encircled the beautiful, well-watered San Bernardino Valley.

Others had here envisioned magnificence and treasure through the centuries. The Jesuits had founded the San Bernardino Mission and converted a number of Indians. When the order was expelled from Mexico in 1767, the padres told their wards that they would return some day, and to keep a fire burning at the Taiopa mine nearby to guide their return. Of course, the Jesuits never came back to northern Sonora, but pretty legend has it that the fires long continued. Some insist that they still burn in the mountain fastnesses round about San Bernardino. In any case, no record was kept of the shadowy mine. Persistent tradition

---

[3] Bernice Cosulich in *Arizona Daily Star,* Tucson, February 19, 1938. See also Bechdolt, *op. cit.,* p. 171. As late as 1888, G. Andrade was selling part of his remaining San Bernardino acres, Tombstone *Prospector,* October 23, 1888.

claims also that the fathers buried its best bullion somewhere on the mission grounds. Thus the tract around San Bernardino has been well burrowed.

On December 16, 1820, a petition was presented to the governor of Sonora and Sinaloa by Ignacio de Perez for "four sites in the depopulated place of San Bernardino in said province." Two months later, an examination was ordered and a survey made. In March of 1822, the ranch was established by Perez who had received a grant from Emperor Augustin Iturbide's short-lived imperial Mexican Government. This first owner paid only $90.00 for the *sitios*. The Perez family was familiar with the story that there was treasure somewhere on their nearly 75,000 acres. According to this tapestry of semi-fiction, Rafael Perez claimed to have a parchment which he at first believed a hoax. Two adventurers, Feliz and Tomas, convinced him that it was genuine, and he promised them each one third of any fortune found. Upon the aged chart there was a cross just outside the San Bernardino church altar. The letters "DESSPE, EAVGEN, ECAISP, ARREOA, JUANSR, OZSMOR, DOOIRA, and EOOLOS" appeared at the top of the parchment, while below them was a Jesuit symbol. Deciphered, it read, "Debajo de la cruz, dos varas, dos cien mil pesos oro en barras" – "Below the cross, two varas, two hundred thousand pesos in gold bullion." Although Rafael had located the cross among the mission ruins, he was almost caught by Mexican officers at Agua Prieta, for like his two companions, Rafael was a fugitive, living none too well by his wits. Feliz and Tomas sold their possessions, bought food and digging supplies, borrowed mules on credit, and left for San Bernardino. They struck something metallic! Unfortunately, they got into an argument and their mules ran off. Thus the hectic pair disappear into the mists of Southwestern mystery.[4] Maybe they were a mirage. Perhaps their doings are accurate to the last painted detail; at any rate, years later, so goes the legend, a hole the size of a metal box was found newly dug at the place marked "x".

History as well as greed and romance lurk in the corners of Slaughter's place. "X" marked the spot for destiny. Captain Bautista de Anza, founder of San Francisco, knew the region well. He was quartered there in 1773, while campaigning against the Apaches. From this site he wrote, on January 22nd, a letter to Viceroy Bucareli.

The strategic harbor of San Francisco, established by Anza, was one of the reasons for American acquisition of California. The notable Mormon Battalion, which volunteered to help conquer California for the United States, crossed the San Bernardino Ranch on December 3, 1846.

As if destined so, gold was discovered in the new Pacific acquisition a few days before the Treaty of Guadalupe Hidalgo made California permanently American. In the gold rush that followed, the San Bernardino Ranch was traversed by hundreds of Argonauts. H. M. T. Powell, a '49er who led a party from Illinois, passed this way and perpetuated through his diary the scene he saw on September 23rd. Powell was pleased with the fine spring a quarter-mile north of the ranch, and his stock was foddered with the rich, abundant grass. Rare for Arizona, this was gramma type grass, young and tender. Even then he saw many cattle tracks worn in all directions. No rancher was this Illinoisan, so these signs meant little to him but a good day's rest. In Powell's day, the mission was already an adobe ruin enclosing three acres. On the west side he noted the main building and offices; on the north was a range of adobe partitions or

---

[4] Cleve Hallenbeck and Juanita H. Williams, *Legends of the Spanish Southwest* p. 98.

rooms, extending the whole length of the structure. On the southwest end was the crude abandoned furnace for smelting ore. It all seemed a wreck, not a promise.[5] For years the Slaughters could point out the old emigrant trail which for miles showed on their land as a distinct yellow line east of the ranch house.

Mexico and the United States were at peace, but a definite boundary had to be made. In 1851, the San Bernardino Ranch was still entirely on Mexican soil. Commissioner John R. Bartlett was appointed by the American Government to help survey the line. Twice he visited Rancho San Bernardino, first on May 21, 1851, and again on August 2nd. He described it as "a collection of adobe buildings in a ruined state, of which nothing but the walls remain. . . . The whole extending over a space of two acres was inclosed with a high wall of adobe, with regular bastions for defense." He had heard that cattle had been raised there by the Perez family shortly before he came, but the Apaches had forced them to abandon their herds. Colonel Philip St. George Cooke, in his march to California, however, had been able to supply his Mormon Battalion with beef from the wild herds in the neighboring valleys and plains.[6]

After the Gadsden Purchase, the new international border went through the dormant estate. In 1854, boundary commissioners met there and fixed part of the line. In 1857, Julius Froebel passed that way. He was even more enthusiastic about the "copious springs, green meadows," and

---

[5] Douglas S. Watson, ed., *The Santa Fe Trail to California, 1849-1852: the journal of H. M. T. Powell,* pp. 200ff. Title to this grant was finally confirmed by the Court of Private Land Claims to "Ignacio de Perez, his heirs, assigns, and successors in interest" on February 10, 1900. It was surveyed by the United States government on June 13, 1902 and declared to be situated "approximately in Township 24 South, Ranges 30 and 31, East of the Gila and Salt River Meridian . . . and contains 2,382 acres." The grant was patented by the United States on May 22, 1913. See the National Resources Records Branch, General Services Administration, National Archives, Washington, D.C.

[6] Frank C. Lockwood, *Pioneer Days in Arizona,* pp. 225-227.

interesting Mission ruins. "There," he wrote, "together with a large tract of land, which is amongst the most valuable in Northern Sonora, is the deserted Hacienda of San Bernardino."[7] Thus went the tale when Andrade acquired the land and did little with it but sell it to John Slaughter. In 1884, after indifferent decades, San Bernardino was owned by someone who could appreciate and use it, fully.

Slaughter started off modestly. It wasn't until 1892 that the family built a real ranch mansion. At first, John lived in an adobe with few conveniences. Nevertheless, the real source of opulence was already there – water. The Slaughters had always been blessed with good water supply, in Texas and later in New Mexico. This had been more a matter of wise choice and planning than mere luck. At San Bernardino, this was even more important, for artesian wells were scarce indeed, in Arizona. John was lured by these waters. Generally, southeastern Arizona was treeless, but the ranch had a large number of giant cottonwoods, which added beauty and pointed to possible agriculture. Slaughter set out to develop the potential flow of water. In time, hundreds of acres were irrigated by artesian wells, and some of these fountainheads yielded four hundred gallons a minute. He was one of the earliest Arizonans to perfect a private irrigation system.[8]

When John Slaughter established his great ranch, he had few neighbors. The San Pedro Valley was more than a hundred miles long and perhaps the best potential farming district south of the Gila. He was now in the Sulphur Springs Valley. Slaughter's second ranch, in the early

---

[7] Julius Froebel, *Seven Years Travel in Central America, Northern Mexico, and the Far West of the United States* (London, Richard Bentley, 1859), pp. 487-488.

[8] William G. Sanderson, a native of Alabama, settled in Soldier's Hole in Sulphur Springs Valley and won, in 1885, a government-sponsored prize of $3,000.00 for developing artesian wells. His deepest borings were eighty-three feet. See *Journals of the Territory of Arizona, 1885*, 13th Legis., I, p. 131. Also interview with Hugh A. Taylor, San Antonio, Texas; and Roy Sanderson, Phoenix, 1950.

'eighties, was in this area, a little above Hereford. The San Pedro Valley, where John Slaughter had first settled, was especially rich. Since buffalo had never ventured that far south and west, the valley had never been grazed before the 'eighties. Then the San Simon Cattle and Canal Company, organized in January 1885, turned loose its first herds on the broad, grass-covered acres. By 1889 the company began to ship cows, heifers, and steers branded H on the left shoulder. Their returns were great during the "fat years," but the 1892-1893 drought was disastrous. Sixty to seventy percent of all stock was lost when supposedly permanent springs dried up. Slaughter's abundant waters saved him. Yet elsewhere water was so scarce that a sack was used to filter dirty water and keep out the *cresas*, or maggots.

Another successful group organized the Chiricahua Cattle Company with its home ranch called El Dorado, also in Cochise County. Their capital stock was $500,000, divided into twenty thousand shares. Thus, the "Cherry Cow," or the three C's, as cowhands liked to call the outfit, began business well staked out. Other big outfits were the Vail Brothers, the Empire Ranch, Erie Cattle Company, and the Babocomari Company, and the Diamond – A, all of them running at least twenty thousand head.

Almost from the beginning all John Slaughter's fellow cowmen were big operators. Jacob Scheerer was one. Coming to the then Pima County in the late '70s, Jake located first at Morse's Mill in the Chiricahuas, where he started with his bull teams freighting lumber and mining ore. This paid so well that in 1883 he bought a half interest in a sawmill at Mormon Canyon. Three years later, Scheerer sold it to purchase a Sulphur Springs Valley spread within a day's ride of what would later be Douglas. Jake began gradually on his Double-Rod Ranch, but, like Slaughter, his herds developed rapidly, both in size and in breed. In 1906, he was able to sell the Double-Rod for $100,000.[9]

When John Slaughter crossed Sulphur Springs Valley to the San Pedro in 1879, he passed near the outfit of another trail blazer, who was to be his neighbor on the north. This was Henry C. Hooker, seven years at his Sierra Bonita Ranch. Like Slaughter, he prospered by selling his cattle to Arizona army posts. He had found Sierra Bonita's fortunate site during a stampede. Springs had made San Bernardino a great ranch; they did the same for Hooker's spread. In time, he ran twenty to thirty thousand head. When Slaughter moved to his final ranch, Hooker was already becoming the cattle king for southern Arizona. Early he recognized that longhorns were poor in saleable meat. Thus, he brought purebred Herefords from Iowa, Illinois and Missouri. Still, water was too valuable to waste, so Hooker built swinging gates so that a man sitting behind a blind could separate Hooker's cattle from neighbor's stock and keep the strays from drinking. They were corralled and notice was sent to the owners to remove their pesky property. Hooker had no Apache scares at first, but later learned to cope with them. His philosophy was similar to that of Slaughter – better to give an Indian a few beeves than risk his taking them all. Then, too, he was like John in never showing Indians any fear, thus gaining their respect. Geronimo never bothered the ranch of either man, and this was certainly a coveted distinction in those parts. If John Slaughter's was the most historic ranch in Arizona, H. C. Hooker's remains the oldest one continuously operated and handed down in the same family to the fifth generation.[10]

[9] Richard E. Sloan, ed., *History of Arizona*, IV, p. 320.
[10] See Mrs. Harry Hooker, "Five Generations of Hookers," *Arizona Cattlelog*, Phoenix, December, 1949. Hooker had gone to California from Hinsdale, New Hampshire, in 1853; was a merchant in Placerville, for 15 years, then went to Arizona. He used a small H brand for young or small cattle, and a large H for large and old ones. He was considered an expert on fine horseflesh, and he raised excellent mounts. Hooker died December 5, 1907, on West Adams Street, Los An-

George D. Stephens was another Slaughter favorite. Like old John, he had come to Cochise County partly for his health. His father had been a '49er driving a herd of cattle from Missouri to northern California. Though not always healthy, young Stephens had the pioneer urge like his father. His herd of a thousand was driven to southeastern Arizona where he established a ranch just northeast of the San Bernardino. Slaughter was Stephens' guiding influence in the cattle business. The two went on many a roundup together. Stephens hated to get up early, but Slaughter had old Pochie saddled and ready by 4:00 a.m. This he did from early youth, following in Old Ben's footsteps. Stephens kept his stock on public domain, later taking squatters' rights. Meanwhile, he and Slaughter for a time held some cattle in partnership.[11]

From Silver City, New Mexico, came Mormon Ross Sloan, a tumbleweed Texan. He bought the Skeleton Canyon land not many miles from Slaughter's. Sloan prospered modestly.

Of course, John's father-in-law, Amazon Howell, was more than a neighbor. John's promises of good rewards in Apache land were fulfilled. Howell had recorded during 1869 in Nevada a "Z" brand on left hip and jaw. This was toted to Arizona, and John Slaughter himself used it, too, but branded his cattle on the right shoulder. Amazon even went in for dairy cattle, supplying neighboring towns. Around Tombstone, he became known as "milk and water Howell." He was a lively old fellow; even in his later years, "Cap" was supple enough to turn cartwheels and ride a horse like a young Comanche.[12] Howell Spring, near Charleston on the San Pedro River, preserves his name.

geles. Los Angeles *Evening News,* December 5, 1907; *Arizona Daily Star,* Tucson, January 12, 1879; and Pima County, Book of Misc. Records, A, page 329, June 7, 1895, for record of his brands.
[11] Interview with George Dickson Stephens, Douglas, Arizona, 1950.
[12] Reminiscences of Cora Viola Slaughter, February 5, 1939.

The first man John Slaughter met when he visited the Dragoons was "Uncle Billy" Fourr. The latter's family had come from France, and Fourr was born on a Missouri farm in 1843. During the Civil War, he had gone west, driving a herd to New Mexico. In time, he drifted to Tucson, a pueblo of just a few stores and fewer dollars. In 1868 "Uncle Billy" Fourr went out to the Dragoon Mountains. After finding permanent water, he started a ranch with eighty head which he had bought in Yuma. Sycamores were a good sign of water, he knew, and his place was covered with them. Here was the only sign of civilization as the road from Tombstone wound to Summit Station.[13]

Of Scotch-Portuguese blood was Slaughter's friend, Manuel Joseph King, a native of Oakland, California. Like Stephens', his father had also been a gold-seeker. In 1885, Manuel went to Arizona, leased open ranges, stocked his ranches with Texas mixed breeds, and in 1895 took over a homestead at Redondo. Later, he turned to Herefords, as most other cowmen did. In those days, local ranchers, like John Slaughter, would send thirty to forty cowhands to help each other in the spring and fall roundups. Usually, a spread hired ten or a dozen men steadily. Slaughter's and Hooker's cowboys were always scouting and kept tab on fresh Indian trails to protect their herds, which lessened the loss of their stock to marauders.[14]

Good neighbors were a great help in any frontier times, and Slaughter had a real knack for making lasting friendships. His skill in judging good ranch hands was even better. Men stayed with him at San Bernardino for many years, and they were usually loyal.

"Old Bat," who was one of the two faithful negroes Slaughter had brought from Texas, was probably the most useful man of all. His full name was John Battavia Hin-

---
[13] Cochise County Minute Book 1, page 523, September 24, 1884.
[14] John Myers Myers, *The Last Chance: Tombstone's early years*, p. 85.

naut, but he never used it. Born in Louisiana, he was a slave until the Civil War. At its end he was discharged at New Orleans. Billy Slaughter had hired Bat in San Antonio, and he became a first-class ranch hand on Billy's spread. Old Bat came along with John's second herd and had Billy's permission to remain. He always went on roundups as cook. When a stampede occurred, he was the first man in the saddle, although on someone else's horse, for he, unlike the rest, didn't keep one saddled for such emergencies. Being camp cook, Old Bat was king of the range. Still, he certainly was never temperamental. Rather, he stuck by Slaughter like a watchdog, since he knew old John kept his gold in a money belt. When his boss slept, Bat kept awake, guarding the treasure. No banks were within hundreds of miles, and those few seldom were trusted. Dubious Mexicans who sold cattle to John Slaughter insisted on being paid for one animal at a time to avoid cheating. Bob Lauderdale, who had known all Slaughter's family in West Texas, tells of John's coin belt earlier on the Nueces. Getting tired of carrying two thousand dollars in gold one day in 1875, he asked Bob to tote it for awhile. Lauderdale said it would have been easier to carry a couple of six-shooters on a belt. At the day's end, he used the burden for a pillow.[15]

Once Old Bat was driving the chuckwagon when he heard some shots which he thought had been made by Indians. It was the cowboys having some fun. He was always prepared anyway. Optimistic, he thought he could do anything; but, panic-stricken, he drove the chuckwagon right into a wash in the Morita Draw, near Packard's ranch. "Why did you drive in that hole?", the foreman asked him. "Well, Boss, it's like this, I thought sure ah could straddle it," was the kindly old fellow's reply. Unfortunately, the

---
[15] R. J. Lauderdale and John M. Doak, *Life on the Range and on the Trail*, pp. 118-119.

chasm was about twelve feet wide and the four-mule-team wagon had to be dug out with a pick and shovel.[16]

Truly Old Bat was a character. He always carried his toothbrush sticking out of his shirt pocket, and in later years around Douglas, had an old-fashioned phonograph beside him on the wagon seat. On a trip to Cuchuverachi, a small town in Sonora, a little Mexican boy became fascinated by the big morning-glory-shaped loudspeaker. When Old Bat was not looking, the waif tried to crawl down the horn to find out where the voice came from.

Since he loved music, Old Bat fancied himself a musician. Somewhat of a natural-born showman, he was eager to make a tune on his squeaky fife. Even a tin-eared desert rat would have known that the notes were not always soft and sweet. John Slaughter was about as fond of Bat as the negro was of his boss. John used to buy him full cases of soft drinks, which Bat would guard even more carefully than he did his "music makers." Though he doted on children as much as Slaughter did, Bat was hesitant to share his sweets with his little friends.[17] Like a gentle nurse and a practical valet, Old Bat saw to "Uncle John's" needs. John was careless about his health, so Bat filled a real need in that respect.

John Swain, the colored boy given to Slaughter in his youth, caught onto Arizona ranching about as fast as any old-timer. Soon he was an expert tracker. He became as much a part of the landscape as a Saguaro cactus. When crossing a cattle trail, Swain could determine as precisely as a mathematician the number of cows ahead. Like his namesake, he could sense whether the tracks left by unknown hoofprints were those of a cow pony, of the steed of an Indian, a vaquero jogging up from south of the border, or an honest gringo rancher. Immediately, he would report

---

[16] Letter from Artie Slaughter Roberts, Pearsall, Texas, November 15, 1950.
[17] Bisbee *Review*, May 27, 1934, containing Jim Brophy's memoirs.

all this to "Mist' John" who kept tab on about everything happening in southeastern Arizona.

One time, Slaughter, John Swain, and Old Bat, with several Mexican hands, tracked a large herd far into Mexico. They found that the animals were being grazed by a couple of herders, who fled to the nearby village to report the intrusion to their chieftain. This hombre was a notorious bandit with a hardened crew of renegades. Slaughter approached the herdsman, uttered a little profanity in Spanish, backed by a piercing glare that looked convincing enough, and Slaughter headed his cattle back toward the San Bernardino. Perhaps it was because his Mexican cowhands felt homesick for their native land, or more likely, fright on their part was the real answer – in either case, when the chief of the rustlers appeared, John's own Mexican vaqueros quickly disappeared into the dense thickets. His two loyal colored servants bravely stood by their boss. The three next turned their cattle into a box canyon and quickly took up positions to resist a possible attack, which might be expected from these Mexican marauders. Sure enough, they came in a full charge, but Slaughter was prepared. The roar of the double-barrelled shotguns soon echoed in the canyon, and this time the bold bandits did not return. The plunging of hooves, yelling of the bandits, and the curses in two tongues signified the skirmish had abruptly ended. John Swain was a schooled marksman. Asked how killing a man felt, he mused, "Ah cain't say; co'se I helped kill a few triflin' 'Paches and no 'count thieves, but no, sir, ah didn't never kill a man." No wonder Slaughter thought him a good man to have along in such cases.[18]

---

[18] Los Angeles *Times,* September 1, 1940. In old age, Swain moved to Los Angeles, where, at about 95, he lived in the slums. This didn't squelch his fine sense of humor or jolly philosophy. He recalled his garden and orchard near Tombstone's court house, and his days as a small ranchman after he left the Slaughters.

Tad "Talt" Roland was also a worth-while hand. He had come to Arizona on the first trip. John always trusted him fully, and an unwelcome test proved his confidence well based. In his early Arizona days, when Slaughter couldn't afford a loss of any kind, John sent Tad to Charleston, a small village on the San Pedro, to collect a bill of $500. Roland went into a saloon and came out of it in a couple of hours without the money he had collected. He probably was doped there, for he said his drinks made him very drowsy. Desperately ashamed, he promised, "I'll work it out, Mr. Slaughter. I'll work it out if it takes the rest of my life." Cowboys then got only $30.00 a month, so his word had to go a long way. It was as good as the gold he had lost, and far less elusive. Even after the cash was all paid back, he felt indebted to John Slaughter for his kindness and confidence. He could never settle up for that. In his middle age, Roland was crippled with rheumatism, but he worked on. Finally, Slaughter showed his own gratitude. He sent his old friend to Indian Hot Springs, for treatment. Though the healing waters helped, Tad never again was entirely well.[19]

James Howell, Viola's brother, was also a big help. He was always with Slaughter on the big roundups. Jimmy kept books in both Spanish and English, and because of his linguistic abilities was invaluable in business deals. Arthur Fisher, Sr., and Jess Fisher, cousins of Mrs. Slaughter, rounded out the number of chief cowboys, though Steele Woods was another favorite of the Slaughters, and would often go to the ranch from Douglas to help out in the busy season. The regular everyday life wasn't easy in those days, working stock; for Slaughter, ranching in Arizona was just as hard as it was in Texas. Arizonians used the same kind of rig, a high-cantled double-cinched saddle with the old-

---
[19] Cora Viola Slaughter reminiscences, February 5, 1939.

fashioned A-fork, which often had steel rings for stirrups. Cowboys preferred the stovepipe, or shotgun-leg leather chap in preference to the hairy angora of the northern cowboy. A low-crown hat, campaign-style, with wide brim and no creases was the pride of every man on the range. There was little difference between the Arizona cowboys' regalia and that of the Texans.[20] Most cowboys carried one sixshooter and a saddle gun, usually a Winchester carbine; some preferred the old Henry rifle. Slaughter preferred California riding pants, inside of high half-box-toe boots; he never removed the spurs from his boots when he retired, and seldom was he ever seen without his boots or six-shooter. When he came to Arizona he had a saddle made especially for his comfort by Kengla-Martin Saddlery on Meyers Street, in Tucson.[21]

If John heard any music besides Old Bat's fife and phonograph, it came from Mexican workmen who had adobe shelters all over his ranch. Though Slaughter was no hand at singing, he would whistle softly as he rode about. In his youthful days he had learned the bed-down song and the soft lullaby of the night herder. This soothed the flighty longhorns and kept them from stampeding. Each morning he would visit the Mexican share-croppers on his ranch, who always bowed their heads as they politely greeted him, with "Buenos Dias, El Petron," or "Don Juan," as they affectionately called him.

Roundup cooks in Arizona were as much at a premium in Arizona as they were in Texas. They got the best of everything as Old Bat knew. No one argued with them, if he didn't want starvation or dyspepsia. A boss might fire a good hand to keep a cook, for if this specialist in "Son-of-a-Gun stew" quit some seventy miles from the home ranch,

---
[20] Interview with Fred Moore, Douglas, Arizona, 1950.
[21] Interview with Manuel King, Tucson, Arizona, 1949.

they all went hungry. Slaughter never had this trouble. At the home ranch John could proudly exhibit his very temperamental but artistic Chinese cook.

Although Slaughter suffered few droughts, windstorms or Indian fights, there were always other perils to combat. Prairie dogs, those little satans of the plains and foothills, had their maze-like metropoli in Arizona. Little could be done on a mass scale against them, but at least everyone helped liven conversation with his latest scheme to annihilate them. How John Slaughter must have chuckled over the old Englishman who came to Willcox in 1885 with his two pairs of ferrets. He tried to rent them out to ranchers to use in ripping the jugular veins of the clever prairie dogs. He claimed that they could kill twenty to fifty before tiring out or getting their bellies so full of blood that they couldn't work. Apparently, his plan of sending them underground to invade prairie dog cities didn't quite work out.[22]

Cattle diseases, however, were no joke. Blackleg, or "symptomatic anthrax," appeared with its high fever, loss of appetite, stiffness, and an increasing soft tumor on hip, neck, shoulder, loin, or flank. In Slaughter's day there was no blackleg vaccine, but cattle getting plenty of exercise seldom contracted the disease, and his were usually active. Barium, the inorganic substance in loco weed, killed many cattle. In Arizona, the flower blooms in May and June, and sometimes one steer will lead others to it.[23]

Arizona tick fever was fairly easily controlled, so no

[22] *Southwestern Stockman,* Willcox, Arizona, February 28, 1885. Exciting little incidents were always happening. Once a Slaughter herd coming in from the east was in the center of Animas Valley when two bulls from the herd started down into a canyon. They amazed the cowhands with their sudden duel. One was finally killed and the other animal was injured.

[23] They can scent it from a great distance. It affects the nervous system, causing the animal to step high. The beast's eyes get glassy, vision becomes defective, and he is always excited, sometimes going into convulsions. In time, the animal becomes emaciated, due to the action of the disease on the stomach walls, and eventually dies.

quarantine line was ever established. The Texas fever, however, had never been a threat that far west. In 1885, the infected area was quarantined. Some fifteen and a half million cattle were south of the Federal quarantine line. Flanking the Slaughter ranch was a quarantine fence, built by the Erie Cattle Company. This blockade was on the north side of San Bernardino and ran from the international border on around to Silver Creek, then northeast, and headed due east. The San Bernardino-Chiricahua fence ran between John's ranch and San Simon Valley. Other ranchers considered this fencing a great public benefit, and they all signed a petition asking that it not be taxed. The Cochise County Board of Supervisors agreed, for it protected the ranges from the fever tick existing in Mexican herds only nine miles distant, south of San Bernardino. Still, it did not prevent free access to the public domain, as some claimed, for the only water in the vicinity was controlled by Slaughter anyway, as he held deeds to all the well-watered land nearby.[24]

At least once the cattle tick did real damage to Slaughter's famous luck. He had sent five thousand head to Pomona, California, where they were to be fed with beet pulp. Willie Slaughter was supposed to feed them at the other end. Slaughter's nephew, Bob Hiler, said the cattle cars had quarantine signs on them, but they blew off enroute, and upon arrival in southern California, many steers were found dead from the fever.

Another bad break from usually beaming Nature was the earthquake menace. A string of natural springs often indicates an earthquake fault. In Slaughter's case, this was true. He had been blessed with water by the same thing that threatened destruction. On March 3, 1887, the Sonora earthquake began to rumble with terrifying results, and was

---
[24] Bisbee *Daily Review*, February 13, 1907.

BRANDING TIME ON THE SAN BERNARDINO
John Slaughter at center. Note the typical mesquite corral of the time.

JOHN SLAUGHTER CHECKING THE FLOW OF ONE OF MANY
ARTESIAN WELLS ON THE RANCH

followed by a series of smaller quakes. The main quake lasted about as long as many a speedy draw, but was considerably rowdier than any human disturbance. Its epicenter was at Bavispe, Sonora, and the diameter of activity was 300 miles. Seismologists fixed the intensity as 10 at epicenter – strong enough to demolish a small kingdom. Fortunately, the temblor occurred in a very sparsely settled region. There had been an extremely heavy rainfall that season and this damage was an additional woe. Movements were felt all the way from Toluca, near Mexico City, to Albuquerque, and Santa Fe, and west to Guaymas and Yuma. The central tract of maximum intensity, however, was in John Slaughter's San Bernardino Valley and in the neighboring part of the Teras Mountains. In the recent past, many big shakes had been felt in that valley, but this was the worst one of all. There was a single large fault on the eastern margin of the San Bernardino Valley where the mesas merge into the foothills. Now, great numbers of cracks were found in the narrow river bed, and there were outbursts of water and sand through fissures and holes which allowed the abundant subsurface water to spout forth. Here were some unexpected springs for John! Sulphur Springs Valley also gained new gushers. At Batepito Ranch, not far off, an area two miles long by one mile wide was covered with water averaging four inches in depth. All over the region cliffs of solid crystalline rock were shattered.

In Bavispe, adobe walls two feet thick came down with creaks and dull rumbles, but most damage was done by rafters which collapsed with the lateral movement of the earth. The two-hundred-year-old church there was completely destroyed. At Tombstone, Dr. George E. Goodfellow noted sounds like prolonged artillery fire coming from the south and dying away in the north.[25] Some thought

---

[25] N. H. Heck, *Earthquake History of the United States, Exclusive of the Pacific Region* (Washington, Government Printing Office, 1928), pp. 51-52.

that it was a runaway mule team. A lady walking on Fremont Street near John Slaughter's town residence fainted. Walls of the Occidental Hotel swayed. Bottles were jiggled from drugstore shelves. W. D. Monmonnier, Slaughter's deputy, was struck on the head in Schieffelin's Hall by a hook shaken from the wall.

At 2:13 p.m. the Howells were living in a sturdy adobe on their in-laws' San Bernardino Ranch. A few minutes later they were homeless! As a local newspaper soon reported it:

> Mrs. Amazon Howell was in the house at the time of the shock, and calling to her husband who was sitting just outside, both fled from the building, which fell with a crash before they had escaped it thirty feet.

It went on to say that a man occupying John Slaughter's house was sick in bed at the time. In a few seconds, he was up and running like a college athlete. Then he stumbled and fell. Down with him and around him went a shower of adobe bricks. None struck the lucky invalid.[26] The new sheriff's stable, smoke house, milk house, and home were also wrecked. John Slaughter built new ones a few hundred yards across the creek from the ruins. Typical of himself, he built better and bigger than before.

Though he trusted Divine guidance, "Don Juan's" nature did not generally take to superstition. Therefore, these omens meant nothing to him. For that matter, dangers in human form were no more disheartening. Many a rancher feared to venture into Mexico with too many "dobe" dollars, to do business with their neighbors to the South – but not John. His trips were more than rugged adventures; they were colorful vacations to him. Some of the most persistent anecdotes and most revealing true stories came out of these mercenary pilgrimages.

---

[26] Tombstone *Prospector*, May 3, 1887.

Viola often went with her husband. Sometimes she took Addie along as far as Hermosillo and then came back with the herd. One night the cattle stampeded and Viola hastily climbed into the wagon. After it was all over, Slaughter came up, as cool as you please, and helped her down. Now he could afford to laugh at her and observe that "if the cattle had come that way they would have trampled that wagon down as if it had been a cracker box."[27]

This probably seemed a mere incident to the veteran of many hazards. For instance, Colonel B. A. "Daddy" Packard, a fellow cattleman, at one time accompanied Slaughter to learn how he operated on his cattle buying trips into Sonora, Mexico. He found that the San Bernardino Ranch loaded a mule with "dobe" dollars in custody of Old Bat, put a few supplies and bedding on other pack animals, and rode across the border. Slaughter never followed the same route twice, fearing ambush by Apache or bandidos. Only four men started out this time, for Slaughter found it cheaper to hire vaqueros in Sonora and discharge them on reaching the border, thus paying trail-drivers one way only. After a rugged jaunt, they entered the bastion of a typical Mexican hacienda. Greetings in the established code of polite Spanish formalities were exchanged. In this case, the joviality was not all twenty-four karat. Slaughter, always alert, had ordered his men to stay mounted. Climbing a short ladder leading to a walk above the adobe corral walls, the Mexican cattle baron and Señor Slaughter examined the cattle below them in their pens. "This is not the young stuff you promised to round up for me," said Slaughter in good but plain Spanish. He had been promised two-year-olds and these were old steers. "Si, si, Señor," insisted his host, "all very young and very good. You may as well take them," he grinned. Then, like the thin steel of a gleaming stiletto, he

---
[27] Cora Viola Slaughter reminiscences, February 5, 1939.

added, "My vaqueros will relieve your burro of his plata before you leave." This put a period to his hospitality, but for John Slaughter this was not a conclusion. With a sly glance, Slaughter had already seen a mounted band of vaqueros behind an adobe wall, heavily armed, wearing cartridge-laden bandoliers over their shoulders. This called for some cool acting and quick thinking on Slaughter's part. Here he had walked into an ugly trap. It was gold coin they were after, and dead men don't talk. Perhaps Slaughter would buy these worthless cattle, and no bloodshed would be necessary, but if he objected, the men in the back awaited the signal. Slaughter calmly stepped down, got on his horse and rode to where the Spanish Don stood. Quicker than a flash he had his sawed-off shotgun pointing at the man's head, and ordered his men to ride out and meet him at a certain spot a quarter of a mile off. In blunt Spanish, John then said to the Mexican, "Now, you S.O.B. you dare make one signal for your men to fire and I'll blow your G-D head off." Said Packard later, "We looked back all the way, and pretty soon here came old John alone puffing on his cigar." [28]

Needless to say, Packard was more scared than impressed! This proved conclusively that John Slaughter was just as brave when all odds were against him as when he rode with a company of Rangers or a bunch of deputies.

This plucky little Texan could be just as relentless to a thief on his own ground. Once, John's nephew, Hugh Taylor, captured a border thief who was making off with one of Slaughter's horses. "Don Juan" conducted his own barnyard trial, tied the border ruffian to a gatepost, and then gave him a good thrashing with his rawhide riata before turning him loose with the warning that a second offense would mean death.[29]

---

[28] Interview with George D. Stephens, Douglas, Arizona, 1950. See also Charles A. Nichols memoirs, MS in Arizona Pioneers Historical Society, Tucson.
[29] Interview with Hugh A. Taylor, San Antonio, Texas, 1950.

Leonard Alvorsen, who in the early 'nineties came to work for the big Chiricahua Cattle Company (CCC) outfit in Sulphur Springs Valley, had long heard of Slaughter's cunning. In the early spring cattlemen of the vicinity went below the border to haze north all their cattle that had mosied there. One year after returning to the American side, Alvorsen and his buddies dropped in at the San Bernardino Ranch, as the CCC had bought two thousand steers from Slaughter and wanted to move them to their new range. In this Alvorsen worked for John's outfit and took tally, trimmed the herd and receipted to John for them. After the trim and the misfits had been rejected, not enough were left out of this particular herd to fill the requirements of the CCC. Some three hundred head were lacking. Taking his cowboys, Slaughter rode onto the Mexican side of the San Bernardino and soon rounded up the wildest, saltiest stock Alvorsen had ever seen. But instead of bringing them to the American side of his ranch, he put them in a strong corral a quarter of a mile below his barn on the Mexican side, and instructed his boys to come in for supper. That night, as the two men sat talking on Slaughter's front porch, two U.S. customs line riders came up with a pack horse. "Well, gentlemen," said John, "You see how I am fixed here; I guess you appreciate my position. The line runs through the center of my ranch. I have cattle on both sides. I have to be very careful and not incur the enmity of the Mexicans, and now if you will keep my name out of it and not implicate me in any way, I think I can give you a tip you've been waiting for all these months." They promised excitedly to keep his faith – mum was the word. Then Slaughter told them that Concho, a slick smuggler they had been trying to catch for years, was coming out with a big pack train near Silver Creek, a half-day's ride from San Bernardino. The Whiskey Fox was supposed to bring 110 gallons of mescal into the country. The line riders quickly deputized Alvorsen to help them and Slaughter nodded his head – "That's right, Leonard. If they asked you, you gotta go," as he laid his shotgun in Alvorsen's arm. The three rode till dusk and camped at Mud Springs, near Silver Creek Spring, but located no one. When the customs men released Alvorsen of his duty, he hightailed scornfully back to the San Bernardino and returned the shotgun. John Slaughter asked him if he had seen Concho. "Hell, Slaughter, what do you take me for anyway?", asked Leonard. Slaughter just chuckled and went into the house. But as Alvorsen had expected, the cattle from the Mexican side had all joined the purchased stock of the CCC cattle, making up the two thousand head – no duty, no red tape, no veterinary inspection.[30]

For a good many years Slaughter sold cattle to the government at the San Carlos Indian Reservation. On one of these deliveries, a young second lieutenant from Fort Thomas with more brass than cow sense, wanted to show off his authority and alleged knowledge of cow country lore. Playing cattle buyer for his glorious moment, he would point to an animal and say, "Cut that one out; we won't take it." Viola Slaughter was there too, watching the little play. Her heart sank as she saw one after another of her husband's best animals rejected. As usual, Slaughter never said a word. His customary poker face was up to par. Quietly, he drove the steers back to the main herd, but on his return, with all

---

[30] Meanwhile, Slaughter had got the rest of the steers on to the American side of his layout for Alvorsen. He sent two of his men to help take the beeves to the CCC outfit. One of these men was Joe Fateley, "a rough, reckless, yet true friend," a real cowboy. He predicted that he would die in a stampede one dark and devilish night, for he'd read the Bible "clean through" and it did not mention cowpuncher even once, though their rivals, the sheepherders, were gently referred to lots of times. He seemed to have been a good prophet too, for Fateley's death came as predicted, several years after he left Slaughter. He punched cattle on the Rio Grande for some time. There he was when a stampede crowded him into the river and he was never seen again. Alvorsen says that Slaughter's ranch 3H horse liniment was the only medicine! See "True Experiences of Leonard Alvorsen," MS dated 1938 in the Arizona Pioneers Historical Society.

the deftness of a magician, he always brought a few rejects back with the new cut which he paraded for inspection before the gloating young cavalry officer. This time the previous rejects were accepted. Time and again Slaughter repeated his trick. When the whole herd had finally been delivered, all had been accepted and the men went back to the ranch empty handed. The young officer had his thrill and kept face, while the Slaughters got their money, a good long chuckle, and a story to tell for years.[31]

Quite a source of joshing too was Hugh Taylor's horse breaking. One day, John Slaughter put an outlaw horse in his corral with a bunch of green colts. Hugh, acting as bronc peeler, told his "Uncle" John, "That horse there don't look like a mere colt; besides, he's sure enough salty." Old John didn't reply, but walked sheepishly away, chuckling and grinning from ear to ear. When Hugh left the corral on the steed, he was in for a bad day. Here was a sunfishing outlaw for sure. That pony unwound a dozen times that day, but Hugh stuck to him every jump.[32]

Slaughter himself was the source of many a laugh, but none of these guffaws ever lowered his dignity or people's respect for him. Like his father, Ben, he looked like a man born to the saddle. He sat at the table with spurs, and never without his six-shooter. In his later years, he would drop in suddenly at ranches to buy blooded stock. One day he went to the Hillman ranch for a carload of Durham bulls. Now a deputy sheriff, he had his old six-shooter on, but age made him a little more grim, and he scared Mrs. Hillman into hysterics. She believed that Slaughter was a hold-up man. He looked to her like Old Ben did to young J. H. Cook, the eastern lad back in Texas.

John Slaughter didn't have to be dishonest to make a real

---
[31] Reminiscences of Cora Viola Slaughter, February 5, 1939.
[32] Interview with Hugh A. Taylor, San Antonio, Texas, 1950.

fortune. When he began, the range was unfenced and cattle might drift anywhere. He made conditions very discouraging for neighboring squatters. His range was enormous. Slaughter's saddle string were kept in a remuda in the Playas Valley of New Mexico. Animas Valley, much closer to the home ranch, was more convenient and useful. His stock ranged far into Sonora, Mexico, and as far north as Galeyville, and then to the Huachuca Mountains and even to the Whetstones.

Until 1885, all the beef cattle grown in Arizona were consumed locally, or shipped to Kansas and California, or driven to nearby Indian reservations. By 1883, there were 23,000 cattle, 4,000 horses, and 2,200 mules in Cochise County. Thus, slowly a great surplus developed which army camps, mining centers, settlements and Indian reservations could not absorb. From 1885 to 1891, the excess beef was shipped to Kansas and Nebraska. These were Hereford and shorthorns which brought good prices. Quick profits, easy money, and newfound enthusiasm helped develop great ranches. After the Sonora earthquake of 1887, Slaughter built his big ranchhouse, entertained like a New World grandee, and busied himself improving his vast holdings. The 1891 calf drop was the biggest in Arizona history. By that fall there were a million and a half cattle on the range, and there hadn't been a bad blizzard in years. Slaughter economically was riding high at the same time that he had gained great prestige as an eradicating sheriff. Then came 1892 and the great drought. The year 1893 saw even less water. Skeletons were found in dried-up water holes, and when the rains finally came pelting down, they fell on only half as many cattle as before.[33] A couple of years later, bone gatherers passed by San Bernardino, piling bleached skulls

---
[33] Sharlot M. Hall, "Old Range Days and New in Arizona," *Out West*, XXVII, no. 3, March, 1908, pp. 181-204.

and leg bones in pyramids. Soon trainloads of jumbled skeletons were sent east to bone factories. Better years followed, but here as elsewhere in the great cattle empire of our West, the open-range days had come to a close. Many cowhands had to turn to farming. Great new ranches arose where thoroughbred stock was pastured, fed and made into "baby beef" for that new market.

Fortunately for John Slaughter, San Bernardino was almost unique in its tremendous water supplies. Like Col. Hooker, he had always believed in investment in blooded stock. As early as 1889, he was reported selling a brand of 108 fine horses, mostly mares, to an investor in Washington Territory.[34] At the same time, he sold five hundred head of steers.[35] The next year, Slaughter was selling stock at $13.00 a head.[36] That April, 450 head of steers went to Kansas by way of Deming. There were then not enough cars to carry his and his neighbors beeves fast enough to the East.[37]

Still, in the thin years, 1892-1893, Slaughter mortgaged his property. In the first year, he mortgaged eighteen hundred of two, three, and four-year-old steers with several brands, and four hundred head of cows branded LCA, 74, IN–, CA, A, and 55, to secure a note for seven thousand dollars, and interest at ten percent per annum, plus fifty cents commission per head of stock.[38]

In 1893, John and Cora Viola mortgaged six thousand head of steers and stock cattle, part of which were branded COD on the left side, part L on the left side, and part Z on right shoulder. Others included 150 head of horses branded

---

[34] *Southwestern Stockman*, Willcox, Arizona, October 5, 1889.
[35] Tombstone *Epitaph*, April 20, 1889. That December he got $16.00 for a lost shipment to Kansas City. See *Southwestern Stockman*, December 28, 1889.
[36] This was in a deal with R. W. Wood, also of Cochise County, for 250 steers on the San Bernardino Ranch. See Cochise County Record Book 1, page 451, May 31, 1890.
[37] Tombstone *Prospector*, April 11, 1890.
[38] Cochise County, Record Book 1, December 7, 1892.

z on the right shoulder, or COD on the left shoulder or hip, and 801 mares and colts with the same brands. The mortgage secured $4,500, and was fully repaid sixteen months later, on May 9, 1894. Slaughter recovered faster than most cowmen.[39]

The new century found him on top again. At one time he sold ten thousand head in a single year. Now he had five hundred acres in hay, barley, wheat and vegetables, and was supplying Bisbee and the new town of Douglas, which he had helped found in 1902.[40] Meanwhile, John Slaughter had run a store known as the Wholesale and Retail Meat Market. Established at Charleston, it made good from the beginning. When the railroads came, he hustled to get their trade. First the Santa Fe, and later the Southern Pacific, between Benson and Nogales, were his steady customers.[41] Hides also brought in the dollars. William Henry, a hide dealer,[42] used to drop into the San Bernardino Ranch and stay several weeks. His business was as welcome as his company.

Slaughter's luck seemed phenomenal, but it wasn't luck that kept him from failing a dozen times. Health and wealth were won at San Bernardino, but only through the more important health of an active mind, and the more basic wealth of unlimited courage.

---
[39] Cochise County, Mortgage Records, May 9, 1894.
[40] Bisbee *Daily Review*, February 12, 1907.
[41] Cora Viola Slaughter reminiscences, February 5, 1939.
[42] Bisbee *Daily Review*, December 8, 1901.

6

Territorial Apache Troubles

It seemed no matter where John Slaughter was to make his home he would be confronted with marauding Indians and stock thieves. His trips down into Mexico after cattle kept him heavily armed. His marksmanship is still being talked about by those who remember him. In the area of the San Bernardino Ranch, the Apache chief, Geronimo, had met for once a white man whom he could hold in great respect, only to flirt with his adversary to the extent of bringing about his own surrender. Slaughter could not have taken up a more dangerous position when he built his final headquarters directly on the path the Apache took to commit his depredations. It was all right for John Slaughter to tell the bad man to clear out of Cochise County when he became sheriff, but the same warning to an Apache was like conversing with a stone.

The Apache lived a life of starvation and disease. He had not the ambition or the common sense of the Pima. On the whole they were superstitious, lazy, cunning and bloodthirsty; they lived the life of nomads, refusing to accept the white man's ways. Though Geronimo, toward the end of his career as a prisoner at Fort Sill, Oklahoma, told his people to follow the ways of the white man, he was a poor example, having left a bloody trail in Arizona, New Mexico and Old Mexico. Being harassed to the extent of surrender, this spelled a bad ending for Geronimo and his people. To be loaded like cattle on a white man's train and to be shipped miles away from his homeland, was Geronimo's saddest moment.

The Apache felt strongly about the intrusion by the white

man, and found it more difficult to adjust himself to the changes taking place around him than did his northern cousins. The U.S. Cavalry was not going to permit another Custer Massacre, and handled the Indian affairs with the Apaches in a much more stringent manner. The Apaches were not well organized, and the method in which they committed their depredations and their sneak attacks caused the settlers a great deal of unrest. It was a certainty that something had to be done with them, for the livestock industry to flourish. John Slaughter was one of the most active ranchmen in bringing about a solution.

In the earlier days, when Cochise and Ezkimizin sold wood to the Government, they did so with sincerity and trust. Then came the lust for silver and gold causing the white man to barter guns and ammunition in return for this gleaming metal. In 1857, Captain Benjamin Bonneville made the initial expedition against the Coyoteros and other bands of hostile Apaches. A treaty was made, then disregarded, and the Apache went on the warpath in southern Arizona. Of these bands the Chiricahuas' Chieftain, Cochise, was the most brilliant and trustworthy. All he asked of the white man was for him to keep his word. His list of eighty-seven people killed was a severe measure of retaliation.

Billy Fourr, who was a neighbor to Cochise in the Dragoons, learned that Cochise was a true friend. Had Geronimo followed in the footsteps of Cochise, there would have been less bloodshed and trouble. Cochise was level headed and probably as well thought of among his peoples as Chief Joseph of the Nez Perce tribe. His castle was no more than a wickiup. Though his encampments were large, it would be difficult to tell his hut from any other. Cochise had a straight, trim figure and the bearing of a chief. With neck straight and head erect he had the poise and dignity of a prince of the plains, which he was. His hair was neatly kept,

TERRITORIAL APACHE TROUBLES   169

and a bluish shining braid of his locks were neatly tied at the back with a rawhide thong. His voice was clear and, in all, his demeanor was impressive. Faced with many ordeals by the white man, to the extent of trying to poison him, he passed this aside and took up with Captain Thomas Jeffords whom he looked upon as a blood brother.

But "Red Beard," as he referred to the captain, was not alone – until 1859 he had also trusted other white officer brothers. At the time Chief Cochise had a contract with the Butterfield stage line to supply the stage station at Fort Bowie with wood. A boy was carried off from there and the soldiers blamed Cochise's Apaches. Lieutenant Bascom arrested Cochise. But his incarceration was short, as it only took one sweep with a sharp hunting knife and Cochise walked through the white man's tent to freedom. Five thousand Americans suffered, and great property damage was the Indians repayment for this.

During the Civil War, King Woolsey was the hero of many attacks against the Apaches. Using Indian tactics, he killed many savages, and seldom lost a man.

Cochise's successor, Geronimo, through his escapades, became the best remembered of all Apaches. He claimed to have been born on the Gila's headwaters in Arizona, but actually first saw light on the Janos in Mexico. As an Indian he felt he was a citizen of the continent, and no white man was to curb his wandering habits. Although no hereditary chief like Cochise, his military skill made him into a natural leader of Apache tribes united with the Chiricahuas.[1] Geronimo never could endure restraint. For a time he was at the Turkey Creek Reservation under Captain Crawford and Lieutenant Britton Davis. These two officers recognized Apache hatred for the drudgery and boredom of plowing,

---
[1] Joe Chisholm, *Brewery Gulch: Frontier Days of Old Arizona.* Here is a very good account of Apache days. References to John Slaughter are scattered throughout.

planting, harvesting and storing. They wanted to train the Apaches as stock raisers with Indian Bureau sheep and cattle. That was one of the first really sensible ideas on the problem, but still it was not compatible with the Apache custom of living. White contractors, however, played the villain here. They did not want the Apaches to become self-supporting and self-sufficient. That would have prevented the sale to Apaches of shoddy merchandise at handsome profits. Added to this was the white man's persistent prohibition of tizwin, the Apache's fermented drink. Meanwhile, the Pimas were always friends of the whites and allies of the United States government. They acted as scouts and performed other services. In general, however, the Arizona settler was in constant danger of attack and massacre, from the Mexican War to the mid-'eighties.

Slaughter and his neighbors knew excitement and tragedy. They were caught in the middle of this hodgepodge of hatreds, tricks and errors. In the 'eighties, Geronimo and his braves were constantly beating through Cochise County, stealing horses and cattle and committing other depredations. The CCC outfit organized a military unit to resist the hostiles, with Jim Brophy, James Maxwell, Walter Fyfe, Judge Tom Blake, Billy Riggs, Jim McClure, and others leading it. Fyfe's mother was killed by Indians at their home.

Brophy and his men had hoped to take Geronimo near Turkey Creek. Thirteen cowboys waited downtrail for the cunning leader and his eighty-three braves, but the palefaces easily tipped their hand, and the Apaches scampered away to safety.[2]

---

[2] Bisbee *Daily Review*, May 22, 1934. The CCC's wise and witty Chinese cook, Sam, was a small but brave fighter against the Apaches. In height, humor and guts, he resembled John Slaughter. One day, he ordered a fellow Celestial not to flee the fray, for if he did, a sharp point of steel would come from the rear, not the fore! Brophy later established a ranch in Sulphur Springs Valley, specializing in Herefords.

TERRITORIAL APACHE TROUBLES 171

The Apaches next rode into the Mule Mountains and killed Bill Daniels below the present Forrest Ranch. This was poetic justice, for Daniels, an enthusiastic young Easterner, had come west declaring he wanted only to kill an Apache.

During Slaughter's days, he was deputy sheriff of Cochise County, but when he heard that the Apaches had left the Dragoons, he departed Tombstone for the scene of action. Geronimo and his warriors had circled Charles Bulle's ranch house, firing shots with each passing. Bulle rode to Bisbee, warned the town, and tried to get help for the Forrest Ranch. As he rode through Tombstone canyon toward Sac Hill, crying, "The Apaches are coming," the signal whistle of the Queen Mine wailed. Women and children scurried for hideouts in a large cave in the neighboring hills. Daniels rode with Bulle to Forrest's, but the Indians had departed. That was Bisbee's closest scrape with the Indians.[3]

Col. "Daddy" Packard, John Slaughter's old crony and fellow ranchman, had plenty of exciting Indian stories to recount. His Cochise Stronghold Ranch was not misnamed. It was just about impregnable, but that did not guarantee his stock. A ranch hand raced to tell him one day that a small party of Apaches had come. Packard set out to rescue his favorite saddle horse. Rifle, six-shooter and field glasses were enough against this band, he calculated. The binoculars showed him that three Indians were only three hundred yards from his outpost. Seeing him, they scampered. Packard later found the colt, a large slice of living flesh cut from its side. Yet the two-year-old survived. Like others, Packard lost more cattle than horses to the hostiles.[4]

---
[3] Bisbee *Daily Review*, April 1, 1948.
[4] Douglas *Daily Dispatch*, December 2, 1928. Packard was president of the First National Bank of Douglas. Slaughter was also one of its founders. Packard's ranch was established in 1882. Four times he served in the Arizona senate.

Another knight-errant against the Apaches was Pete Kitchen. He had come to Arizona in 1854, a soft-spoken, spare, five-foot-ten youngster. Typical of many mild-mannered gentlemen, he was unbending. He began a ranch near Nogales, called the Potrero, and another at Canoa, and fortified them. They had fortress-thick walls of adobe, built higher than the roofs to allow defense from atop the buildings; loopholes were provided, like Slaughter's, to help stand off attacks, and many times they had to be used. Like Slaughter, Kitchen lived in the heart of Apache trail grounds, and refused to leave. Sentinels guarded his stock, while his plowmen tilled the bottom lands with rifles on their backs. After the 'seventies he prospered, as if Providence wanted to say, "Well done!"[5]

Slaughter's own men had their close shaves. He had bought a bunch of steers from one Señor Molina down Mexico way. Tuck Potter of the Erie outfit made a fine hand for Slaughter, and doctored them. One day he saw Indian signs off on the right hand prong of Cottonwood Canyon (now on the Geronimo Trail). A white oak growing behind a boulder seemed to have a fox sitting in a branch. Each time Tuck fired at the cottonwood, the fox disappeared. His 40-60 Marlin rifle was a good one, and he couldn't understand it. All his shooting scared the cattle, diverting his attention to the herd and saving him from a massacre. The Indians were hoping that the boys would climb the hill and fall into a neat trap. Disappointed in their lack of success, the Indians got some satisfaction by rolling rocks down toward Potter and his companions.[6]

In many ways, these tragedies and close calls touched the Slaughters' lives. About 1888, Bunk Robinson and Jack Bridges, cowboys for a neighboring outfit, discovered a

---
[5] Thomas Edwin Farish, *History of Arizona*, II, p. 195. Pete Kitchen's son was killed by the hostiles, but the old man died of natural causes.
[6] Interview with Tuck Potter, Douglas, 1950.

COWBOYS WHO WORKED FOR THE CHIRICAHUA CATTLE COMPANY
AND FOR JOHN SLAUGHTER
Standing, L to R: Jim Pursley, foreman, Walter Fife, Jim Maxwell.
Seated: Billy Riggs, James McClure, Judge Tom Blake.
Photo by C. S. Fly of Tombstone.

CAPTAIN HENRY WARE LAWTON, UNITED STATES CAVALRY
As he appeared during the Geronimo Campaign in 1886.

freshly killed calf. They reported it, returned to the place, and both were killed on the spot. Gus Hickey, a prospector who had gone along with them through curiosity, made it to the San Bernardino spread, fifteen miles away. John and his men patched up Hickey, and brought in the bodies. As usual, their heads were mashed in with rocks, Apache fashion. About the same year, Apaches killed one Jake Bowman, a Bisbee officer, near the San Bernardino.[7] John never lost but one man in his employ, though from 1882 to 1886 the final bloody Apache campaigns were fought in his region, and Geronimo's band shuttled between San Carlos where Slaughter sold beef, and the Sierra Madres of Mexico, where John's herds and buying expeditions passed. Several times he scouted for the United States Cavalry on marches into Mexico against them, but there were no reprisals against him. Often he and his brother, Charley, would remember the early days when they had rescued Mormon settlers, and Charley had exclaimed in his soft, low voice, "We made Christians out of them Injuns!"[8] Knowing that Apaches did not fight after dark, John would be up and aboard his horse by 4:00 a.m. Late sleepers were often jumped just at daybreak.

Viola was a part of this dangerous scene, too. She rode beside her husband on many expeditions into southwestern New Mexico or down into northern Sonora where she saw smoking wagons and bodies of Apache victims. Slaughter decided to make his ranch and family safe. He turned to Apache strategy, and made forays on them in their own way — preying upon their camps. One time his vaqueros wavered in attacking an Apache hide-out, and Slaughter promised to kill the first Mexican who hung back. The Indians decided to give his spread a good wide berth.[9] Geron-

[7] Jim Brophy memoirs, *loc. cit.*
[8] Interview with Mrs. Nancy Slaughter Tubert, Tombstone, Arizona, 1950.
[9] Bechdolt, *op. cit.*, pp. 175-176.

imo knew his match. He gave specific orders to his warriors to keep away from this bad medicine.[10]

Geronimo used to make cattle raids in Mexico and bring the stock back to the San Carlos Reservation. On one occasion, he told Tom Horn, herder and friend of the reservation's chief of scouts, Al Sieber, that they were planning this. Horn sent some customhouse men from El Paso to San Bernardino Ranch. There on the border they collected duty on the rustled herd. Luckily for Geronimo, the Mexican soldiers following the Apaches had turned back and the customs officials let the Indians enter.

Horn knew Slaughter well. On a tracking trip with a military company, in the mid-'eighties, he stopped at the ranch, saw old John, and told him that he wanted the best horse he could lend. Slaughter gave him a good breakfast first. Then he told the scout to keep the animal, as he had three thousand more. At Tex Spring, Horn camped. General George Crook sent a Lieutenant Wilder to command the enlisted men with Horn in command of the outfit. Shortly, six cowboys came across the flat. They were Slaughter's men, bringing Tom the two saddle horses he left at San Bernardino.

These five Mexicans and one "gringo" wanted to get in on the fight, sharing as they did their boss's tradition for cleaning up the region of Apaches. They were heavily armed. This, too, was a tradition among Slaughter hands. All his employees could take care of themselves in any situation. These San Bernardino cowboys thought that the Apaches would come in from the Pillares via Dry Creek and knew that they would bring many horses, crossing the border at night near San Bernardino.

The best route to the San Carlos Reservation was through Don Juan's spread, too. Thus the cowboys and soldiers kept

---

[10] Chisholm, *op. cit.*, p. 51.

a good lookout. Next morning, they struck the Apaches by surprise. From all sides the white men attacked, and the Indians were driven into flat country. Only one squaw was not killed of a party of fourteen – eleven men and three women. The only American casualties were a dead cowboy from San Bernardino and two wounded hands from the same place. The Slaughter hands had put on the best show as fighters and horsemen. They retook 118 head of stolen horses. Since the San Simon Ranch boss would not accept them, and the Army through its "red tape" could not, Horn trailed the beasts to San Bernardino and had them turned loose on Slaughter's range. It seemed a San Bernardino victory all around.

Horn arranged next for meeting Geronimo on the Bavispe. They had a long talk and Geronimo arranged to go with him to Skeleton Canyon in the United States, to meet General Nelson Miles in a dozen days. Miles would not guarantee the date of meeting, and Geronimo grew disgusted. Horn rode back to Slaughter's ranch, got a needed rest, and found a cavalry troop camped there. A dispatch from Miles arrived, so Slaughter awakened Horn and told him he was wanted. The dispatch said, "Make any arrangements you want to for me to meet Geronimo. I will go where and when you say to meet him." Geronimo and Horn had ridden in opposite directions since last meeting, but Horn relocated him and gave him the message. With but four days notice, Miles did meet Geronimo on time at Skeleton Canyon. Horn was the interpreter. Geronimo agreed to surrender.

This conference was held on the San Bernardino ranch, with John Slaughter, as a scout, witnessing it all. It was September 3, 1886. The troops marched grandly to the San Bernardino, accompanied by Indians, while Lieutenant Gatewood came with the Geronimo party. He took his life in his hands in doing so. When Mexican soldiers arrived, Lawton told them to halt. His request was honored after promising their prefect an interview with Geronimo. Mexico, too, considered him a public enemy. Miles took the Apache chief and his people to Fort Bowie, where the soldiers formed on the parade ground and the braves laid down their arms. Miles wired the Southern Pacific Railroad station at Bowie for a special train to send away all the Chiricahua Apaches in locked and guarded cars.[11]

Arizonans had clamored for riddance, and Miles had ordered the removal as much for the Indians' protection as for the Arizona clamor. President Cleveland was out of Washington, so Miles had received no official advice. The general had assumed a responsibility not specifically ordered. When the President learned of this, he objected. Orders were sent to stop the train at San Antonio. Despite the political-military mixup, the Indians did not return to their old homes. Cleveland never forgave Miles for the incident.[12]

Many men remember that John H. Slaughter had helped send the Apache hostiles out of the West. When Captain Henry W. Lawton was sent in May, 1886, to command the expedition against the reservation fugitives, he took but thirty-five men, twenty Indian scouts, and a couple of pack

---

[11] Tom Horn, *Life of Tom Horn*, p. 150ff.

[12] Thomas Cruse, *Apache Days and After*, pp. 201-212. Here is a good account of the last Apache campaigns. Tom Horn had gone to work for Al Sieber in a government pack train in 1882. The next year, he helped Sieber track Chiricahua Apaches and bring them back to the White Mountain Reservation in Arizona. In 1885, when they broke away from there, causing war, Sieber followed them into Mexico with Captain Crawford. Horn went along. He returned the Indians and would have delivered them to the reservation had some whites camped near the San Bernardino Ranch not sold them whiskey and mescal. They soon broke away and returned to Mexico. Later, Horn worked as a cattle ranch hand in Pleasant Valley, getting into the sheepmen-cattlemen war raging there. As a result of conviction on allegedly circumstantial evidence, Horn was hanged on November 30, 1903, in Colorado.

trains into Mexico. They marched from Fort Huachuca into country so rough that mounted troops were useless. Dismounted with the scouts, they took the trail. The soldiers concentrated on getting the Indians' animals and supplies. Through good scout advice, they did so. By July, the army had reconnoitered 1,396 miles through the roughest country, with its scarcity of water and grass. Despite every Indian device to throw them off their trail, the troopers and scouts made the pursuit close and never let the savages rest. Heavy rains nearly destroyed the trail, but the scouts picked it up and never fell for the Indians' elusive devices. Scouts now pushed on alone as heavy rains made the Sierra Madres almost impassable. In these mountains were almost vertical cliffs, thousands of feet high. Some of their canyons rivaled the Grand Canyon. In many places the trail, if it existed at all, was but a few feet wide, and the rainfall made this indistinct. Still, the scouts kept going. Couriers were efficient, too. They gave news of Mexican negotiations with Apaches and helped Gatewood communicate with the Mexicans. When surrender was finally achieved in September, the campaign had covered 3,041 miles of marching and scouting. John Slaughter had a good part in this, though he seldom spoke of it. He scouted for Miles and Lawton, and the latter said of him and his fellows that their work had made safe the whole region, making it impossible for the Apaches to escape.[13]

John Slaughter's role against the Apache, and as scout,

---

[13] See the "Report of Captain H. W. Lawton, 4th cavalry en route to Fort Marion, Fla., September 19, 1886." Congressional Record, 56 Cong., 1 sess. Lawton, born March 17, 1843, served in the Union army in the Civil War, studied law at Harvard, but became a second lieutenant in 1871. He got his first Indian war experience under General Ranald S. MacKenzie. He saw action in Cuba during the Spanish-American War and became military governor of Santiago city and province. Ordered to the Philippines, he fought insurgents but was shot through the heart on December 19, 1899. Oliver L. Spalding, Jr., "Henry Ware Lawton," *Dictionary of American Biography*, (New York, Charles Scribner's Sons, 1943), XI, pp. 62-63.

was never forgotten by Geronimo. While Geronimo was a prisoner at Fort Sill, Oklahoma, and charging fifty cents to let soldiers and tourists take his picture, John Slaughter's niece, Mrs. Nancy Tubert, met him. The exiled chief looked at her glumly and said that there were only two things he would like to do before he went to the heavenly hunting-ground – die in Arizona and kill John H. Slaughter![14] As a pacifier of the great Southwest, Slaughter needed no further tribute.

[14] Mrs. Nancy Slaughter Tubert, interview.

7

The Dutchman's Town

Ed Schieffelin, the father of the town of Tombstone, had this to say in his will:

> It is my wish if convenient to be buried in the garb of a prospector, my old pick and canteen with me, on top of the Granite Hills about three miles westerly from the city of Tombstone, Arizona, and a monument such as prospectors build when locating a mining claim built over my grave, and no other monument or slab erected – and that none of my friends wear crape; under no circumstances do I want to be buried in any cemetery or grave yard.

This epitaph tells the story of the kind of a man Schieffelin was. Plain, ordinary and simple, preferring to be buried alone like the life he had led, usually by himself and close to nature, with mother earth close at his side. Prospecting is what he loved in life. He wrote a friend:

> I am getting restless here in Oregon and wish to go somewhere that has wealth, for the digging of it. I can't say that I care to be rich, it isn't that. If I had a fortune, I suppose I'd not keep it long, for now I think of it, I can't see why I should. But I like the excitement of being right up against the earth, trying to coax her gold away and scatter it.

Schieffelin was born October 11, 1847, in Tioga County, Pennsylvania. He came with his parents and brother, Al, to Jackson County, Oregon, by emigrant ox-train of covered wagons. He next went to Nevada but had little luck, having to spend much of his time working to get a grubstake. After securing enough supplies for a long trip, he next set out for the newest strike at Signal in western Arizona, at the McCracken Silver Mine. Here he again met with disappointment, and having worn out his clothing and boots, and used up his grub supply, he tramped off across the desert to Wickenburg.

Here he met Al Sieber, whom he called one of the greatest scouts in the West. Sieber, at the time, was taking a party of Indian scouts to explore the region of the Huachuca Mountains to select a suitable location for a military post. The area in between had been virgin country and little was known about it, and that appealed to Schieffelin. He asked Sieber if he might go with him, so he could do some prospecting and still have some protection. Sieber was delighted with this suggestion and gladly gave his consent. Sieber told the Dutchman he knew the country quite well, and that he had acquired a knowledge of how to locate the rich minerals. This proved false, as Sieber was a much better scout than a prospector. However, the two became very good friends.

Upon reaching the foothills of the Mule Mountains, Schieffelin observed in the distance what appeared to be an outcropping along a wash which led toward the San Pedro river. Sieber advised him that to leave the scout party was a foolhardy idea, for the Apaches were very bad in that part of the country. But the Dutchman was badly in need, and the prospecting urge overshadowed the dangers of being killed by Indians. They shook hands and Sieber yelled to Schieffelin as he departed with his mule, "Remember, I warned you, all that you will find out there is your tombstone." [1]

But the big Dutchman paid little attention. He soon found the silver mine he had been hunting. He took in with him as partners, Al Schieffelin, his brother, and Dick Gird, an assay man from Tucson. This strike caused a stampede to

---

[1] Ed Schieffelin was preceded in the area by Estaban Bronkow, or Bronchow, a trained mineralogist, who in 1860 prospected in the perilous land, located in the San Pedro Valley a mine he called the Bronkow, and set to working it. It was only seven miles from Schieffelin's later Tough Nut site. Bronkow later was murdered by his Mexican employees, who stole his bullion and stock.

the area. When a tent town went up, and finally a town of buildings, Schieffelin remembered what Sieber had told him he would find, so he named the town "Tombstone." When Schieffelin died the wishes in his will were carried out, but the marker was quite large. It had a monument twenty feet square, about three feet high, grounded on solid granite. The pinnacle reached only twenty feet above the rich rock beneath. Here, in frontier garb, his remains rested. The words were almost his own:

> Ed Schieffelin, died May 12, 1897, aged 49 years and 8 months. A dutiful son, a faithful husband, a kind brother, a true friend.[2]

Nearly a half century later, this might have been said of John H. Slaughter, whose marker is as simple.

Yet a living monument for both breathed on. Many said Tombstone lived too fast, but there was much good in the ornery mining camp that dared become a city. It was filled with miners from every mineral section of America and parts of Europe. Cowboys enjoyed its rough entertainments. Dancehall girls were none too ladylike, and justice often winked behind her flimsy blindfold. But there was much progress – and no boredom!

Laid out in 1879, the camp had over a thousand inhabitants before the year was over. By 1880, three thousand were there, and the number had grown to about eight thousand when the census count was taken. Tombstone was built on a rolling mesa, rising gradually from its 4600-foot elevation into the Tombstone Hills. One could look across the valley to the north, and there some fifteen clear miles away were the Dragoons, stronghold of old Cochise and his belligerent followers. To the south and west the Huachucas

---

[2] When Schieffelin's body was found, a little sack of ore assaying $2,000 was discovered near it. Probably he had uncovered a rich pocket. Generous all of his short days, he left all his remaining property to his widow, except fifteen University of Arizona bonds of $1,000 each, which went to his brother Jay, as trustee. Ed left no children.

towered, and on their blunt and barren peaks could be seen Indian signal fires, a more potent sign of danger than any mine whistle might be some day.

Politically, the town began in 1881 when on February first it was incorporated. A mayor, four councilmen, a police judge, an attorney, a chief of police and an assessor were provided for. Only twenty-four days later the territorial legislature made it the county seat of the new Cochise County, cut from older Pima and named for the unforgettable Apache. In the beginning this new county was larger than Connecticut, and almost as big as that state and Rhode Island combined.

In that day, physical appearance was often a determinant. Men took each other at face value when there was no other clue. Again Tombstone was disarming. It looked fast-growing and busy enough, but hardly history-making. The tenderfoot could not see that the town was more undermined with silver diggings than it was with crime. Its streets were always safe for good people, IF they minded their own business. Houses were made mostly of wood, a few of adobe, and all shaded over with wooden awnings extending beyond the sidewalks. The new courthouse, finished in 1883, was the finest edifice, a two-story brick affair, costing $43,000. Then there was the city hall, which cost another $15,000. Two banks and a couple of good hotels added an "Eastern" air.

Boston might have its Brahmins, but it didn't possess Tombstone's good, straight streets. To cut down on the bullwhacker's cuss words, they were plenty wide, too. Blocks were three hundred feet square. That universal shade tree of the old West, the cottonwood, stood before most residences. Slaughter knew the tree well. His windbreaks at San Bernardino were of it.

A sightseer would be interested but hardly excited. On the corner of Fremont Street and First was the public school, supported as much or more by gamblers' chips as by more respectable coin. Slaughter's young ones knew this place for a time. St. Paul's Episcopal Church, on the corner of Safford and Third, welcomed John and Viola. The Tombstone *Epitaph,* which would preserve on paper Slaughter's doings, could be found between Third and Fourth on Fremont. In its columns booms, blood, and blessings got their squibs and editorials. At Fremont and Fourth streets was the Shieffelin Hall, where citizens would gather for heated meetings. There old John might meet his cronies. There, too, politics grew sometimes grimy. Fortunately right next door was a Chinese laundry – cleanest place in town in many ways. Farther away was Billy King's blacksmith shop, where many a badman's horse was shod. The bloody OK Corral stood between historic Allen and Fremont. For good food, one might try the Can Can restaurant, a regular honky tonk, but he probably would prefer respectable Nellie Cashman's American Hotel. She was the soul of charity as well as the spirit of Irish fury, as those who tried to charge admission to grandstand seats at a hanging discovered. She wrecked the place.[3]

Tombstone's water supply was excellent. It was brought eight miles by pipe from Sycamore Springs near the Dragoons. Another water company had spent $500,000 to carry it from the Huachucas, thirty-one miles distant.[4]

For those with a more violent thirst, saloons were plentiful. Some say that the Crystal Palace was as good as any in fabulous San Francisco. William Henry Bishop, who visited Tombstone in 1882, counted on one block of Allen Street:

> . . . the barrooms of two principal hotels, the Eagle Brewery, Can Can Chop-House, French Rotisserie, Alhambra, Maison Dore, City of Paris, Brown's Saloon, Fashion Saloon, Miner's Home, Kelly's

---

[3] R. N. Mullin, *Tombstone in 1882.* (n.p., 1916) p. 3ff.
[4] Jules Baughman. "Tombstone, Arizona," *Mining and Scientific Press,* San Francisco, LIX, November 23, 1889, p. 399.

Wine House, The Grotto, and Tivoli, and two apparently unnamed saloons. Gambling was carried on at all of them.[5]

Still, there was an ice cream factory, a skating rink, a Turners' Hall, and dignified parlors for the Masons, Odd Fellows, Knights of Pythias, G.A.R., United Workmen, Daughters of Rebakah, and Patriotic Order of Sons of America. Four religious denominations were represented.

The needed fire house was on Toughnut and Fifth. The year 1881 and 1882 had witnessed two serious fires ,so Tombstone was taking no more chances. Its engine by 1883 was the best of the day.[6]

In an adobe on the corner of First and Fremont Streets John H. Slaughter later lived as sheriff. In these early days, though, he visited Tombstone only on business, and knew by sight the half-villains and semi-heroes who passed beneath its wooden verandas.

Slaughter understood what made the desperado and what he became, once he had been "completed." John was to "finish him off" in a more final sense. He knew, as fiction writers refuse to learn, that the wild and wooly gun-toter was not all bad, nor all good. The Southwest may be a land of bright sunshine and deep shadow, with clear contrasts and distant vistas, but the arid atmosphere cannot change human nature. Little is all black or all white. There is much gray in a man's character. Slaughter was no saint. Yet he had the abundant common sense and perfect balance to weigh right and wrong on a delicate scale.

The "cowboy element," as it was called, made up the small but loud proportion of Cochise County's outlaws. Mostly, they were from Texas. Like Slaughter, they had come to Arizona to seek new fortunes and for their "health," but unlike him, the cause was not always literally medical.

[5] William H. Bishop, *Old Mexico and Her Lost Provinces: Journey in Mexico, Southern California, and Arizona by way of Cuba*, pp. 491-492.
[6] Mullin, *op. cit.*

THE DUTCHMAN'S TOWN

As a result, Texas drew the undeserved notoriety. But a cross-section of the Lone Star State could be found there in southeastern Arizona; it supplied more of good and more of bad than any other State. Today, Arizona is grateful.

One day a little Texas cowhand was hailed before a Tombstone jury for failing to pay his debts. Uncle Billy Plaster, a real Lone Star enthusiast, was one of the "twelve men, and true." Mary Tack, the defendant's German-born landlady, testified in broken English, "Well, Chudge, de poy ain't to plame; hees fadder ist frum Texas and hees mutter ist frum Texas, so I dun't tink de poor poy is to plame. I tink he shud pee oxcewsed." Billy leaped up and clapped his hands. With a Texas yell he exclaimed, "By Gawd, if he's a Texan, turn him loose!" [7] Still, most of the Texas cattlemen were like Slaughter. They did not have to be "oxcewsed." A visitor described them as perfect gentlemen, some of them good at the bar for as high as $20.00 or $25.00 per day.

Murders and robbery were usually due to drunkenness. The main form of theft was rustling. In the early days, ranchers wanted to buy cattle cheap, and it was hard to get them delivered from Texas, California, or Sonora, so they were not too fussy with their supply's origin. They might buy from the badmen — prices were right, usually one third the market value. In other cases, they were afraid not to do business. Being mostly Texans, cursed with a border hatred of Mexicans, they felt a certain reluctance in purchases from below the border. Rustling was conducted on a gang-like basis. Mexican thieves would bring the cattle from Mexico, and meet the gringo rustlers on the Arizona side, usually east of Slaughter's ranch. One of the favorite meeting places was Skeleton Canyon.[8]

---

[7] Interview with Tuck Potter, Douglas, Arizona, 1949.

[8] Interview with Fred Moore, Douglas, Arizona, 1950. See also Carlisle S. Abbott, *Recollections of a California Pioneer*, pp. 205-235, for a little-known account of Tombstone.

Lois Hunsaker of the old Hermitage Ranch in Rucker Canyon has many interesting tales about the conduct of these cow thieves. One time they rode up about sundown, and acting very polite and mannerly, asked if they could have something to eat. After washing and combing their hair, until the meal was prepared, they sat around like prominent ranchers of the neighborhood, and talked about everything else but stealing. After mealtime they offered to pay, but, in accordance with western tradition, payment was refused. They then went out to the corral, and there they left their jaded horses and saddled up Mr. Hunsaker's best saddle string – without asking permission from the owner. A week or two later, when the boss of the Hermitage outfit went out to do the morning chores, he saw all his saddle horses had been returned. The rustlers had taken their own and gone, leaving a note on the gatepost; simply scribbled, "thanks." When Hunsaker needed any help at roundup or branding time, he could count on the rustlers to assist. At no time would they accept payment from the man who tended to his own business without shouting, "Sheriff."

Fred Moore of Douglas, recalls his boyhood days when he used to saddle up his pony, and take a basket of food out into the hills to feed the outlaws. As a boy he refused to give the officers any information about Grant Wheeler and Joe George, two noted train robbers. It was a strange relationship between the ranchers and the outlaws in the hills. However, this type of courtesy extended to the lawless kept them from stealing from the ranchers who befriended them.

Buckskin Frank Leslie who later registered a brand nearby calling his ranch the Seven-Up, would drop into the Hunsaker place now and then. He was soft-spoken, mannerly, immaculate in dress, and extremely polite to the ladies. When Lois first saw him, she asked her father who this gentleman was. When Mr. Hunsaker replied it was the notorious Buckskin Frank Leslie, she found it hard to believe that this quiet gentleman was a murderer. Later on, the canyon where Leslie had his ranch, was named after him.

Buckskin Frank Leslie, in the 1882 census records of Cochise County, was listed as Nashville Frank Leslie age 40, U.S., saloon keeper, Tombstone. He went by the name of Frank Leslie, and because of his buckskin clothes was known as Buckskin Frank Leslie. He tried his best to keep his past concealed, but Jim Brophy of the Chiricahua Cattle Company told of when he knew Leslie in San Francisco. Leslie was very much disturbed when the Tombstone *Daily Prospector* on Monday, July 15, 1889, gave a sketch of his background. It stated he was born in Galveston, Texas, and although he once gave his name as Franklin Nashville Leslie, his real name was Kennedy. The Leslie was his mother's maiden name. His father was Thomas Kennedy, and Frank had an uncle in Houston who had a great deal of property. Though Frank Leslie looked a gentleman of his time, with his long moustache, chiselled nose, and big blue eyes, he was nevertheless dangerous. An excellent shot, he was one to stand up to his foe, take a long steady aim and fire. The rapid-shooting artists were easy prey for him. He had found out that in order to stay alive in a gun battle, he must draw fast, take time in aiming the weapon and then fire. The first bullet was usually the one that counted. While Leslie was friendly towards Slaughter, although he was later hauled off to the Yuma prison by the sheriff, it seems that his shooting of an ex-Slaughter cowboy named Billy Claiborne was never questioned by John as being anything other than self defense. Slaughter at the time, was not yet sheriff of Cochise county. Like so many of these killings, the facts became distorted and eventually the truth becomes so entangled with opinions, that the real facts are never established. It is for this reason that quoting the findings of a coroner's jury, and hearing the testimony of the witnesses is what gives the telling ring of authenticity. In the case of Billy Claiborne's gunfight with Buckskin Frank, the latter being the winner, Claiborne lived long enough to say something. Witnesses of the fight rounded out the rest of the facts as they saw it. The facts of the shooting are here made available in print for the first time. The event illustrates the type of trouble which would later be dealt with by John Slaughter when he became sheriff.

November 14, 1882
Tombstone. A.T.

W. J. Mason duly sworn says: He resides in Tombstone and recognizes the body submitted as that of William Claiborne. He states he has known Claiborne for three years. He goes on to say:

I, this morning came to the Oriental saloon. While I was drinking alone, Mr. Claiborne came into the saloon and had some words with Mr. Leslie – and Mr. Claiborne, said, "I will see you later!" – Mr. Leslie replied, "While I am in Tombstone, you can see me anytime." Mr. Claiborne then left the saloon, and I left the saloon to see Mr. Brophy, and met Mr. Claiborne on the corner near the Oriental, 5th and Allen – I advised him to wait; I would buy some fish, and we would go to breakfast together; I advised him to do nothing, but drop the matter, and have no trouble. He said, he did not propose to drop the matter but would go and get his winchester and would settle the matter at once. – That is the last, I seen of Mr. Claiborne in good health – I saw him next lying before the fruit stand beside the Oriental, he complained he was mortally wounded, saying, "my back bone is shot out." I got on the ground in time to see Mr. Leslie hand his six shooter to the officer – and being taken off by the officers, the next I saw of Mr. Claiborne was in the undertaker's office dead. I did not see the shooting. I do not know of my knowledge who killed Mr. Claiborne. Claiborne said that he had some trouble with some one, and he was going to get his winchester and settle the matter. Mentioning no names, he passed down Allen Street with his gun in his hand towards the Oriental saloon.

I was in Mr. Brophy's saloon when I heard the shots – I think there were three shots – I did not know of any ill feeling existing between the parties before this morning – I saw the officers take a rifle from the ground where Claiborne lay – I do not know the officer's name who took Leslie away, I only seen one rifle on the ground.

(Signed) W. J. MASON

Doctor G. C. Willis, a surgeon and physician, was next called to tell what he had known about the situation. He saw Claiborne a little before 8 o'clock at his office being brought there by his friends, after the shooting. He stated Claiborne was in a shock bordering collapse. Dr. Willis cut open his shirt and found a gunshot wound in the left side and an opening in the back close to his spinal column, probably the wound of the exit. Claiborne was bleeding profusely, and wanted to urinate, which he did; the urine was found to contain blood. After that act his prostration was more complete. The doctor gave him some stimulants and dressed his wounds. More relaxed now, Claiborne talked of his opponent calling him "a murdering sonofabitch." As there was no convenience at Dr. Willis's office, he had Claiborne taken to the hospital. Willis found no pulse at the wrist from the time Claiborne came in until he went out. The action of his heart was feeble, and it could hardly be detected. He did not probe the wound. In his opinion the ball passed through the spleen and through the left kidney; in all probability it accounted for the blood in the urine, according to Willis. The ball had injured the spinal column, and it was his opinion the shooting was fatal. Before Claiborne was to be transferred to the hospital he began giving his belt to a Mr. Herring; he was not wholly conscious at the time. After relinquishing his belt, Claiborne relaxed, took a deep breath and died.[9]

Otto Johnson, a Willcox saloon keeper, was in Tombstone that morning and was leaving Judge Mose's saloon to catch a snack of breakfast at the Can Can chophouse. He saw Claiborne on the corner of Fifth and Allen, near Joyce's

---
[9] Cochise County, Arizona, Court Record Book 2, page 414, November 22, 1882. See Coroner's Inquest death of *William Claiborne,* Bisbee, Arizona.

Oriental Saloon, with a gun scabbard slung over his left shoulder, and a Winchester in his right hand. He noticed Billy Claiborne had his thumb on the trigger, gun pointing downward. "He said," "Hello Bill, where are you going?" Billy walked up to Johnson and remarked that he did not allow any man to push him around, and said that if Leslie wanted to fight he should come out on the street, otherwise he (Claiborne) would go inside to make the fight. Johnson tried to talk the red-headed Texan out of it, told him to take a walk and cool off, or to come along with him down the street. Claiborne got nasty then, and told Johnson if he poked his nose in his business that he would turn on him. So Johnson left him, and walked into Joyce's saloon. In the saloon, Johnson saw a friend named Percy talking with two other men at the bar. Johnson walked up and shook hands with Percy, and asked him if he knew a man by the name of Leslie. Percy said, "Why yes, I do." He turned to one of the men he had been drinking with, who happened to be Frank Leslie, and introduced Johnson. Not having been able to stop Claiborne, Johnson thought he would now warn Leslie, as a good upright citizen. He told Leslie to be careful that outside there was a man after him with a Winchester. Leslie asked Johnson the whereabouts of this man. Johnson said he was just outside the saloon. Leslie walked through an arched door into another room, where there was a side entrance that opened on Fifth Street. He opened the door, looked around, then pulled it shut, stepping out on the sidewalk.

 The next thing the men inside heard was the sound of gunshots. Johnson immediately went outside and saw Claiborne lying on the sidewalk, and Leslie about two feet from him, with a man holding up the hand that Leslie had the pistol in. Johnson took one quick look and walked hurriedly away. He testified that Leslie had left the saloon by the side door on Fifth Street.

William Henry Bush, a colored man who was shining shoes, saw Claiborne come up the street with a gun on his shoulder, saying, "I am going to kill Frank Leslie." The shoe-shine man pleaded with Claiborne not to go and asked for his gun. Claiborne, obviously in a nasty mood, refused. The colored man next saw Billy across the street with his Winchester and at the same time hollered to the barkeeper of the Palace Saloon that there was going to be a shooting scrape. Bush saw Claiborne raise his rifle to shoot Leslie and saw the smoke when he pulled the trigger. Claiborne, in a fit of anger, had missed, his bullet hitting the sidewalk. Next Bush heard two more shots, then he saw Leslie near the Oriental Saloon with a pistol in his hand. Bush could not tell who fired those two shots, but he did testify Claiborne fired first.

John J. Reilly, a laborer working in Tombstone, first spotted Claiborne beside a fruit stand with a rifle in his hand. The fact he remained so long in the same position drew the attention of Reilly. He soon realized he was in range of the rifle, so retreated behind the corner of the Crystal Palace Saloon. He saw Leslie emerge from a door and then heard the shots. He, at first, seemed sure he heard three shots, then he changed it to four shots being fired. He knew both of the men doing the shooting, and testified Claiborne shot first.

James Coyle, a Tombstone policeman, was on the street at 7:30 that morning and was standing opposite Cohen's cigar store on Allen street talking with Dave Cohen, with his back to the Oriental Saloon. He heard a shot fired, and quickly turned. He saw Frank Leslie close to the sidewalk with a pistol in his hand, and saw him fire. Coyle ran toward him, but before he could reach Leslie, he had fired again. Leslie then turned to Coyle, saying, "Jimmy, here is my pistol. Be careful – it is cocked." Leslie then laid the hammer down, and handed the pistol to policeman Coyle.

He said, "I will go with you Jimmy. I could have done more, but I couldn't have done less. He was laying to kill me." Coyle next picked up Claiborne's rifle that was laying across his thighs. He then walked Leslie as far as the police courtroom, and turned his prisoner over to Deputy Sheriff Cory, handing him Leslie's pistol, and Claiborne's rifle. Coyle could not see what Leslie was shooting at as Claiborne was down behind the fruit stand. Coyle testified that there were only two empty chambers in Leslie's six-shooter.

Dave Cohen, who had been conversing with officer Coyle, saw Claiborne raise his rifle and fire the first shot. Then he saw Leslie fire two shots. He observed Claiborne was back at the end of the fruit stand near the door of the Oriental saloon. He said that Leslie was standing facing him, but he did not spot Leslie until the first shot was heard. He saw Claiborne fall backward as soon as Leslie fired. Leon Jacobs story corroborated that of Cohens.

The evidence in the case was climaxed by additional light on the scenes that led up to the shooting, as testified to by E. H. Dean, a barkeeper at the Oriental. He stated that Leslie was in the saloon for an hour before Claiborne came in. He said Leslie was with three others at the bar down toward the end. Claiborne stepped up to the four men at the bar and interfered with their conversation. Nosing his way into the circle, Claiborne made a remark about a man named Dave Neagle, who was running for sheriff against a man named Ward. Claiborne said that any man that would vote for Ward was a sonofabitch. Leslie told Claiborne to go away, as they were discussing politics. Billy said he would not go away. Then Leslie warned Claiborne he was apt to get in trouble with the other parties. Billy went on with his interference. This time Leslie grabbed Claiborne and shoved him toward the opening into the next room. Claiborne again bounced back saying he would allow no man to handle him in this way. Leslie then told him it was for his own good

THE DUTCHMAN'S TOWN

that he treated him as he did. Claiborne stomped out then, in a huff, and shortly afterwards Dean saw Johnson come in and warn Leslie that a man was outside with a rifle to kill him. Leslie went out one side door and E. H. Dean went out by another side door, both opening on Fifth Street. Dean's testimony differed as to Claiborne's position, stating he was standing at the end of the fruit stand near the third door. H. M. Mathews acted as coroner in the case. Leslie got off, having acted in self-defense. It later was rumored that Billy Claiborne had accused Leslie of waylaying his friend John Ringo. Whether this is so, leaves room for doubt and speculation.

Politics are always strange. In Tombstone, they were downright bizarre. When Cochise County was organized in 1881, the Republicans hoped to hold most of the public offices. This seemed logical, for although the people were mostly Southern Democrats, the territorial governor, John C. Fremont, was an appointee of the Republican president, Rutherford B. Hayes. Fremont was one of the West's famous explorers, and this last frontier seemed appropriate for him. Still, his actions were original, to say the least. The office of sheriff was much coveted. It paid $4000, for the sheriff was also assessor and collector of taxes. The board of supervisors allowed him ten per cent of all collections. Strangely enough, it seemed, Fremont appointed a controversial Democrat, Johnny Behan, as first sheriff of Cochise County. Wyatt Earp was a Republican, which might have been at least one reason these two lawmen were at loggerheads.

This even more controversial Westerner was much more than just a party man. Wyatt had been lawman at the last of the long-trail cow towns, Dodge City. His brothers, James, Virgil, Warren and Morgan and his chief aide, Doc Holliday, had also played bit parts there. After a couple of years as that town's lawman, Wyatt landed a similar job in Tombstone. He came late in 1879, as United States Deputy Marshal.[10]

John H. Behan was a jolly, kindly fellow, brave but somewhat easy-going. He was a natural-born politician and came to be nominal leader of the opposition to the Earps and the atmosphere they imparted.[11]

The Tombstone *Epitaph* was a Republican paper. It supported Wyatt Earp and gave him good publicity. He declared himself the nemesis of the "cowboy faction," while Behan insisted that the Earps were in league with stage robbers. Johnny Ringo challenged Holliday to a duel, but was refused, for Ringo was more than an even match. Holliday apologized for a remark he had made, and the matter ended. Later, Indian Charlie and Frank Stilwell were accused of killing Morgan Earp while he was chalking his billiard cue at Bob Hatch's poolroom. In vengeance, Wyatt and Doc Holliday killed Stilwell at the Tucson depot, while taking Morgan's body to the family home in Colton, California.

With such violent men, a feud was explosive. The Clantons, once neighbors of John Slaughter, were the Earps' special foes. Old Man Clanton, as he was always called, headed his family and led the Earp opposition. His sons, Ike, Phineas and Billy, were eager pupils. Billy was only a boy, trying hard to grow whiskers. Wyatt wanted Ike Clanton to confess that his chums, Leonard, Head and Crane had robbed the Bisbee stage sometime earlier. Earp wanted to clear his friend Holliday of the same charge. The deal got out, and the Clantons were furious and in danger. Ike later claimed that the Earps had confessed to him that their men were in on the holdup. Ike Clanton was often drunk. Being

---

[10] Stuart N. Lake, *Wyatt Earp: Frontier Marshal* (Boston, Houghton Mifflin Company, 1931).

[11] See "John H. Behan," in *Arizona Biographical Dictionary*, (New York, S. J. Clarke Company, 1916), III, pp. 200ff.

THE DUTCHMAN'S TOWN

so, he threatened to kill Doc Holliday the next time they met. To make things worse, a rumor got out that Ike was trying to court Earp's sister.

Wyatt was sober, but he could not always control his temper. He lost it and struck Frank McLowery, a friend of the Clanton boys, who also threatened the Earps. There was no fight then, but it was brewing to a fast boil, as everyone in Tombstone knew. October 26, 1881, is the town's most famous date. Here was the showdown. The Earps wanted it as much as the Clantons. In front of a gunsmith's shop, appropriately enough, Wyatt came face to face with Ike and Billy Clanton and Tom and Frank McLowery. What happened then? He told them to get a horse off the Tombstone sidewalk! That was strictly against the law! Still, history is often sparked by such little things. There was plenty of gunpowder for a little spark to set off. The sheriff, John Behan, was determined to stop any fracas, so he went to find the boys and discovered Ike and Tom unarmed. Only Billy and Frank had weapons. Suddenly, the three Earps and Holliday approached down the street. Behan tried to stop the fatal meeting, but he was turned aside, so the story goes. Within about five feet of the Clantons, Virgil Earp demanded they raise their hands. The Earps claimed that Billy and Frank now drew their six-shooters and fired. In any case, Billy Clanton and the two McLowery boys were killed. Ike, however, tried to grab Wyatt's gun arm, and ruin his aim; then ran into Fly's photo gallery and then across to "Daddy" Packard's office. Here he hid until night. Packard gave Ike a horse and he left town.

This ended the two factions forever. Ike was killed six years later trying to escape a posse. His less notable brother, Finn, was shot by Ballard Pierson. The Earps found refuge in Colorado after a warrant was issued for their arrest. Their apologists still take sides, though the six-shooters have been silent for seventy-five years. In Boot Hill is the grim reminder of what happened. It is a marker over three rock-covered graves. "Tom McLowery, Frank McLowery, Billy Clanton, murdered on the streets of Tombstone," it declares. Some still argue about the truthfulness of its wording.[12]

John Slaughter himself was given a wide berth. He never bragged, but things no doubt would have been different had he been sheriff at that time. Slaughter was for minding his own business. He saw the killing of Billy Clanton and the McLowerys as a lawless blunder. John Slaughter had no trouble with the Clanton family.[13] Anyhow, Jimmy Howell, John's brother-in-law, lived with his father, Amazon, near the Clantons and was certainly chummy with young Billy. Howell was all broken up when his youthful pal was killed.

John Slaughter kept an eye on Doc Holliday, the Earps' right-hand gunman. After a famous Benson stage robbery, John and Viola were returning from a visit. Mrs. Slaughter had objected to going, as she had a premonition of danger, but John only believed in his own hunches. It was a fully moonlit night along the Charleston road as the couple headed for home. Suddenly Viola heard hooves beating behind them. Neither said anything, but on a curve a lone horseman came alongside. Viola noticed the shining pistol that he was holding in his hand. Suddenly the stranger spurred his horse and rode away in a gallop. Mrs. Slaughter

---

[12]The coroner's report on the battle of the O.K. Corral "is now missing" from the court house records at Bisbee, but it used the spelling "McLowery" as on the grave marker. They were always called Frank and Tom Laury; however, "McLaury" is the proper spelling. They both worked for John Chisum at his Bosque Grande Ranch in New Mexico before coming to Arizona. – Interview, 1952, with W. J. Chisum, nephew of John S. Chisum.

Douglas *Daily Dispatch,* Dec. 2, 1928. See also Walter N. Burns, *Tombstone,* Chs. XII, XIII, and XIV. Burns is partial to the Earps. John P. Clum in "It all Happened in Tombstone," *Arizona Historical Review,* II, October, 1929, also supported the Earp faction. His *Epitaph* had always been their chief defender. Judge James C. Hancock point by point disputed much of Burns' contention. See his interesting article in the *Arizona Republican,* Phoenix, March 4th, 1931.

[13] Burns says Slaughter hated the Clantons, but Hancock categorically denies it.

whispered, "Why, that man had a gun in his hand." Slaughter grinned. "That's fine. I have one, too," he said. He had recognized Holliday's horse even before Viola saw the night rider.[14]

Slaughter always hated the vigilante spirit, although as a lawman he later upheld the statutes as *he* saw them. It couldn't be any other way if it was to be at all. Tombstone had a "Citizens' Safety Committee" of about 200 businessmen to support law officers in maintaining order. As mayor, John Clum headed it. All met in front of the *Epitaph,* of which he was editor. Whenever there was trouble, they appeared there, fully armed, ready to march in twos. The editor-mayor claimed that the Clanton gang tried, after the big feud, to kill him as he rode in a Concord coach, but they had fired so excitedly that they missed and frightened the horses. Bolting, they carried Clum to unexpected safety.[15]

In the county that Slaughter was destined to clean up, Tombstone was not the toughest town. Galeyville probably deserved "top honor." John H. Galey, a Pennsylvanian, had entered the oil and gas business at its inception and later pioneered in Kansas fields. Seeking further wealth, in 1879 he went to burgeoning Tombstone, where someone told him of a silver prospect in Turkey Creek Canyon. There, Galey built a smelter. A quartz mill soon followed, and Galeyville had sprung up.[16]

---

[14] Bisbee *Daily Review,* April 22, 1934. See also Bechdolt, *op. cit.,* p. 181.

[15] Clum, *loc. cit.*

[16] In the 1880s his brothers, Bill and Jim, arrived in Galey's new town with $1,500 but were advised by an assayer not to invest, so they put their money in the Bradford oil field in northern Pennsylvania. When Galeyville failed and the smelter moved to Benson, the town swiftly emptied. Later, Galey was a partner of Colonel James M. Guffey in the historic Midcontinent oil field at Neodesha, Kansas. In 1901, he was instrumental in putting Texas oil on the map, and in drilling the famed Lucas Gusher at Spindletop near Beaumont. He also developed oil at Coalinga, California. See Thomas Mellon Galey, Owensboro, Kentucky, February, 1942. "Historical Outline of the Petroleum Industry in Oklahoma and Kansas," MS in W. M. Mills files of the Gulf Oil Corporation, Gypsy Division, Tulsa, Oklahoma.

The wicked town was beautifully situated on the eastern slope of the Chiricahuas, surrounded by shady groves of aged oak. Begun in November, 1880, in six months it had four hundred people, half a dozen stores, four restaurants, a couple of blacksmith shops, a trio of butcher shops, thirteen saloons, and barber, bakery and boot shops. It never grew larger, though briefly the Galeyville *Bulletin* was published during 1881. A post office flourished for a year. Next they planned a school, but the town hardly had a kindergarten atmosphere. The Cosmopolitan Hotel raised its shoddy roof, but was not much to look at.[17]

The town needed beef. John Slaughter knew the place, but he was not its main supplier. The rustlers took over. Using Galeyville as their chief headquarters, they built corrals in nearby gorges and canyons and adopted a brand. The rich San Simon Valley to the north was handy grazing ground. A Galeyville Militia was organized in 1881 by Joseph Bowyer and other merchants. Unfortunately, its purpose was to fight Apaches, not bad hombres. They scared off the former, but didn't even twit the latter.

William Graham, or Curly Bill, alias Broscius, was chief of the Galeyville gang, and his rule took in all the main camps: Charleston, old Hughes ranch, and others. Meanest of all the badmen, he was also the best liked. Curley helped a young lawman, Billy Breakenridge, collect taxes and recover a horse stolen by his own men![18] Curly was a perfect shot, never rattled under any circumstances.[19] Once he vowed to kill John Slaughter and take his herds. Needless to say, it was all hot air. As with all the rest, temper was his weakness. One day in July of Galeyville's big year, 1881,

---

[17] Patrick Hamilton, comp., *Resources of Arizona*, 1881, pp. 50-52.

[18] Lorenzo D. Walters, *Tombstone's Yesterdays*, p. 140ff. It is said that Wyatt Earp shot and killed Curly Bill, but there is no substantial evidence to prove it. Others say the rustler went back to his Montana home and died – supposedly of measles!

[19] Frank C. Lockwood, *Pioneer Days in Arizona*, pp. 280-281.

Curly and his men rode into the camp. Jim Wallace was with him, and the two were disagreeing. As Curly Bill felt more and more the flame of firewater, he began to bawl out Wallace. Friends separated them, and Jim went to the corral. He saddled his horse, led him around in front of the saloon and stepped up on the little porch. Bill, in another saloon across the street, spied him. Wallace then waited until his boss was about half-way across the dusty street. Then he leaned over his horse's back and shot Bill with a .45 Colt six-shooter. A bullet went through Curly's cheek, but he still lived. Russian Bill, a would-be-desperado, but really a fugitive Muscovite nobleman, nursed his pal back to health. Again, Curly Bill was shot while raiding in Mexico, and though the slug clipped through both hips just below the spinal column, he luckily survived once more.[20]

There were notorious characters looked down upon even by the standard gunmen like Curly Bill, Bud Snow, Joe Hill, and others. Cherokee Jack, a thorough drunk, picked on innocent citizens. He made an old miner get down on hands and knees in a saloon and pray, while Jack hit him over the head with his pistol. John Ringo was a man of better breeding. A tall, reddish-blond, soft-spoken and well mannered fellow, he was Curly Bill's admirable friend. He had come from a good family. Though suspected of rustling livestock, Ringo's word was better than his notarized signature. He borrowed money from rancher Hughes near Galeyville and repaid the $1,500 on the day he promised.[21] When it came to marksmanship, Johnny was even better than Curly Bill's gang, or any of the Tombstone crowd. Known as the county's best pistol shot, he was always asked to entertain, which he did by holding .45 Colts on the index

---
[20] Tombstone *Epitaph,* April 29, 1926. Herein is an article by George H. Kelly, the state historian, entitled *"Galeyville."* Russian Bill and Sandy King were hanged at Shakespeare, New Mexico, on suspicion of horse stealing.
[21] He also bought cheese and butter from Nick Hughes quite regularly. Interview with Nick Hughes, Jr., Prescott, Arizona, September 20, 1950.

fingers of each hand, barrels down, then giving the two pistols a three-quarter turn, firing both of them simultaneously at beer bottles spaced three yards apart. The latter always tottered a second later, without necks! Ringo would shoot bullets into the open necks of bottles, placed on a post, twice out of four times, and at twenty-five feet. His binges never seemed to unsteady his hand or eye.

A. M. Franklin's stock once found their way into Ringo's corral. Having lost about two hundred head, Franklin went to Galeyville to the saloon and, without proof, confronted Ringo with his story. Johnny looked at the rancher with his large steady gray eyes, asking, "Did you see anything as you were coming up the trail?" Franklin said that he wasn't sure. Ringo then wanted to know why the other man had not sent his Mexican vaqueros to get the cattle. Franklin replied that they had other things to tend to, but if Ringo would help round up the lost beeves and deliver them to the San Carlos Reservation, it would be worth $10.00 a head to him. Then Ringo asked Franklin how much money he had. The cash on hand amounted to about $100 which Ringo gave to his boys to fulfill the rancher's wish. It was all done without delay.[22]

John Ringo was neither reckless nor mercenary. He did not approve of Doc Holliday's ways. As "King of the Cowboys," he once challenged this "King of Gamblers" to a handkerchief duel, but the shooting was prevented by Wyatt Earp. When law officers once came to question him, Ringo held them at Charleston and invited them to drink at the bar. Finally, because he liked Deputy Sheriff Bill Breakenridge, he allowed this plucky young lawman to serve a warrant on him. Johnny even showed up in Tombstone for trial, since he didn't want Billy to suffer any embarrassment before the Earp clan. Later he rode with the law and order

---

[22] "Story of Ringo and the Cattle Thieves, as told by Mr. A. M. Franklin, 1925," written by A. M. Widdowsen. MS in the Arizona Pioneers Historical Society.

league in an attempted cleanup. Ringo's intentions were to reform and settle down, but his conscience bothered him, as he was still wanted for murder and was a fugitive from justice, having broken out of jail in Texas. Also, his family believed he was a respected cattleman in Arizona. They found out differently, when, only two weeks before his death, he paid them his last visit. Wearing a big royal moustache, and his nostrils flaring like a wild bull, he sat down with a brace of pistols beneath his coat for a last final photograph. No longer did he look like the little blond boy his mother had known, nor like the boy mule skinner at the age of fourteen – he looked so vicious. But what would drown out all the demons was a good many shots of mescal whiskey. From then on he had the blues. His feet painfully pinched by the new boots he had bought in Shakespeare, New Mexico, a jilt from his lady friend, a ruckus with his partner Joe Hill, and a chilly sendoff by his family, could all be settled simply by pulling the trigger of that same .45 that gave Louis Hancock such a severe headache.

B. F. Smith had a fine drinking place at Morse's Mill, and many freighters stopped by to wet their whistle. Only John had indulged in several too many. Then Alfred Smith heard a shot ring out. A little while later Ringo's horse was caught nearby with reins trampled off. The coroner's jury made its report:[23]

Turkey or Morse's Mill Creek
July 14, 1882

STATEMENT FOR THE INFORMATION OF THE CORONER AND SHERIFF OF COCHISE COUNTY, ARIZONA TERRITORY.

There was found by the undersigned John Yoast the body of a man in a clump of oak trees about 200 yards north from the road leading to Morse's mill and about a quarter of a mile west of the house of

---

[23] There has been much controversy on how Ringo met his death. The following official report is from the files of the District Court, Cochise County Court House, Bisbee, Arizona.

B. F. Smith. The undersigned reviewed the body and found it in a sitting posture facing west, the head inclined to the right. . . . There was a bullet hole in the right temple, the bullet coming out on top of the head on the left side. There is apparently a part of the scalp gone, including a small portion of the forehead and part of the hair, this looks as if cut out by a knife – These are the only marks of violence visible on the body.

Several of the undersigned identify the body as that of John Ringo, well known in Tombstone. He was dressed in light hat, blue shirt, vest, pants, and drawers, on his feet were a pair of hose and undershirt torn up so as to protect his feet.[24] He had evidently travelled but a short distance in this foot gear. His revolver, he grasped in his right hand, his rifle rested against the tree close to him – He had two cartridge belts, the belt for the revolver cartridges being buckled on upside down.

The undernoted property were found with him and on his person: 1 colts revolver Cal. 45, No. 222, containing 5 cartridges; 1 winchester rifle-octogon barrel, Cal. 45, Model 1876, No. 21896, containing a cartridge in the breech and 10 in the magazine; 1 cartridge belt containing 2 revolver cartridges; 1 silver watch of American watch company, No. 9339 with silver chain attached; 2 dollars and 60 cents ($2.60) in money; 6 pistol cartridges in his pocket; 5 shirt studs; 1 small pocket knife; 1 tobacco pipe; 1 comb; 1 box matches; 1 small piece of tobacco.

There is also a portion of a letter from Messrs. Hereford & Zabriskie, Attorney's At Law, Tucson (to the deceased John Ringo).

The above property is left in the possession of Frederick Ward, teamster between Morse Mill and Tombstone. The body of the deceased was buried close to where it was found – deceased, had been dead about 24 hours.

CORONER'S JURY:

Thomas White	A. E. Lewis	W. J. Darril
John Blake	A. S. Nieghbors	J. C. McGregor
John W. Bradfield	James Morgan	John Yoast
B. F. Smith	Robert Boller	Fred Ward
W. W. Smith	Frank McKinney	

---

[24] Douglas *Daily Dispatch,* January 31, 1939. Mrs. Rosa Anna Smith, daughter of B. F. "Coyote" Smith, says in her reminiscences that one of Ringo's boots was found five miles down the valley, and his horse was discovered by Alfred Smith a week later. "Reminiscences of Robert M. Boller, as told to Mrs. George F. Kitt" is also useful. Arizona Pioneers Historical Society, MSS.

THE DUTCHMAN'S TOWN

The above report was properly certified and signed on July 15 by George H. Daily, clerk of the county.

Several have claimed killing John Ringo. Some of these are Wyatt Earp, Buckskin Frank Leslie, Johnny Behind-the-deuce, Joe Hill, Doc Holliday, and certain members involved in the "Hoo Doo," or Mason County War in Texas. Though John Slaughter was friendly with both Joe Hill and John Ringo, it is definite that he had nothing to do with it. It was generally supposed that the most logical candidates to have murdered Ringo would have been the friends of Louis Hancock. The *Arizona Miner* on Friday, December 19, 1879 published an account of the Ringo-Hancock shooting affair.

> Last tuesday night a shooting affair took place at Safford in which Louis Hancock was shot by John Ringo. It appears that Ringo wanted Hancock to take a drink of whiskey, and he refused, saying he would prefer beer – Ringo struck him over the head with his pistol and then fired. The ball taking effect in the lower end of the left ear and passed through the fleshy part of the neck – half an inch more, in the neck would have killed him. Ringo is under arrest.

This action on Ringo's part brought the Territory of Arizona against him. During the March term, 1880, when court convened in the First Judicial District, County of Pima, an indictment was brought, charging him with assault with intent to commit murder. It stated that this fracas took place on December 9, 1879, at Safford. Most writers have given vague accounts of this event, placing it at Tucson. So that he would not be inconvenienced and still remain loyal to his friend Sheriff Charley Shibell, of Pima County, Ringo wrote the following letter:[25]

San Simon Valley. N.M.
March 3, 1880
Mr. C. Shibel:
Dear Sir: Being under bond for my appearance before the Grand Jury of Pima County, I write to let you know why I can not appear –

---
[25] District Court, First Judicial District, Arizona Territory, March term, 1880.

I got shot through the foot and it is impossible for me to travel for awhile. If you can get any papers for me, and will let me know, I will attend to them at once. As I wish to live here. I do not wish to put you to any unnesescary trouble nor do I wish to bring extra trouble on myself. Please let the District Attorney know why I do not appear for I am very anxious that there is know forfieture taken on the bond.
Respectfully Yours, Sir.   JOHN RINGO

Whether an excuse or a valid reason, the letter demonstrates Ringo's loyalty to his friends. His only summons was a letter from Shibell. Ringo had Zabriskie, a famous criminal attorney from El Paso and Silver City and still later from Tucson, to represent him. Some writers stress that Ringo was well educated, some going as far as stating that he was a university man. The truth is he stopped going to school at the age of fourteen. All of his family were bright and studious, and John Ringo made good use of his home studies, but it is absurd to say he received a college diploma.

One of the local ballads, sung in the saloons and around the San Bernardino Valley campfires, reflects the outlaw lore. It was sung to the tune, "Goodbye, My Lover:" [26]

>John Ringo went over the hill,
>Goodbye, my lover, goodbye,
>And there was Johnny behind-the-deuce,
>Goodbye, goodbye.
>
>He darn near stuck his head in the noose,
>Goodbye, my lover, goodbye,
>The strangers came on him with a rush,
>Goodbye, goodbye.

---

[26] As sung to Allen Erwin by Charles Lockling with his own accompaniment. As for Boot Hill, not all of its quiet population were evil in this world. John Swain's stone was erected there by the personnel of Fort Huachuca. He was born July 18, 1845, served John Slaughter as cowhand most of his life, and reached the century mark, minus a few odd days. He died on February 8, 1945. The old Tombstone Cemetery contained, and contains still, the remains of most of the respecable citizens. Viola's brother, Stonewall Jackson Howell, lies there. His stone reads: October 2, 1863-October 22, 1889. His father's grave is nearby, as is his mother's. She was born July 29, 1836, and lived a long and useful eighty-four years, dying on April 9, 1920. Tombstone Cemetery is not to be confused with "Boot Hill," as this is an entirely different burial ground.

And Johnny-the-Deuce took to the brush,
Goodbye, my lover, goodbye,
And Doc Holliday was thin and frail,
Goodbye, goodbye.

But his scatter gun made brave men quail,
Goodbye, my lover, goodbye,
And old man Clanton and Curly Bill,
Goodbye, goodbye.

They'd ambush Mex and shoot to kill,
Goodbye, my lover, goodbye,
Now they all are dead, their guns are still,
Now they are sleeping on old Boot Hill,
Goodbye, goodbye.

Ole Phinn Clanton and Black Maria
He was a pretty good boy but a Gol darn liar,
Goodbye, my lover, goodbye.

The court records showed many charges of grand larceny, robbery, rustling, and murder, all tried in the Justice Court, Third District, for Cochise County. Loquacious lawyers like Al English and Mark Smith could sway juries in that era of the master spellbinders.[27] The famous Bisbee Massacre at Goldwater and Castaneda's store, the town's largest, had taken place December 8, 1884. Three citizens never saw Christmas. The next February 22nd, a mob, determined that John Heath, the ringleader of the murderers, should not escape by a technicality, took him to a pole just below First and Toughnut Streets, where a man named Dutch Bill threw a rope over the crosspiece and prepared Heath for the eternity he met so coolly. The condemned man requested that his body not be fired upon.

Elsewhere in Arizona, violence flared as never before. Holbrook had its only lynching in 1885, and the next year Tonto Basin heard the whine of feudists' bullets in the sheepherder-cattleman war begun by the Tewksburys and

---

[27] James Wolf, "Tombstone," *Arizona Highways*, XVI, March, 1940.

Grahams.[28] Many times half-buried bodies were found near the Charleston road. An arm or a leg stuck out was the only tombstone. These deaths were often laid to the Apaches, but probably rustlers were responsible for many roadside graves.

The Tombstone *Epitaph* constantly called for cleaning up the county. On April 4, 1882, it warned, "The recent events in Cochise County make it incumbent upon not only officials, but all good citizens, as well, to take such positive measures as will speedily rid this section of that murderous, thieving element which has made us a reproach before the world, and so seriously retarded the industry and progress of our country."[29] Four years later the paper might have reprinted these words with current accuracy. Some feared that federal intervention loomed, as it had in the earlier year.

Willcox was its rival for notoriety. Nestled in the heart of Sulphur Springs Valley, where Slaughter's early herds had grown fat, the town was noted for rowdyism, more than for murder. When William M. Stewart, United States senator from Nevada, visited the place, he saw the cowboys take after a somber, clerical-looking gentleman in a tall silk hat as he stood on the Southern Pacific train platform observing the scenery. The cowpokes got the drop on his Lincolnesque "stovepipe" headgear, and in a matter of seconds had riddled it. A local merchant fared as badly. After he had opened a general store in a tent, the cowboys ransacked his goods and then demanded he treat. Unlike a would-be Marshall Field, the storekeeper didn't think the

---

[28] Territory of Arizona versus Ed Tewksbury, Precinct Court of Maricopa County, Phoenix, August 29-September 8, 1892. See in the Arizona Pioneers Historical Society, John S. Merril MS.

[29] Tombstone *Epitaph,* April 4, 1882. In Bisbee, it was not safe for a man to leave his horse tied on the street without keeping watch over it. Cattle and horse thieves had become so daring that they would ride into town just at dusk and drive the mounts away! Douglas *Daily Dispatch,* February 17, 1922. In Tombstone, however, housebreaking and horse stealing were fairly rare. Outside the town's limits, rustling was a different matter.

customer always right, so they made him stand in back of the tent, holding a lighted candle. That seemed easy enough, but it got decidedly harder when they took pot shots at the flame to see who would snuff it out. Since their host trembled like a hummingbird, the flickering light was a mighty poor target even for these well-practiced marksmen. Next morning the one-day storekeeper was on the eastbound train![30]

In time, John Slaughter would quiet the rambunctiousness of Willcox. However, in addition to frightening greenhorns, at one time Willcox shipped more range cattle than any other Arizona town.[31]

Finally, there was Charleston. Slaughter had a butcher shop there in the early days, before he moved to the San Bernardino. The twin of Tombstone, this mill and smelter town was born of a bonanza in 1879. Only eight miles from the larger town, it served the outlaws even better. They could escape surer justice and still be in good rustling grounds. While they lasted, the banks of the San Pedro were never peaceful. Yet the man with the wildest heart of them all was John Law himself — Justice Jim Burnett. Burnett was not as colorful nor nearly so witty as Judge Roy Bean, but he did his best to serve the same clear purposes. As a lawman, he was unlike the Earps, nothing like jovial Johnny Behan, and not a stickler for the finer points of jurisprudence. John Slaughter later would interpret justice and make it work, but Charleston's arbitrary purveyor of justice was not his ideal. For instance, as soon as Burnett assumed his office, he made himself actual dictator of the whole area. He prepared only one quarterly report to the board of supervisors at Tombstone. When Burnett asked for fees due him for the revenues he had collected, the board

---

[30] William M. Stewart, *Reminiscences*, (New York, Neale Publishing Company, 1908), p. 267.
[31] Nat McKelvey, "Willcox: Portrait of a Cattle Town," *Arizona Highways*, XXVII, September, 1951, pp. 10-15.

cut down his total. After that, he collected and kept both fines and fees. As John Slaughter would later do, Burnett endured no legal delay, but carried simple and swift justice to the offender. Unlike the Texan, though, he helped stir up some rumpuses just to give the court profits and dissolve the boredom. Burnett served warrants with a shotgun and "just looked for trouble." Court was held whenever and wherever he pleased, and there were no appeals. He is said to have stocked his ranch with "strayed" cattle, and those beeves paid as fines, in lieu of cash.

William C. "Cananea" Greene had grown rich as a cattle king and silver tycoon. He, too, was used to having things his own sweet way. When Greene's San Pedro irrigation dam was mysteriously blown up and his little daughter drowned in its broken spillway, he blamed Judge Burnett. When "Cananea" went gunning, somebody died. It was never "Cananea." Appropriately enough the lethal rendezvous was Tombstone's OK Corral's entrance on Allen street, the opposite end from where the Earps, Clantons and McLowerys had fought. Burnett was unarmed, but he died anyway, for a crime he had not committed.[32]

Today, Charleston is in ruins, and Bill Greene's old ranch is marked by desert foliage.[33]

John Slaughter had always done his duty to his neighbors, but he was not a civic-minded man. Only when it was necessary did he go to Tombstone, and he had kept out of all the gun-play which had built up the present troubles. So far, sheriffs and United States marshals, vigilantes, individual merchants, and ranchers had all failed to bring good order. Slaughter, it seems, had always succeeded in accomplishing his aims. So far, his fights against American and Mexican outlaws had been private, but the honest cit-

[32] Hal Mitchell, "Justice Jim," *Arizona Highways,* XXI, July, 1945, pp. 33-37.
[33] Interview with John Ross, Tombstone, Arizona, 1950.

izens were aware of his modesty, and the integrity and pure courage it hid. Why couldn't the rancher from San Bernardino clean up Cochise County? His brother Charley was in politics – but John was no speaker, no hand-shaker, no vote catcher. He worked cattle, and what he knew of horse trading deals was mighty different and of a less shady type, than that of the rustlers.

In 1886, when Tombstone's civic leaders were looking for a qualified man to run for sheriff on the Democratic ticket, in their opinion Slaughter was the only man for such a job. This meant much more than just mingling in politics. It meant that John Slaughter would be away from his ranch most of the time. San Bernardino Ranch was really beginning to prosper with the "fat years," and the herds were now safe from any danger of Apache raids. Singlehandedly, Slaughter had made his spread immune. The army had just made the territory so. For a long time John fought the idea of public office. He tried to dissuade his friends, but he was hardly the one to be coy, and Slaughter was no man to delay a decision any more than he was born to back down. He knew that it was his duty, so he agreed to run.

"It is said that Slaughter will be nominated by acclamation, but we arise to remark that there will be an election later on, in which this acclamation business will cut no figure," declared the Republican Tombstone *Epitaph* in September. Yet Slaughter was the man who would lead the crusade it had always called for! A couple of days later, when he had been nominated, it noted, "John Slaughter is a good citizen and a deserving man, as far as the *Epitaph's* knowledge of the gentleman extends, but Bob Hatch has made a fearless, competent sheriff, and the people of this County are not going to defeat him."[34]

There is little record of Slaughter actively seeking the

---

[34] Tombstone *Epitaph,* September 16 and 18, 1886.

rough peace-officer job. He was no campaigner. Indian campaigns were his only experience. Still, his record was better than platform orations. So he sat calmly on the platform while the politicians took the bows. Meanwhile, the *Epitaph* punned: "After the smoke is lifted from the present campaign, the Democratic party will learn with sorrow that several of their pet candidates are SLAUGHTERED."[35] The paper was wrong. Bob Hatch was politically scalped.

November 16, 1886, the board of supervisors and the probate judge met in Tombstone, canvassed the election and certified that John Horton Slaughter had won the election.[36] He won more votes than any other Democrat before him.

Right after New Year's in 1887, when his brother Charley was becoming a legislator in New Mexico, John Slaughter solemnly took his oath of office. Third sheriff of Cochise County, he was the most important public servant in an area the size of some states, and with crime problems big enough for a metropolis.

---

[35] *Ibid.*, September 23, 1886.
[36] Cochise County, Book of Supervisors, Minute Book, 2, p. 408, November 13, 1886.

8

Bullets and Justice

The question of what qualifications make a good sheriff, especially to enforce law and order in Cochise County, Arizona Territory, in the 1880s and 1890s, would have been difficult to answer. Lawbreakers were as seasoned to their profession as an Indian scout in an Al Sieber scouting party. The outlaw who had his stronghold in the mountains and hills was as cunning as any fox that might be found in the Huachucas. If it takes a fox to catch a fox, the same would not necessarily go for John Slaughter. At the same time in his lifetime he had known John Wesley Hardin, John Selman, Sam Bass, Bill Longley, Joel Collins, John Ringo, Black Jack Ketchum and a score of men that at one time or other would not be considered law-abiding.

John Slaughter had a brand of psychology that could not be taught in a classroom, simply because it did not run true to form. He was a mysterious man in many ways. His actions and personality were so irregular that it would automatically throw a person off guard. He had certain habits and ways that could be followed, such as rising before sunup, carrying his money in a money belt or in canteens on a cattle buying trip, and sitting at the end of the table at meal time. On the whole, these habits were quite permanent, but every now and then he would do such odd things as transfer his saddle from one horse to another at the last minute, or make a complete change in plans. There seemed to be an intuition that motivated his actions. He called this behavior the instructions of his "guardian angel." His impulsive action in changing sides of the buggy with his wife, or in turning off on a side road instead of continuing on, indicated he had confidence in his powers of instinct or clairvoyance. The latter action on occasion saved him from being waylaid. This, along with the fact his aim was excellent with a six-shooter or rifle, plus being a superb horseman, would make the outlaw wary of him. There was no question that the Democrats in Cochise County had put up the right man to run for sheriff.

A particular peculiarity in addition to his high and low tone of speech, climaxed by a guttural growl and a grunt or two, was his way of starting out to say something. Almost invariably he would begin with, "I say, I say, I say, –," winding up with the given name of the person to whom he was speaking. To receive a rough or insulting reply from an outlaw meant immediate action. An illustration of this is given in testimony in some of the coroner's inquisitions into the matter of how some of his enemies had met their deaths in the course of his official duties. An example of John Slaughter's manner of carrying out his duties can be summed up in giving the following illustration – the coroner's jury report on the death of one Guadalupe Robles, a noted bandit.[1]

County of Cochise,
Arizona Territory

In the matter of the Inquest on the body held June 7, 1888 before W. D. Shearer, J. P. Ex-Officio (Coroner)

First Witness Tesana Lucerio being duly sworn deposes and says:

Q. What is your name?
A. Tesano Lucerio
Q. Where do you reside?
A. Tombstone.
Q. What is your occupation?
A. Mining

---

[1] Cochise County Records, Inquest on a Body Held, June 7, 1888, before N. D. Shearer. This includes Tesana Lucerio's testimony as well as Slaughter's.

Q. Go ahead and state all you know in regard to the death of the deceased.
A. We, Slaughter, Burt Alvord, and another Mexican got in the morning about daybreak in the Whetstone Mountains. When we got within fifteen yards of their camp, Mr. Slaughter called them to, "Wake up", and throw up their hands; and the party answered, "We will throw up our hands with our guns", and Mr. Slaughter gave orders to fire. We fired and that is all I know of it.
Q. Did any of you have shotguns?
A. Mr. Slaughter had one.
Q. Did any of them run after you commenced firing?
A. Yes, he run (the deceased) after they commenced firing. One was killed in bed, and the other ran out of the corral and got his gun and he tried to get behind a big rock that was about ten steps away; and when he jumped from that rock, Mr. Slaughter shot him, and he fell down. Mr. Slaughter gave orders not to shoot him any more. The other one stood behind the rocks and he shot twice, and Mr. Slaughter gave orders to go around and stop the man. When we started to stop him, he started from the rocks, and Mr. Slaughter shot at him, and hollered to us to stop him, and not go any further. He fell down, and we took the wrong road down, and he went down the canyon; so I stopped right then, as I had no shoes on either, and nor did the other boy, and I could not go further.
Q. Was there any shooting before Mr. Slaughter asked them to hold up their hands?
A. No sir.

(Signed – Teserio Lasceria)

Sheriff Slaughter called to testify after being duly sworn deposes and says:
Q. What is your name?
A. John H. Slaughter.
Q. Where do you reside?
A. Tombstone.
Q. What is your occupation?
A. Sheriff.
Q. Go on and state all you know in regard to the death of the deceased.
A. This morning, after daylight, I crawled up to within fifty yards of the man. I asked him to get up. I asked them then if they would

surrender. They answered with their guns in their hands. Just at this time, one of the men fired a shot, and knocked the bark off the tree close to my ear. Just about that time I shot him. About a second afterwards (the deceased) jumped up with a six-shooter in his hand and I said, "Burt, there is another Son-of-a-bitch, and I shot him. Just after that this man Manuel ran down the Canyon, probably about a hundred yards away, and I said, "Burt, there is another Son-of-a-bitch. Shoot him!" and I shot him. As I shot him he fell on his left side. After that I told Burt to follow him down the canyon, and kill him, and I would stay where I was, and watch those two fellows that were there. Burt and the other Mexicans fired about twenty shots, at this fellow down the canyon, and came back and said, "He got away".
Q. What was the name of this man?
A. Guadalupe Robles.
Q. Did you have a rifle?
A. No! I had a breech loading shotgun.

(Signed – John H. Slaughter)

Verdict of the Coroner's Jury:

A jury of the Inquest duly impanelled and sworn by W. D. Shearer, J.P. and Ex-Officio-Coroner to inquire as to whose, the body submitted to our inspection, when, where, and by what means he came to his death after viewing the body, and hearing the testimony as has been brought before us, find that his name was GUADALUPE ROBLES, age about forty years, nativity – Mexico, and that his death in the Whetstone Mountains on the 7th day of June, A.D., 1888, from gunshot wounds inflicted by the Sheriff of Cochise County in the discharge of his duty as such sheriff.

       Foreman – Ben Cook
       G. W. Alkiting
       John S. Williams
Coroner's Jury – J. B. Hennessy
       Smith Gallen
       Chas. T. Hine
       Ridjely Tilden

John Slaughter had obviously drawn upon his previous experiences with bad men in the Rangers and on the Texas frontier. A man seldom ever went for his gun without intent to use it. Slaughter seldom waited for the other party to

BULLETS AND JUSTICE

make the first move. Still toward the end of his law enforcement days he found himself staring down the muzzle of a six-shooter held in the hands of a Texan named Arthur Finney. Quick action was all that saved his life.

Historians still wonder what would have happened to the Earp party at the OK Corral if John Slaughter had been present and had sided in with the two McLowery boys and Billy Clanton. To John Slaughter the Earps were tinhorn gamblers, who could not stand up to a real showdown. Nevertheless, they left him alone and that was all that mattered. He had seen enough fighting in Texas, and his ambitions were that of a stock raiser. Running for sheriff was far from his mind, until enough of his Democratic friends pleaded with him to run for office.

Many of those he had asked to "hit the road," he had known in Texas and New Mexico, and they knew his background. Until the time he became sheriff his own sense of justice guided his actions toward those with whom he had contacts or dealings. It was pretty well an established fact that if a person was shot by a lawman, the officer would be exonerated, as the coroner's juries found almost invariably that a killing when done by a sheriff or constable, whether right or wrong, was justifiable. Burt Alvord found this fact a great convenience when he played the twin role of constable of Willcox and train robber.

On the whole, riding on the side of the law was a tiresome job. Lawmen and outlaws alike covered as much as eighty miles in a single day.[2] An early-day report indicating the distances showed that from Tombstone it was 30 miles to Benson; 28 to Fort Huachuca; 65 to Willcox; 64 to Slaughter's San Bernardino, and even eight to nearby Charleston. Not even fabulous Pecos Bill could have covered this ground and made it peaceful in that generation.

---
[2] Interview with Nick Hughes, Jr., Prescott, September 20, 1950.

Slaughter had no modern communications system to use. He depended on men who were as good with a gun as they were astride a horse.[3]

He did appoint many men to assist him. But they were better in ability than in numbers. Although Slaughter's deputies might not always remain honest, they were loyal to him and the public as long as they were under him. His first appointment on January 1st, was G. W. Farrington as deputy-sheriff to act in the capacity of jailer at Tombstone. Just two days later he named his first under-sheriff, Enoch A. Shattuck, to be followed before Spring by Deputies Ed Barker, James Scow, W. J. Showers, Edward R. Monk, and D. Johnson.[4] Probably because he knew their honesty and ability best of all, John Slaughter appointed several in-laws to office. If this was nepotism, he made the most of it – for the public's benefit. Tommy Howell, Viola's cousin, was for a time, jailer. Young Howell let the Mexican prisoners play their guitars and fiddles. It was a jolly jail in his time, but poor Tommy did not enjoy life for long. He soon was dead of tuberculosis. Jesse Fisher, in-law and good friend of Slaughter's as well, and his ranch boss for many years, was also a jailer. Stonewall Jackson Howell, Viola's young brother, was also a deputy under his famous brother-in-law. He served almost from the beginning and proved a good choice. Stonewall could ride a bucking bronco to a standstill and seemed to be afraid of nothing, so Slaughter

---

[3] See Tombstone *Prospector*, October 30, 1888. Fairbank was nine miles from the county seat, Contention ten miles, Soldier Holes twenty-one, Bisbee twenty-nine, and it was twenty miles to the Pima County line. Cochise County then measured 75½ miles north to south, and eighty-three miles east to west.

[4] Enoch A. Shattuck was required to post a $2,000 bond on March 11, 1887; James Scow posted $1,000 on January 20; W. J. Showers put up the same amount of bond February 12; Burt Alvord, appointed by Slaughter, did the same. Old John himself had to post the substantial amount of $10,000 bond for his first term, naming W. W. Pardun as surety. When he entered his second term in January, 1889, he posted another $10,000 naming this time as sureties W. C. Greene, E. A. Shattuck, E. R. Monk, and A. B. Burnett.

made him his ranch foreman for a while. One day, he gave the Tombstone citizens an exhibition of bronc riding at the OK Corral. He also served Slaughter as his ranch foreman. The boisterous life he loved ended quickly, too. While still prime ranch hand and deputy, he died of pneumonia at Tombstone. The whole family seemed destined to die unbooted.[5] The Howells all spent much time in Tombstone while Slaughter was sheriff. Viola, Addie and Willie lived in town at the time, too.

The work done by these deputies would in itself make a book.[6] Lorenzo Paco, a clever old vaquero, was one of the sheriff's hard workers. He did much of the routine work, tracking and trailing. There was more sweat than water on the trail of a rustler. Another special deputy was Jim Kreigbaum. One day in the late 'eighties, Tip Lowther, constable of Bisbee, tried to arrest a gunman named Daly, but died in the attempt. The murderer then escaped on horseback and headed east. When the appeal came to Slaughter, he sent Kreigbaum to take Daly. The deputy knew him. Kreigbaum went twice to San Francisco and once as far as Kansas City, but persistence did not win out. The culprit was never caught. Cochise County lawmen could not claim perfection.

Another wild chase was more typical of Slaughter achievements through his deputies. Reilly Dutton had clubbed a man to death in a railroad camp near Charleston.

---

[5] *Southwestern Stockman,* Willcox, October 26, 1889.

[6] Other appointees of Sheriff Slaughter were: In 1887: P. Michelana, as deputy-sheriff; D. Johnson, the same; H. D. Simmons, ditto; Ed Rockman, deputy-constable; A. J. Ritter, deputy poll tax collector. In 1888: W. D. Monmonier as special deputy-sheriff; Lou E. Gray, as deputy-sheriff; Frank P. Lynch, as constable; and George D. Machin, deputy-constable. In 1889: Jesse Fisher, as special deputy-sheriff. In 1890: W. W. Woodman as deputy-sheriff; Hugh A. Taylor, special deputy-sheriff; John Sellers, the same. Also briefly appointed deputies by Slaughter were: Allison Thomas, Frank Castle, S. L. Carr, R. E. Cole, Alex Freeman, L. E. Gray, Lorenzo Paco, H. S. Kemp, C. B. Kelton, Frank L. Lynch, W. W. Lowther, J. H. Martin, L. V. Wilkerson, and W. W. Woodman. See Cochise County Misc. Records Book 2, pp 729ff.

Then he fled. John Slaughter located him and sent to Phoenix for the necessary papers to bring him back from that place. The papers were issued, but somehow through some leak in the governor's office, the news leaked out and was made public in the Phoenix *Herald*. Angry, Slaughter asked the Tombstone papers not to publish anything that Dutton's friends might use to further his escape. Unfortunately, a Tucson newspaper copied the data. Slaughter had sent his deputy Walker there posthaste. Again Dutton got the news and fled. Now Slaughter was determined to arrest Dutton. He told Walker never to return to Arizona without the murderer. Weeks later, a telegram came from Guaymas reporting that the deputy had captured Reilly Dutton at Chimpas, Chihuahua, and wanted $70.00 to get home! He had gone three hundred miles to the south, through rough Mexican country. The order of a field marshal couldn't have been better obeyed.[7]

Jeff Milton was one of Slaughter's most famous friends and helpers. Old John used to say that when a shooting was in the wind, he always liked to have Jeff with him. In those daring days of his early sheriff's duties, there was a gang of outlaws in the Whetstone Mountains some thirty-five miles from Tombstone, and the two men went to take them. As the lawmen approached, the sun was setting. The desperados' fires glowed in the twilight. Slaughter took one side of the narrow arroyo and had Milton defend the other. "Alto, alto," yelled Jeff at the Mexican *ladrones,* and all hands raised toward heaven – except one. Suddenly this fellow reached into his pocket, pulled out a handkerchief and wiped his brow! Later John told his companion, "I say, I say, Jeff, why didn't you kill him?" Jeff had waited to make sure, preferring to put his life in danger than regret for the remainder of that life having killed an unarmed man.[8]

---

[7] Tombstone *Prospector,* July 19, 1889. *Ibid.,* January 28, 1890, for an account of the murder of David Duncan and Slaughter's trailing the murderer.

BULLETS AND JUSTICE

Still, John Slaughter's greatest adventures were followed through in solitude. His old gray horse was a familiar sight. He kept it in a barn beside his Tombstone home at First and Fremont and took care of it himself. Slaughter's even more memorable Colt was probably the single-action army revolver popular at that time.[9]

It is said that on one occasion the new sheriff came riding into town with three horses – astride his own and with two very dead hombres tied over the other two Mexican nags. When he had been a peace officer only three months, Slaughter already had nineteen prisoners in the county jail and had plans to put restraint on thirty more horse and cattle pilferers.[10]

Most of the prisoners he had taken himself. Others were not lucky enough to land in jail. Jim Wolf, who knew Slaughter for years, said that once Don Juan rode up to his ranch house after a Mexican had trotted by on the prettiest black pony Jim Wolf had ever seen. The sheriff mentioned that he was on this particular vaquero's trail, for he had stolen the horse of Slaughter's father-in-law, Amazon Howell. The next time Wolf and Slaughter met, the Texan said he had recovered the mount. "What happened to the thief?" inquired Wolf. John chuckled, "That's one horse thief that will never steal again."

Apparently he never went farther than a lonely canyon in the Mule Mountains. There some cowhands found the remains. Viola Slaughter always denied that her husband left his foes wherever they had fallen. Slaughter, however, never

---

[8] Walter P. Webb, *The Texas Rangers*. Milton's adventures are briefly recounted here. His widow told this particular story. At another time, Slaughter's deputies brought in one Calagia, a rustler who had escaped the sheriff in December, 1877, and had remained free in Sonora for a dozen years. Tombstone *Epitaph*, September 12, 1889. Mrs. Jeff Milton in an interview at Tucson, 1949.

[9] Charles H. Coles, curator of the Colt Museum, Hartford, Conn., in a letter to the author, April 13, 1950.

[10] Tombstone *Prospector*, April 14, 1887.

discussed his work with his wife; affairs like that the sheriff would keep to himself — at least as far as the ladies were concerned.[11]

Another Latin American who did not want to follow the "good neighbor" policy was Eduardo Moreno, an in-law of Curly Bill. This horse thief held criminals' rendezvous on the west side of the Huachucas, and laughed at the threats of lawmen. Since Burt Alvord was his most helpful assistant, John Slaughter took him along. In their peculiar "thunderbolt" fashion they scaled the aerie-like hideaway. The three Mexicans were in their blanket rolls, and when Slaughter shouted to get up with their hands in the air, they threw off the covers and started shooting. The sheriff's aim was as good as his trailing, and the battle ended quickly. Back in Tombstone, Slaughter and Burt tied their horses to the courthouse rack, and reported to District Attorney W. H. Stilwell that there had been a fight in which Moreno and two of his bandits had died. That was that. Slaughter never told the details to anyone, but Burt had a bit looser tongue. One afternoon he dropped into the harness shop of his friend, Charles L. Blackburn. While Blackburn got to work on some stitching on Alvord's strange new cartridge and money belt, Burt explained that it had belonged to one of the rustlers. When he got it, the belt had contained $500 in gold coin![12]

In talking about this, a Tombstone wit said of the sheriff, "His name was Slaughter all right, but he wasn't in any way the sort of a man we used to call a 'killer'. He didn't like to

---

[11] MS in the Arizona Pioneers Historical Society, dictated by Charles A. Nichols. See also Cora Viola Slaughter's memoirs in the Bisbee *Daily Review*, April 22, 1934. She claimed that Slaughter killed fewer men than some sheriffs who are almost unknown.

[12] Bisbee *Oasis*, February 22, 1922. See also Jim Brophy's reminiscences in Bisbee *Review*, May 27, 1934. John Slaughter himself reported in October, 1889, that Moreno had been killed by Mexican soldiers at Mescal Springs — *Southwestern Stockman*, Willcox, November 19, 1889.

JESSE FISHER'S APPOINTMENT AS SPECIAL DEPUTY
Fisher, cousin of Cora Viola Slaughter, was later murdered
outside the San Bernardino ranch house.

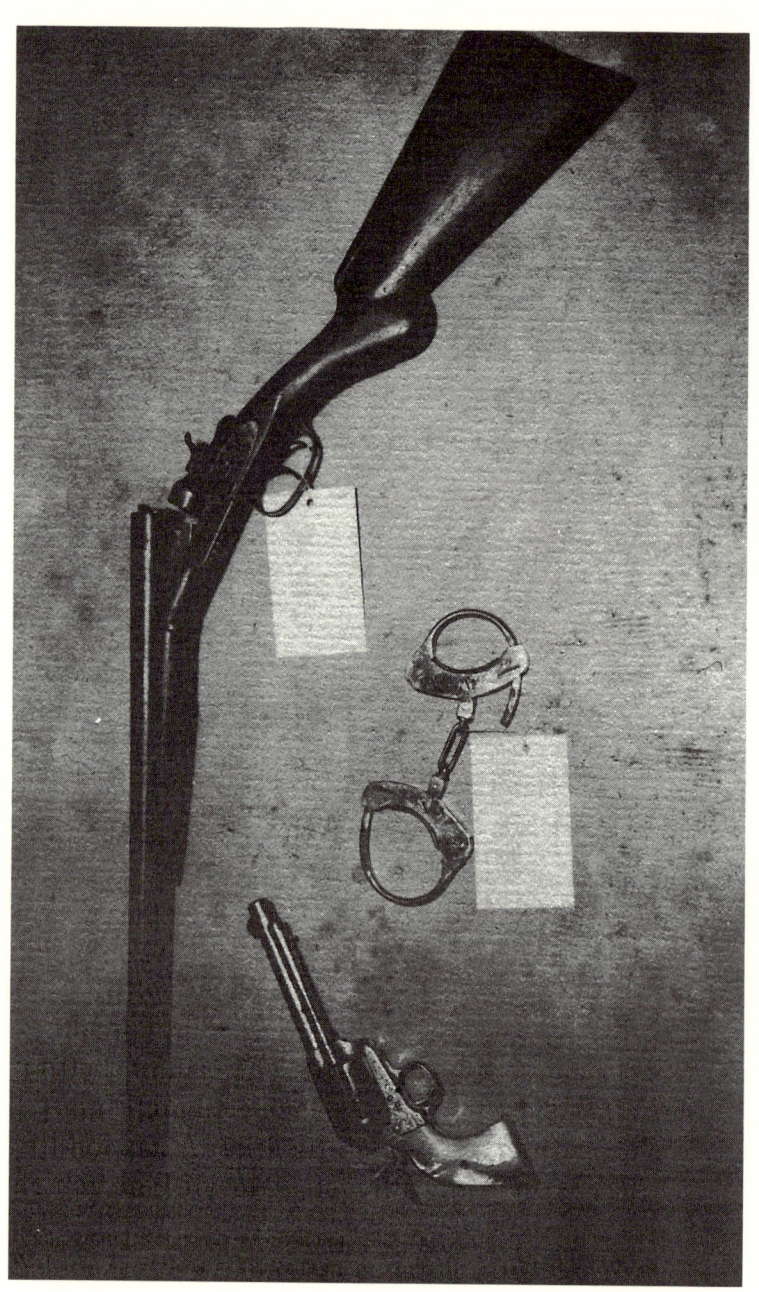

SAWED-OFF SHOTGUN, PISTOL, AND HANDCUFFS USED BY SLAUGHTER AS SHERIFF OF COCHISE COUNTY

The pearl-handled six shooter is worn thin at the muzzle from usage, and no doubt is the gun which killed Berney Gallagher.

shoot people. He did it simply because it was in the day's work, was his duty and was for a good purpose."[13]

Soon another "good purpose" developed. This time the "day's work" had to be done on John Horn, a Fort Huachuca bully. "French Tom" Simmons complained that Horn had threatened him with a six-shooter and had beaten him. A shady lady named Frankie evaded her duty as a witness against Horn when he threatened to do the same to her. Immediately, Slaughter arrested the small-time tough, "who was very badly used up, and is now lying at his room at the Way Up Lodging House."[14]

Another 1887 duty of minor import was his arrest of L. Larrieu. With Charlie Smith and Fred Dodge, Slaughter went to Contention, and at Larrieu's slaughterhouse arrested him, his son John, and employees John Foster, John Galin and Rafael Varela. They were suspected of supplying their abattoir with cattle they had rustled from John Vaughn of the Vail Cattle Company, but there was not sufficient proof for a conviction.[15]

That little jaunt was a picnic. Later in the hot summer of that first year he got a heap of excitement in the taking of Carmen Mendibles, a Sonoran, whose father had named all his six sons Carmen. Now Carmen I had started out to found a tradition. He had been shot. Carmen II dangled by a hangman's hempen loop. Carmen the elder was said to have killed his own wife with an axe. What Carmen III's future would be only John Slaughter was able to predict. Carmen Mendibles III had put an end to Tomás Salcido at Fairbank in early July, stabbing him through the heart in a house of ill fame. Not long afterwards, Slaughter discovered that the murderer had gone to his native Sonora, thus getting out of

---
[13] Brophy, *loc. cit.*
[14] Tombstone *Prospector*, July 7 and 12, 1887.
[15] *Ibid.*, April 9, 1887. Fred Dodge later assisted in hanging Black Jack Ketchum at Clayton, New Mexico.

the sheriff's jurisdiction. Strategy being his long suit, Don Juan by some unrevealed scheme enticed the culprit across the line near his own San Bernardino spread. There he took him. John found that Carmen III was at least as tough as his elder brothers. Slaughter had to chain and handcuff him while he fought like a mountain lion. Sullen and docile, he remained silent once John's deputy had locked him up at Tombstone.[16] That fall Mendibles was sentenced to life imprisonment at the Yuma penitentiary, and five days later, on November 21, Slaughter and Stonewall Howell took him and three other captives to that prison on the Colorado's shore.[17]

That same busy summer, Slaughter received a telegram from a fellow sheriff in Socorro County, New Mexico, asking him to look out for a cattle and horse thief who had stolen some animals in New Mexico and was heading toward the Cochise region. John Slaughter recalled that he had seen some animals bearing the brand of the stolen cattle, so he sent a deputy to look around. Having found two of the stolen horses at a ranch of the Erie Cattle Company, he reported it to Slaughter on August 2nd. A. M. Whitney, of the same cattle outfit, arrived in Tombstone and saw the man who had sold the horses to him. Immediately he notified Slaughter, who soon had the thief in his custody. This fellow turned out to be none other than William Palley, a Pecos outlaw, who had begun calling himself Billy the Kid after the original's sudden demise.[18]

Next, Slaughter was off after some train robbers up Willcox way. He and Constable Fred Dodge took five of the gang at Stein's Pass. They had been hiding out at the ranch of one of their number, named Hughes. As usual, Slaughter used surprise to make the capture quick and bloodless, if

---
[16] *Ibid.*, August 12, 1887.
[17] *Ibid.*, November 22, 1887.   [18] *Ibid.*, August 3, 1887.

possible. This succeeded, but Hughes escaped while another outlaw rode hard for liberty. Slaughter's cutting horse was faster. He overtook the runaway after firing two close shots. Now there was time to be "properly introduced" to his unwilling guests. They were J. T. Blunt, Dick Johnson, Joseph Brooks and L. M. Sheehan, to all of whom he gave a free ride to Tombstone, and as official host provided a stout lodging and confining hospitality in the county jail. Larry Sheehan seemed to be the leader, and was held on $2000 bail.[19]

Only once did Viola go with her husband when he took in a prisoner. Slaughter had heard that José Lopez, wanted for a murder committed near Willcox eight years before, was at this time hiding out in Clifton, Arizona. John and Viola went to Willcox by team, taking along with them their son Willie. Upon reaching there, they left Willie with friends, then boarded a train for Clifton. At Bowie station, Viola and John went to visit some friends. Slaughter then went to Clifton by himself to see what he could learn about the bandit. His capture was quick, and soon Slaughter brought him into Bowie. Here he picked up his wife, and after placing her on the forward wagon seat, and with Burt Alvord at the reins, they proceeded to Tombstone. On the way Lopez asked Viola how her brother Stonewall was, pretending he knew him. This attempt to gain sympathy failed miserably, as all he got was a scowl from the sheriff's wife. Upon reaching Willcox, John decided it would be best to stop and rest. There was the problem of what to do with the prisoner. Lopez was handcuffed, then paraded to the back of a combination general store and saloon, with Burt Alvord to watch him. When Slaughter returned, he

---

[19] Willcox *Warblings,* August 23, 1887. Even Slaughter could make a serious mistake. A couple of weeks later he took one Charles Wilson prisoner for the murderous assault on a cattle inspector at Willcox a few months earlier. It was the wrong man!

found Alvord drinking in the front at the bar, while three Mexicans in the rear chatted a mile a minute with their fellow countryman. Once more the sheriff was not slow in drawing correct conclusions. The culprit's three visitors were plotting with him to waylay the Slaughters the next day and free the captive. They actually tried, but found that Slaughter had forestalled them by getting up at an early hour and was already far away. This time, Alvord drove with the prisoner beside him, while Viola, Slaughter and Willie sat in the back seat. Presently, John nudged his wife and pointed to Lopez. At first she didn't know what he meant, but then she noticed that the murderer was trying to pull his hand out of one of the cuffs which hadn't been snapped tight after his captors had loosened him to eat breakfast. Viola was fascinated but frightened. Still, John said nothing. Then, just before the moving hand came free, Slaughter had his gun muzzle in Lopez's side, ordering him not to move a muscle. He froze! Viola's blood ran cold for a second, too. Once more the persistent Lopez was to furnish a scare. At noon they stopped to eat a lunch they had brought along. Again the captive's hands were freed. Suddenly, Slaughter stepped around and faced Lopez and Alvord as they ate, for Burt, being left-handed, was carrying his pistol on that side, and Lopez's free right hand was within grabbing distance of the deputy's equalizer. Slaughter scolded Burt for his carelessness.[20]

It was harder to send Juan Soto to a Yuma exile. Burt Alvord, despite occasional carelessness, was useful in finding desperadoes and getting evidence against them. This was his specialty, since he was a real back-slapping self-styled investigator, always at his best in a warm and spirited bar-

---

[20] Reminiscences of Cora Viola Slaughter, February 5, 1939. Lopez was sentenced on May 28, 1887, to 15 years at the Yuma Penitentiary. The Globe *Democrat*, January 30, 1888, mentioned the break from Yuma of Slaughter's captives, Jose Lopez, Fernando Vasquez, Leopoldo Baca, Albino Villa, and Ricardo Padilla.

room. His undercover man soon learned all that was needed about Soto the cattle thief. He knew Soto's movements better than the rustler himself. Then when a couple of stock buyers in Charleston were murdered and robbed near the border, Slaughter and Alvord mounted and went to that town, where Soto was taken into custody. Evidence showed that he had been a bandit leader in California. Still, despite all the sheriff's and Burt's brainwork, the jury was swayed by oratory and found Soto innocent. Once more vigilanteism rose, but Slaughter, a worse foe of a mob action than of criminals, soon silenced that. He was his own "law and order" committee, so one night he went to Soto's house and gave him ten hours to leave the country. The rustler took the advice.[21]

Slaughter had better luck in getting a conviction for George Cleveland who had stolen a horse from the Grand Central Mine early in April, 1887. Constable Bill Showers was sent out from Benson. Though the culprit had a twelve-hour start, Showers got him in the San Pedro River valley. Cleveland claimed that he had bought the mount from a Mexican who was going to Sonora and didn't have enough money to pay for it. That was an old alibi! Judge Richard E. Sloan of Cochise county had heard it as many times as Slaughter. The Mexican border looters had this as a stock excuse. As Sloan tells it:

> Invariably they accounted for the possession of a stolen horse in this wise: the defendant met another Mexican on the road and traded his own horse for the one found in his possession. The name of this other Mexican was invariably Manuel. On being asked what became of him, the defendant always answered, "Yo no se," or "Quien sabe?" It became a current joke.

---
[21] Frederick Becholdt, *When the West was Young*, p. 160ff, especially 186-188. Jose Soto had sworn out warrants for Slaughter's arrest, that of Constable Fred Dodge, and Undersheriff Shattuck, County Jailor George Farrington, and a clerk for false imprisonment for eight days. He was fluent in English as well as Spanish. Later he was accused of murder and horse stealing. See Tombstone *Prospector*, April 20, 25, and May 7, 1887.

When not wanting to tell the whole truth, cowmen joshingly cracked, "I got it from Manuel." As the good Judge noted, Slaughter wasn't hindered a bit by such a ruse. In this case, Cleveland got quick justice. Cleveland had sold the stolen horse for twenty dollars to one Nicholson. On May 18, 1887, Cleveland, charged with grand larceny, was sentenced to a year at Yuma.[22]

No man could be so thorough in his job against so many vicious characters without rousing fury like the fires of hell. Many desperate men were out to get him, threatening death in a dozen forms. Vengeance inspired a gunman to throw down on him as he was entering a saloon. Caught unawares, as the sheriff flung up his hand he grasped the other's pistol, thrust his thumb under the descending hammer, while he drew his own weapon and calmly placed the furious hombre under arrest. That took nerve, but no more than at another time, of which Frederick Bechdolt tells.

A couple of train robbers tried to coax Slaughter to Willcox by sending a letter telling him that his nephew had been killed. Once more he was quicker of mind than they. Slaughter investigated, learned that his kinsman was alive, and got a deputy to go with him. They left the stagecoach from opposite doors, each man with a double-barrelled shotgun under his arm. The vengeful badmen retreated in undignified haste![23]

Agustín Chacon was a more relentless enemy. Perhaps Slaughter may even have been nervous about him. Surely Chacon was the only man who ever upset the sheriff. It is not clear just why the Sonoran hated Slaughter so deeply. It may have been that he couldn't stand to see a friend of

---

[22] Tombstone *Prospector,* April 13 and 14, 1887. See also Richard E. Sloan, *Memories of an Arizona Judge,* pp. 94-95. Of Slaughter, Sloan said, "I unhesitatingly say that his wide reputation as a fearless and effective peace officer was fully justified."

[23] Bechdolt, *op. cit.,* p. 189.

BULLETS AND JUSTICE

the law and an enemy of his own kind succeed so completely. More likely still was the natural vanity of the criminal. How he could have bragged if he could destroy Slaughter. He, Agustín Chacon, would indeed then be king of Tombstone. Certainly, Chacon was egotism itself, his boasts had to be backed up, and he went to Tombstone. When Slaughter heard the challenge, he was furious, but he kept his head. In such cases, the Earps hadn't. In a hurry, though, the sheriff ran into his office, where Alvord was seated, quickly placed a shotgun in his deputy's hands and said, "Follow me." The two went up a gulch back of the courthouse, where they saw a small, dimly lit tent. Slaughter told his deputy to go to the front, demanding that Chacon come out, as he was under arrest. The sheriff would get the man if he came out the back way. Alvord shouted out the ultimatum, and the next thing, Slaughter's shotgun discharged in the darkness. Of course Alvord thought Chacon was a bit heavier with lead, but when he came up in the dark to see his boss, he found Slaughter in as mad a mood as man can be. Chacon had come out, but in his rapid departure had tripped over a guy wire of the tent and had been pitched headlong into safety in the shallow bottom of the arroyo. Chacon's pony was saddled and ready, awaiting his master in the arroyo. The rapid hoofbeats that echoed in the direction of Charleston were ample proof this rider was well on his way. Chacon must have used good judgment to put the rear exit next to the gully. By now he was on his retreat through the Tombstone hills, heading for Mexico.[24]

This was one of John Slaughter's few fumbles, and he couldn't take it as a joke. Pablo Salcido of Morenci wouldn't have laughed either, had he known then what Chacon's flying exit would mean to him. On Christmas Eve, of 1895, Chacon and his gang were still molesting Arizona.

[24] Brophy, *op. cit.*

They robbed the store of a Mrs. McCormick that night. The manager, Paul Becker, refused to open the safe, and was mortally wounded. Next morning, in a Mexican house at Morenci, they fought off Constable Alex Davis. Before it was ended, sheriff's men and citizens struck in pitched battle against the robbers. Two of the latter were killed. Chacon shot Salcido while the peacemaker was going up to persuade the outlaws to surrender. In time, Chacon was caught and jailed in Solomonville. On June 9, 1897, just ten days before he was to be hanged for murder, the desperado escaped to Sonora and eluded capture for another five years.

A strange aftermath occurred, after Slaughter's time as sheriff. Two versatile lawmen, Burt Alvord and Billy Stiles, decided to try outlawry, which resulted in their capture and confinement in the Tombstone jail, the same hoosegow Alvord had once guarded for John Slaughter. Knowing the weaknesses of the jail, the two ex-lawmen escaped, after wounding the jailor, and went to Mexico. Chacon, being aware of their activities around Willcox, joined up with them. The three men made a fine combination, for both the inside and outside of law and disorder were united. Slaughter by this time had left the sheriff's office and spent most of his time at the San Bernardino, although he carried a deputy sheriff's commission until his death. A protege of Slaughter's was Captain Burton Mossman of the Arizona Rangers. He was appointed by the governor to captain a ranger force in Arizona. Mossman had been foreman of the Hashknife outfit at Holbrook, and had the pick of cowboys as his rangers. But now he was to follow in Slaughter's footsteps and perform a job as a lone hand. Chacon was at large, and news had leaked out that Stiles and Alvord were with him.

Quietly and bravely, Mossman rode down south of the border in the direction of Cananea. Here in Col. Greene's mining town he learned the whereabouts of the outlaw camp. With his life in his hands, depending upon his six-shooter and his ability to use it, "Cap" Mossman approached the old rambling shack where Alvord was busy preparing a noonday feast for his henchmen. Mossman, who had seen photographs of all three wanted men, recognized Burt at once. Burt was equally suspicious of Mossman and had the drop on the ranger before the latter could dismount.

Mossman had learned from Slaughter the type of man Burt was. He soon found out that the old sheriff had him pegged right. Slaughter had hired Burt because he knew Burt was well informed on outlaw activities. And they knew that Alvord would sell his best friend down the line for a fee. This time his freedom was the fee. Mossman placed his cards on the table, and told Burt he was Captain Mossman of the Arizona Rangers. He promised that if Alvord could bring Chacon to a certain spot on the plain, south of Naco, that he (Mossman) would do everything in his power to have both Burt and Billy Stiles acquitted, offering them a new trial, and change of venue. Thus they could come back to Arizona to live without any further bother of the law. At first, Burt was dubious about the whole affair. Finally, Mossman told him that one Chacon was worth a dozen Alvords to the Arizona Rangers. This did it. Burt agreed.

Just about that time, in rode the Chacon gang and Billy Stiles, all laughing, cutting-up, with a few good snorts of mescal under their belts. They swarmed around Mossman. "Who's this guy, Burt? Think we'll kill him now, and save him explaining," said Chacon. "Leave him alone," demanded Burt, "he's my guest." "Well, then," shouted Chacon, "introduce us." A phony name had been agreed upon by Burt and Mossman, plus a hoax that sounded mighty convincing. But Burt managed to wink at Stiles, and Stiles kept mum. He went on to tell that the visitor was an old pal of his, that he broke out of Tombstone jail with him, and now wanted to join up with the "boys". "Well, he's your problem," said Chacon.

The bandit never did take his eyes off Mossman. After dinner, one of the border ruffians lifted Mossman's pearl handled pistol out of its holster, and replaced his rusty old weapon in the ranger's holster. "Wahl, Burt," exclaimed the tough, "think I'll see my lady friend. Won't she think I look a might bit purdy wearin' this classy hogsleg?" Mossman quickly showed how tough he was, as he cussed the bandit and ordered Burt to either make his man give him back his six-shooter or there would be a killing. After a few cuss words, the gun fancier apologized and gave the gun back.

It took half a day before the bandits accepted Mossman. Looking like an ordinary saddle-tramp, unshaven and with tattered old range garb, Mossman played his part well. Alvord told the gang that the new recruit had some good plans concerning a hold-up and a cattle stealing venture, that would set them up in business. Mossman was to leave and look the situation over; Stiles, Alvord and Chacon were to meet Mossman near Naco when things looked ripe. A couple of weeks elapsed before Mossman dispatched a message to Alvord for the meeting. Mossman laid out in the hills for three-quarters of a day before the men showed up. When they did, Chacon still had his eyes fixed on the newcomer. With horses hobbled, they built a little fire in the shallow depression between the slopes of two buttes. Mossman gave Stiles the price of a bottle of whiskey and a sack of grub. Stiles rode in to Naco and after getting in a hilarious mood, returned to camp with the supplies. The night passed slowly – drinking, card playing, feasting – the preparations of outlawry were in full swing.

Alvord and Mossman had planned that daybreak would

be the signal to break camp. To make things worse, Chacon stayed wide awake, refused to drink, and glued his eyes on Mossman. Here Mossman was with three dead shots, who could shoot him down in cold blood, bury his remains on the desert without fear of apprehension. His whole life rested upon Burt Alvord's final decision. Daybreak arrived, and a ghastly feeling overtook Mossman. This was the showdown. Here it was September, 1902, and Chacon had still gone unpunished for his crimes.[25] Suddenly, Alvord arose, walked over to his horse. This was the cue for his departure. Mossman broke out in a cold sweat, but kept his head. He walked to where Burt was straightening his saddle blanket. "Watch Billy Stiles; don't trust him," warned Alvord, "I brought your man here; now I am going."

Mossman walked back to the campfire and squatted down cowboy fashion, while Stiles and Chacon sipped hot coffee. The fact that Alvord went over to his horse, prompted Chacon to become uneasy, as if he were going to saddle up also. Now the opportunity had arrived, thought the ranger. Slowly, he walked over to a dead bush and broke a twig off; then with his left hand he carefully placed the twig on the hot embers. He lit his cigarette and placed the burning stick back on the fire again, at the same time springing to his feet, and with six-shooter drawn, covering the surprised Chacon and Stiles. Immediately Mossman began to cuss the lanky bandido, as he ordered Stiles to handcuff him, unbuckle both their gun belts, and throw their rifles in the brush behind them. By this time, Burt had taken out on a slow jog. Chacon asked Stiles what all the cussing was for, saying he did not do anything to arouse the man's temper. "I'll answer that," said Mossman, "I'm Captain of the Arizona Rangers, and you're under arrest." Stiles was ordered to prepare the horses, or be killed.

---
[25] Brophy, *op. cit.*

Soon they were on the way to the border, Stiles leading, Chacon in the middle, Mossman in the rear. Stiles was not handcuffed, but Chacon was. When approaching the border, Chacon kept looking back over his shoulder. Mossman did not learn why until some time later. It seems Chacon had been a former member of the Mexican Border Rurales, and this was directly in line with their patrol. Mossman later said, "Had the Rurales seen us, I undoubtedly would have ceased to be Captain of the Rangers." As luck would have it, the train was coming along, enroute to Benson. Mossman ordered Stiles to flag down the freight, and went aboard with prisoner and horse. Stiles was released to rejoin Alvord. When the train arrived in Benson, by sheer coincidence Jim Parks, the sheriff from Solomonville, was standing on the platform. He had just returned from taking some prisoners to Yuma. Mossman turned the shackled Chacon over to Sheriff Parks, who later hanged the desperado at Solomonville on November 22, 1902. Mossman had performed his feat, and immediately took a vacation to New York City. Before he left, he gave John Slaughter his famous and most cherished horse, an honor and high tribute on the range.[26]

Chacon came to the end of his rope quite literally. Like many another man whose life contained not one whit of nobility, he died bravely, saying just before the trap was sprung, "I consider this to be the greatest day of my life." Slaughter joined heartily in the sentiment.

In life's race, vengeance never did catch up with the fast-riding Slaughter. Ed Lyle thought it could, and tried to outdo Chacon. He and his sidekick, Cap Stilwell, had heard that Slaughter was on the road between Fort Huachuca and Patagonia, so they set a trap. Saddling up well in advance, they rode far ahead and sat beside the road to challenge him.

---
[26] Bisbee *Daily Review*, November 22, 1902.

John Slaughter's intuition was an asset, but good planning always helped out more than he would admit. He never went out in a rig without having his saddle horse ready, tied behind and saddled for an emergency. That quiet evening all seemed as calm as Boot Hill, and many times more cheerful, as John and Viola drove along. Viola's brother was with them and decided to ride ahead. Suddenly the unintended advance lookout spied half a dozen horses saddled and bridled off to one side of the road. The site was a small spring which trickled down from the Huachucas. They asked Howell to get down from his horse, remove the bridle and water it, but he was too wise for the road agents. He calculated that his horse could drink with a bridle on. A bit later, when the Lyle gang saw Slaughter coming, they were a little taken off guard. Slaughter, noting that it was Lyle and his pals, swung his team sharply to the right and around them, but always keeping his hand on the shotgun trigger. "Well, I guess we had better be riding," Lyle drawled to Howell, and the five horsemen departed. Still, they continued to cross the lawman's trail several times during the evening's ride. They never broke down his nerve. As he approached a narrow canyon the sheriff thought a showdown would come at last, so he gave the reins to his wife, telling her he would mount his horse and give them chase. The criminals would not shoot a woman, as Slaughter well knew. "But they may kill you," she cried. "They just can't hit me, Viola. Don't worry, I'll be all right," he assured her. The Lyle gang soon outdistanced Slaughter. They passed by the danger point safely, which greatly relieved Viola.

That night John and Viola stopped and slept at the Downing ranch. The next morning they saw three men, two mounted and one leading his horse. They had probably gone to Sonoita, since Howell had told them that the Slaughters were bound that way. Later, the sheriff's party saw three more perched on their horses atop a little rise. Viola felt sure it was part of the gang, and bravely she grabbed the reins and started right for them! Slaughter calmly sat beside her, shotgun ready. But calmly he replied, "Why, Viola, don't get excited; I have my gun." He was ready to mount his pony again, but the three strangers departed. Viola drove the rest of the trip, while her husband kept alert, ready for action.[27] Slaughter never forgot this challenge. A few days later he saw Lyle in Charleston and threw down on him. Lyle said that he had no pistol. The sheriff told him that if he had, by now he would be a dead man. Another day, he saw Lyle again, this time in a wounded condition. When you get better, I want you to leave Cochise County, demanded Slaughter. Told to get out, in the plainest of words, Lyle left as simply; Stilwell got the same ultimatum, and followed suit.[28]

The sheriff also had trouble with Geronimo, the bandit. No, Slaughter was not seeing double, though this Mexican *ladron* was more a headache to Don Juan than the Apache commander had ever been. Not long after the latter had been expressed to points east, this Geronimo Baltierrez with Nieves and Miranda, his compadres, robbed a gold-laden burro train and took some Wells Fargo express money amounting to several thousand dollars. Slaughter promptly sent two deputies onto the trail. Quite easily they got the minor menaces, but not Geronimo, the bandit. Señor Baltierrez seems to have had the slipperiness of his Apache namesake. Backtracking in good Indian fashion, the bandito returned to Tombstone and hid out in the home of one Doña Irena. Maybe it was a new Slaughter strategem, or simply disgust for bad outlaw manners. Anyway, it was soon being reported to Geronimo by his friends that the sheriff

---
[27] Reminiscences of Cora Viola Slaughter, February 5, 1939.
[28] Bisbee *Daily Review*, April 22, 1934.

was saying the Mexican was yellow to the core and would rather hide behind a woman's skirts than fight out in the open like a man. Baltierrez denied this, but said he did not want to be the moving bulls-eye for Slaughter's sharp shooting deputies. One night, however, he was in Page's blacksmith shop where John Slaughter always passed on his way home to Fremont Street. As the hour arrived, Slaughter came by briskly. Geronimo called out, "Amigo, Slaughter, I am Geronimo Baltierrez. I understand you are looking for me, and that you say I am afraid." Slaughter replied that he didn't want Geronimo; the law did. Then Geronimo suggested they shake hands and be friends. Like a king snake facing a rattler in the desert, they advanced cautiously, as Slaughter dropped a hint for Geronimo to leave town. A crack of a twig might have set off a gun fight. Neither would admit their tenseness. Next morning, Slaughter sent his able deputy, Cesario Lucero, to tail Geronimo. Someone warned the outlaw, who paid Lucero a surprise visit at a spring while he was washing his face. Smiling as if he were greeting a brother, he observed, "I understand you are after me." Lucero didn't answer, but went for his pistol – too late.[29]

This was not the end of the Geronimo affair. He turned to train robbery. "Doc" Benjamin Franklin Hall had come from Kentucky to Tombstone in September, 1881. When he saw a cold-blooded murder the next day, Hall wanted to leave town, but he had no money. Later, he climbed under a billiard table when a pistol fight took place in the Oriental Saloon. One had to learn fast to live in the "town too tough to die," and "Doc" was educated quicker and better than most newcomers. For a while he ranched in Guadalupe Canyon, but in 1887, while on leave from the Copper Queen mines at Bisbee, he met John Slaughter and Burt Alvord.

[29] Dan de Lara, *South From Tombstone* (Tombstone, privately printed, n.d.).

The sheriff offered Hall the then regal sum of $2.00 a day. After a great deal of persuasion, he became a special deputy. This lasted a month, but it was thirty days full of action.

To start off, Slaughter informed Doc, "I want you and Burt to meet me here at the office." He never explained more. There was no need. That day they rode off to Fairbank, and the sheriff looked up an old Mexican whom he asked in Spanish where Geronimo was. Being loyal to both Baltierrez and his own perishable hide, the elderly man wouldn't talk; claimed he didn't know. Slaughter was used to this kind of dodge. He looked the old man straight in the eye and demanded a reasonable reply. The Mexican finally told the sheriff that Geronimo was in a tent, visiting with his senorita, camped about a half-mile from Fairbank. When the three lawmen found the tent, it was getting on toward dusk. After some brief instructions, the men knew what to do. Doc took the front entrance, Burt the opposite end, and Slaughter was standing back to stop him on the run. The sheriff and men had to be careful not to harm the girl. About thirty feet east of the tent was a pagewire fence which anyone inside would have to clear. Geronimo slit a hole in the tent and made it to the fence. Slaughter let go with both barrels of his shotgun and nearly cut him in two. Then old John had them take him on a spring wagon back to Tombstone. This wild-and-wooly-west display was too much for Doc. Back in Tombstone, he took off his borrowed gun belt and pistol and put them on the sheriff's desk. "This is enough for me," he said, tossing down his deputy's badge. Old John chuckled for a minute, then he joshed, "Why, you wouldn't let a little thing like this stop you or make you quit?" [30]

---

[30] Interview with Benjamin Franklin "Doc" Hall, 1950. Later, Hall got in a scrape stealing cattle from one Sanderson, but never told of it until October, 1950. Once, Doc shot his employer, who had drawn a gun when Doc demanded back pay. Thinking he had killed the fellow, Hall fled Arizona, went to Oklahoma, there to

Mexican wood camps were often hideaways for criminals. Manuel Colorado was "one of the most dangerous outlaws that ever infested this country.[31] Slaughter found his whereabouts, and late one January evening, crept up on the camp somewhere in the Dragoons. The jailor made ready another Tombstone cell.[32] Soon the *Prospector* newspaper was calling the lockup, "Hotel de Slaughter!"[33] Into this hoosegow went Librado Marrojo, captured by Slaughter and his men in 1889 for the usual offense, horse stealing.[34]

Guilty of the same charge were a couple of Mexicans who held up and robbed Henry Schultz in Sulphur Springs Valley that same summer. Slaughter kept on the trail day and night until a heavy rain turned it into a river. Then he sent a couple of deputies to Sonora. This time, good cooperation with the famous Mexican Rurale colonel, Emilio Kosterlitzky, solved the crime. This Russian-born Mexican army man sent Slaughter a letter saying that he had recovered the two horses, but had to kill one of the outlaws to do it. Slaughter and Jess Fisher left at once for the border to get the thief at Arispe. Schultz had his mounts returned after only a month's absence.[35]

Drunkenness was the cause of many beatings and cracked heads. John Slaughter was pestered with many of these annoying cases. They were usually harder to deal with, too,

---

remain until his brother Jim told him in a letter that the man had recovered. Once accused of stealing a hundred head of cattle, Hall was locked up by Sheriff Slaughter until a friend bailed him out and proved his innocence. His mine foreman at the Copper Queen in Bisbee testified Hall had not missed a shift, thus he could hardly have been committing a crime eighty miles away in Guadalupe Canyon.

[31] *Southwestern Stockman*, May 24, 1890.
[32] Tombstone *Epitaph*, January 14, 1888.
[33] Tombstone *Prospector*, October 7, 1887, and November 6, 1889.
[34] *Ibid.*, November 6, 1889.
[35] Tombstone *Prospector*, July 15 and August 17, 1889. At the time, Deputy Jess Fisher returned with Youngman, a fellow indicted by the grand jury. Slaughter recovered many fugitives this way. A Chinese murderer of Sam Shang, was recovered in Magdalena – *Ibid.*, January 2, 1890.

since assault and battery was charged, and the devious processes of the law took over. Here, where he could not be so fast and direct, Slaughter was at a disadvantage.[36]

Through many of John Slaughter's years as sheriff, Burt Alvord was his star deputy. It must have been disheartening to him when his able companion finally went bad. He was kindly toward Slaughter and showed concern for his boss's health. John Slaughter had had asthma since the Civil War, so Burt carried a special coat and muffler for him at night in case of a bad attack.[37]

Alvord had come west with his parents, a sister, Mae, and a brother, Will. Burt's father, who was briefly a justice of the peace, had been known to his cronies as "Judge" Alvord. Burt had a tendency to hang out in a bad environment around Tombstone's dives. At eighteen, his greatest thrill was seeing John Heath lynched at First and Toughnut Streets. For a living, young Alvord worked for John Montgomery, owner of the fatal OK Corral, where Burt fed and saddled horses, cleaned the stables, and prepared buggies for trips. In front of his boss's place, he witnessed the Earp-Clanton feud. Slaughter watched Burt grow up, and they hit it off from the first. He liked twenty-year-old Burt's straightforwardness and ability to learn all about the people in Cochise County. Both had a good sense of humor, though Burt's was boisterous. He once spread a rumor, after he had turned outlaw, that he and Stiles had been killed, and he shipped two coffins to Tombstone with their names on them. He then rode the same train, to get the full benefit of the citizens' reaction.

Under the new sheriff's watchful eye, Burt got full training in strenuous and dangerous duties. Alvord got his first lesson in the methods of train robbers in 1888. Jack Taylor

[36] *Ibid.,* February 11, 1889.
[37] Bernice Cosulich in *Arizona Daily Star,* Tucson, February 19, 1938.

and his five thugs held up a train of the New Mexico and Arizona Railroad at Agua Zarca, Sonora, on the night of May 11th. Three trainmen were murdered. Taylor, however, was soon captured in Nogales, and sent to the penitentiary for life, but the four others, all Mexicans, fled their native land and took refuge in Tombstone. Now they were under John Slaughter's jurisdiction. Clever, if not wise, they suspected that he was watching them, so they lit out for the rugged Whetstones where they were provisioned by a brother of one of their number. The sheriff was not far behind, and with him came deputies Alvord and Lucero. They trailed the wood-hauler brother to his camp and surprised three of the robbers in their blankets. They arose shooting. One of their number was badly wounded.[38]

After Slaughter's time as sheriff, Burt must have grown bored. Most deputies took brief vacations from official duties. They had their own cattle business which kept them busy during these off days. Alvord was a town man. His idle hours were at a bar, not a corral fence. When Slaughter cleaned up Cochise County, Burt was kept too busy on the law's side to think up much deviltry, but soon he was drifting back with the shady friends of his youth for a more lucrative way to make money. In the mid-nineties he went down to Mexico rustling cattle. At that time this was not looked upon too severely. Just as many a pirate in past centuries was considered a patriot, now many a cattle robber was thought to be avenging Texans and Yankees for Mexican misdeeds. Furthermore, Alvord kept his doings pretty quiet. Besides, already he had cleaned up Pearce. His credit was good and he paid all his bills on time. Nobody asked where the cash originated. Then again, Alvord's fine reputation as Slaughter's assistant was much more durable. It was well known in tough Willcox.

---
[38] Charles A. Nichols memoirs, *loc. cit.*

As late as 1896, that town was still the largest cattle shipping center in the territory. Five hundred head was a trainload, and 24 cars made a heavy pull. Many shipments pulled out from the depot in those days. There were many cowboys on the dodge and a tough man to calm the rowdy was needed. The citizens thought of Burt Alvord. He might be Slaughter's gun-toting heir apparent. The good people hoped so. Thus they chose him as constable. Alvord took office on July 12, 1897, after resigning as deputy-constable of Pearce. On November 22, 1898, he was officially elected. Burt began in his familiar way. George Raum's saloon was the favorite hangout for the noted and notorious. In the back end was a wine and whiskey cellar.

One day, Andy Darnell, an Erie Cattle Company cowhand, and Billy King, his sidekick, entered the place. King was likeable but wayward, "variable as the whirlwind." Andy was harder to handle than a stampeding longhorn, when the firewater burned from within him. Andy didn't like Alvord's bright new star so, foolishly, he tried to bully this killer of rustlers. "There is that bad constable and his two deputies. Let's show the people how harmless they are," he snarled. Darnell was no common mouth fighter. He and Billy had Alvord covered before he could turn. That nice cool cellar could store lawmen as well as liquor, and maybe all Burt needed was a little aging, so the cowboys herded Alvord and his deputies down there, locked the trap door, and took over the saloon and its liquid treasures. Ignominiously, the constables were liberated by friends.

Being confined like a mouse in a trap in a dark cellar was just too much. It slapped at Burt's reputation as nothing ever had before. King wouldn't leave town, so there had to be a showdown. Next morning, Burt told Billy what he thought of that kind of treatment. King regretted it somewhat. "If I hadn't been drunk it wouldn't have happened," he halfway apologized. Then he promised to buy the drinks and put his six-shooter behind the bar. After that he'd buy Alvord a new hat. Burt thought this fair, or pretended to, so they shook. All that was promised was done. Then back again at their saloon headquarters, Burt got serious and told King he wanted a good long talk with him. Alvord then ushered King down a narrow hallway, opened the door for him to step out first. As soon as they were in the back yard, Burt shoved his six-shooter in King's face and emptied it, killing King instantly. That evening, sixty or more cowboys swarmed into Willcox to hang Alvord. When Leonard Alvorsen, who observed the whole affair, suggested they draw straws for the honor, time and thought in doing so calmed them down and nothing was accomplished. Alvord had the law on his side.[39]

Burt's pistol had gotten him into an earlier mess. Having the law on his side had saved him then, too. It was 1889 when Slaughter was sheriff. Alvord was off duty as deputy, and as was his custom, was having a high old time. It was in the home of one Fuller and his brother-in-law, named Fortino. Liquor had flowed too freely. When Fortino went to the door to go out, Fuller seized his hat, wanting to exchange sombreros. A scuffle followed, turning into a general row, and Fuller grabbed Alvord's pistol. Burt had been toying with it, perhaps bragging of his great deeds. Fortino was shot twice. He died shortly after midnight. Fuller got away with the deputy's pistol. John Slaughter's town house was only three doors away, and when he came running and found Alvord's role in the whole mess, he was raving mad. Since Alvord was only a special deputy at the time, Slaughter was saved some embarrassment.[40]

[39] Leonard Alvorsen, "Alvord's Killing of Billy King," Douglas, Arizona, 1938. Ms in Arizona Pioneers Historical Society. See Coroner's inquest of Billy King at Bisbee Court House. Cochise County records.
[40] Tombstone *Prospector*, February 15, 1889.

Now, Burt went to work cleaning up Willcox. His gun could be very useful here. He did a good job, too, but built up a gang of outlaws, as he added to his reputation cleaning out the riffraff. It was exchanging old dirt for new. Billy Stiles, a wild young fellow, became deputy, as did Bill Downing, a ruthless gunslinger from Texas. Another Texan of no principles was Matt Burts. All had drifted in between the swinging doors. Alvord was now ready for bigger things. He knew criminals from every angle. He had fought them, killed them, jailed them, and joined them. As for the law, he had viewed it, too, as a pupil of Arizona's most renowned sheriff. He thought he knew how both sides would react in any given situation. Furthermore, he knew the lay of the Cochise County land. Smarter men have tried for the perfect crime, but none was more optimistic than John Slaughter's deputy-gone-bad. Half an hour before midnight on September 1, 1899, four men held up the westbound passenger train at Cochise Station just west of the constable's newly cleaned up Willcox.

They used dynamite to blow up the baggage car. Getting $30,000, they rode toward Willcox, but disappeared a half mile from town. C. L. Sonnichsen calls this "one of the most brilliant pieces of planning" in the history of American banditry. When Burt was informed of the robbery, he was in a saloon, calmly taking his ease. He pretended shocked indignation. He had heard many on the other side of the fence, so Alvord had many alibis, as did Downing, who was on duty that evening. All had been planned for months. Downing supplied the horses and had stolen blasting powder from a local store. Matt Burts and Billy Stiles had done the robbing and delivered the loot to Alvord, the recognized brains behind the scheme. It was a masterpiece. How he would have liked to brag about it! Could John Slaughter have thought out such a campaign of sheer genius? It was not a perfect piece, though. Stiles got only $480 as his share, and this weakened a link. To carry off the illusion of righteousness, lawman Alvord rushed to join and head a posse.

Next, the would-be mastermind planned a holdup on the southbound for Benson It was to be taken at Fairbank, a cattle loading point. Alvord and Stiles sent their henchmen, Three-Fingered Jack Dunlap, and George and Louis Owens, Bravo Juan Yoas, and Bob Brown. Bravo John was elected captain. On February 15, 1900, they ordered Jeff Milton, Slaughter's old friend, who was loading the freight car, to surrender. He held fire to avoid hitting bystanders, but the badmen did not. Milton finally did get Jack Dunlap with eleven bullets and sent a volley, hitting Bravo John's pants' seat. Bravo was captured by Mexican officers at Cananea, Sonora. Three-Fingered Jack soon died, but in revenge for being ditched by his comrades, told the whole story of Alvord's and Stiles' criminal campaigns.

On March 2, 1900, Alvord and Downing were charged with obstructing the United States mails. Stiles turned state's evidence, admitted his complicity, and told of Alvord's role. Regretting his treachery, on April 8th he drew a gun on jailer George Bravin, and freed Alvord and Juan. The rest refused to flee. Soon the Arizona Rangers were organized with Burton C. Mossman as its captain. Contacting the two outlaws, Mossman offered clemency and arranged a mountainside meeting below Naco. Badmen and lawmen schemed for Chacon's capture. The latter was taken and eventually hanged, as mentioned earlier, while Alvord and Stiles dropped once more into jail. But not for long. December 15, 1903, they broke out after digging through a building and making a drop rope to freedom. No wonder John Slaughter had recognized Alvord's resourcefulness.

Never daunted, they returned to the old routine and

robbed a Mexican bullion train. They got an $8,000 bar of gold. On February 17, 1904, Alvord was taken by two rangers in Nigger Head Gap, Mexico. Wounded and tired of running, Burt spent a couple of years more in prison, but managed to evade several criminal charges and was finally freed at Yuma.[41] Stiles had escaped, but was finally killed in January, 1908, in Nevada. Before his end, though minus two fingers, Billy had done a take-off on Alvord's old trick – he had turned lawman and was deputy sheriff, serving the public faithfully. As if in ironic justice, a prisoner riddled him.[42]

What became of John Slaughter's old friend, Burt Alvord? Well, Sheriff John may have often wondered about that, too. Certainly other people did, and "accurate" reports of his whereabouts kept cropping up. Some say Burt went to Barbados and died of tropic fever. Others claimed that he settled in Panama where he oversaw canal workers.[43] Then again, he was reported headed for Alberta, Canada, and later supposedly turned up in Venezuela. Rumors filtered back that Alvord had married a Honduras lady and died in that banana republic about 1910. His nieces, Mrs. H. H. Spohr and Mrs. Jacob Nordleman, insisted years later that indeed he had passed away in the fall of 1910, but on a small island off the Atlantic coast of Panama.[44]

---

[41] C. L. Sonnichsen, *Billy King's Tombstone*, pp. 67-70. See also James H. McClintock, *Arizona*, II, p. 487. This tells of "Burnett: The Czar of Charleston." See also Douglas *Daily Dispatch*, May 4, 1941, for Sam J. Hayhurst's life story. He was one of the rangers sent to capture Alvord and Stiles after their 1900 jail break. In a true life comedy of errors, they got on the trail of several horsemen reported to be outlaws. The "badmen" turned out to be a couple of teen age boys out rabbit hunting! On another occasion friends of Alvord sent the lawmen on a wild goose chase. Finally, they camped near the rangers, and Stiles and Alvord watched them over their evening coffee. They could have killed the rangers and no one would have known their whereabouts.
[42] J. Evetts Haley, *Jeff Milton: A Good Man with a Gun*.
[43] McClintock, *op. cit.*, II, p. 487.
[44] Tombstone *Epitaph*, January 21, 1938.

BULLETS AND JUSTICE 249

Sheriff Slaughter's life was not all smoking six-guns, although he was never given to twirling in a swivel chair. Still, there was much routine, even some dull paper work. The local court was always issuing orders for him to carry out. Glad enough he was to offer rewards for desperadoes. Usually, these sums ranged from $250 to $500. For instance, during 1887, Slaughter offered $250 for the arrest of those who had tried to kill J. S. Clark and his wife; $500 for the murderer of Nicholas McCormick; another like sum for the killer of Alfred Richards, and $500 for the "unknown killer" of Tomás Salcido. In 1890 he offered $200 for the return of one Thomas Forget, who escaped Cochise County jail. A French Canadian of small stature, his only distinguishing characteristic in that cow country was that he had on a pair of shoes.[45] Popular W. W. Lowther was murdered near Bisbee that spring, and the Copper Queen Mining Company, along with Bisbee citizens, had the sheriff offer $500 for the capture of James Daly, who had done him in.[46] Lowther had been a constable there under Slaughter.

Such trivia as buying five pairs of handcuffs required a special court order and its red tape, as did Slaughter's buying new matting for the guard's room floor.[47] There were always sheriff's sales that he had to arrange, announce and theoretically conduct, ending up with certificates of the transactions. Since most of these sales involved livestock, he was just the man to do it.[48]

Coroner's juries were much more interesting. Slaughter was often named as one of the half dozen or so jurors to go

---

[45] Tombstone *Prospector*, May 12, 1890.
[46] *Ibid.*, April 14, 1890. Billy King was briefly jailed by Constable Lowther as witness to the murder of a miner named Hines – *Ibid.*, January 12, 1890.
[47] Cochise County, Record Book 2, pages 126, 200, 224, 602, 611 and 620. See also Tombstone *Prospector*, October 7, 1887.
[48] Cochise County, Misc. Records Book 2, page 23ff.

to the death spot, examine evidence, and make a decision. As sheriff, his testimony was most important.[49]

Antagonizing to a straight-shooting man of simple justice must have been the technicalities and loopholes, the red tape and double-talking lawyers of that region. A habeas corpus has often left the goddess of justice not only blind, but paralyzed. Still, a free country such as Slaughter loved, must suffer a little for its freedom. Istacio Inyana claimed that he was illegally imprisoned and restrained by Sheriff Slaughter, and called for a freeing writ.[50] H. E. Jones also claimed that Slaughter had no legal warrant or judgment to imprison him, and he gained his liberty. Obviously, John Slaughter was no diplomat. He did not understand completely all the technicalities that lawyers wove into a net.

Even the swift sheriff could be tripped up with red tape. Politics, too, confounded him. As 1888 slipped away, the public called upon him again to run for office, and since he did not think his work done, he agreed to do so. In that year the Democrats were not as popular nationally. It seemed that they were weak in Arizona, too, so even John Slaughter had to join other candidates in traveling about and campaigning. Against him ran Silas H. Bryant, a well-known Republican. He was only forty years old, seven years

[49] These Cochise County coroners reports give a voiceless history of that rugged territory in its goriest and "gloriest" days. No. 48 of 1881 showed Billy Clanton's decease on October 26; 1882 chronicled Billy Claiborne's exit from gunshot wounds, as well as John Ringo's strange end, and that of Morgan Earp. In 1887, Slaughter's first shrievalty year, Nicholas McCormick died of pistol wounds, Joseph Smith of gunshot wounds. In 1888 Guadalupe Robles, Ramon Carisoso, John Doe and Richard Roe (very often present in the rolls due to the anonymity of many corpses in that rough era), James Barrock, J. M. Martin, and others went the same way, but Ramon Basquez died of the "stab of a knife." In 1889, there were recorded grimly Juan Castalum, Jose, an unknown Mexican, Muk Hock Ching, a Chinese, Florentina Rodriguez, all victims of hot lead; 1890 carried out Patrick Brown, alias Joseph S. Lotritz, of California. More honorably that year, Robert Hardy, N. H. Robinson, and John Bridges died at the hands of some still untamed Apaches. See Cochise County Coroner's Reports, nos. 32-236, 1882-1891.
[50] Cochise County, District Court, First Judicial District, April 9, 1887.

younger than the incumbent. Campaigners compared his six-foot frame with Slaughter's but they could not compare the records. Bryant was a good enough man, but his only fame was as a deputy under Bob Hatch, who had preceded Slaughter. Like "Don Juan," Bryant was a rancher; his spread was in the Dragoons.[51]

Even before the campaign was under way, public opinion was overwhelmingly for Slaughter. The *Prospector* was a Democratic paper, but it hardly exaggerated when it said:

> If the Democrats nominate John Slaughter for sheriff this fall, they will have the consolation of knowing that they can elect one man, whatever may be the luck of the others. Thus said yesterday a strong Republican in the presence of half a dozen men. The man said, "the reason I say this is because he has made a splendid sheriff. No one could do better, and I don't know of a man in the county who would have done so well. His thorough knowledge of the whole county, his familiarity with the Mexican people and their language, and his great courage has of course given him an advantage over many men, who while they may be as brave, don't possess the other advantages. He has brought more criminals to justice than all the other sheriffs, principally because he knows the haunts of that class, and spares neither horse flesh nor money when he goes after them. I am not disparaging the sheriffs we Republicans have elected, for except Slaughter, the Democrats have never had a really good man in that office. But they've got one now, and I really think he'll be in there another term.[52]

The anonymous Republican was a good prophet. Slaughter got 882 votes against the 785 of his Republican opponent. Before the votes had been counted, he had made up his mind that he would not run again. Only Slaughter's spirit was still strong. He never was entirely well, and in October, 1887, his resistance surrendered to cholera morbus. He had been on the trail of some train robbers, but all the grit in his system could not fight this plague. A stagecoach brought the

---

[51] Territory of Arizona, Cochise County, District Court of the First Judicial District, May 1, 1888. See also Tombstone *Prospector*, October 5, and 11, 1888.
[52] Tombstone *Prospector*, June 9, 1888.

seriously ill sheriff back from Fairbank. Slaughter had backtracked before, but never surrendered. Under good care, he won out again, and was soon back on duty.[53]

There were other good reasons why John Slaughter wanted to retire. His job as sheriff was financially a handicap. Of course, he was doing well with his San Bernardino range, but he had to be away most of the time, leaving his herds to helpers, and for a man who wanted to be in touch with every detail of his interests, this was hard to take. Furthermore, there were official expenses that he had to bear until slow judicial procedure let the public reimburse him. For instance, the case of Kelton vs. Cochise County cost him $1,647.30, which he settled for only $823.65 from the board of supervisors. And the expense fund warrant was slow in being issued to him. His bills for fees mounted up, as did his salary bills.[54] Yet, his hustling helped swell the county treasury. For instance, for his criminal work up to October, 1888, he got for the year, $4,670.11. For the same period, he paid into it $22,072.25.[55]

Most important of all, Viola was against his running for a third term. When the Democratic leaders came to his home, seeking the nod of their one sure winner, she exclaimed, "Gentlemen, it would kill him, and perhaps me." She explained further that his business and family needed his time more than the county he had made calm and honest. Knowing that this husband and wife would not change their minds, the boosters dropped their draft campaign.[56]

John Myers Myers has said in our own day that the tale of Sheriff Slaughter, the Lone Ranger of lone rustlers, is a

---

[53] *Ibid.*, October 4, 1887.

[54] Slaughter's salary bill was for $2,000 on October 8, 1887. His bill dated January 7, 1888 was for $820 in fees. Tombstone *Epitaph*, October 8, 1887 and January 7, 1888.

[55] Tombstone *Prospector*, October 24, 1888.

[56] Bisbee *Daily Review*, April 24, 1934, and Bernice Cosulich, *op. cit.*

BULLETS AND JUSTICE 253

great tale of Cochise County, "but not the whole story of Tombstone."[57] Certainly that is true, for there were many of note in the mining city. Slaughter should have been appointed when the Earps were in Tombstone. Perhaps conditions would have been different. Accurately, though, he put the final period to a whole book of violence there. After him it opened a new volume of orderly living. At the beginning of 1895, John Slaughter's successor, the photographer, C. S. Fly, made a public effort to reward the hero and at the same time make good use of him. On January 5, Allen English, criminal lawyer and notary public, swore in "Don Juan" as deputy-sheriff: Slaughter would hold that responsibility the rest of his life, and like Tombstone would begin another volume, as exciting in its way as the first.

Tombstone was full of memories. Boot Hill was crowded with epitaphs, but the rustlers occupying the plots got no better send-off than a poem published in the *Prospector* in July of the year Slaughter became sheriff. It could better have been written four years later, as a tribute to his undeniable efficiency:

THE RUSTLER

The rustler sat on his old gray horse,
    And afar off viewed the town,
And softly sighed as he noted that
    Its color was mostly brown.
"Oh, for a glimpse of the good old days,"
    The sad-eyed rustler said,
"When me with a gang of bullies brave,
    Used ter paint the old place red.
"We'd spur like mad up the busy street,
    Make the sheriff hunt his hole,
Shoot glasses and hats and their damage pay,
    From a big fat greenback roll.

---
[57] Myers, *The Last Chance: Tombstone's Early Years,* p. 236.

"The store man he would lock his door,
 The tenderfoot run like hell,
And the barkeep buckle on his gun,
 When he heard our rustler yell.
"The perleece would suddenly disappear,
 The dance hall man would grin,
And the monte bank would open up,
 To swallow in our tin.
"The girls would holler 'Hells old punch'
 And we'd shoot out all the lights,
The restaurant man would take in his sign,
 Fer he knew our appetites."
And the rustler felt in his pockets deep,
 In search of vanished wealth,
And said, as he turned his back to the town,
 "I guess the valley's best fer my health.
"No, I won't go to town for a couple of years,
 I'll stay out at the old ranch instead,
And besides, two dollars is mighty few paint,
 Fer to paint the whole town bright red.
"The rustler he hain't got no show eny more,
 The country's a settlin' too fast,
He'll go where the buffalo and injun hev gone,
 But he'll be a bully boy to the last." [58]

---
[58] Tombstone *Prospector,* July 7, 1887.

9

Outlaws and Apaches

Marion Williams was an oldtime rancher in Arizona. He knew every cow outfit in the country, and its owners. After John Slaughter had passed on to greener pastures, Williams bought the San Bernardino. Except for putting on a new screen porch it was left about the same way as the former owner had it. Looking toward old Niggerhead Mountain, Williams pointed to a graveyard that was surrounded by a rusted barbed-wire entanglement. The graves were unmarked. There were thirty-three there in all. Mostly Mexican share croppers, some were killed by Indians. Two were of interest. One of these was the grave of Apache May the little Indian girl; the other was where Arthur Finney was buried. The latter was an outlaw better known as "Peg Leg," simply because he had a wooden leg of the old peg-shaped kind.

Finney had shined shoes in Bisbee. However he was a tinhorn gambler and thief in his spare time. Tired of it all he decided in 1898, to go to Nogales on the border and hold up a bank. However, when it came to the moment of the holdup he was scared off by officers. His next move was to ride down along the border to Naco. Here he stole a horse and a Gallup-Frazer saddle belonging to Marion Williams. He then headed toward El Paso, which would take him by way of the San Bernardino. The theft was reported to Judge Starr Williams at Bisbee.

John Slaughter, because of his sheriff activities, had the first telephone line put up in his section of the country. It was made of iron poles, and had cut across the north part of his ranch straight to Bisbee. It would be easy for Williams therefore to convey a message to John to be on the lookout for Finney. As suspected, the thief did go by way of San Bernardino Ranch.

As usual the boss was up early and so were his employees. One, by the name of Rios, first spotted Finney and was talking to him when a man named Gillman, who had been out that morning at 6:30 to drive some stock, rode up. Finney wanted Rios to get a horse for him, which he, no doubt, wanted to add to his loot. He bargained with Rios, who was a Mexican, by running down the American rancher whose property he was on, thinking that Rios would respond to his wishes in this manner. However, Rios was loyal to Don Juan, and Finney made the mistake that cost him his life.

Peg Leg was a man who had a few tricks of his own. He had been tired after his experience and decided to find a nice shady tree on the edge of the ranch where no one would see him. To have this sleep he felt it necessary to make certain that, should he be caught unawares, he would not receive the bad end of the surprise attack. He put his pistol in his right hand with finger on the trigger and thumb on the hammer, and lay down with the gun in hand beneath him so as to conceal it. Then he rolled on his right side, facing partly downward. If anyone came by, all he had to do was raise up and fire his pistol, should the visitor be unfriendly. Finney knew he was on John Slaughter's place, and knew the type of man he was where thieves were concerned. The inquest over Finney's body gives an accurate account of what really did happen. Here, in the following, we view the results of the Slaughter-Finney shooting affair:[1]

---

[1] Cochise County Superior Court Records, August, 1898-December, 1899. Each of the three depositions was signed and sworn to before "S. K. Williams, Coroner-Ex-Officio," Gillman's on Sept. 20, and Howell's and Slaughter's on Sept. 19.

IN THE DISTRICT COURT, FIRST JUDICIAL DISTRICT
COUNTY OF COCHISE, TERRITORY OF ARIZONA
INQUEST HELD ON THE BODY OF ARTHUR FINNEY (Alias "Peg Leg")
Filed September 28, 1898
A. H. Emanuel (Clerk)

In the Matter Of the Inquisition upon the body of Arthur Finney (Deceased) Before S. K. Williams (Coroner)

Lloyd L. Gillman, being by me first duly sworn deposes and says:
Q. What is your name?
A. Lloyd L. Gillman
Q. Where do you reside?
A. I reside in Guadalupe Canyon, Grant Co., New Mexico.
Q. What is your occupation?
A. I am a sheep raiser.
Q. Did you know Arthur Finney during his lifetime?
A. I did not.
Q. Please state all the facts connected with the same, to the best of your knowledge to this jury.
A. Well, this morning, at about 6:30 o'clock a.m. as I went to the field to drive some stock out, I met the deceased, in conversation with Rios. I went on to the house, and met Mr. Slaughter, who told me that he had telephoned to the custom house, to get information as to the character of this strange man that just passed by, and shortly afterwards, a message came from Judge Williams of Bisbee, stating to arrest the man, and take him dead or alive. So Mr. Slaughter told me to get my gun, and to get ready to go with him, and we proceeded to carry out your instructions in the message.

We found Finney about one mile east of here, apparently asleep, under the shade of a tree, with his horse tied near him. We surrounded him, and advanced toward him, and as Mr. Slaughter got near him, he picked up his gun (Finney's gun) and threw it back from him about seven or eight feet. As he threw the rifle back, he told Finney, "You are under arrest", and as he spoke these words Finney raised up, and flashed a six-shooter, cocked and pointed it directly at Mr. Slaughter's face. And as he did this, Mr. Slaughter, Rios, and myself, all three shot at him, of which three shots took effect. The deceased fell back lifeless.

We then returned to the house, and sent Judge Williams a message and received instructions to care for the body as best we could, which we complied with, by beginning to bring the body to the house and laying it out.

Q. Have you stated all facts within your knowledge regarding the killing of Arthur Finney?
A. I have.

Lloyd L. Gillman

Sec. Witness Called
James A. Howell, being duly sworn by me deposes and says:
Q. What is your name?
A. James A. Howell.
Q. Where do you reside?
A. In Cochise County, Arizona.
Q. What is your occupation?
A. I am a sheep rancher.
Q. Did you assist John H. Slaughter in making an arrest of the person of Arthur Finney, this date?
A. I did.
Please state all the facts connected with the same, to this jury.
A. Well, about 7:30 a.m. this morning, Mr. Slaughter told me to saddle a horse, and to go up to a Mexican's house about two miles north of here, and see if this man (Finney) was up there, as he had told Rios, that he was going there to meet another man, so I went up there. And after staying there a while no one showed up, so I came back home. When I returned here, Mr. Slaughter stated that he had received instructions from Judge Williams of Bisbee, to arrest Finney. So I told him that I would go with him. So we proceeded at once to make such arrest. Mr. Slaughter ordered us to shoot him (Finney) if he began to shoot in resisting such arrest.

We found him about one mile from here, in an easterly direction. He was laying under a tree in Mr. Slaughter's pasture. We supposed that he was asleep. We surrounded him, and proceeded to close in on him, as we all got up near him Mr. Slaughter picked up his (Finney's) Winchester which was lying right by his right side, nearly against him, and threw it back behind him. And as he done this, it seemed to awaken him, and Mr. Slaughter told him, that he was under arrest. And as Mr. Slaughter said this, he raised up, with a cocked revolver in his hand, and aimed it at Mr. Slaughter. Mr. Slaughter then shot him in the hand, and the bullet passed through his hand and entered his breast on the right side. And about this same time that Mr. Slaughter shot, Mr. Gilman and Mr. Rios shot, of which all three

shots took effect, and Mr. Finney, fell back dead. We all came back to the house and stayed here until we received orders from you to take care of the body.
Q. Is this all that you know regarding the shooting of the deceased?
A. Yes, sir.

J. A. Howell

3rd Witness Called
John H. Slaughter, being by me first duly sworn deposes and says:
Q. What is your name?
A. John H. Slaughter.
Q. Where do you reside?
A. In Cochise County, Arizona.
Q. What is your occupation?
A. I am a cattle-raiser.
Q. Did you know Arthur Finney, the deceased, during his lifetime?
A. No, sir.
Q. When did you first see him?
A. I first saw him at about 7 o'clock a.m. this 19th day of September, A.D. 1898.
Q. Where?
A. Here at the San Bernardino Ranch.
Q. Did you speak to him then?
A. No, sir, I did not, because he passed too far away from the house where I was.
Q. Did you then have reason to suspect that he was a fugitive from justice?
A. Yes, sir, I did.
Q. What caused you to have such suspicions?
A. Because he passed as far from the house as he possibly could. He even went on past the corral, and off the road.
Q. What did you then do?
A. Well, shortly after he passed, a Mexican by the name of Rios (who works for me) came in, and I asked him, what this strange man wanted, and he told me that he (Finney) had one leg off, and that he wanted him (Rios) to furnish him with a horse. He also told me that the strange man did not want me or any other American to know that he was here.

I then came to the house and telephoned to the American Custom House, and also to Bisbee to find out what he had done. And in response to such telephone call, I received information from the

American Custom House, that he (Finney) had stolen stuff from there, and was wanted. And later I received orders from Judge Williams to arrest him as he was a bad man and would probably make a fight, and to enforce such arrest, and if he resisted, to take him dead or alive. And in obedience to such orders, I spoke to Mr. Rios, and Mr. Gillman, and asked them to go with me and help arrest him.

And just at this time, W. J. Chillis came along, and told me that, that was "Peg-Leg" and that you can't take him alive. I then told Mr. Chillis to come and go with me, if he knew the man, and at this time J. A. Howell came along, and told me he would go along too, and I told him, "All right".

So we went to make the arrest, as ordered. And found him about one mile from here, in an easterly direction, in my pasture. He was laying down under a tree, supposed to be asleep. So I walked up to him and took his Winchester rifle from near him and threw it about eight feet back, behind me, it was the only gun I seen, until I told him, that he was under arrest, and as I told him this, he came up with a six-shooter in his right hand, which was cocked and pointed his pistol at me. As he done so, I then shot him with my 45-85 calibre Marlin rifle.

The shot which I inflicted struck him in the right hand in which he held the pistol, and passed on through the right side of his breast. My instructions to Mr. Rios, and Gillman, was to all shoot if Finney showed fight. And as I shot they both shot too.

I cannot tell which wounds were inflicted by any certain one, but he was wounded once in the head, once in the breast, and once in the hip. We then telephoned to you (S. K. Williams) and informed you, as to what we had done, and at your instructions brought the body to the ranch and cared for it as best we could.

Q. Have you stated all the facts connected with the killing of Arthur Finney?

A. Yes, sir, all that I know of.

J. H. Slaughter

The above testimony is followed by the official coroner's certificate of death, including the statement "I caused to be interred his body on the 20th day of September, A.D. 1898, at San Bernardino Ranch in said County and Territory." The final paragraph of the coroner's jury report reads:

That he was a Native of Texas, aged about 28 years, that he came to his death, on the 19th day of September A.D. 1898, in said County and Territory. . . From the effects of three gunshot wounds, while resisting arrest. Inflicted by Deputy U.S. Marshal John H. Slaughter and his assistants, Lloyd Gillman, and one Rios while in charge of his official duties as such officer, and we hereby unanimously exonerate the said officer and party of all criminal proceedings. All of which we fully certify to by this verdict, in writing, by us signed this 20th day of September, A.D., 1898.

   Ed A. Wittig (Seal)   H. B. Strauss
   David Johnson   Art Markeim
   Peter Hanson   Charles L. Jones

John Slaughter admitted that Finney's six-shooter looked twice its size as he momentarily stared down its muzzle. The nervy little peace officer said that "it was the closest call I ever had." Perhaps his age suddenly made him realize a loaded pistol looked dangerous.

The Southwest has been full of Black Jacks. John J. Pershing comes to mind on the hero side, but before his days, there were at least three by the same nickname who are classed as villians. The original was Bob Christian, a Texas cowboy who had been imprisoned in Oklahoma for supposedly killing a deputy. He broke jail in the early 'nineties and came to southern Arizona. Christian got the handle because in the Chiricahuas he became a champion cutter of Black Jack timber, a scrubby oak used in building corrals, such as Slaughter's. A good-looking, easy-going fellow, expert at roping and riding mustangs, he was liked by all the cowboys and cattlemen in the San Simon, Sulphur Springs and San Pedro Valleys. He would often help ranchers at roundup time, shoeing horses, branding and cutting out from the herd. There was hardly a ranch house where Black Jack could not get a horse. Like Curly Bill, he was dangerous only when he drank. One day John and his brother Charley heard that Black Jack was over in

Silver Creek, somewhat inebriated, and invited ex-Sheriff Slaughter to drop by. John only chuckled, for Christian was not that bad, he reasoned.[2] Christian is supposed to have been shot to death in the spring of 1897 by "Crick Neck" Johnson near Clifton.[3] His gang left Arizona.

That same year another band arose, led by Tom and Sam Ketchum, cowboys from Tom Green County, Texas. It was this kind who gave Texas a bad name. They were broke and desperate when the gang reached Pearce. As Tom was very dark, the citizens there said he was liable to be taken for Black Jack, and so the nickname, temporarily without an owner, was adopted. The brothers held up a stage in the Stein's Pass country and later robbed a bank.[4] Their gang of four never mixed with anyone. Cowboys called them the "Snaky Four." Outside of stealing horses, and a few provisions, they did not bother the local ranchers. The Chiricahuas was their base, for robberies in New Mexico and Texas. The Tom Ketchum Canyon, striking out from the San Simon Valley, today recalls their route. Slaughter was out to get them, and they hated the relentless deputy. They, too, were friends of Burt Alvord.

Fred Moore, who in his wild younger days rode with the outlaws, was with them one day near Mud Springs when the famous rancher's name came up. Ketchum darkened and suggested, "Let's go down and kill that little rat-headed S.O.B." Moore had always admired John Slaughter, and he now tried to get away to warn him. Keenly observant, they

---
[2] Interview with Nancy Slaughter Tubert, Tombstone, Arizona, 1950. Charley Slaughter was appointed deputy-sheriff of Cochise County and sworn in January 5, 1901.

[3] Douglas *Daily Dispatch*, May 4, 1941. Contained herein is a story of the gang by Sam J. Hayhurst. He knew Christian. Interview with Mrs. Sam Hayhurst, Douglas, 1949.

[4] Tempe *News*, May 1, 1897. The *News* reported the supposed death of Black Jack, killed by a posse 19 miles from Clifton. Probably, though, he went to Cliff, New Mexico, ranched for awhile, and was killed by a posse there.

wouldn't let him slip off. As if Slaughter's Western magic was working, the deputy and Viola came riding along, Slaughter driving. As John spied the robber bunch, he handed the reins to his wife, just as he had done so often, and put his shotgun across his lap. Then, as if to dare them to the limit, he slowed his mule team as he passed the house and looked right at the bandits. Not a word passed until they were over the hill. The four men stayed silent until one spoke up, "Well, there he is, fellers; if you want him, go get him." No one volunteered. Slaughter's luck and nerve again succeeded. Not long afterward, the Black Jack gang broke up. Tom was captured and taken to the New Mexico penitentiary. He had a shattered arm from a gunshot wound after a train robbery, and was finally hanged at Clayton, New Mexico. His brother, Sam, died in prison.[5]

There was only one Apache Kid, but he was more elusive than a whole deck of Black Jacks. His raids were the last serious ones after Geronimo's surrender. Still, this Indian was not typical — nor were his maraudings really Indian raids. He was a renegade. He would as soon kill his own Apaches than massacre white men, and he was pretty much a lone wolf. Black Jack Pershing added much to his military experience dealing with this robber and murderer; yet cavalry, Indian scouts, frontiersmen, and two nations' governments failed to check him.

At fifteen, the Apache Kid had come to Globe. There he became an expert herder, learned English well, and then

---

[5] Leonard Alvorsen memoirs. Alvorsen joined the gang and soon learned all its ways and tricks. Once he shaved Black Jack with a dull razor. Alvorsen, knowing John Slaughter's reputation, warned them not to start anything in Cochise County. They never even stole one cow there! Alvorsen was eventually arrested by a posse, taken to Silver City, New Mexico, found not guilty by a jury, but jailed by the district attorney on a new charge. Later Sam Ketchum confessed on his deathbed that Alvorsen had nothing to do with the charged train robbery. Theodore Roosevelt signed his pardon March 29, 1904. Back in Douglas, he was made deputy-sheriff almost immediately.

fell in with Al Sieber, chief of the scouts, who liked him as well as the gamblers, miners and cowhands generally did. In 1878, the Kid was a member of Sieber's scout company and soon became top sergeant in the trailers. For unruliness at the San Carlos Indian Reservation in June, 1887, he was disarmed and put in the guardhouse. Furious at being humiliated, he stole a rifle and fled. Soon he was captured by Lieutenant Carter Johnson and sent to San Diego, but was returned when the Supreme Court declared for local jurisdiction. Although President Cleveland pardoned the Kid, the county court sentenced him to seven years at Yuma.

With other Indian prisoners, he disarmed his white guards on the way to prison and escaped. Now he turned to murder, and may have killed a number of persons. The Kid was feared from the Tonto Basin to the Sierra Madres. Occasionally, he returned to San Carlos to steal squaws, whom he sometimes killed, to avoid being betrayed.

John Slaughter knew this Apache well. When Slaughter had assisted Crook and Sieber in trailing Geronimo, the Kid and John passed many a pleasant time on the trail. In December of 1890, the Kid and his bunch penned up three white men on a hillside twenty miles southwest of the San Bernardino Ranch. Only one, Gus Hickey, escaped alive.

Hal Kerr said Slaughter wanted him to settle on the Cajon Bonita in Sonora, about thirty-five miles southeast of San Bernardino, since that would protect his lands as a buffer against the Apache Kid! Kerr hastily declined.

Fred Moore, Slaughter's neighbor, had several near escapes from the Kid. Three miles from Whitewater, he went into a Mexican's house to get a bridle. Something, maybe a share of Slaughter's premonition, told him to skedaddle. He ran half a mile. Later, Moore found that renegade Indians had followed him in an attempted cut-off. The tracks proved it.[6]

When the Kid used to hole up in the hills near Slaughter's place, the former sheriff wouldn't let his friends or hands go into Mexico by that route. However, he would let them go along with him when he passed that way. Viola's cousin was a victim of the Kid's party.[7]

In 1894 the Kid seemed to be dying of tuberculosis. A squaw he had finally freed told reservation officers the whole story. He recovered, though, and fled to the Animas.

Once Jess Fisher had trailed him through Mexico into the border regons, and Slaughter, with the cavalry, hoped to take him. Some of the San Bernardino cowhands were to scare the Indians into a camp below where the small army force was located. Slaughter was among them. Since they were still in Mexico, the soldiers knew that they had to be extra cautious. A squaw came down to gather the horses for her bucks, and seeing the troopers, she yelled back to the braves to warn them. Like a tornado, Slaughter leaped on a horseback Apache pony and raced after her. Leaning way over its side, he caught her by her long, black hair. Suddenly her resistance pulled him from the horse. In the commotion, she got away, but the cowboys began shooting and the soldiers failed to see what they were aiming at. At least one marauder whom they had mistaken for the Apache Kid, was killed. At this time, John Slaughter couldn't walk very far with his small and sore feet and a bad case of asthma, yet he managed to catch the pony – about the only victory in one more fruitless chase against the slippery Kid.[8]

Now, John Slaughter and Captain Benton studied the Apache Kid's movements. Slaughter felt it his old duty, for he had chased the Kid for many a year. His friend, Ben

---

[6] William Kent, *Reminiscences of an Outdoor Life*, (San Francisco, A. M. Robertson, 1929) for a good account of the Apache Kid; and William A. Keleher, *Fabulous Frontier*. Interview with Jim Hiler, jailor at Silver City, N.M., 1952.

[7] McClintock, *Arizona*, I, p. 269.

[8] Interview with George D. Stephens, Douglas, Arizona, 1950.

Williams, Bisbee's chief of police, had been killed in Guadalupe Canyon while chasing the lawless Apache.[9] Needing a fellow expert in range lore and mountain craft, he looked to Benton, who promised abundant help. In time, the Kid's trail was picked up, bit by bit. It was a geographical jigsaw puzzle. He had stolen a Mormon's horse. A trapper had seen his cohorts near Skeleton Canyon. Into the Sierra Madres, Slaughter and Benton went. Now the confusion develops rapidly. Joe Chisholm insisted that Slaughter lead the search afoot. His asthma and painfully sore feet would have made this seemingly impossible. Anyway, according to the legend, Slaughter and Benton dressed in woodcutter's garb. Hours of stalking followed. John recognized that someone had changed the Indian directions to water holes and was sure, according to Chisholm, that the Kid had done so. He also recognized crushed shrubbery. At dawn, his usual fighting hour, Slaughter is supposed to have built a shrub fire and crept two hundred yards farther south. The Kid, creeping toward the smoke, exposed his back to Benton. Due to the dim light, Slaughter failed to kill his prey at once. Reconnoitering, he fired at half-minute intervals, thus preventing the Apache from hiding himself. Driven delirious by thirst, the renegade finally dragged himself to the south end of his gorge. Four bullets were found in his body.[10]

Probably no one can ever prove the real end of the Apache Kid. Movies, fiction and studied history will try. Tom Horn, who knew most of the characters important in the story, said that the Kid finally did die of tuberculosis.[11] Others said that a posse made up of Ed James, John James, Walter Hearne, Charlie Anderson, Jim Hiler, Jim Keene and Burt Slinkart killed the Kid on September 20, 1907,

---
[9] Tempe *News*, April 29, 1893.
[10] Joe Chisholm, *Brewery Gulch*, contains this latest version.
[11] Tom Horn, *Life of Tom Horn*.

in San Juan Canyon, New Mexico.[12] In any case, John Slaughter's place in history is secure without this extra and uncertain credit.

In his later years, Slaughter was worried by George Musgraves. This fellow had gone outlaw when a man named Parker traded him a bunch of horses which he had stolen. When Musgraves found out and Parker refused to confess, he killed the thief. Musgraves then was only a boy, yet he threw a dare at Slaughter, telling the former sheriff's nephew that if the great lawman wanted him and a fat reward, he should come right out and get him. Slaughter sent word that he would do just that if it took twenty years.[13] Musgraves also became known as "Black Jack."

Bob Stevens, known in Cochise County as "Little Bob," was a noted Tombstone gambler. He had held up a roulette game in Bisbee, then stole a horse and had the nerve to ride out to San Bernardino, where Slaughter, on guard against the robber, killed him. The last fellow that John shot was a youth of about eighteen who had murdered a mother, son, and daughter for $300. Slaughter joined the posse and helped them hunt him down. Afterwards, despite the wild youngster's terrible deed, John Slaughter said he had hated to kill anyone so young, and would have liked to have taken him alive, but that the youth showed fight. The hangman would have done the job anyway. Even in his later years, John Slaughter was occasionally called upon to do his duty. In January, 1901, he was reappointed as deputy-sheriff, and once again on August 31, 1921, Sheriff J. E. Hood swore him in, along with his ranch foreman, George D. Stephens. The fighting spirit stayed, though he was in his eighties.

---

[12] Art Leibson, told this story, a supposed forty-year "secret." This was revealed in a series of letters from Ed James, a member of this posse, to the author, and also by interviews with Jim Hiler and Walter Hearne. — See Allen Erwin Collection, Arizona Pioneers' Historical Society, Tucson.

[13] Interview with Nancy Slaughter Tubert.

10

Business and Politics

A busy career as lawman may have somewhat interfered with John Slaughter's chores as ranchman, but it certainly gave prestige to his name, helping him politically. As a respected citizen, it also gave him business contacts which were later of value. In 1906 the Cochise County Democrats asked him to run for the territorial assembly, and John consented, though half-heartedly. What did this lack of enthusiasm mean to his backers? After all, they reasoned, he had been opposed to running for sheriff too, but his vote-getting and job accomplishment had certainly been satisfying. As Arizona was strongly Democratic anyway, they knew that he would have little difficulty in winning without a whirlwind campaign. He was no spellbinder, but his name and reputation were much in his favor. With little trouble, he won. The other member from his county was to be Owen Murphy, of the same party.

The next January, Arizona's 24th territorial legislature convened. The capital had been moved from Prescott to Phoenix a decade before, but this year the new location proved inconvenient, due to bad floods. Cochise County was almost isolated, and Slaughter was late to his first session. Along with John went his wife, Viola, and their friend, Edith Stowe, who expected a position as an employee of the legislature. She was not disappointed. The body appointed her fifth committee clerk.

Even in the role of legislator, Slaughter could not escape his old pastime, or his own great reputation. While the Bisbee *Review* was saying that he had "more to do with the capture of the Apache Kid than any other Arizonan" the Slaughters were passing through Casa Grande from Maricopa to Phoenix. Billy Stiles, outlaw partner of John's old aide, Burt Alvord, was then hiding out at Casa Grande, and Slaughter might have taken him, had he known this. Later, on the road to Florence, the stage driver told him. Since Edith Stowe and Viola were along, Slaughter dared not go back and try a capture.[1]

As member of the assembly, John Slaughter let others make the speeches and introduce the complicated bills. Meanwhile, he felt stiffer and more useless than his new fancy collar. Still, he was very rarely absent from sessions. Of course, his main interests were in irrigation and agriculture, and his chief proposal was to establish a state penitentiary branch at Benson, in his own county. Yuma was a poor location, as climate experts had told him, and he knew first-hand how far off it was. During his four years as sheriff, Slaughter had noticed the heavy county expenses entailed in transporting prisoners clear across the territory.[2]

Appropriately enough, he was made chairman of the assembly's County Boundaries, Agricultural and Public Buildings Committees.[3] When his two-year term had ended, John gladly came home.

As a businessman, John Slaughter was more active. His butcher businesses were usually very profitable. In February of 1910, he bought from J. E. Mosher of Bisbee for $2,500 the latter's one-story concrete butcher shop and equipment, including horses, wagons, and harness and supplies.[4] Five days later, he purchased from F. W. Arndt his butcher

[1] Bisbee *Daily Review*, January 18, 1907 and February 1, 1907.
[2] *Ibid.*, February 1, 1907.
[3] *Journals of the 24th Legislative Assembly of Arizona*, (1907), House Journal, p. 27.
[4] Cochise County, Bill of Sales Book 5, page 237, February 16, 1910.

business and equipment for only $650.51, in addition to his Johnson addition in Bisbee. The Central Meat Market contained scales, refrigerators, hooks, racks, two delivery wagons, a couple of delivery horses, a stable in the rear, and the business.[5]

Of greater financial return was the town of Douglas. Douglas grew out of Bisbee. The town was named for James S. Douglas, a Canadian who developed a new copper refining process and came to Bisbee in 1880 to procure new ores. He soon became a mineralogical expert connected with Phelps Dodge, which in 1885 absorbed the Copper Queen Mining Company. Eventually, Douglas became president of Phelps Dodge. His faith and courage, copper in the nearby Mule Mountains, and Nacozari, Sonora, as a shipping center, combined to furnish the base on which the city of Douglas was founded.[6]

In October, 1900, Douglas, with W. J. Brophy, John H. Slaughter, M. J. Cunningham, S. W. French, S. W. Slawson, and C. D. Beckwith, met in Bisbee and decided to start the town. To do so, the International Land and Improvement Company was organized, with James Douglas as president. The townsite was soon laid out by this company, and on January 12, 1901, a map was made of the original acreage by E. G. Howe. The new smelter was conveniently close at hand.

Slaughter and his associates knew frontier hardships as few can today, yet they planned a modern border city with no background of struggle. To accomplish their purpose, the Douglas Improvement Company was established. The streets were fixed to be so wide that the twenty-mule teams

[5] *Ibid.*, page 239, February 21, 1910.
[6] Glenn Dumke, "Douglas, Border Town," *Pacific Historical Review*, XVII, pp. 283-298.

could turn around in the middle of a block.[7] The Company was interested moreover in maintaining electric light and power, a telephone system, ice plant, and water works.[8]

On May 15, 1905, the town was incorporated. The founders might have minimized frontier hardships, but, like all border towns, Douglas had its rough side. The Cowboy Saloon, run by Tom Hudspeth and Lon Bass, was a nucleus of crime. Lon Bass was rumored to be a brother of Sam Bass, of Indiana and Texas. However, this was never proved.[9]

John Slaughter was also one of the organizers of the Bank of Douglas. Besides that, he and Charley Clawson, the superintendent of the Copper Queen, had taken up much of the land around Douglas.[10]

On May 19, 1906, however, for a nominal sum of ten dollars, Viola and John sold to Billy Slaughter lots 21, 22 and 23, in Block 74 in Douglas.[11] Meanwhile, Charley and his wife, Rebecca, had come in on the original division of Douglas. In November, 1904, they sold for $500 cash lots 2 through 7 in Block 22, of the Musgrove Addition of Douglas.[12] Still, John Slaughter acquired more land there. He built the San Bernardino Building, named for his ranch, on Nineteenth Street, between F and G Avenues. In

---

[7] Robert Glass Cleland, *A History of Phelps Dodge, 1834-1950*, pp. 135-137.

[8] Douglas *Daily Dispatch*, May 4, 1941. An article in this issue by S. P. Applewhite is entitled "City of Douglas."

[9] Captain Thomas H. Rynning, *Gun Notches*, p. 75ff. Rynning speaks of Douglas and of its badmen.

[10] Nancy Slaughter Tubert said that she took up a homestead at Douglas but that John Slaughter held her off. Nonetheless, she stood on her land with a double-barrelled shotgun and wouldn't let officers approach. A judge in Tombstone declared that she might remain. After that, she gave Slaughter a good piece of her mind. Mrs. Tubert was Charley Slaughter's daughter.

[11] Cochise County Records of Deeds, Book 35, page 289, recorded July 18, 1906.

[12] Cochise County, Real Estate Book 31, page 65.

JOHN H. SLAUGHTER IN 1907
As he appeared in the Arizona
Territorial Legislature.

FRANK "PANCHO" ANDERSON
AND THE AUTHOR
Pancho was raised by Slaughter,
and served him faithfully as
chore boy and chauffeur.

A Typical Saturday Afternoon Scene in Douglas, Arizona, in 1903
John Slaughter's white horse is seen at the left.

1912 he was renting it for $75.00 a month.[13] John Slaughter dealt in mortgages with many of his neighbors, producing an important source of income for him during these early years of the twentieth century.

By 1910, Douglas had begun to consider itself the "Gateway to Sonora."[14] That was probably an unfortunate achievement, for that very year the Mexican Revolution commenced. Francisco I. Madero, dreamy apostle of the first movements, found a great deal of his support in Sonora. Agua Prieta, just across the line from Douglas, was valuable to both Mexican factions, since it commanded one of the best passes in that region and had grown wealthy through Arizona's progress and its copper mines. Bullets buzzed across the border in April, 1911, when 250 Mexican rebels attacked the Mexican town. Six persons were accidentally shot in Douglas. Four years later, General Plutarco Elias Calles, who would be president of Mexico within a decade, retreated toward Agua Prieta, while General Maytorena chased him. Refugees poured into Douglas. Calles remained entrenched at the Mexican post. On November 1, Pancho Villa threatened to take Agua Prieta, and once more artillery and rifles kept Douglas residents indoors.

Bombastically, Villa threatened to seize Douglas if United States troops stationed nearby dared to interfere. Viola Slaughter could see American soldiers camped on a mesa close to her San Bernardino living room. Many Cochise County citizens were considerably jumpy about the situation. But former sheriff John Slaughter, sat on his porch and glared south to the Mexican side of his vast domain, watching the rebel soldiers. When he saw these

---
[13] This was leased to Russell Meadows, also of Douglas, for five years, beginning June 15, 1914. See Cochise County Record Book 7, page 116.
[14] Dumke, *op. cit.*, p. 299.

thieving soldados killing his cattle, he said to a colored cowpoke, "Pancho, go saddle my horse, and bring your horse, too." Then he put his shotgun in its saddle scabbard and mounted his pony. "Mr. Slaughter, what are you going to do?" asked Pancho. "I am going down and jump old Pancho Villa," replied his boss. He did just that! When the Mexican guerilla chieftain saw Slaughter, whom he had met many times before, he exclaimed, "If it's all the same to you, Mr. Slaughter, I'm staying here." The former sheriff was not moved by the rebel leader's thinly disguised threat. "You get into that saddle and vamoose, pronto," he said. That was the end of the stealing. Slaughter rode into the midst of the guerillas and came back with United States twenty-dollar gold pieces in his saddle bags, in ample payment for his slaughtered beeves! This, said Fred Moore, who can stand as an expert, was John Slaughter's "nerviest deed." [15] It was probably his most dangerous piece of practical business too! When Villa's gang threatened to take Cananea, Colonel Bill Greene, who had a big ranch there, told Mrs. Nancy Hunt Tubert, Charley Slaughter's daughter, "Well, if I had John Slaughter and his shotgun, there wouldn't be many left." [16]

Even without Slaughter's firearms, Villa's campaign failed. On November 4, 1915, he retreated to Naco. The next year, on March 9, he invaded New Mexico and attacked Columbus, where several Americans lost their lives. Pershing led a campaign against him, but since the Mexican government would not let United States troops use the Mexican railroads, and the American army officers refused to occupy villages, the wily rebel escaped. Slaughter and Arizona never saw him again, and in time he was killed by his own Mexican enemies.

[15] Interview with Fred Moore, Douglas, 1950.
[16] Mrs. Nancy Slaughter Tubert interview.

Meanwhile, Slaughter's opulence grew with Douglas. The town reached greatest prosperity in 1917 and 1918 with a population of 15,000.[17] John Slaughter spent much of his time there on business.[18] His old friend, Jim East, was chief of police there. It was, however, on his great ranch that Slaughter was happiest, and there he always seemed most like himself. He was born on the land, and thrived best when his roots were deep in the eternal soil.

---

[17] Dumke, *op. cit.*, p. 295.

[18] As early as August, 1887, John Slaughter's assessments by the Board of Equalization of Cochise County were raised to $600 – Tombstone *Epitaph*, August 18, 1887. With Herring and Shattuck, Slaughter purchased a quarter interest in the Guilding Star Mine – Tombstone *Prospector,* December 16, 1888. While in Sonora on sheriff's business in January, 1889, Slaughter bonded a valuable mining company. As a veteran, John Slaughter got soldier's homesteads. The first was Lot 2, Section 11, Township 24, S, Range 30 E, nearby, containing 21.17 acres. His second grant was of 80 acres, and the third for 40 acres in Arizona. See U.S. Department of the Interior, General Land Office, Serial Numbers 026075, 022521, and 026074.

At her death, Viola Slaughter left a large estate in stocks and bonds, many of them purchased by her late husband. She held: 1,167 shares of Devon Gold Mines, Ltd., 200 shares of San Diego Gas and Electric, 40 shares of Pacific Gas and Electric, 400 shares of Yuba Consolidated Gold Fields, 50 shares of General Paint Corporation, 200 shares in Shattuck Denn Mining Corporation, 100 shares in Dominguez Oil Fields, 15 shares of American Telephone, 80 shares of Walt Disney Productions (obviously purchased after Slaughter's death, since it did not exist in his lifetime), 40 shares of Creameries of America, 20 shares in Bank of Douglas, 12 shares of United Aircraft, 3½ shares of Boeing Airplane Company, 80 shares of Kern County Land Company, 354 shares of Douglas Investment Company stock, 25 shares of Tolan, Incorporated, 2½ shares of Talon, Inc., 500 shares of Jerome Bisbee Copper, 10 shares of Buick Mack Oil Company, 1,000 shares of Medine Oil Company, 300 shares of Cancelograph Company, 200 shares of Bisbee Consolidated, and 2 shares of Peoples Light and Power Company.

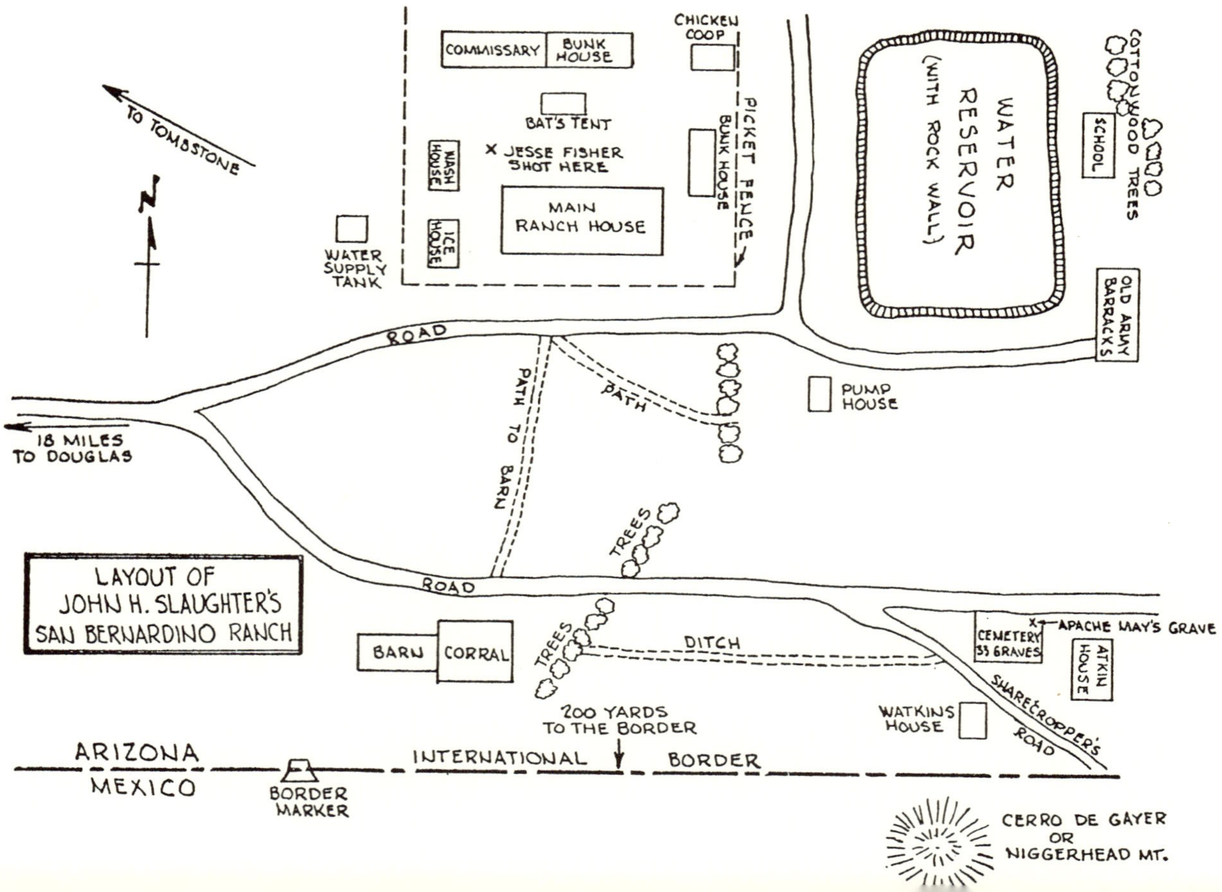
LAYOUT OF
JOHN H. SLAUGHTER'S
SAN BERNARDINO RANCH
COMMISSARY
BUNK HOUSE
CHICKEN COOP
BAT'S TENT
X JESSE FISHER SHOT HERE
WASH HOUSE
ICE HOUSE
MAIN RANCH HOUSE
BUNK HOUSE
PICKET FENCE
WATER SUPPLY TANK
WATER RESERVOIR (WITH ROCK WALL)
COTTONWOOD TREES
SCHOOL
OLD ARMY BARRACKS
TO TOMBSTONE
N
ROAD
PATH TO BARN
PATH
PUMP HOUSE
18 MILES TO DOUGLAS
TREES
ROAD
TREES
DITCH
BARN
CORRAL
CEMETERY 33 GRAVES
X APACHE MAY'S GRAVE
ATKIN HOUSE
SHARECROPPER'S ROAD
WATKINS HOUSE
200 YARDS TO THE BORDER
ARIZONA
MEXICO
INTERNATIONAL BORDER
BORDER MARKER
CERRO DE GAYER OR NIGGERHEAD MT.

II

Life on the San Bernardino

Viola had shouldered her responsibility since that day she promised to marry her cowboy friend at Howell's Arroyo west of Seven Rivers, New Mexico. She proved not only to be a good wife, but an excellent horsewoman. She would ride either side saddle or in cowboy fashion. The residents of Douglas, Arizona, still speak of her fine posture astride a sixteen-hand-high Morgan horse, riding in the parades. In many respects she was as daring as her husband. She would jump her horse over fences, water holes and cactus, when she first came to the San Bernardino. Later on she had all she could do simply to run the household and provision the commissary. Bat was always handy should she decide to pay a visit to the Hampe family or to the Raks she frequently visited.

Ranch life suited the young Missouri lady. As a girl, her mother, Rachael Howell, often had Viola ride to the Beckwith ranch, or to visit the Olingers at Seven Rivers. Her mother told her if she fell off she would get a whipping. Viola never did. In fact, she liked to jump her mount and was thrilled with the most spirited horse. If spankings came, it was because she took too many chances.[1]

Viola was a brunette, with expressive dark eyes. Unlike John Slaughter, Viola was emotional and temperamental. She liked to have her own way, but her husband always knew just when and where to put his foot down. He also used to make peace between his wife and the elderly Mrs. Howell, who was quite set in her ways, also. No one in the

[1] Cora Viola Slaughter memoirs, September 27, 1937.

family seemed to be weak-willed. Viola was changeable. She was a good friend and a hard enemy, a trait she shared with her great husband. However, even she admitted her self-indulgence in whirlwind whims. She might on the spur of the moment decide to go to town with Slaughter after she had already definitely refused. She liked to travel, too, and would sometimes suddenly decide on a long jaunt. Without much planning, she would leave. Slaughter, used to such quick trips in his sheriff's business, saw nothing odd in that. Together they traveled much, too.

John Slaughter was as completely devoted to his lovely wife as she was to him. Often before dawn he would leave to hunt, and later would serve her, and any guests, quail on toast. He took great pains in fixing this delicacy himself, instead of having the very capable Chinese cook do it. Being temperamental, the Oriental chef did not care much for this.

If Slaughter had any domestic sin, it was extravagance in the name of love. Whenever he went to town, first to Tombstone and later to Douglas, he came back with his road wagon loaded down. One jolly day he bought a surrey and drove it home for his wife to see. It was a shiny city affair with fancy new black running boards. Viola give it one long look and said, "But Mr. Slaughter, what did you get this for? We can't even get a suitcase into it." "Well," he reasoned, "I bought it for you so you could be comfortable and not be packed in with the provisions." [2]

Since Cora Viola was easily riled and was perfect for a tease, John frequently would play jokes on her. One day when she and her friend, Ethel Macia, were walking down the street with him, his sharp eyes caught sight of a little owl. "Do you see that?" he asked. They said, "No," so he whipped out his sixgun, saying, "Well, I'll show you," and

---
[2] *Ibid.*

immediately dropped it at their feet. On another trip to town, Viola was accompanying him down Allen Street in Tombstone, when he reached down and picked up a quarter, saying, "What's the matter, don't you pick up quarters on the street?" He made good use of the good that the Lord had given him. One annoying but amusing habit of his was to exclaim, "My God, Vi, don't you know one of your stockings is down?" She countered on one occasion with "Yes, but yours are down all the time." With high-topped boots, they never showed anyway. Disgusted with an old pair of pants he used to wear at the ranch, Viola grabbed a pocket and tore a hole from top to bottom. He chuckled, then reached for her apron and tied her to the gatepost with it.[3] After a little joke like this, he would pat her cheek and pin a flower in her long brown hair.

Other people used to josh Viola Slaughter, but this was perilous. One of John's cowboys told her that a little hotheaded ranch hand about Slaughter's size, named A. B. Carey, had four or five orphaned children in Texas whom he had deserted. Carey was working for the Lazy F outfit near Elfrida. Viola waited, her motherly instinct and natural sense of fair play making her boil inside. When she met him at Slaughter's dinner table, she gave him a generous piece of her ample mind, causing a tense situation between John and Carey. Fred Moore, a friend of them all, spoke up and explained everything. Slaughter and Carey at last cooled down.[4]

Generally, Viola's temperament was kindly. On their way to visit another ranch one afternoon, the Slaughters came upon Fred Moore, who had stopped his horses to wind them and was squatting just inside the quarantine fence near Silver Creek. Viola leaned from the wagon and called to

---
[3] Interview with Cora Gray Henry, Douglas, Arizona, 1950.
[4] Interview with Fred Moore, Douglas, 1950.

him, "Fred, you know I ought to take this buggy whip and wear it out on you." Her look was very grim. Moore replied, "Well, that's okay with me, Mrs. Slaughter." He feared a row with the famous marksman's wife. Then, with a gentle smile she could no longer hold back, she continued, "You have been here seven months and have never once been to our place." After that, Moore went to San Bernardino frequently.[5]

Viola certainly was a wonderful mother, although she never had any children of her own. When she married John Slaughter, his family resented her about as much as her own had opposed the wedding. They thought her too young, and there were various personality clashes.[6] This did not apply to Eliza Harris Slaughter's two young children. They always loved their stepmother. Addie was only about four, and Willie a little nineteen-month-old mite when they lost their mother, and they never thought of anyone but Viola as "Mama."

Mrs. Howell had thought that the two children might come between John and his second wife, but her fears were groundless. He had told Viola right after the marriage, "Why, Viola, I am not asking you to take the children. I intend sending them to my brother in Texas. Don't think I am marrying you to be a nursemaid." When they reached their new Sulphur Springs ranch, Addie and Willie were brought to them, and Viola tended to their many needs, until Slaughter could find an opportunity to send them on to his relatives. At first, his wife had thought this might be best, but it was not many days before she became very attached to them, and dreaded the time when she would have to give them up.

---

[5] *Ibid.*

[6] Georgia Hiler Hays, Stayton, Oregon, niece of John H. Slaughter, in a letter to the author, September 7, 1951.

She worried and worried, and finally sobbed out, "The children." John was startled and bewildered. "Why, Viola, don't be unreasonable. I will send them to my brother Billy the very first chance I get." Then she hurriedly protested, "No, I don't want them to go. I want to keep them myself." A big smile broke out on his tanned expressive face. In relief he caught her to him, and said happily, "Now, Viola, we will keep them, but if at any time you feel that they are interfering with your happiness, we will make arrangements with their uncle." Both had dreaded their leaving. For the first time, they had kept a secret, and a silly one. Needless to say, the children remained.[7]

Not long after that, Viola went with her husband on one of his trips in connection with his San Carlos government beef contract. The two children were left with Grandma Howell, who had plenty of valuable experience rearing her own brood. They had happy times, and probably were well spoiled. However, when the Slaughters returned, little Addie ran down the hill and threw her arms about Viola's neck, sobbing, "Grandma has been very nice to us, but I am so glad to see you."

Willie Slaughter was John's only living son, and naturally he became a rancher. For a time in 1898 he was a registry officer at San Bernardino.[8] He was about as short as his famous father, and quite a scrapper, too. He liked to get into fights with men twice his size, and Tuck Potter, whom John Slaughter also looked upon like another son, used to have to help him out. Viola often blamed Tuck, thinking he had caused the rough-and-tumble rows, but later found out that Willie was to blame.[9] Willie's temper made him some enemies, but none of them ever called him a coward. Un-

---

[7] Cora Viola Slaughter reminiscences, *loc. cit.*

[8] Cochise County, Records Book 4, page 342.

[9] Interview with Tuck Potter. Douglas, Arizona, 1950. Potter used to carry telegrams for Slaughter when he was sheriff.

fortunately, he had not only his dad's great heart, but his weak chest. Although Arizona proved a curing medicine for the elder Slaughter and his asthma, it did not stop young Willie from developing tuberculosis. Despite his weakness, in 1907, young Slaughter left the San Bernardino Ranch and bought the Douglas Hardware Store. He had a good business head, like his father, but the humdrum and confinement palled on him, and in 1909 his health broke completely.

Willie sold the business and moved to Phoenix where he hoped the dry climate would restore his health. Receiving no real relief, he returned to Douglas and gradually grew weaker. His wife and one son were with him, and did their best to help, but in vain. At 4:00 a.m. on August 25, 1911, the white plague carried him off. He was only thirty-three years of age.[10] Willie's wife bought a plot in the Douglas cemetery where he was buried.[11] Still much hurt by his first wife's death, Slaughter refused to go to the funeral if his son were buried beside his mother.

Addie was Slaughter's pet. Named for her beautiful mother, she reminded John Slaughter of the youthful young ladies in Texas so many years before. With her little brother, Addie had attended school in Tombstone during its hectic gun fighting days, when her father was sheriff. Addie was in town most of the time, helping her new mother as hostess during the leisurely, prosperous and hospitable San Bernardino ranching days. Then she went away to Oakland, California, where she attended Field's Seminary, a fashionable finishing school which her father had approved. Like many other well-bred young ladies of that day she liked to

---
[10] Bisbee *Daily Review*, August 25, 1911. Willie was quite a joiner. He was an Elk, a Mason, and an Oddfellow, active in all three until his health broke. The funeral was well attended on August 27th, in Douglas Masonic Hall, at Eighth and G Avenues.

[11] Cora Viola Slaughter reminiscences, *loc. cit.*

paint on canvas and china. She and Viola hit it off well all their lives.

Then, when Addie was thirty she met a young doctor. He had been born on Long Island and was four years her senior, but already William Arnold Greene was becoming a successful surgeon. His career was interesting and proved that he had lots of gumption. With little money and, formally, only a grade school education, he had become a druggist's apprentice for three years; then he was made a registered pharmacist. At twenty-two he had gone to Bisbee, studied a year under the Copper Queen Consolidated Mining Company's chief surgeon. Three years more at the University of New York, and a surgical internship at Bellvue Hospital, completed his medical education. Greene's first position as surgeon was on the staff of the C & A Hospital in Bisbee. The level-headed doctor was in love with John Slaughter's daughter, and she with him. Apparently the Slaughters were as well pleased with the prospect as was the happy couple, and a large wedding was planned.

Addie's nuptials offered Douglas society a big thrill. This was the first Episcopal marriage ever performed in the new city of Douglas. There on September 9, 1903, at 9:00 a.m. in the Roy Hotel the ceremony was performed. Only the closest friends and families of the couple were in attendance, but among these were Cochise County's most famous builders and pioneers. Of course, John Slaughter gave the bride away, while the bridesmaid was Edith Stowe, then of Bisbee. Willie Slaughter, the groom's good friend, who naturally had helped on the wedding, served as best man. Addie wore a pretty traveling suit and carried a prayer book given her by the Rev. Joseph McConnell, who performed the ceremony. She preferred this to the conventional bridal bouquet. The traveling suit was appropriate, too, for the newlyweds departed that morning on a two-week honeymoon to Chattanooga and Lookout Mountain, and to their future home, Chicago. Greene was about to start his new practice there.

Before they left, however, there were gifts to be seen – a generous check from John Slaughter, a chest of silver, cut glass and a luncheon cloth from Viola, and a silver coffee service from the bride's brother, Willie. The Howells gave a candelabra. Jimmy Howell brought a silver mounted buck horn cutlery set. Edith Stowe provided a cake dish and silver candlesticks, while the Minus family presented the bridal couple with assorted silverware. Other guests gave various treasures which would become heirlooms. At the time, Jimmy Howell was an assemblyman in the territorial legislature and made a special effort to attend.[12]

The marriage proved to be a very happy one. Greene served as medical examiner for the Equitable Life Insurance Company in Chicago for almost two years. They had three children, John Slaughter Greene, William Arnold Greene, Jr., and Adeline Howell Greene, the firstborn named for his famous grandfather, and the only daughter given her middle name in honor of Addie's beloved Viola. Greene died after a generation of marriage.[13]

John Slaughter's love for children was not selfish. He did not limit it to his own flesh and blood. When Addie and Willie grew up, he quickly acquired another big brood by informal adoption, and this ranch yard full of youngsters represented three races – dark, white, and red. He loved them all and treated them equally. They knew he loved them, and all children would come into his arms at first

---

[12] Douglas *Daily Dispatch,* September 9, 1903. See also Cochise County marriage license records for September 4, 1903; made out on that date in Douglas.

[13] Bisbee *Daily Review,* February 28, 1941. Addie died February 28, 1941, in Douglas. Her daughter, Addie, became Mrs. Parks of Washington, D.C., and was at her mother's deathbed. John S. Greene moved to Santa Barbara, and William A. Greene to San Francisco.

meeting. Perhaps inborn wisdom, the lore of childhood, told them that he, like they, was naturally what he seemed. He donned no adult's pose and polish.

John Slaughter was fond of dogs, too. One of his was called Bonita. It was a friendly little spaniel who followed the rancher everywhere. Another of his favorites was a little brown water spaniel named Curly. It would fetch out of the water, ducks that Slaughter had shot. The lawman always had a small pack of dogs about him and taught them tricks. Curly was friendliest of all and shook hands with all the guests. A well-trained cutting horse named "Scissors" was his lasting pride.

Mrs. Slaughter owned a parrot. The parrot was one with an extraordinary vocabulary and a keen memory, and did not need coaxing to speak. Mrs. Slaughter had her pet names for the beautiful bird, and much of her affection was lavished in kind words as she spoke to her parrot. She usually opened up her conversation with, "Do you love muzzer?" and "Muzzer's little darling, Muzzer's little pet." A few hours of this sort of bird talk was too much for Lt. Emory, who was camping with a company of soldiers on the ranch during the Pancho Villa uprisings, so he watched his chance, and got a private hearing from the fine-feathered, much-pampered pet. Emory would have daily consultation with the parrot when Mrs. Slaughter went about her household duties. He taught the bird a phrase that was very unpopular, and was contrary to what the parrot had been learning. One morning Viola went to the cage and lifted up the woolen shawl she had used to screen out the light. She greeted her pet by saying, "Good morning, Muzzer's little darling"; "Did Muzzer's little pet have a pretty sleep?" The parrot responded with unexpected sarcasm, "Muzzer, you go to hell – hell – hell."

Among the children John Slaughter brought up was

Arthur Fisher, Jr. He had come to the ranch when only a baby of two. His father was Viola's cousin who had had trouble with his wife, leaving no one to care for his little boy. Fisher, Sr. developed a large ranch in Mexico and took part in several campaigns against the Apaches. Slaughter was with him on some of these forays. Much later, he was shot while enroute to the Gabilondo Ranch. Little Arthur, too, was born for the saddle and spurs. Even before he was big enough to saddle his own horse without climbing into a wagon to do it, Arthur, Jr. was riding John Slaughter's milder mounts. One day he rode away and was never heard from again.

John always believed in giving the younger generation as fine an education as the children wanted and could profit by. He sent the Fisher boy to several schools, but he didn't care for learning and never would stay. Even in the lean years, Slaughter sent his son Willie, Viola's brother, Jimmy Howell, and Cora Gray to the General City Business College in Quincy, Illinois. He always felt that he could afford to provide money for learning. Cora was at the college for a year and later worked for a newspaper, the Bisbee *Orb*. After a time she met William R. Henry, a hide buyer, at the San Bernardino Ranch, where he was doing business with Slaughter. They were married soon afterwards and ran a hardware store in Bisbee. Often they stayed a few days at San Bernardino. On one occasion, they turned the trick on prankster Slaughter by pushing their porch chairs together and making him think they had stayed up all night.[14]

There was even a little adobe school built on the ranch. Slaughter, after some unsuccessful efforts, got the Slaughter School District established at his ranch on October 8,

---
[14] Cora Gray Henry interview, Douglas, Arizona, 1950.

LIFE ON THE SAN BERNARDINO 289

1902.[15] Edith Stowe, who had been educated at Tombstone and lived at the ranch most of the time after her mother died, seemed ideal to teach school there. For a time, she was the ranch's bookkeeper and helped run the commissary; then she finally agreed to teach in the adobe. It was built so that one could drive through the center in a buggy.[16]

Mae Watkins was no orphan, but just the same she became one of the Slaughters and received Miss Stowe's teaching. Her father, William E. Watkins, was one of the ex-sheriff's ranch hands. The Watkins and their three little daughters lived about a mile from the big house, but Mae, the youngest, was up on John's front porch most of the time. Mae had been only ten months old when she had a fast horseback ride one Sunday morning in 1901. Slaughter rode over where the Watkins lived on the ranch, and brought her back on a pillow. This became a regular weekend custom, and she loved to spend the day with Slaughter's increasing kindergarten. When Mae was 16, she learned to drive Slaughter's Model-T Ford and took him all around in it.[17]

Jimmy Howell was Viola's very young brother. He spent most of his early years there too, when his parents lived in Tombstone, and later moved to within a mile of John Slaughter's home on the San Bernardino. From the time he was seven in 1879, he saw a lot of John Slaughter. The latter sent him to St. Matthew's Military Academy at San Mateo, California. Later, Jimmy took a business and banking course at Quincy with the other youngsters. After that, John Slaughter helped him get an appointment, in 1895, as road overseer in the San Bernardino Ranch vicinity. Thus began a career that led to being manager and owner of the San

[15] Cochise County Minute Books, Book 5, page 215, October 8, 1902.
[16] Edith Stowe told Frank C. Lockwood, on October 9, 1931, the story of her life, in a letter. See Frank C. Lockwood, *Pioneer Days in Arizona,* p. 281.
[17] Interview with Mrs. Hal Burns (Mae Watkins Burns) Tucson, Arizona, 1950.

Bernardino Market, City Clerk of Douglas, and eventually to the Arizona Legislature. In his middle years, Howell settled down as a successful rancher in Sulphur Springs Valley.[18]

Viola's cousin, Henry Woods, had come to Arizona in 1879 and soon ran some cattle with his Texas in-law; Henry's son, Steele, was born at Slaughter's and became one more of the youngsters. When he grew up, and became as good a cowman as his dad, Steele was chosen by John Slaughter as his ranch manager, a *caporal* whom all the vaqueros respected. He stayed on for several years.

After Addie had married, and Greene had returned to Arizona, Mae Watkins used to go to their place and the family rode over to Paradise to spend their holidays. The Fourth of July was ever the big day.[19] Still later, little Billy and Johnny Greene were at the ranch, and nothing need be said about how fond John Slaughter was of his grandsons.

Often sources for the famous Slaughter chuckle were Blanche and Frank Anderson, a couple of little Negro children who loved John Slaughter. There were four offspring in the Anderson family, two boys and two girls. They were Ruby, Blanche, Andrew and Frank, arriving in that order. They were very poor and had no schooling whatever. One day Cora Viola Slaughter went to Piedras Negras where her cousins, the Fishers, had a coal mine. The Anderson family lived close by. When Viola saw them, she wanted to take them home right away. Blanche was nine in that year, 1894, and seemed the brightest and most winsome, so Viola asked Mrs. Josephine Anderson to let her go to San Bernardino. To back up the plea, Mrs. Slaughter promised the

---

[18] Bisbee *Review*, January 25, 1906. Only his wife and Viola survived him. The widow remarried, this time to Jack Stillman, friend of the Slaughters. See *Who's Who in Arizona*. (Phoenix, 1913) p. 547.
[19] Mae Watkins Burns interview.

JOHN SLAUGHTER AND HIS
GRANDSONS, THE GREENE BOYS
Teaching them some cow sense
on the San Bernardino.

JOHN SLAUGHTER SEATED
IN HIS FAVORITE ROCKER
With him are John and Billy Greene
and Gladys Watkins. The boots are
typical of those he wore all his life.

THE ADOBE SCHOOLHOUSE ON THE SAN BERNARDINO RANCH
Long since melted away. Shown here is Bess Nooningham who
shared the teaching duties with Edith Stowe.

child would get good schooling, free board, room and bringing-up. That same day they caught the train at Eagle Pass for Arizona. When Blanche arrived in the home where she would stay for six years, John Slaughter asked her, "Are you gonna like us, Blanche?" She said, "Yes," and she meant it, for she liked the old rancher the minute she saw his rough but kind face. Blanche had been brought up among Mexicans and knew Spanish about as well as English, so she could chat with Slaughter in either tongue. By washing, ironing, making bread and milking, she helped considerably around the house. Still, Blanche always had plenty of fun. When she first arrived, Slaughter had an old gray horse named Muggins. When he told a cowhand to go get Muggins, Blanche shouted, "Here I am," and ever after that she was known as "Muggins" to all the San Bernardinans!

John Slaughter enjoyed giving a child a gift even more than the young one was thrilled in getting it. When he went to town the kids went along, and he let each of them pick out their candy. Sometimes that almost proved a day-long chore. A Papago Indian used to come to the ranch. From him, Slaughter bought for little Mae Watkins a pair of beaded moccasins. He got Blanche a nice gold ring with green stones in it for Christmas, as well as good clothes from Bisbee. It took them a whole day to go to town, and they usually stayed two or three days, making a real holiday of the trip. On one of these jaunts, Viola bought the little girl a silver thimble and a doll, which she still had in 1952.

In 1900, when she was nearly fifteen, Blanche got homesick. She hadn't seen her mother in a half dozen years, so the Slaughters, sadly but with understanding, gave her train fare and off she went. Viola missed Blanche, and two years later tried to coax her back, but she was working for a family miles away and did not want to leave. This time little Frank said he wanted to come. He begged and cried until his mother gave her permission. Frank never went home again and bade his mother boodbye for the last time.[20]

Frank was always "Pancho" to John Slaughter, for that is the Spanish and Mexican nickname for Francisco, or Frank. Everyone soon knew what a lazy boy Pancho was. He slept in an adobe bunkhouse with Old Bat and some other hands, and resting there was his chief accomplishment. All the children had chores to do, but Pancho seemed to have been born tired. John Slaughter showed his sense of humor as well as mild disgust for a lazybones when he got a basin of ice water from the spring and dashed it in Pancho's drowsy face. After that, he got up early.

Slaughter bought him his first pair of shoes. When the boy was quite small, Slaughter left him in a wagon, while he went to buy a watch. Suddenly he looked around and there was Pancho. "What do you want, Pancho," asked Slaughter. "I want a gold watch, like yours," said the boy. Pancho still treasures the gold watch and chain with the original $20.00 gold piece attached to it. Even earlier he had wheedled some jewelry from Uncle John. Viola had wanted a diamond at Lloyd Gillman's store in Bisbee, but Slaughter, always the tease when his loved ones were concerned, just grinned and pretended to pass it by. In a few minutes, however, he telephoned the jeweler and asked him to bring the diamonds out to the ranch. Still he said nothing to the folks. Viola was as surprised as one of the children when he held it up to her, grinning like a ten-year-old with his first valentine. Now this didn't end the issue. Little Mr. Anderson wanted a diamond ring, too. How could John Slaughter tease so much! First he told the boy that his hands

---

[20] Interview with Mrs. Blanche Anderson Rogers, Van Nuys, California, March, 1952. Blanche was born in 1885; Frank in 1889.

were too big for one, but that was a pretty weak excuse for the little fellow, so the old rancher went to town and splurged $150 on a yellow gold ring with a genuine sparkler in it. Pancho's eyes outshone the diamond and were much bigger than the present. Though he was proud as a king, Pancho became careless. While swimming in Slaughter's reservoir, he lost the diamond and put his godfather into quite a huff.

Lloyd Gillman, the amiable jeweler who got all this business, was one of "Uncle John's" boys, too. He had come to the ranch as a young fellow with shoes worn through, hungry and tired. Liking him, Slaughter gave the boy a job and later sent him east for an education. He was with Slaughter at the Peg Leg Finney shooting. Slaughter gave him many a boost and started him in the jewelry business at Bisbee.

Just like little Pancho Anderson, John Slaughter liked things fine and shiny, so in 1912 he bought his first Cadillac. Earlier, Pancho had driven the wagon into town with all the youngsters scrambling over it. Now Pancho was elected to be the family's chauffeur. Even this did not satisfy the opulent ranchman. When the car got a little shabby, he bought another for $1,400. Viola was much more practical about such things. She knew a Cadillac was not built for rumbling over chuckholes and dry gullies, so she went out and ordered a Model-T Ford for ranch use. When Pancho wasn't showing off as a chauffeur, he had two horses of his own, given him by Slaughter, a black and a brown one.[21] John Slaughter had a sulky for his own prized racehorse.[22]

---

[21] *Ibid.*

[22] A Chinese youth driving the sulky from the truck garden was shot when his rifle accidentally discharged. He was hit in the leg and gangrene set in. Despite the herbs of an elderly Chinese from below the border and the help of Mrs. Franke Stillman, he died. Interview with Franke Howell Stillman, 1952.

For years, Pancho lived on at the ranch. He was good natured and willing to work, even if he was slow, and never outgrew his love for sleeping. When first asked by Slaughter if he could milk, he said no, but he would try. Asked if he could ride, he gave the same answer. Before long, Pancho was an expert at both, and lived at San Bernardino until he was drafted in World War I. Then he took a course in shoeing army mules and was sent to France. The first day back in Arizona, he put back on his favorite cowboy clothes, got drunk, and put up a good exhibition of early-day cowboys' fun by shooting up Douglas. John Slaughter was notified, chuckled, paid Anderson's $500 fine, and brought the returned hero back to the ranch. "Don't you know, Pancho," he commented, "that all the bad men are dead?" Then Slaughter who had made Pancho a cowboy, joined him in a good, long laugh. Pancho, however, didn't want to stay at the old ranch. A soldier's life had made him restless, so he got a job in Douglas. Afterwards he often came back to help Viola and John when they needed him.[23]

Another broken home like little Arthur Fisher's added one more child to John Slaughter's impromptu nursery. This was Lola Robles. It was a Mexican custom in the case of separation for the man to keep the daughters and his wife to take their sons. Thus, in 1895, Señor Robles was left with his little girl, an untidy child of five or six. Viola spied her and decided that she should live with the Slaughters. The poverty-stricken father agreed. Lola stayed with her foster parents until she married a man who proved to be unkind to her. Later she remarried and had several children in Tucson.[24]

---

[23] He would cook, wash and iron for them when needed. When their foreman, Jess Fisher, was murdered in 1921, Pancho dropped everything and without being asked came to the ranch and worked for several months. Cora Gray Henry interview.

[24] Cora Viola Slaughter reminiscences.

LIFE ON THE SAN BERNARDINO 297

Curiously enough, John Slaughter's most devoted youngster was born among the hated and feared Apaches, and it all began with the most brutal forms of murder. It was a full decade after Geronimo's surrender near Slaughter's place, but the Chiricahua Apaches were still restless. One bright winter day of 1895, a small band of them left the reservation and went wild with their new freedom, robbing and marauding throughout southeastern Arizona. A few innocent settlers got in their way and perished. A sad tragedy befell the Merrill family.

Horatio Merrill and his fifteen-year-old daughter, Eliza, were living on a Mormon settlement near Pima, Arizona. They had farmed in Cottonwood Wash, after coming from their native Utah a short time before. The father was on his way to Clifton with a load of grain when the Apaches struck. The Indian problem was something considered as being in the past, with the exception of a few young bucks straying off the reservation now and then.

Eliza Merrill was quite happy the day she sat up on top of the load of grain beside her father. She was dressed in her best clothes. Even though Clifton was a small mining town, to her this was a big event, and she was anticipating her impending employment with a Mr. Whipple who had a family and lived in town.

Horatio Merrill and daughter, Eliza, started out on December 3rd. They planned to go part way on the first lap, then spend the night above Solomonville at the Parks ranch. That next morning early, the horses were hooked up to the grain wagon, and with Horatio Merrill at the lines they were making excellent time. It was just six miles out that they were ambushed, at a point in the road west of Ash Springs. An account of the affair was published in the *Bulletin*.[25]

---

[25] Solomonville *Bulletin*, December 6, 1895.

H. H. MERRILL AND DAUGHTER, OF PIMA, KILLED BY INDIANS

Friday, Dec. 6th, 1895 (The Bulletin)
(Found dead in the road six miles west of Ash Springs – Moccasin Tracks Discovered – The Coroner's Inquest)

Wednesday morning, Frank Courtney of Duncan brought the news to Solomonville. . . It was at once surmised that the murdered parties were Mr. Horatio H. Merrill and his daughter, who had camped near the residence of John Parks, Monday night.

The dead bodies were discovered in the road near their wagon by J. L. T. Watters about 7 o'clock Tuesday evening as he was going home from Solomonville. When he rode up, the wagon was standing across the road and the horses had whirled and locked the front wheels and one of the horses had fallen under the tongue where it yet lay. The bodies of the man and woman were yet warm – and the killing had been only a few moments before. Mr. Watters hurried on to Duncan and notified the officers there, and Justice Haynie and Deputy Sheriff Black gathered a coroner's jury and came at once to the scene of the murder.

An examination showed that the parties who did the killing were composed of five or six persons, all wearing moccasins from which the natural inference is that the Indians are responsible for the bloody deed and have added two more atrocious murders to the already long list of human butcheries in Arizona.

The man was identified by papers found on the body as H. H. Merrill and his wagon was loaded with grain which he was hauling to the Clifton Market. He was shot twice, once through the heart and once through the head. His companion was his sixteen year old daughter. She was shot twice through the body.

In the wagon was a provision box. It was carried away some two hundred yards and left empty. What provisions were not eaten were carried away. Further on the trail some distance, a pocketbook belonging to Mr. Merrill was picked up. It contained only some papers and a small lady's ring.

CORONER'S INQUEST

The following is the proceedings of the coroner's inquest held on the Solomonville and Clifton road six miles from Ash Springs towards Solomonville. The following jury was sworn to inquire into the cause of death of a man and a woman found in the road: Tom Windom, W. Holland, Joe Terrell, Lee Windom, John Clay, Chas. Holmes,

Sam McMillan, John Woods, J. Putman. After viewing the dead bodies and wagon and discovering moccasin tracks of six persons, J. L. T. Watters of Duncan, Graham County, Arizona was sworn and testified:

Last evening as I was riding home from Solomonville, I came to this wagon about 7:00 o'clock and discovered two bodies lying in the road.

After trying to arouse first the man and then the woman, I discovered blood issuing from the man's mouth and was satisfied he was dead. I was not certain whether the woman was or not.

I placed a quilt under the head of each and covered the bodies and then released the horse from the wagon, it having fallen under the tongue. I then unharnessed the near horse and transferred my saddle from my horse to it and rode to Duncan and informed J. W. Black, the deputy sheriff.

I recognized the man as one who told Mr. O'Brien and myself on Monday, at the waste ditch of the Montezuma Canal, on the Safford Road that his name was Merrill and that he lived in Pima. This same woman was with him but I didn't know who she was. (signed) J. L. T. Watters.

J. T. Black of Duncan was sworn and testified:

I passed these two persons on this wagon on the mesa below here about 4 or 4:30 o'clock and exchanged a few remarks with them. I was on my way to Duncan from Solomonville. (signed) J. T. Black.

The verdict of the Coroner's Jury was as follows:

"We, the jury, find that this man and woman came to their death, from effects of gunshot wounds, fired by persons unknown, supposed to be Indians."

Sheriff Wight organized a posse immediately after receiving the news and started early Wednesday morning on the trail. The posse consisted of James V. Parker, W. H. Parks, Joe Terrel and John Woods.

Horatio H. Merrill, the murdered man, has been a resident of this valley for the past five years living in the vicinity of Pima. He was probably 60 years old. A hard worker, and a tender father to his family. He came here from Utah and settled on a piece of land in the vicinity of Cottonwood Wash where he spent his last dollar trying to make a home. He made a failure and moved into Pima where he has since lived. His daughter who was murdered with him was only fifteen years old, and was going to Clifton to work for W. Whipple and family. Father and daughter left Pima Monday morning in a loaded wagon of grain and camped at the residence of John Parks above Solomonville the same night.

Mr. Merrill leaves his wife and five children in destitute circumstances. The oldest child is a boy 17 or 18 years of age.

The Apache Kid is known to travel this trail when going to and from Mexico where his headquarters are believed maintained in the Sierra Madre Mountains.

Sheriff Arthur Wight and posse and manager of the Gebhard Cattle Company and several boys from his ranch came upon the Indians about 2 o'clock Wednesday the first day out. The Indians had stopped at the foot of the Witlock Mountains. The Indians saw the posse first and started on a run up the mountain, one on foot and one on horseback. Only two were seen. The posse pushed hard up the mountain but the Indians easily distanced them over the rugged rocks and finally disappeared over the summit. Where the Indians were camped they left a pair of moccasins, one blanket and a Bear grass saddle such as are used by the Apaches.

A black horse belonging to W. H. Parks' herd had been killed there and some of his ribs taken out which were left laying on some rocks. The posse followed the trail as fast as they could on their tired horses until dark when they spurred into camp for fresh mounts and grub supply. The point where the Indians were encountered was fifty miles from Solomonville.

Considerable time was lost at the scene of the murder before hitting the trail which first went north and then turned south.

Thursday morning the posse was back on the trail at daylight, which they followed to the valley south of Whitlock Cienega. After leaving the mountains the trail was plain and was followed on a gallop. During the day they found where the Indians had killed a steer and cut out a chunk of meat. But no sign of any stopover was discovered and the fleeing Indians had evidently traveled in the night. When dark came Thursday night, the posse went to Whitlock Ranch to camp and get fresh horses.

Not finding any horses there, Sheriff Wight and John Parks rode that night ten miles to a horse camp, secured mounts, and was back ready to again start the trail Friday morning. The trail turned west and north toward Solomonville and then back east into the Whitlock Mountains through which they had been Wednesday. The trail in the mountains was lost Friday and was not regained that day.

On Saturday, Frank Richardson of Whitlock Ranch reinforced the posse with several of his cowboys and Whitlock Mountain was thoroughly searched in an effort to regain the trail but neither was accomplished and reluctantly the posse disbanded and returned home. Joe Terrel was boss of the Gebhard Cattle Company.

There was general quiet throughout that winter. Then, on March 28, sixteen-year-old Alfred Hand was home alone, pondering over an especially tough algebra problem on his slate. The Hand's simple cabin at Cave Creek was not far from Slaughter's. Poorly furnished, its only decoration was a silken election poster on the wall. Even that was eight years out of date. They had some goats munching on the hillside and down the valley, and Alfred noticed that it was time to go get them. As he went about his humdrum task, some Apaches slipped up on him and clubbed the youth to death. Then they ransacked the cabin, taking the election poster.[26]

As spring grew middle-aged, the Apache menace became more than red-blooded pioneers could stand. John Slaughter had not grown soft with his fifties, so now he was ready to lead an expedition against the marauders. People had suspected the Hand murderers had gone to Mexico and were followers of the Apache Kid. Slaughter knew that he could find the trail. Not only did he feel duty-bound, but the Indians had stolen some of his best horses. Certainly the army had made good use of his services as scout before, so they were not hesitant in asking his assistance. Jess Fisher and Arthur Fisher, Sr. also went as army guides. John Slaughter was up long before the soldiers. Sleepy and grumbling, they started from his ranch. A few of John's Mexican vaqueros also accompanied the expedition.

---

[26] Rube Hadden, last man to leave the ghost town of Galeyville, knew the Hands well. He remembered Alfred's funeral and the G.O.P. poster which had been nailed to the cabin wall. Mrs. Walter Reed today owns the slate with the algebra problem still on it. Interview with Mrs. Earl Reed.

They rode through the Guadalupe Mountains until dark. Then on May 7th at 9:00 a.m., they found the first Indian camp. "It was on the highest peak in the country and a solid, almost perpendicular wall of rock on three sides from the south. It could be gotten to only by a narrow winding trail. There were two lookouts where the Indians had evidently posted men," reported Lt. N. K. Averill, who was by Slaughter's side. Where the rocks were not a natural protection, the Indians had built small fortifications of boulders. This made them almost invisible. In time, these were captured. Then the party went on to the next camp. By now they were about fifty miles south of the border. Once again it was the old Slaughter trick of a sunrise surprise. Before the Indians could give warning, the whole force swept in upon them. Slaughter, Arthur Fisher, Sr., and some vaqueros took the left flank, while Averill, Jess Fisher and the troops fell upon them from the right. Suddenly the Indians made a break. It was no rout, though, for only one was hit by the white men. As best they could, the braves and squaws rushed into the safety of the hillsides and sagebrush thickets.[27]

Now the party climbed up into the Indian camp where everything except firearms had been left behind. Even mother instinct was forgotten in one wickiup. As John Slaughter was searching through the abandoned camp he heard a cry, like that of a lost kitten. He knew a baby's whimper too well to be fooled. And there it was, a little copper-skinned girl, wild as a puma kitten. Beside her was an even more savage girl of about five, whom the party had to hold like a frightened deer to keep her still until an Indian scout could take her to the San Carlos Reservation. One Indian hater wanted to kill the girls, but Slaughter covered him with his pistol and roughly warned the man

---

[27] Cora Gray Henry interview.

not to try anything. Suddenly, some bucks with the canyon ledge as their target, began firing on the scouting party. About fifteen or twenty shots were exchanged. The soldiers were better marksmen – an Indian who may have been the baby's father tumbled down the Sierra slope.[28]

More calm than Slaughter with the infant find, Averill officially reported:

> We found a little girl, about two years old, and everything else they had in the world, four or five wickies full, a large supply of dried meat, mesquite and large hides full of water. Many large canteens and ollas full, several hides, etc., and a great deal of food packed up as if they were just going to start on a long trip. Seven saddles and bridles in good shape, a large quantity of plunder in Indian saddle bags and bags the squaws carry, most of which was evidently American with a few Mexican things, a complete reloading outfit for a 45-75 Winchester with powder and balls, shoeing outfits, hatchets, needles, thread, scissors, everything that one could think of; blankets, parts of carpet, fresh leather, etc., and also $1.25 in U.S. coin.
>
> We took what we could, threw everything else into the wickies with the straw, and burned it up, so that they were left without a thing in the world but what they had on.

In conclusion, he gave great credit to John Slaughter. "If it had not been for Mr. Slaughter," he reported, "and his man Fisher, we would never have been able to do anything, as they knew all the water holes and country, and took us by the cañons, as the Indians could have seen the horses if we had attempted to cross the hills." [29]

Already John Slaughter had made up his mind that the little Apache wouldn't be an orphan long. She was a bit over a year old, he judged, and dressed in outlandish garb. To keep her warm, John wrapped her in a brown woolen shawl and hoisted the little bundle up before him on his

---

[28] *Ibid.* See also Tombstone *Prospector,* May 12, 1896, for "A Papoose captured."
[29] Department of the Army, Office of the Adjutant General, National Archives and Records Service, No. 38312, file with 29451. To Fort Grant, Arizona Territory, N. K. Averill, 2nd Lieutenant, 7th Cavalry, made this report, May 9, 1896. He was at San Bernardino.

horse. Now, one would have thought the tough old rancher-trailer-sheriff had captured a vault full of silver and gold. He was happy and proud as a discoverer, but there was no vanity in this kind of pride, just tenderness, love, and bubbling humor. He sent a runner the fifty miles to his ranch to tell the folks of the baby's capture. All afternoon Viola shaded her eyes with her hands, looking for him. When finally she glimpsed him approaching, she peered forward to see the captive. Up he galloped, and there was the baby, dark and a little frightened, yet quiet. She seemed to know what was expected of a tight-lipped Apache. Raising the bundle like a trophy, he yelled, "Here, Vi, here is a little Apache for you."

Evidently his wife didn't think it such a prize, for she only answered, "Now, John Slaughter, you can just take that child down to a Mexican family and let them raise it." Cora Henry, her girl visitor, had taken in the whole sight, and ran up crying, "Aunty Slaughter, I'll take care of her and bathe her if you will just keep her." Well, Viola's heart was tender, and she melted as easily as butter in the Arizona sunshine. She grumbled a little, for after all, the hard work and responsibility would be on her.

Immediately she went to her sewing machine and began fashioning a dress of red calico with white flowers, while Cora Henry, then about sixteen, gave the Apache waif her first good Christian bath. From then on, "aunt and niece" shared the task of caring for the baby. Addie Slaughter had been visiting on the San Pedro River at "Cananea" Greene's home, but when she returned she made unanimous the plea to keep this Indian child. Since Addie was the favorite of both John and Viola, that decided the issue for good.[30]

When Viola went to remove the Indian baby's clothing, she discovered something that not only surprised everyone,

---
[30] Cora Gray Henry interview.

LIFE ON THE SAN BERNARDINO 305

but was the topic of local conversation for years. The infant's blouse was made from the top of Eliza Merrill's garment, taken after the roadside massacre that past December. Her full skirt was the silk election poster ripped from Alfred Hand's cabin on Cave Creek. Viola could still read the names of the Republican candidates of 1888; there was the name of Si H. Bryant, candidate for sheriff, whom Slaughter had defeated. The brown wool, fringed shawl which he had used to wrap the baby also belonged to the dead Mormon girl. Some other Indian effects were also picked up by the soldiers and ranchers. Among them were a couple of buckskin papoose carriers, which so fascinated Viola that she had her picture taken with the baby in one of them. A handmade wooden comb, one buckskin gun scabbard, an Apache necklace made from jumping beans, and manicure scissors – Indian style, made up the loot. Mrs. Slaughter also saved a pretty little pair of buckskin moccasins made for the new baby by a couple of Apache scouts who had accompanied the cavalry party and became attached to the child.[31]

The baby was soon a legend in Cochise County. On June 3, Viola and Addie took their combination pet, mascot, and daughter to Tombstone. It made a bigger stir than if the Earps had returned. As the *Epitaph* chronicled it:

> As soon as it became known that the papoose was in town, a steady stream of people visited Fly's Gallery to catch a glimpse of the young captive. "Isn't she cute," said each of the ladies in their turn, and the youngster merely calmly munched some cake. When our office devil, besmirched with ink and his new shirt daubed in spots came, the papoose immediately cast a smile of recognition – her features were covered with a most propitious smile and seemed tickled to death, which in turn was contagious to the ladies present.
> When George Thomas arrived, he brazenly made some remark

---
[31] Cochise County Probate Records. Last Will and Testament of Cora Viola Slaughter.

about her ladyship, to which the heroine took decided exception – proceeding to frown and at last to wreak Apache tears. George was driven out by the ladies.

The papoose is a chubby girl about two or three years of age, with a good head of coarse, black hair, large beautiful eyes, and for her size is strong and healthy, complexion that color which distinguishes an Apache.[32]

Probably John Slaughter never enjoyed playing with a youngster as much as he did with the little Apache. Right away he dubbed her "Apache May," because she was a Chiricahua Apache and he had found her in May of 1896. Before long, though, he and the other ranch folks affectionately shortened it to "Patchy."

Patchy's first English words were, "Look at the moon," or more literally, "Look, Moo." For a while, though, she was like a little wild animal and never did like to go indoors. After dinner, when the rows of oleanders about the house were watered, she would lie down flat on her stomach and drink muddy water from the ground.

In time, her beautiful, glossy, thick black hair had to be cut short in front, but the Slaughters always let it fall behind to her shoulders. This, her crowning glory, was the child's only vanity. Patchy certainly never was finicky or temperamental, and she didn't like strangers to fuss over her. She would eat anything, even scraps off the floor. When the sandman followed the sinking sun, she would curl up and go to sleep anywhere. In time, she did learn to eat from a dish and drink out of a cup. Mentally, she was a normal child, with any young one's interests, excitements and imagination. She finally had her own bed with Lola, but often slept with Blanche.

Patchy's only deity was "Don Juan" and she followed him all around the ranch. Second favorites were Slaughter's ranching neighbors, the Gabilondos. These jovial

---

[32] Tombstone *Epitaph,* June 3, 1896.

Latin Americans had a family of eleven – six girls and five boys – and brothers Rafael, Edgardo and Hilario helped make the clan complete. Their brother-in-law, Francisco Elias, was governor of Sonora. They used to buy beeves from Don Juan and run them with the 3G brand on their Guadalupe Canyon Ranch. All of them really loved the little Apache May and sometimes came all the way from their distant spread at Cuchuverachi, Sonora, to see her. To delight the baby, they once brought three little chairs forty miles by pack mule.[33] Josephine Gabilondo used to comb Apache May's beautiful hair and put her to bed. When Patchy would cry, all Slaughter had to do was place his hand lightly on her head, and she stopped at once.

All in all, the little Indian had a very happy childhood. Lola Robles, Arthur Fisher, Jr. and Blanche Anderson were her playmates. Slaughter was always good for some candy or a little story, and they could all stand in awe before Old Bat as he played his fiddle or cranked his sorry old gramophone, and as he made up his own words and sang in a creaky voice. They would always remember the "dimple" made in his cheek by an Apache bullet and his scuffed up old cowboy boots and high crowned hat. They liked to hear the old fellow's long winded conversations with his mules.[34]

As always, the ranch was full of enough pets to make up a small menagerie and entertain the young folks. Certain it was that animals and children would never be hungry. Slaughter's commissary had quarters for hanging beef, storing jars of butter, jellies, jams and other preserves, crocks of eggs, and shelves full of bottles and canned foods. By Patchy's day there were nine gushing artesian wells which allowed John to raise almost every kind of vegetable and

---
[33] Cora Viola Slaughter reminiscences, September 27, 1937. *op. cit.*
[34] Tombstone *Prospector*, June 19, 1888.

fruit. As an active sportsman, he kept their larder full of the best of game.

Old Bat too was a good hunter. Ranchers used to go with him. One of them, Charley Lockling, once shot Viola's pet cat for a rabbit. She never stopped teasing him about that. Another cowhand drank a whole pan of milk and his stomach puffed up so big that after that his chums all called him "Doggie." Not so funny was the time that Lockling was charged by a wild hog he had shot and thought dead. Only by an inch did he escape a tusk. More fun were the domestic kind of pigs. Slaughter used to hold greased pig chases at his ranch, and Bill Nash was the champion.

The youngsters even had an artificial lake or reservoir near the house, and it was ideal for hot days. The rambling main house was big enough to be cavern-cool in summer, and the harness shop had rows of saddles, blankets and ropes. Sturdy corrals were adjoining.[35] The children had a limitless playground on the ranch, and were never bored by cramped quarters. It was a peaceful ranch, too. John Slaughter spoke softly and never spanked his brood. It seems he didn't have to. They didn't always appreciate Edith Stowe's grammar lessons, but they were good on the whole. Blanche Anderson used to hide behind the stable and smoke where Viola couldn't see her, but this was a minor sin. Contentment was the rule.

Then came San Bernardino's saddest tragedy. Viola used to heat water in the ranch house yard in a big iron kettle. It was an enormous pot with four legs lifting it a foot or so off the ground. Here the help would heat water for washing clothes, and at other times lye was prepared for the family's soap supply. Patchy was always entertained by watching the big bubbling monster and the leaping red flames beneath it. One day in 1900 she played too close to

---

[35] Bernice Consulich in *Arizona Daily Star,* Tucson, February 19, 1938.

CORA VIOLA SLAUGHTER AND ADDIE
A photo taken at St. Louis,
Missouri, during the Fair.

ELIZA MERRILL
Daughter of Horatio H. Merrill. Both
were massacre victims of Apaches.
Eliza's dress was used as a garment
for the Indian baby, Apache May.

APACHE MAY
After she had been washed and groomed by Blanche Anderson and Cora Gray. This photo, taken shortly after her capture in 1896, was one of several taken by C. S. Fly.

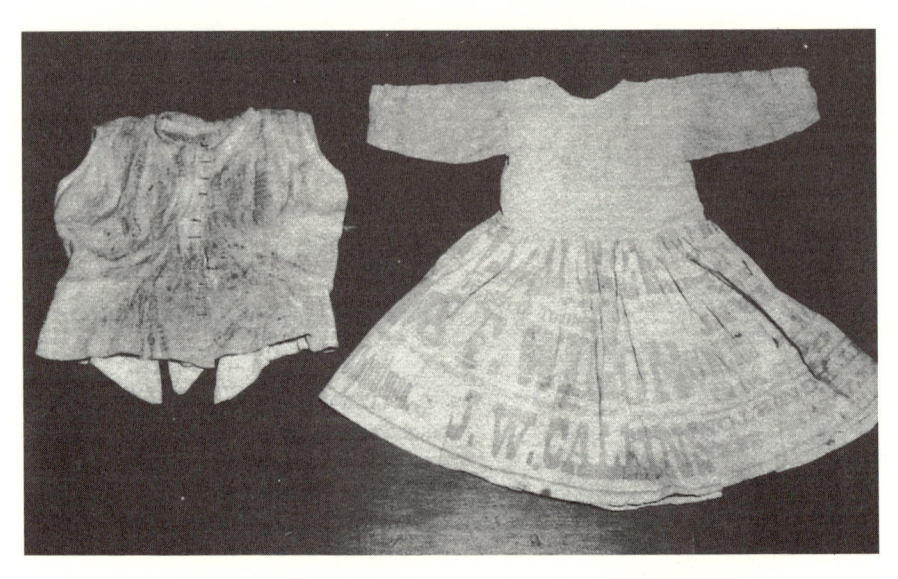

APACHE MAY'S CLOTHING WHEN SHE WAS FOUND
The blouse was made from Eliza Merrill's dress, and the skirt from the election poster, stolen from the Alfred Hand cabin on Cave Creek.

it, and her dress caught fire. Little Arthur Fisher was blamed for pushing her into it. Patchy began running and screaming. Jess Fisher, the foreman, raced after her, caught her in his arms, and finally put out the flames. It was too late. Her little body was terribly burned. They called into town for the doctor, and in a few hours he arrived. Patchy overheard him say that she couldn't live, so she called Slaughter and whispered, "Don Juan, I'm going to die. I heard the doctor say so. Goodbye, Don Juan." Then she said farewell to Jess Fisher. All through her last hours, she never cried aloud, and died as bravely as any Spartan-like Apache warrior. When Jess was making her little coffin, tears ran down his face every time he drove a nail, and John Slaughter wept in earnest. He didn't play cards for at least six months after her death. Quietly, she was buried in the ranch's cemetery.[36]

Like some people, Slaughter felt most sentimental at sunset. For months, at this time of day, he would sit in his old rocker on the ranch-house porch facing Mexico. He looked toward the country where he had first seen Patchy, and slowly, silently rocked. His face showed nothing, and only Viola knew what was going through his mind, and why his eyes were damp.

In time, though, John Slaughter returned to his old ways, and the big ranch family returned to its normal activity. The fighting rancher always loved to gamble. When he married Viola, he promised her that he never would bet again, because her mother objected. This was the only known time he didn't keep a sober promise. Then he began staying out late in Douglas; the excuse always was "business." One of his hands told Viola of her husband's cleverness at poker, and how he won a big herd of cattle in Mexico. When Viola asked her husband, he could hardly

---
[36] Cora Gray Henry interview, and Blanche Anderson Rogers interview.

face his angry spouse. At first her husband denied it, but later admitted his act. "I won't deny it any longer," he said, "but if I knew who the blabber-mouth was who told you, I would kill him."

Later, when soldiers were stationed on his ranch, Slaughter would go over for a game with the officers. Capt. Henry Ware Lawton was his favorite poker partner. It got to be a habit. He was gone every evening, and sometimes until two o'clock in the morning. As Viola and Addie used to take evening rides, he could hardly wait to see them gone. When the troops were moved away, John missed them so much that he taught his wife and daughter the wiles and worries of poker. He always put up the money for them and at first gave out forty chips at ten cents each. As they progressed in true Slaughter fashion, becoming real players, the amount was raised to a half dollar per chip. Then they began playing with other people, and since Viola was a reckless player, John finally said that she was too extravagant. After that, she kept careful track of her gambling bill for a year, and totaled up that she was eleven dollars and a few cents ahead.[37]

Steele Woods used to drop over at noontime to play cribbage. Fred Moore was a frequent player at the Slaughter table, his favorite being penny ante, and he marveled that John could round up cattle all day and play poker until after midnight. Slaughter and his cronies called it "saddle blanket poker" on the range, but it was just plain draw poker. Viola liked to bluff a lot, and this helped her win many pots. When she lost, Slaughter would observe: "You oughtta know better," and then follow it with a severe scolding.[38]

Not all of John Slaughter's card games were so Sunday-

---
[37] Cora Viola Slaughter reminiscences, February 5, 1939.
[38] Fred Moore interview.

school-nice in their outcome. He liked to bluff too, and would bet just as much on two deuces as on a full hand. Then at the end of the game he would settle up with gold currency and later checks. Five hundred dollars was not an unusually large pot to him. Sometimes Slaughter's poker parties upstairs in the old Gadsden Hotel in Douglas lasted twenty-four hours or more, while the players ate and drank at the card table. Slaughter was a good loser if honestly beaten. To catch a cheat in the game might suddenly inspire him to high-jack the whole crew and relieve them of their gambling money at pistol point. Barney Gallagher had been no exception. George Spindles liked to crowd danger, but was canny enough to know just how far he could go. Spindles was no gunman, but his personality and easy-going ways were perhaps more satisfactory to get him out of scrapes, and less dangerous. A great one to chew tobacco, he kept his light blond handlebar mustache well-dyed by the juice. He bragged he had the longest and fullest mustache in all Arizona. With his right arm he would mop his prize face-piece with a mighty swish in an angular cross-sweep to the left, so that the tips of his mustache joined together both on the left side of his face. In this position it hung oddly. Spindles was a remarkable story teller besides being a natural wit, and it was this bit of talent that could have cost him his life. Two card sharks blew into town; they had learned of Slaughter's wealth and his great desire to play poker. How to get Slaughter to play with them was something that took some careful planning. In their own professional sly manner they learned of Spindles, and after they flourished a good-sized greenback roll, he became interested in their proposition. Slaughter's usual hangout was in the old Gadsden Hotel, upstairs overlooking the main street. Like a fox, Spindles lured the tiger of the Peloncillas into what Spindles thought was a fine trap. The four men sat down and a new deck of cards was opened; the first few hands Slaughter won very easily. The card sharks knew how to take a sucker, and were gleeful to see the size of Slaughter's roll. The first half-hour all was in order; then as previously agreed upon, Spindles was dealt the top winning hands to offset any suspicion. What the card sharks forgot was that Spindles was a poor poker player, and Slaughter knew it well. The cards were dealt around until the stakes became bigger and bigger. As they grew, the beads of sweat began breaking out on Spindles' forehead, and the more violently he brushed into a vanishing point the corners of his much-tangled mustache. Things were getting just too hot, so a window was opened to welcome the cool breeze. With several thousand dollars on the table in the pot, each man built up the ante. There sat Spindles holding a royal flush. As he studied over his pat hand he became more nervous by the second. Suddenly the wind came up and made the money flutter. Slaughter reached in his back pocket and brought out a $500 bill, at the same time placing his pistol on top of it so it would not blow away. This was too much for Spindles. He jumped up and threw down his winning hand, cursing his bad luck, saying, "Dang those bum hands you fellows are dealing me. I quit!" Slaughter raked in the pile of money, holding two deuces. After the game the bewildered card sharks asked Spindles the reason for his action. His only reply was, "I like to live too well." Spindles later told his cronies that Slaughter ruined all his chances by putting that six-shooter on the table.[39]

Still, John didn't drink heavily when he played. He took his liquor diluted with water and kept up his spirits with high-priced Cuban cigars. One night steady nerves served

---
[39] Interview with Frank E. Hillman, Douglas, 1950. Hillman was foreman for B. A. Packard, 1917-1934.

him well. He had been gone from the ranch three days. He had a good foreman he could depend upon, and Viola was now spending most of her time at Dr. Greene's place in Douglas with Addie. This was one time Viola did some sobbing and pacing the floor. John had been fairly well intoxicated in this length of time, but he knew what he was doing. He had lost a fortune those three days up above Jim Graham's restaurant and bar, with some sharp poker players who were masters at swindling in a naive sort of way. The cards were coming from the barkeep down below, and Slaughter finally observed that not only were his drinks spiked, but that the keeper was in cahoots with the card sharks, giving them marked decks for new card packs.

On the afternoon of the third day of Slaughter's disagreeable poker venture, Bob Hiler, a nephew, had returned from the St. Louis Fair. He had just come in from Bisbee by carriage, where he got off the train. Viola pleaded with Bob to go to Jim Graham's and bring her husband home. Young Hiler consented even though he was tired from the long trip. He stopped the buggy in front of the restaurant-bar and entered. Here he found his Uncle John at the bar alone, just ordering a drink.

As Hiler entered, Slaughter perked up for a moment with surprise. "Why, Robert, what brings you here?" he inquired. "Auntie Viola," exclaimed the nephew, "she wants you to come home." "Well, you go back and tell Viola that I said she can go to hell." Then Slaughter told Bob to have a drink with him. Young Hiler never had a drink in his life, but thought this might be a diplomatic time to start. Then the foxy bartender brought up a half bottle of whiskey from under the bar, which Slaughter figured was the spiked variety. Hardly had the barkeep removed his hand from the bottle, when the angry Uncle John swept it to the floor with his six-shooter, breaking the bottle into pieces. "You damn sonofabitch, I ought to kill you now. You set up a new bottle and open it on top of the bar," growled Slaughter. Then he walked behind the bar and knocked off the glasses and mixed containers with his weapon. He ranted on and on, trying to get the saloon man to go for his gun. Finally Slaughter approached the bartender behind the bar, slowly advancing, his eyes narrowed, his footsteps firm, his hand by his holster, ready for action. Hiler quickly saw what was happening and ran behind his Uncle John, throwing his arms around him, locking them down. Hiler at the same time motioned the barkeep to keep quiet and leave by the back door. His gestures were obeyed in haste, and Slaughter was helped into the buggy. As they drove toward Dr. Greene's house the still angered Slaughter ordered Hiler to drive him by Luke Short's place. Short was a customs-house inspector and Slaughter figured this was as good a time as any to get him out of his hair. For thirty-one years the Texan had no one to spy on him as he drove his cattle back and forth on his ranch that straddled the border of Mexico and United States, and now he was having difficulty with the customs on his own ranch. Hiler was panic-stricken; he had just helped his uncle out of one mess, and now he planned another. Had Slaughter visited Luke Short, it is hard to say how much trouble he may have gotten himself into. As luck would have it, daughter Addie and Viola were standing out in front of Greene's house as the vehicle was about to pass, en route to Short's place. As if nothing had happened, Slaughter had snapped out of his fighting mood, quickly regaining a posture of sobriety. The incident was forgotten, but it left Hiler weak with fright. Ordinarily Slaughter was a quiet man, who stayed clear of trouble, but losing a few thousand dollars to crooked swindlers had revived his memory of more youthful days.[40]

---

[40] Interview with Robert Hiler, nephew of John H. Slaughter. This Luke Short is not to be confused with the earlier Luke Short of Dodge City.

On one occasion when Mrs. Slaughter was in a quarreling mood with "Don Juan," she threatened to leave her husband, so she ordered Old Bat to hitch the horses to the surrey and take her to Willcox to the train depot. All morning she ranted and raved about her husband playing poker and coming home late at night. Now she had packed her suitcase and was bidding John farewell. To make things worse, he just chuckled and said with little concern, "Well, have a nice trip, Viola." Soon she was leaving the yard, whipping the horses on a gallop in a fit of anger. Slaughter sat on his old gray horse with a big grin on his face and shouted, "Bon voyage." In about an hour the carriage with Bat at the reins drew up in front of the San Bernardino house, and Mrs. Slaughter got out, banged the screen door a few times to announce her return, and walked briskly into the cowboys' dining room, where her husband was peacefully having a snack. He did not look up or pay any attention – just kept right on eating. This got the best of Viola; things had gone just too far. She suddenly reached out and grabbed the tablecloth and at the same time, with a vigorous motion, spread food and dishes all over the floor. Now John got mad. "I say, I say, I say, Viola. I can get nasty too." With that, he put his number six boot up against the kitchen stove, and pushed it over. The lids, burning wood and ashes dumped right in the middle of the floor. With both of their tempers having found an outlet, they made up for the time being. Every once in a while, Mrs. Slaughter would have one of these tantrums, but John usually would just laugh.

There was always some sort of entertainment at the ranch. If it wasn't a card game, the folks were playing croquet in the afternoon. This wasn't for Slaughter. At home, John himself lived very simply, almost like a monk. He could never get used to most modern comforts, though he was lavish with his wife and family. John slept on a crude pallet on the bedroom floor. Ever since he attended a cattlemen's convention on a trip to Denver he was cautious. He had fallen out of an upper berth and broken a bone in his leg. No more high sleeping for him he said. He did like the color and happiness around him, though. Sometimes at night the Mexican hands would entertain with guitars and sing gay ranchero songs. Lanterns were strung and lighted to make the outdoor get-together brilliant. Slaughter served hard liquor, of course, but almost always held his own. As a steady drink he had adopted his Mexican neighbors' mescal, well aged.[41]

Slaughter always liked company, and when sitting in his front porch rocker he might glimpse some people driving up. He would rise with dignity and a big grin. If a stranger tried to be too personal, he would draw in like a terrapin. Generally, though, he went all out. Following the old Southern and Western traditions which all his people knew, he would ask anyone, stranger, friend or kinsman, to have dinner, and "stay a spell."

The house was often crowded, but there was no cramping of space, or stinginess of hospitality, for the table would seat twenty-five. The dining room was immense. The Chinese cook put all the food on at once. Its variety was astonishing. As host, John Slaughter was friendly, but not talkative. He never had been born a gossip or chatterbox, and he would not talk about himself. It took him some time to get to know a man, although he usually sized him up at first moment of meeting.[42]

At the Slaughters', dignity never climbed up to affected elegance, but everyone at Viola's table had to come properly dressed. All the men wore coats in that huge cowboy dining room. The master of the house sat at one end of the long, heavy dining table and Viola at the other.[43]

---
[41] Cora Gray Henry interview.
[42] Fred Moore interview.

LIFE ON THE SAN BERNARDINO 319

Mae, the Oriental cook, was a severe taskmaster. He would not allow anyone to enter his kitchen after he had cleaned up. No matter who the person was, if he or she used the stove, it had to be polished to its usual spotless shine. Lee, a Chinese gardener, delivered fresh vegetables weekly. He worked for Slaughter on the Mexican side of the spread, and had to return daily in keeping with the immigration law. Slaughter kept his money for him in a strong, old trunk, which was his personal bank vault, by his pallet.

There were many notables among the San Bernardino guests. Among them were Generals Gomez and Emilio Kosterlitzky, chief of the Mexican rurales. Many a time the Russian-born Emilio, who had trailed with and helped Slaughter, told big whoppers at the table, and even as the food passed around, he recounted stories too gory to believe. Each course brought half a dozen more oral killings. His experiences were elaborate and dramatic enough without the embroidered edges. He had deserted a Czarist man-of-war in 1872 to join the Mexican army. In 1886, Diaz had placed him in the border service. When President Diaz was overthrown, Kosterliszky was the last remnant of the old regime to give in. He did not surrender, but rode proudly across the border on March 13, 1913, and stacked his weapons near San Bernardino.

The Reverend Mr. Nugent, of Tombstone's Episcopal Church, held evening vespers for Slaughter's cowhands, and Captain Thomas H. Rynning, of the Arizona Rangers, who succeeded Mossman, was a welcome visitor, too. He made benches for the ranch school that the Slaughters had gotten Cochise County to support. Then the army of "brass" sparkled in all its military glory. Generals Crook and Miles

---

[43] John's brother, Charley Slaughter, whose ranch was twelve miles from Bisbee in an old fort area, was a frequent San Bernardino guest until his departure in 1905. Charley took carloads of horses to the shipping points and sold them at good prices at about this time. Bisbee *News,* November 9, 1901.

and their notable subordinates, Lawton and Crawford, dined with their old scout and his lady. Villa lurked about, but was frowned upon. After the bandit's defeat at Agua Prieta, a Mexican general dropped by the Slaughter home and handed them a sword with ornately-decorated handguard and scabbard. All he asked in return was some food. The officer refused to give his name.[44]

Not so illustrious, but quite as memorable, was a Dr. Rohn, one more of Arizona's tuberculosis health seekers. This dentist used to come out to the ranch just to drink the fresh, hot blood of cattle newly butchered there. He thought it gave him strength, and it seemed to. After a few months, the frail, pallid consumptive took on color, filled out to a muscular two hundred pounds, and declared himself recovered.

This was the life on John Slaughter's ranch. There were dull days, as well as hours of laughter and color, as there are in most people's lives, but even the humdrum wasn't boring when John Slaughter was about. He seemed to be everywhere too, for no cattleman was more active in tending to details and demanding as good work from his hands as that which he himself gave. He liked them all, and they returned the compliment.[45]

Full years are fast years, so the decades flew by at San Bernardino. Of all his enemies, only passing time could be the one his sixth sense and six-shooter would fail to stop.

---

[44] Bernice Cosulich, *op. cit.*

[45] Tad Roland, who had come to Arizona with Slaughter's first herd, died on December 20, 1888. Only 34, he was already withered away by rheumatism. Slaughter cared for him and was with him in his last hours. Tombstone *Prospector,* December 22, 1888.

12

The Final Roundup

There is nothing more beautiful to a man who has been a witness of the Creator's work of art, than an Arizona sunset. So picturesque is this magnificent sight, that it defies description. The purple haze of the Arizona mountains, and the colors that fall over the deserts and prairies when evening draws nigh is a spectacle no nature lover could forget. Perhaps the pioneer may have had hard times, but the compensations and beauties have been written in the pages of many an old diary. There comes the time when the body grows tired, but the mind remains active. At this time of life John Slaughter rocked in his chair looking off across his cattle kingdom. He must have enjoyed these beauties, with his confident feeling of accomplishment to compensate for his hardships, sadness and misfortunes. However, his days were finally coming to a close. Perhaps without knowing it he was contributing to a final chapter in the more rugged period of western history.

Toward the last the boss of the San Bernardino had been bothered by foot trouble. The thousands of times he had gone without taking his boots off had now had its effect. Sometimes his feet were so swollen he could not get the boots on. Toward the last he was using slippers, and sometimes used crutches. His feet were in such a condition he could only with great difficulty put them in the saddle stirrups; nevertheless he would manage to get himself mounted. His last ventures were accomplished in the back seat of an automobile. He made two trips back to Texas. One was in 1914 and the last in 1920. He had to see Pleasanton and Friotown. On the last visit he mustered up all his humor, and joshed with the old-timers, recalling days long gone by. As he rode around in a surrey he had remarked about the country. Not much had really changed except there was more brush land than he recalled, and quite a few buildings and barbed-wire fences. Still, many of the old landmarks were as he remembered them.

This being Prohibition time was hardly noticeable to John Slaughter. He had plenty of liquor on hand. He had Bat and Steele Woods help him bury many barrels of whiskey. Many spots on the ranch are said to have mescal jugs buried. Markers would either be moved or wiped out and the liquor remained hidden. Typical of old-timers of his status, he liked good whiskey. Often a good cattle or land deal was swung over a few jiggers of it, and border line riders that dropped in would be treated to a shot or two of this illegal contraband. The border rurales also were treated.

In May, 1921, Mary (Mamie) Fisher heard the telephone in their big white house in Douglas. She was the wife of Jess Fisher, a relative of Viola's. John Slaughter was on the other end of the line, and wanted to speak to Jess, his old deputy and ranch foreman. Jess had not been feeling too well, and had retired after many years of hard work. Don Juan explained that his feet were in bad condition and that he needed Fisher just one more time to conduct the spring roundup. Jess Fisher was reluctant, but just could not refuse his old boss. He went over to help out. John Slaughter was finally tiring. He was now eighty years old. Fisher was sorry for him, and understood the frustrating need of a man who had always been active. And now, Don Juan was sleeping way past daybreak.

His vast cattle spread needed a trusted and efficient hand, and there was nobody more first-rate than Jesse H. Fisher. Besides, Slaughter wanted Jess to help him with his land markers on the border, and Jess was a man familiar with the bounds. The Mexican Revolution was just winding up,

THE FINAL ROUNDUP

and John feared that if he wasn't mighty careful, he would lose much of his valuable land to the south.

Jess Fisher's past proved that he was the right man. A six-foot, two-hundred-pounder, with blond hair, light skin, and a jolly personality, Fisher was respected for his character, sobriety and strict truthfulness. Slaughter had gotten to know him well in the early 'eighties, for Jess was a relative by marriage. He had come to Tombstone to visit cousin Viola. Jess liked the country and stayed on. Slaughter sized him up immediately as a good man to have around. If anything, Fisher was too kind-hearted. Everyone knew it, and some took advantage of him. He would even back up their worthless notes. Slaughter made him his foreman, and Jess soon was carrying $10,000 in gold stuffed in his money belt. Old Bat went along with him, as he had with Slaughter. The sheriff gave Fisher the privilege of buying cattle for himself and running it on the San Bernardino range. He did not have to pay for their keep, as he would today. The Lazy B was Fisher's brand. The ranch hands liked Jess so much that they gave his bride a horse worth $175, with a hand-tooled Western saddle trimmed in silver.[1]

Jess had always vowed he wouldn't marry. During 1907, on visits to Mr. and Mrs. George Kelley of Douglas, they joshed him on his bachelor tendencies. Soon the pair had good reason to make it a joke. Mrs. Kelley's sister, Miss Mary (Mamie) Graham, of Columbus, Ohio, came to town. Within three months Fisher was a benedict!

The wedding was a quiet one at the parsonage of the Church of the Immaculate Conception in Douglas. It was October 24, 1907, and the Slaughters attended, along with all the Fisher clan.[2] Of the wedding gifts, the Fishers prized most highly a sterling silver flatware set, given them by John and Viola.

[1] Interview, George D. Stephens, Slaughter's former foreman, Douglas, 1950.
[2] Douglas *Daily Dispatch*, October 24, 1907.

The newlyweds spent a three-month honeymoon in Douglas. When they returned to the ranch, John Slaughter, who thought of Jess as another son, eagerly planned a big fiesta. Now, Jess was a very temperate man, almost a teetotaler. Still, he had a boundless sense of humor, as good as Slaughter's. His friends planned a little joke. With her wonderful imagination, Viola engineered the masterpiece. It seems that the Gabilondo brothers had given Jess a five-gallon jug of mescal, in jest, during his bachelor days. Since he wouldn't take a snort, they made him promise not to open it until his wedding day. This seemed a safe enough promise to him. With no delay he buried and forgot it. Now Viola had the ranch hands dig up the long-forgotten jug, and secretly stored it in her attic. Finally the big homecoming party took place. Everyone was invited, cowboys, Mexicans, neighboring ranchers, servants and the whole Fisher-Slaughter tribe. Tom turkey and cranberry sauce, pies of every description, pastries and punch were prepared by Viola and Mae, the cook. Then, in holiday spirit, Viola produced the jug for Jess, to the merriment of all the guests. Everyone had some of the ancient stuff. These frontier people really looked upon aged mescal as if it were Napoleon brandy, for it was rare. Some modest if not too truthful guests produced bottles to take samples home for their "complexions," and for possible "snake bite" use.

Fisher returned to his one-room meat market on Tenth Street in Douglas. When the town was founded, he had left Slaughter's employ and established this business, selling beef to the El Paso and Southwestern Railroad. Shortly after his marriage, Jess bought a small ranch near Douglas and erected a big slaughter barn to serve his market. Some distance away he built a big house with eleven rooms.

Now, he had given up his successful business to help out temporarily his old boss and favorite in-law. That spring of 1921, John Slaughter kept gold in his small ranch safe, just as he had for years. He was careful to keep the family valuables locked up, though the cowhands then all seemed trustworthy. Still, there was something in the air that night of May 5th. Things were just too calm. Jess wasn't superstitious, but when he telephoned his wife in town that evening, he said that he was unaccountably apprehensive. She felt the same. As usual, he called Mamie three times a day, the last time about 10:00 p.m. This evening he decided to stay in San Bernardino until late, so he told Mrs. Fisher to kiss their two sons, Gerald and Edward, goodnight for him.

About that time, Viola became a little "jumpy." Manuel, the chore boy, hadn't appeared for supper after he had milked the cows. Slaughter had a flock of young turkeys which might be killed by the predatory animals lurking around the ranch, so Mrs. Slaughter decided to look after them herself. Jess offered to go along and help shut them up, but Viola suggested that he go with Edith Stowe to attend to the chicken coops, another of Manuel's neglected duties.

They all left the house at the same time. Her task done, Viola was starting to return when she heard a commotion at a storehouse next to where Manuel and another Mexican, Pacio, lived. Then Edith called out her name, and in a few moments Jess said mysteriously, "All right." A second or so later, Viola thought she saw Manuel and Pacio rush from the shack, their exit followed by two rifle shots.

What had happened? Edith would never forget a detail of it. She and Jess had closed up the chicken coops and started for the house together. In the dim light they reached the cowboys' bunkhouse, when both were attracted by a rattling of the heavy wooden door. As they reached it, Edith saw it open just a crack, and it frightened her. She called out to Viola and began running toward the house. A few steps later she heard two shots. Looking back, Edith saw Fisher totter and fall to the ground, groaning. "I did not see who came out of the house, nor did I recognize any of the voices," she later testified. Viola, however, was sure that the killers were Manuel Garcia and Pacio Perez. She claimed that the light from the big house and Jess's flashlight beam proved it. Racing into the house, she screamed to Slaughter, "My God, Manuel has killed Jess."

The two trembling women thought that the house was being surrounded by bandits, so they hurriedly barricaded all the doors and refused to let anyone leave the house to investigate. Tired and sickly, John Slaughter insisted on taking charge. Harkening back to his sheriff days, he wanted to search for the marauders, but the women became almost hysterical. It seems that hunch had warned him better than it had Jess. Slaughter's habit was to sit near the north window in his living room, but that night he had gone to the bedroom. A strange warning, perhaps, but it saved his life, no doubt. Were his lifelong hunches still potent at eighty years? Slaughter was sure that he was safe, but to quiet the family, he agreed not to go out and leave the women unprotected. Although he took no more chances, John Slaughter would be ready for any invasion. With his rifle across his knees, he waited, calmly facing the big front door. Though a sick man, he wanted to go outside and shoot it out, but was restrained by his wife.

Now, Viola telephoned the Greenes, saying that they might not see them all alive again, for she thought she had heard Mexican bandits outside. A few minutes later, Douglas' chief of police, Percy Bowden, got a call from Mrs. Slaughter. The chief contacted deputy sheriffs Vernon La More, Ed Leahy and Fred Moore. The party set out in three darkened cars, ready to meet anything at San Bernardino.[3] Still with lights out, they drove to Slaughter's house. They got out carrying rifles, and went through the yard to the main building. "Who's there?" asked Viola excitedly. After

---
[3] Interview with Fred Moore, Douglas, Arizona, 1950.

Application for Re-recording of Brands

STATE OF ARIZONA,
County of *Cochise* } *Z on Right Shoulder*

John H. Slaughter, of *San Bernardino*
Name of brand owner or authorized agent

County of *Cochise*, State of *Arizona*, make the following statement for the purpose of complying with the provisions of House Bill No. 34, an Act of the Fourth Legislature of the State of Arizona, approved February 24th, 1919, which provides for the re-recording of all brands now in actual use, (the words "actual use" meaning only such brands as are kept up and brands not kept up on increase, but are holding brands on cattle, horses, mules or asses now actually owned by recorded brand holders), and which provides that no fee shall be charged or collected for the re-recording of any valid mark or brand which appears of record in the office of the Live Stock Sanitary Board of Arizona.

That *John H. Slaughter*, of *San Bernardino*, County of *Cochise*, State of *Arizona*, the owner, of *said* *Z on Right Shoulder* brand, recorded in the office of the Live Stock Sanitary Board of Arizona, in State Brand Book No. *5*, Page *2336*, and Numbered *16239*.

That the said *John H. Slaughter* is the owner of the above described brand by original record ~~or by purchase thereof from~~, ~~or otherwise~~.

That the said *Z on right shoulder* brand is now in actual use by the person herein named as the owner thereof and is used by *him* upon increase of stock or, (as the case may be), is used by *him* as holding brand upon approximately *2000* head of stock.

That application is hereby made in the name of *John H. Slaughter* for the re-recording of *said* brand, together with all earmarks used in connection therewith, the same being accurately indicated in the following diagrams:

RIGHT SIDE   LEFT SIDE

Brands for Cattle

RECEIVED
DEC 5 1919
LIVE STOCK SANITARY BOARD

Brands for Horses, Mules and Asses

That this application is made by the undersigned on *her* own behalf, or as a duly authorized agent for and on behalf of .... who *is* the owner of said brand and affiant knows of *her* own knowledge and not by hearsay that the statements herein made are true.

John H. Slaughter

Subscribed and sworn to before me this *3* day of *December*, 19*19*.

D. A. Richardson
Notary Public

(SEE NOTICE ON BACK)

RE-RECORDING OF THE BRAND WHICH JOHN SLAUGHTER
BORROWED FROM HIS FATHER-IN-LAW, AMAZON HOWELL

JOHN HORTON SLAUGHTER AT 80
Photo taken by Heath Studios of Phoenix.

JOHN H. SLAUGHTER AND DRIVER IN HIS AUTOMOBILE
At the San Bernardino Station north of the ranch,
a shipping point for his cattle.

THE FINAL ROUNDUP 329

being satisfied of their identity, she opened up, and there was John Slaughter, ready for business! He offered a $1,000 cash reward for the return of the killers.[4]

Addie's husband, Dr. Greene, soon arrived and found by his examination of the body that Fisher had died almost instantly. He discovered that three wounds had been made, two through Jess' shoulder blade and one in the stomach. The first couple of shots had been fired from the rear. There were bloody footprints from the body to the commissary; the killer must have also attempted robbery.[5]

Now a new element entered the tangle. John Slaughter's ranch hands, Manuel Garcia and Jose "Pacio" Perez, came in. They had quite a story to tell. Explaining their disappearance, they claimed that they had been late in their evening chores and did not start milking until about eight o'clock. While the two were doing this, they said five men approached the barn, took the two Mexicans some distance from the barn, tied their hands and left a couple of guards over them. All this lasted over an hour, and then the disguised pair, hearing the fatal shots, fled. In a few moments Garcia and Perez said they too lit out for William Hughes' place. This halfbreed cut their bonds and brought them back to Slaughter's place. As soon as they entered the door, Viola came alive. Pointing at Garcia, she insisted that he had fired the shot which killed Fisher, and in an excited scene she threatened the ranch hand with a gun. Bowden stepped between the upset woman and her suspect, fearing that she might actually shoot him.[6]

When Mrs. Slaughter had been calmed a bit, the Mexicans related that the five masked men in their story had threatened to return and kill everyone at the ranch.[7] Then

---

[4] Charles Proctor, "Murder at Slaughter's, *"Sheriff Magazine,* v, no. 2, June, 1946, pp. 59-63. See also Douglas *Daily Dispatch,* May 6, 1921.
[5] Douglas *Daily Dispatch,* May 6, 1921.
[6] *Ibid.*   [7] *Ibid.*

the officers separated the two, and surprising all present, their stories still matched. Now no one could be sure of anything. John Ross, Cochise County Attorney, began a careful investigation, and called in Lonnie Murchison, a Douglas police officer, and one of the pioneer fingerprint experts in Arizona. J. F. McDonald, also a fingerprint authority, made prints of Perez's and Garcia's digits. He also made one of a print found at Slaughter's commissary, proving it identical with Jose Perez's right forefinger. The two men claimed they had never been near the commissary, yet science had proven otherwise.[8]

The coroner's jury named Garcia and Perez as the killers. Brought to trial before Judge Alfred E. Lockwood the next September, the pair were convicted of second degree murder as accessories, and sentenced to life imprisonment. After about eight years, Garcia was paroled. Certainly the two were in on the killing, but they had not shot Jess Fisher. The murderer was Arcadio Chavez, who had looted the commissary, stealing food, ammunition and clothing. He rode off on one of Slaughter's mounts, leading others with him. One of them later returned, with the saddle dangling from its belly.[9]

For almost a month the true details remained a mystery, for Chavez fled to Agua Prieta, across the border from Douglas. Then, believing himself safe from justice and not wanting innocent men to pay for his killing of the unarmed Fisher, he made a statement of confession to Mexican authorities. Cochise County wasn't going to let it go at that. Immediately the county attorney made application to Governor Pina of Sonora for Chavez's extradition. Meanwhile, the murderer started a writ of habeas corpus proceedings to get free from custody. He failed. The Mexican Government applied to Consul Dyer of Agua Prieta to help them

---
[8] Proctor, *loc. cit.*, and Douglas *Daily Dispatch,* May 7, 1921.
[9] *Ibid.,* May 9, 1921.

in the case. Having all the facts, they moved Chavez to the stronger and safer jail at Hermosillo. There, at Hermosillo, he was tried and found guilty.[10]

Once the confusion about Jess's death was over, all the spirit seemed to go out of John Slaughter. Jess had been his right-hand man on the cattle range, outlaw trail or market jaunt. Even Manuel Garcia, who had so craftily planned to massacre his employers, had been trusted by Don Juan, and especially by Viola, who had brought him up, just as she had Patchy, Blanche and Pancho. The first thing she did when it was quiet again was to go around the house and gather up all the firearms. Apparently Slaughter did not object. In a few days, he left the ranch, never to live there again, although he would visit it and manage its affairs until the day before his death.[11]

As John Slaughter's feebleness progressed, all the soul seemed to go out of San Bernardino. There was little reason for him and Viola to stay on there. His grandson, John S. Greene, remained at the ranch after 1921. Modern conveniences made it easy for Slaughter to supervise and drive out to the place. Besides, Willie was dead and Addie and her family lived comfortably on Ninth Street in Douglas. So it was decided that the Slaughters too would move to the town the former sheriff had helped establish. He had business dealings there which needed him. Since the elderly couple did not need large quarters, they moved into the Fisher Apartments, named for their relatives. John's cronies would drop by in the evening. For a time after Jess's death, John wouldn't play poker, but gradually the late nights and the good times again took over.[12]

Slaughter suffered from eczema of the hands and feet, and often had to bandage them. Sadly, he shed his cowboy

---
[10] *Ibid.*, February 19, 1922, and May 15 and 20, 1921.
[11] Bernice Cosulich in *Arizona Daily Star,* Tucson, February 19, 1938.
[12] George D. Stephens interview; also Mrs. Calishier interview.

boots for carpet slippers. Towards the end of 1921, he was suffering from high blood pressure. The old pioneer could live at high speed no longer. In search of recovery, he made two trips to Indian Hot Springs, in Graham County, Arizona, and made some noticeable gain. After that, Slaughter had these health waters shipped to him. With the new year, he planned to make another journey, but gave it up because of poor accommodations at the springs.

Then, on Wednesday night, February 15, 1922, after getting back from a visit to the San Bernardino Ranch, he complained of a bad headache. Viola called Dr. Greene. The doctor remained with his father-in-law until after midnight, when Slaughter went quietly to sleep. About five o'clock the next morning, Viola tiptoed into the sickroom. In the old days, her husband was up and fed by that hour. Everything was dark and quiet. With his boots off, John Horton Slaughter had gone to the last big round-up.[13]

John and Viola had known almost forty-three years together. Shortly before his going, John knew that he was about to die, but showed no fear. He was sitting with Viola, and suddenly said quietly, "Viola, I want to ask a favor of you. When I die, I do not want to be buried in Tombstone. It will be only a matter of time before there will be nobody left in Tombstone, and I want to be buried where there are people." Only in doing his duty did he like to work alone. Despite his reputation as a lone wolf, Slaughter had always hated loneliness.

The funeral and burial were in growing Douglas. The services were simple, but friends were more numerous than if it had been the most elaborate of burials. It was held at the Greene's home. After the private rites there, the mourners moved to the Episcopal Church, where the Reverend E. W. Simonson conducted the service and followed it with

---

[13] Douglas *Daily Dispatch,* February 16, 1922.

a few simple personal remarks. The choir sang several beautiful hymns that Slaughter loved. The building was crowded, and many late-comers had to stand outside. Many friends came from Bisbee and Tombstone. The list of pallbearers was a roll of John Slaughter's best friends. The active members were: C. A. Overlock, an old pioneer; Rafael Gabilondo; and George H. Kelley, who had grieved with John but nine months earlier when their friend Jess had been laid away. James H. East, captor of Billy the Kid and fellow lawman, helped lift the bier, and John Grigbaum and H. M. Wood stood beside him. The honorary pallbearers were: B. A. Packard, rancher and student of the Slaughter lore; H. C. Stillman, who had known John for many years; and William Lutley, Tim Taft, Hugh Conlin and Judge Fletcher M. Doan. Many of these fellows hadn't cried in years, but tears flowed that sad Sunday afternoon. Finally the coffin was borne to the church door, and the cortege moved to the cemetery, for graveside services.[14]

Many considered the flowers the finest ever brought to Douglas. There were banks of many kinds; wreaths had been arranged as a bower on the altar's right side, and the coffin was covered with a blanket of the most beautiful roses.[15] He was buried beside Willie.

In his rough but far from vicious manner, John Slaughter had lived the Golden Rule. Born, bred and buried a Christian, he had lived in dignity all his days. No one recalled just what the minister said, but some years earlier a suitable verse had been written: "His life was gentle, and the elements so mixed in him that nature might stand up and say to all the world – 'This was a man'." With justice, this can be applied to John Horton Slaughter.

A few days after the funeral, Slaughter's will was read.

---
[14] *Ibid.*, February 19 and 21, 1922.
[15] Douglas *International*, February 20, 1922.

It had been drawn up on September 27, 1920, and left the bulk of his estate to his widow. His granddaughter, Adeline H. Greene, received $5,000; Edith Stowe, $6,000; and half the ranch went to Viola; one eighth to his daughter, Addie; 3/32 to his grandson, John H. Slaughter; 3/32 to the granddaughter above named; 3/32 to John Slaughter Greene; and another 3/32 to his grandson, William Arnold Greene. The residue of Slaughter's estate was divided equally between his widow and only daughter.[16]

Financially, Viola was well taken care of. And despite her loss and grief, she was in her way as brave as John Slaughter. She kept up her interest in the world about her and was as active in many endeavors. The San Bernardino Ranch now became the John H. Slaughter Ranch, Incorporated. On April 29, 1924, she turned the spread over to this company.[17] Then on May 27, 1937, the John H. Slaughter Ranch, Inc. was sold to Marion L. Williams.[18]

After her husband's death, Viola continued living in Douglas. She kept up with the fashions, too – bobbed her hair, and adopted current styles. As John Slaughter would have advised, she never let herself be conquered. She even claimed that she would like to be 104 or more. Just to be prepared if fate disappointed her, Viola went to the Bank

---

[16] The Bank of Douglas was executor of this will and guardian for John Horton Slaughter III during his minority.

[17] This included $111.36, all livestock branded Z on left shoulder, approximately 500 head, and the San Bernardino private land grant lying north of the border in Sections 10, 11, 12, 13, 14, and 15, Township 24, South Range 30, East, and in Section 18, Township 24, South Range 31, East G & S RR. and M., all in Cochise County. The boundary began at a mound of stones, the northwest corner near the head of Aston Springs and near the edge of Aston Gulch, then ran south 55° 16′ 26″ 100 cords, or 13,728 feet to the northeast corner, thence south 0° 11′ west 2,863 feet to the southeast corner at the international boundary, then west along the border 16,176.2 feet to the southwestern corner, then north 10° 45′ east, 1,019.4 feet to a monument of stones, then north 26° 7′ east, 10,705.3 feet to the northwest corner. It thus contained 2,366.6 acres with improvements. See Cochise County, Deeds of Real Estate, Book 91, pages 362, 371, Deed 91, April 29, 1924.

[18] Cochise County, Deeds of Real Estate, Book 123, page 368.

of Douglas in June, 1936, and made her will. This last testament showed that Viola still remembered her friends. To Steele Woods, the little boy she had fed and clothed, she left $1,500; Mae Watkins, who had been abandoned by her mother and had come to San Bernardino in poverty, got $500, and Margaret Watkins received a like amount. George and Nancy Stephens were left the same sum apiece. Pancho Anderson, whose hatred for the three R's had disappointed Viola, was not disillusioned with his $500. Even her maid, Antonia Olivan, got $500, as did Cora Gray Henry, John Hankin and Curtis Woods. The latter appreciated her prized Limoges china pudding set. Addie's doctor husband, whom Viola always greatly respected, received $5,000 and John Slaughter's big solitaire diamond ring which he had worn for half a century on the little finger of his left hand.

Most interesting of all was the large collection of historical material, real collectors' items, which she willed to the Arizona Pioneers Historical Society at Tucson. In this John Slaughter memorial were all the sentimental treasured articles connected with Apache May, her clothing and toys; and John Slaughter's famous equalizer, the pearl handled six-shooter with his name engraved on the handle. What a wonderful biographer of the great sheriff that weapon could be! He carried it every day from the late 'seventies until he took it off after Jess Fisher's funeral. One of his sawed-off shotguns, used when he was a sheriff hunting Chacon and others, now would hang in silence at the museum. An old rusted iron handcuff that Slaughter had found in abandoned Charleston's ruins was mentioned. What memories of badmen that item aroused! Then there were fossil shells, arrows, and pottery estimated at 500 to 1,500 years old. John and Viola had picked them up over the years as they mosied about San Bernardino. These relics had known the ranch even before the Apaches were there. Four Mexican spurs with large rowels had been saved. They were too big for

Slaughter's use on his horses. These objects were like manuscripts of the Slaughter story. They tell of the work and the daily living of the master of San Bernardino.[19]

Cora Viola Slaughter did not live to her predicted 104; instead she died at only eighty, just two months after Addie's death. Quietly she passed away on April 1, 1941. The services were conducted three days later at the Douglas Episcopal Church. By then, many of their old friends who saw Slaughter buried were gone themselves, but Sam P. Applewhite, Henry W. Williams, and George D. Stephens of Douglas, John F. Ross, Tuck Potter, and James L. Powell of Bisbee were pallbearers.[20]

John Slaughter had wanted to sleep where people passed. He was wrong in thinking that Tombstone would be a ghost town. But he was right in believing that Douglas would live and grow. Now that both wilderness and wildness had been taken out of the West by him and his breed, Slaughter knew that its future, like its old-fashioned optimism, had few limits.

There are men and women in the New West just as brave as were the Slaughters. They may not place as much faith in luck and intuition as did John Slaughter, but the fortitude and confidence is equally apparent. Slaughter was of the colorful Old West, and, as that philosopher with a paint brush, Charles M. Russell, wisely said, "The Old West is like a sweetheart. You might lose her, but you will never forget her." That today's Westerners love and remember Slaughter's day is a good guarantee that the West, old or new, has a quality as timeless as its gold.

---
[19] Viola's will was drawn up June 18, 1936 and admitted to probate at Douglas, Arizona on April 21, 1941.
[20] Douglas *Daily Dispatch,* April 4, 1941.

Epilogue

John Slaughter died in 1922. In 1937 Viola Slaughter sold the San Bernardino Ranch to Marion Williams. Subsequently, it was declared to be a National Historic Landmark and The Nature Conservancy acquired the Ranch. In 1982 it conveyed the east portion to The United States Fish & Wildlife Service to create The San Bernardino Ranch National Wildlife Refuge, and the west portion, containing all of the buildings, house pond, and the old military outpost, to a private non-profit foundation, The Johnson Historical Museum of the Southwest. That foundation, which is entirely privately funded, was created in 1978 by Floyd Johnson and Harvey Finks for the purpose of acquiring and preserving historic ranches, stage stations, and homesteads "so that the youth of tomorrow may know what it was like yesterday."

The original historical buildings still standing are the ranch house, ice house, wash house, commissary, granary, car shed and implement shed. Gone are the bunkhouse, blacksmith shop, and schoolhouse. The barn was previously re-built in approximately the original size and shape.

In 1984, complete restoration of all of the historical buildings was undertaken and the next year, the San Bernardino Ranch, as it had looked at the turn of the century, was opened to the public as the Slaughter Ranch Museum. It is the only one of the great Arizona cattle ranches of the 19th century that remains intact today. Its location, in a remote valley in the extreme southeastern corner of Arizona, made it invulnerable to both the vandal and the subdivider. So it remains today, a window on the past.

The Museum is open to the public Wednesday through Sunday, 10:00 a.m. to 3:00 p.m. Inasmuch as it receives no funding from any governmental agency whatsoever, a modest admission charge for persons 15 years of age and older is requested. Drive out from Douglas 16 miles on the Geronimo Trail, which is an extension of 15th Street. For more information, contact:

       Slaughter Ranch Museum
       P.O. Box 438
       Douglas, AZ 85608
       520-558-2474

Bibliography

Bibliography

INTERVIEWS

The following persons kindly gave their time during 1949-1952. Their helpful and irreplaceable information has been of great value. These are in addition to those mentioned in the preface of this book.

Anderson, Frank. Douglas, Ariz.
Barney, James G. Phoenix, Ariz.
Bennett, Fred. Tombstone, Ariz.
Blackburn, Charles. Tombstone, Ariz.
Bowden, Percy. Douglas, Ariz.
Bull, Mrs. J. Reno, Nev.
Burns, Mrs. Mae Watkins. Tucson, Ariz.
Cartledge, Mrs. Nancy Isabelle Harris. Austin, Tex.
Childress Bros. Ozona, Tex.
Church, Mrs. Amelia Bolton. Roswell, New Mex.
Cotulla, Simon and Paul. Cotulla, Tex.
Cull, John. Douglas, Ariz.
Drachman, Harry, Sr. Tucson, Ariz.
Epley, Ed. Paradise, Ariz.
Fisher, Mrs. Jesse. Douglas, Ariz.
Gordon, Jonathan. Tombstone, Ariz.
Greene, John S. Santa Barbara, Calif.
Harkey, Dee. Carlsbad, New Mex.
Harris, Ralph H. Austin, Tex.
Harris, Wayne T. San Angelo, Tex.
Hayhurst, Mrs. Sam. Douglas, Ariz.
Hearne, Walter. Hot Springs, New Mex.
Henry, Mrs. Cora Gray Douglas, Ariz.
Higdon, William M. Pearsall, Tex.
Hiler, Jim. Silver City, New Mex.
Hillman, Frank E. Douglas, Ariz.
Hunter, J. Marvin. Bandera, Tex.
Hunsaker, Lois. Hermitage Ranch, Cochise County

Kerr, Hal. Deming, New Mex.
King, Manuel. Tucson, Ariz.
Krantz, Frank. Texas Canyon, Ariz.
Lamb, Mrs. Mary. Tombstone, Ariz.
Larrieu, Judge. Tombstone, Ariz.
Lauderdale, Nannie. Pleasanton, Tex.
Lutley, Mrs. William. Tombstone, Ariz.
McClure, Mrs. J. Douglas, Ariz.
Merril, John. St. David, Ariz.
Milton, Mrs. Jeff. Tucson, Ariz.
Moore, Fred. Douglas, Ariz.
Paul, Alfred, Sr. Douglas, Ariz.
Pearson, John. San Marcos, Tex.
Petersen, Pete. Douglas, Ariz.
Potter, Tuck. Douglas, Ariz.
Reed, Mrs. Earl. Douglas, Ariz.
Roberts, Ed. Pearsall, Tex.
Rogers, Mrs. Blanche Anderson. Van Nuys, Calif.
Ross, John. Tombstone, Ariz.
Sanderson, Roy. Phoenix, Ariz.
Scheerer, George. Douglas, Ariz.
Slaughter, Mr. and Mrs. George. Roswell, New Mex.
Slaughter, Mrs. Sallie Slaughter. Carlsbad, New Mex.
Smith, Wager. Albuquerque, New Mex.
Stillman, Mrs. Franke Howell. Douglas, Ariz.
Stillman, Jack. Douglas, Ariz.
Taylor, Hugh A. San Antonio, Tex.
Tubert, Mrs. Nancy Slaughter. Tombstone, Ariz.
Walters, Rose M. (Mrs. Lorenzo). Tucson, Ariz.
Woods, Gladys and Steele. Douglas, Ariz.

CORRESPONDENCE

During the preparation of this book the author exchanged correspondence with the following persons, whose information was of great help.

Bagby, Commander Oliver W., u.s.n. Arlington, Va., Jan. 11, 1951
Bergin, Maj.-Gen. William E., u.s.a. Washington, d.c., May-June 1951
Coles, Charles H. Colt Museum, Hartford, Conn., Apr. 13, 1950
Edgington, L. Edward. Alamagordo, New Mex., May 5, 1952
Fulton, Maurice G. Roswell, New Mex., Apr.-June 1952
Fitzgerald, Mrs. Minnie Minus. Yuma, Ariz., Apr.-May 1950

BIBLIOGRAPHY 343

Godbold, Mrs. Annie. Leakey, Tex., Feb. 6, 15, 1951
Hayden, Carl, U.S. Senator from Arizona. Washington, D.C., 1949-1951
Hays, Mrs. Georgia Hiler. Stayton, Oreg., Jan.-March 1952
Hiler, Robert. Douglas, Ariz., Apr. 7, 1950
Jackson, F.R. San Francisco, Calif., June 18, 1950
James, Ed. Chloride, New Mex., March 24, 29, Apr. 13, 15, 29, 1950
Lucas, Mrs. Fannie Slaughter. Carlsbad, New Mex., Feb-March 1951
Rheiner, Dan J. San Antonio, Tex., May 8, 22, 1952
Roberts, Mrs. Artie Slaughter. Pearsall, Tex., Nov. 15, 28, Dec. 28, 1950, Apr. 29, 1951
Veal, Mrs. Minnie Slaughter. Dallas, Tex., April 1950
Witter, Webster. San Antonio, Tex., May 1951

MANUSCRIPTS

The Arizona Pioneers Historical Society Library at the University of Arizona, Tucson, is rich not only in Southwestern newspapers and periodicals, but also in manuscripts relating to Arizonans. Most useful for this study have been the reminiscences of pioneers, now gone – particularly the following:

Alvorsen, Leonard. Ms books of memoirs, Douglas, 1938
Boller, Robert M. Reminiscences, as told to Mrs. George F. Kitt
Breakenridge, Col. William M. Reminiscences, as told to Mrs. George F. Kitt, 1927
Dow, Mary Neatherlin. "Memories of a Pioneer Woman," typescript
Franklin, A.M. "Story of Ringo and the Cattle Thieves," as told to A. M. Widdowsen
Hand, George O. Diary
Merril, John S. Manuscripts
Nichols, Charles A. Reminiscences
Roskruge, George J. Reminiscences, as told to Mrs. George F. Kitt, 1928
Slaughter, Cora Viola (Mrs. John H.) Reminiscences, 1939
Smith, Mrs. Rosa Anna. Reminiscences

OFFICIAL RECORDS

United States, National Archives, Washington, D.C.
Records of the General Land Office, Arizona Private Land Claims
Records of Forts Apache, Bowie, Huachuca and Thomas, Arizona Territory, 1877-1887

Congressional Record, 56 Cong., 1 sess., for "Report of Capt. H. W. Lawton, 4th Cavalry, 1886."
Arizona, Territory of
  Cochise County, Bisbee: Miscellaneous Records, 1880 on
  ———: Court Records, 1890-1896
  ———: Coroner's Reports, 1882-1891
  ———: Sats. of Mtg., 1898-1916
Louisiana
  State Land Office, Baton Rouge: Rio Grande Claims, 1823
New Mexico, Territory of
  Eddy County, Carlsbad: Records of Deeds, 1876-1888
  Lincoln County, Carrizozo: Miscellaneous Records, 1876-1888
  San Miguel County, Las Vegas
  Santa Fe County, Santa Fe
Texas: State Records, Austin
  Atascosa County, Pleasanton: Miscellaneous Records, 1859-1875
  Bexar County, San Antonio: Miscellaneous Records
  ———: Records of Deeds, 1874-1880
  Caldwell County, Lockhart: Records of Deeds, 1850-1855
  Frio County, Pearsall: Bills of Sale Records, 1873-1888
  ———: Poll Tax Records, 1876
  ———: Survey Books, 1885-1888
  La Salle County, Cotulla: Patent Books, 1874-1880
  Medina County, Hondo: Records of Deeds, 1880-

NEWSPAPERS

Many newspapers of West Texas, New Mexico and Arizona were consulted for the general period 1870-1910, but the following were found to be by far the most helpful:

Austin *Tri-Weekly Gazette*, 1863-1865
Bisbee *News*, 1901; *Orb*, 1898; *Review*, 1901-1907, 1921-1922, 1937, 1941-1948
Douglas *Daily Dispatch*, 1903-1907, 1921-1922, 1937, 1941
El Paso *Times*, 1948-1950
Mesilla *Independent*, 1879
Pearsall *Leader*, 1927
Phoenix *Herald*, 1885
Salt Lake City *Herald*, 1878
San Antonio *Express*, 1875-1876; *Semi-Weekly News*, 1863; *Light*, 1951

Santa Fe *Daily*, 1890; *Review*, 1884; *Weekly New Mexican*, 1876-1877
Tombstone *Epitaph*, 1887-1892, 1926; *Prospector*, 1887-1898
Tucson *Arizona Star*, 1879-1882
Uvalde *Leader-News*, 1938
Willcox *Warblings*, 1887; *Southwestern Stockman*, 1885-1891

BOOKS AND ARTICLES

Very little has been published on John H. Slaughter, though brief mentions are made of him, his father, and the George Webb Slaughter branch of the family. In periodicals, brief and popular accounts of his sheriff days are occasionally found. The best accounts, touching on the Slaughter story, were found in the following publications:

Abbott, Carlisle S. Recollections of a California Pioneer (New York, Neale Publishing Co., 1917)

Adams, Ramon. Western Words: a dictionary of the range, cow-camp and trail (Norman, University of Oklahoma Press, 1956)

Arizona Biographical Dictionary (New York, S. J. Clarke Co., 1916)

Barker, Eugene C., ed. Readings in Texas History (Dallas, Southwest Press, 1929)

Barney, James M. "Bob Paul, Early Arizona Sheriff," in *Sheriff Magazine*, IX, Feb. 1949

Baughman, Jules. "Tombstone, Arizona," in *Mining and Scientific Press*, Nov. 23, 1889

Bechdolt, Frederick. When the West was Young (New York, Century Co., 1922)

Belisle, John G. History of Sabine Parish, Louisiana (Many, La., Sabine Banner Press, 1912)

Bishop, William H. Old Mexico and Her Lost Provinces (New York, Harper & Bros., 1887)

Branchstone, Mrs. Cornelia. Early Days in Texas (Galveston)

Breakenridge, William M. Helldorado (Boston, Houghton Mifflin Co., 1928)

Britzman, Homer E. "Trail's End," in *Arizona Highways*, xxv, November 1949

Brophy, Jim. "Memoirs," in Bisbee *Review*, May 27, 1934

Burgess, Opie Rundle. "Miner Foreman's Daring," in Bisbee *Review*, April 1, 1948

Burns, Walter Noble. Tombstone: an Iliad of the Southwest (Garden City, Doubleday & Co., 1951)

Burton, H.J. "History of the J A Ranch," in *Southwestern Historical Quarterly*, XXXI

Caldwell, Laurence. "John Swain Interviewed," in Los Angeles *Times*, Sept. 1, 1940

Chisholm, Joe. Brewery Gulch: Frontier Days of Old Arizona (San Antonio, Naylor Co., 1949)

Cleland, Robert Glass. A History of Phelps Dodge (New York, Alfred A. Knopf, 1952)

Clum, John P. "It All Happened in Tombstone," in *Arizona Historical Review*, II, October 1929

Colton, J.H. Guide to Texas, with a map (New York, 1839)

Consulich, Bernice. Article in 14th Annual Rodeo Edition of *Arizona Daily Star*, Tucson, February 19, 1938

Cook, James H. Fifty Years on the Old Frontier (New Haven, Yale University Press, 1923)

Cruse, Thomas. Apache Days and After (Caldwell, Idaho, Caxton Printers, 1941)

De Lara, Dan. South from Tombstone (Tombstone, privately printed, n.d.)

Dixon, Sam Houston. The Men Who Made Texas Free (Houston, Historical Publishing Co., 1924)

Douglas, C.L. Cattle Kings of Texas (Dallas, Cecil Baugh, 1939)

Dumke, Glenn. "Douglas, Border Town," in *Pacific Historical Review*, XVII

English, Jake. "Trail Drivers from Frio," in Uvalde *Leader-News*, XVI, no. 3, December, 1938

Farish, Thomas Edwin. History of Arizona (8 vols., Phoenix, 1915)

Fehley, Florence. Old Timers (Uvalde, Tex., Hornby Press, 1939)

Forrest, Earl R. Missions and Pueblos of the Old Southwest (Glendale, Calif., Arthur H. Clark Co., 1929)

Fulmore, Z.T. History and Geography of Texas as Told in County Names (Austin, Steck Co., 1935)

Genealogy of Tarlton Fleming of Mannsville, Goochland County, Virginia (n.p., n.d.)

Haley, J. Evetts. Jeff Milton: a Good Man with a Gun (Norman, University of Oklahoma Press, 1948)

Hall, Sharlot M. "Old Range Days and New in Arizona," in *Out West*, XXVIII, no. 3, March 1908

Hallenbeck, Cleve, and Juanita H. Williams. Legends of the Spanish Southwest (Glendale, Calif., Arthur H. Clark Co., 1938)

BIBLIOGRAPHY 347

Hamilton, Patrick. Resources of Arizona, 1881 (Phoenix, 1882)
History of Southwest Texas (1907)
Hogan, William Ransom. The Texas Republic: a social and economic history (Norman, University of Oklahoma Press, 1946)
Horn, Tom. Life of Tom Horn (Denver, Louthan Book Co., 1904)
Hunter, J. Marvin. "Lewis Strickland Tells Experiences," in *Frontier Times*, XIV, no. 1, October 1937
Hunter, J. Marvin. Trail Drivers of Texas (2 vols., n.p., 1920, 1923)
—— same: revised, 2 vols. in 1 (Nashville, 1925)
Keleher, William A. Fabulous Frontier (Santa Fe, Rydal Press, 1945)
Kent, William. Reminiscences of an Outdoor Life (San Francisco, A. M. Robertson, 1929)
King, Frank M. Mavericks (Pasadena, Trail's End Publishing Co., 1947)
Lauderdale, R.J., and John M. Doak. Life on the Range and on the Trail (San Antonio, Naylor Co., 1936)
Laxson, Crawford. "Personal Recollections of Big-Foot Wallace," in *Frontier Times*, XII, no. 4, January, 1935
Lockwood, Frank C. Pioneer Days in Arizona (New York, Macmillan Co., 1932)
Love, Clara M. "The Struggle of the Range Industry for Existence," in *Southwestern Quarterly*, July 1916
Lundy, Benjamin. Life, Travels and Opinions of Benjamin Lundy (Philadelphia, W. D. Parish, 1847)
McClintock, James H. Arizona (3 vols., Chicago, Lewis Co., 1916)
McKelvey, Nat. "Willcox, portrait of a cattle town," in *Arizona Highways*, XXVII, September 1951
Martin, Douglas D. Tombstone's Epitaph (Albuquerque, University of New Mexico Press, 1951)
Maverick, Mary A. and George Madison. Memories of Mary A. Maverick (San Antonio, Alamo Printing Co., 1921)
Mitchell, Hal. "Justice Jim," in *Arizona Highways*, XX, January 1945
Mullin, R.N. Some Locations in Downtown Tombstone prior to the Fire, May 25, 1882. (Toledo, 1916)
Myers, John Myers. Last Chance: Tombstone's Early Years (New York, E. P. Dutton & Co., 1950)
Page, George Hays. "Sabinal, Texas," in *Frontier Times*, XIV, September 1937
Proctor, Charles. "Murder at Slaughter's," in *Sheriff Magazine*, V, June 1946

Richardson, J.C. Article in *Frontier Times,* XVI, September 1939
Rynning, Thomas E. Gun Notches (New York, Frederick A. Stokes Co., 1931)
San Antonio Business Directory, 1871
Sloan, Richard E. Memories of an Arizona Judge (Stanford University Press, 1932)
—— same, ed. History of Arizona (Phoenix, Record Publishing Co., 1930
Sonnichsen, C.L. Billy King's Tombstone (Caldwell, Idaho, Caxton Printers, 1942)
Sowell, A.J. Early Settlers and Indian Fighters of Southwest Texas (Austin, C. Jones & Co., 1900)
Stillman, H.C. "Douglas Pioneer [Stillman] Favors Early Marriages," in Douglas *Daily Dispatch,* December 9, 1928
Twitchell, Ralph E. Leading Facts of New Mexican History (Cedar Rapids, Iowa, Torch Press, 1917)
Wade, Houston. A Book of Masonry, of Members Who Were in the Texas Revolutionary War (Houston, 1935)
Walters, Lorenzo D. Tombstone's Yesterdays (Tucson, Acme Printing Co., 1938)
Watson, Douglas S., ed. Santa Fe Trail to California, 1849-1852: Journal of H. M. T. Powell (San Francisco, Book Club of California, 1931)
Webb, Walter Prescott. The Texas Rangers (New York, Houghton Mifflin Co., 1935)
Wharton, Clarence R. Texas under Many Flags (4 vols., New York, Amer. Historical Soc., 1930)
White, Grace M. "Oliver Loving," in *Frontier Times,* XIX, April 1942
Zipf, Walter. "A Classical Helpmate: Mrs. John H. Slaughter," in Bisbee *Daily Review,* April 22, 1934
——: "John Slaughter, the Man Who Knew No Fear," in Bisbee *Daily Review,* April 22, 1934

Index

Index

ABBOTT, Carlisle S: 187
Abilene (Kan.): 83, 87, 91
Adams, Capt. George: ranger, 63
Agua Prieta (bordertown): 140, 275, 320, 330
Alamagordo (N.M.): 132
Alamo, Battle of the: 32, 37, 65, 88, 96
Agua Zarca (Mex.): 243
Alberta (Can.): 248
Albuquerque (N.M.): 157
Alkiting, G.W: 216
Allen, Billy: 66
Allison, Clay: 76
Altar River: 136
Alvord, Burt: deputy, 215-217, 227-228, 232-236, 239, 242-248, 262
Alvord, Judge: 242
Alvord, Mae: 242
Alvord, Will: 242
Alvorsen, Leonard: 161-162, 245, 263
American Customs House: 259-260
Anderson, Alex: 58
Anderson, Andrew: 290
Anderson, Blanche: 290, 294, 306-08, 311
Anderson, Charlie: 266
Anderson, Frank "Pancho": 273, 276, 290, 294-296, 331, 335
Anderson, Mrs. Josephine: 290
Anderson, Ruby: 290
Andrade, G: 138-139, 143
Anglo-Americans: 39
Animas Valley: 133, 164, 265
Anton Chico (N.M.): 106
Anza, Capt. Bautista de: 141
Apache Indians: see Indians
Apache Kid: scout and renegade, 263-267, 270, 300-301
Apache May "Patchy": 255, 303-311, 331, 335
Applewhite, Sam: 336
Arispe (bordertown): 241

Arizona: 27; Slaughter enters, 120, 132-133; early settlement, 135, 139-143; explorers, 135-136; Slaughter activities in, 138 ff
Arizona Pioneers Historical Society: 160, 162, 202, 204, 245, 267, 335
Arizona Rangers: 247, 319
Armstrong, Billy: 53
Army camps: 99
Arndt, F.W: butcher, 270
Artesia (N.M.): 124
Artesian wells: 143, 156-157
Ash Springs (Ariz.): 297-298
Aston Gulch, and Springs (Ariz.): 334
Atascosa County (Tex.): 58, 60, 79, 94, 111
Austin (Tex.): 39
Austin-San Antonio Road: 47, 90
Austin, Stephen: 31
Averill, Lieut. N.K: 302-303

BABE HAND'S SALOON: 66
Babocomari Ranch: 144
Baca, Leopoldo: prisoner, 228
Baldwin, J.H: ranch owner, 85
Baltierrez, Geronimo: bandit, 238
Bandera (Tex.): 78
Bank of Douglas: 171, 272, 277, 334-335
Barbados: 248
Barbed-wire fences: 322
Barker, Ed: deputy, 218
Barker, Eugene C: 75
Barnes, Jim: murdered, 66
Barnett, Joseph: 43
Barrock, James: 250
Bartlett, John R: 142
Bascom, Lieut: 169
Bass, Sam: outlaw, 213, 272
Bass, Lon: saloon operator: 272
Bastrop (Tex.): 46; cattle markets, 65
Basquez, Ramon: stabbed, 250

Batepito Ranch: 157
Baughman, Jules: 185
Bean, Judge Roy: 209
Beaver Lake: stockman's winter quarters, 95
Bechdolt, Frederick: 116, 139, 229-230
Beckwith, C.D: 271
Beckwith, John: 126
Beckwith Ranch: in New Mex., 279
Behan, Johnny: sheriff, 195-197, 209
Benavides, Capt: Texas Ranger, 62
Benge, Wake: cowboy, 136
Benson (Ariz.): 139, 166, 217, 229, 236, 247, 270
Benton, Jesse James: 265, 266
Bergin, Maj. Gen. William E: 63
Berry, Jim: 66
Bexar County (Tex.): 65, 90-91, 96
Billy the Kid: 24, 106, 108-110, 121, 124-126, 333
Bisbee (Ariz.): supplies for, 166; massacre, 207; murder near, 249; outlaw Finney at, 255, 257-259; business activity, 270-271, 277, 288; Dr. Greene at, 285; Gillman's store, 294; 203, 218, 239, 266, 336; *Orb* newspaper, 288
Bishop, William Henry: 185-186
Bittich, Capt. J: Texas troops: 62
Black, J.T: deputy, 298, 299
Black Maria: race horse, 207
Black River (N.M.): 116
Blackaller, Jim: trail driver, 64
Blake, John: 204
Blake, Tom: 170
Blunt, J.T: robber, 227
Board of Equalization: 277
Boise (Idaho): 133
Boller, Robert M: 204
Bonney, William H: see Billy the Kid
Bonneville, Capt. Benjamin: 168
Boot Hill: 253
Border ruffians: 34, 45, 86, 91-92, 150, 160, 228-229, 234
Bowden, Percy: police chief, 326, 329
Bowdre, Charles: 126
Bowie, Jim: 88
Bowie Station (Ariz.): 227
Bowman, Jake: killed, 175

Bouldin, Lillian East: 24
Boyle, Andrew: 126
Bradfield, John W: 204
Bramlette, M.H: 53
Brands on livestock: 78, 85, 87, 93-94, 107, 119, 136, 144, 146, 155, 166, 226, 323, 327, 334
Bravin, George: jailor, 247
Brazos River (Tex.): 87
Breakenridge, Billy: 200, 202
Brewer, Richard "Dick": 125
Bridges, Jack: killed, 172, 250
Brite, John M: 57
Bronkow, Estaban: killed, 182
Brooks, Joseph: robber, 227
Brophy, Frank Cullen: 23
Brophy, Jim: cowboy, 149, 170, 189-190, 222
Brophy, W.J: 271
Brown, Bob: outlaw, 247
Brown, Henry: 126
Brown, Patrick: 250
Brownsville (Tex.): 81
Bryant, Silas H: ran for sheriff, 250-251, 305
Bucareli, Viceroy: 141
Burleson, Col. Edward: 42
Burleson, J.R: 65
Burnett, A.B: 218
Burnett, Jim: justice of peace, 209-210, 248
Burnett County (Tex.): 62
Burns, Mrs. Hal: 289-290; see also Mae Watkins
Burns, Walter Noble: 116
Burton, H.J: 102
Burts, Matt: 246
Bush, William Henry: 193
Butterfield stage lines: 169

CABEZA DE VACA: 64
Cahill, Frank: 121
Caldwell, Matthew "Old Paint": 41-43
Caldwell County (Tex.): 44
California: 136, 141, 187
Calles, Gen. Plutarco Elias: 275
Calishier, Mrs: 331
Camp, Frank: killed, 65
Camp, Wilson: 61

INDEX 353

Cananea (Mex.): 232, 247, 276
Cardwell, Laurence: 137
Carey, A.B: cowboy, 281
Cajon Bonita (Mex.): 264
Carillo, Concepcion: 101
Carisoso, Ramon: 250
Carlsbad (N.M.): 32, 106; cowboy discovers Caverns, 117
Carr, S.L: 219
Cartledge, Isabelle Harris: 90
Casa Grande (Ariz.): 270
Casey Ranch (N.M.): 115
Cashman, Nellie: 185
Castalum, Juan: 250
Castle, Frank: 219
Castroville (Tex.): 65-66
Cattle: see Slaughter family; cowboys, trail drives, diseases, brands, outlaws
Cattleman's convention: 317-318
Cave Creek (Ariz.): 301, 305, 310
Central Meat Market (Bisbee): 271
Chacon, Augustin: outlaw, 230-236, 247, 335
Chang, Sam: murderer, 241
Charleston (Ariz.): 146, 151, 166, 200, 208-210, 217, 219, 229, 231, 238, 248, 335
Chattanooga (Tenn.): 286
Chavez, Amado: 121
Chavez, Arcadio: 330-331
Cherokee Jack: 201
Chicago: 60, 286
Chief Bowls (Cherokee): 37
Childress, Billy: 93-96, 111, 118
Childress, Molly Harris: 93
Chillis, W.J: 260
China Valley: 84
Chiricahua Apaches: see Indians
Chiricahua Cattle Company: 144, 161-162, 170, 173, 189
Chiricahua Mountains: 139, 261, 262
Chisholm, Joe: journalist, 169, 266
Chisholm Trail: 73
Chisum, Jim: 112
Chisum, John Simpson: 99, 100, 106-107, 111, 198, 225
Chisum, Pitser: foreman of Jingle-Bob, 112
Chisum, Sally: 121

Chisum, Will (W.J.): 24, 113, 115, 121, 198
Chiswell, Solomon: vigilante, 77
Christian, Bob (Blackjack): 261-262
Church, Amelia Bolton: 107
Cibola Ranch: 72
Circuit riders: 45
Citizens Safety Committee: 199
Civil War: 53, 64, 242
Claiborne, Billy: 136, 189, 190-195, 250
Clanton, Billy: 196, 198, 217, 250
Clanton, Ike: 196-197
Clanton, Phineas: 196
Clark, J.S: 249
Clarke, Mary Whatley: 37, 97
Clawson, Charley: 272
Clay, John: 298
Clayton (N.M.): 225, 263
Cleland, Robert Glass: 272
Cleveland, George: horse thief, 229-230
Cleveland, President: 178, 264
Cliff (N.M.): 262
Clifton (Ariz.): 227, 262, 297-299
Clum, John P: of Tombstone *Epitaph*, 198-199
Coahuila (Mex.): 31
Cochino Ranch: 80
Cochise, Chief: 135
Cochise County: 71, 95, 165-166, 171, 191, 256, 283, 285-286, 305, 330, 334; Charley Slaughter goes to, 117; Board of Supervisors, 154; county seat, 184; coroner's jury, 203-204, 214-216, 257-261; outlaws of, 208-209, 238-254; sheriff of, 211-214; deputies, 218-219; legislator from, 269-270; business in, 271-277
Cochise Station: 246
Cochlin, Tom: see Cochran
Cochran, Tom: 124-125, 136
Coe, George: 24
Coghlan, Pat: 127
Cohen, Dave: 193-194
Cole, R.E: 219
Coles, Charles H: curator, 221
Collins, Joel: outlaw, 213
Colton (Calif.): 196
Columbus (Ohio): 323
Columbus (N.M.): invaded, 276

Concho: whiskey smuggler, 161-162
Concho River (Tex.) : 87
Conlin, Hugh: 333
Contention (Ariz.) : 218
Conway, Thomas F: 100
Cook, Ben: 216
Cook boys: 58
Cook, Dr. Harold: 24
Cook, James H: 48, 83, 163
Cooke, Col. Philip St. George: 142
Copper Queen Consolidated Mining Company: 171, 239, 249, 271-272, 285
Coronado, Francisco Vasquez de: 135
Corpus Christi (Tex.) : 81
Cortes, Hernán: 55
Cory, Deputy-sheriff: 194
Cos, Gen: 61
Cosulich, Bernice: 124, 139, 242, 252
Cottonwood Canyon (Ariz.) : 172
Cottonwood Wash (Ariz.) : 297-299
Cotulla, Joe: 78-79
Cotulla, Simon and Paul: 79
Cotulla (Tex.) : town, 79
Cotulla Ranch (Tex.) : 78
Council House Fight: see Indians
Courtney, Frank: 298
Cowboy Dining Room: 317-318
Cowboy Saloon: 272
Cowboys: equipment, 44-45, 48, 56, 68, 74, 81-82, 151-152; cooks and food, 44-45, 56, 152; lingo, 56; lore, 74-75; rustler defined, 75; trail driving, 81-82
Coyle, James (Jimmy): 193-194
Crawford, Capt: 169, 178, 320
Crockett, Davy: 88
Crook, Gen. George: 176, 264, 319
Crouch, Col. B.L: 79, 81
Cruse, Thomas: 178
Cuchuverachi (Mex.) : 307
Cunningham, Mike: 271
Curly Bill: see William Graham

DAILY, GEORGE H: 205
Daly, James: badman, 249
Darnell, Andy: cowboy, 244
Darril, W.J: 204
Davis, Alex: constable, 232
Davis, Lieut. Britton: 169

Davis, George (alias Tom Jones) : 126
Daugherty, W.C: 94-95
Daugherty, George: 65
Dawson, Lieut. Byron: soldier, 128-130
Dean, E.H: barkeeper, 194-195
Del Rio (Tex.) : 67, 95
Deming (N.M.) : 137, 165
Devil's River (Tex.) : 87, 99, 111, 136
De Villis, Rev. John W: 71
De Witt Colony (Tex.) : 88
Diamond-A Cattle Company: 144
Diaz, President: of Mexico, 319
Dilley (Tex.) : 63
Dimmitt County (Tex.) : 112
Diseases: of Texas frontier, 45, 82, 92; of cattle, 74-75, 153-154; of Slaughter, 82, 133, 251, 331-332; malaria, 117; smallpox, 119-120, 123; of Indians, 167, 265-266; tuberculosis, 133, 265-266, 284, 320
Dixon, Sam Houston: 43
Doak, John M: 58, 148
Doan, Judge Fletcher M: 333
Doan's Crossing: 83
Doe, John: 250
Dodge, Constable Fred: 225-226, 229
Dodge City (Kan.) : 81, 87, 316
Dolan, James J: 126
Dolan-Riley faction of Lincoln County War: 108
Dominguez Oil Fields: 277
Double-Rod Ranch (Ariz.) : 144
Douglas, James S: 271
Douglas (Ariz.) : 151, 160, 245, 262, 279, 283, 322, 330; established, 271; Slaughter activities in, 271-272, 277, 332-336; events of, 275-276, 280, 284-285, 290, 311-315, 322-324
Douglas *Daily Dispatch:* 204, 208, 323, 329-330, 332, 336
Douglas Hardware: 284
Douglas Improvement Company: 271-272
Douglas Investment Company: 277
Downing, Bill: deputy, 246
Downing Ranch (Ariz.) : 237
Dragoon Mountains: 135, 147, 183, 185, 251
Dumke, Glenn: writer, 275, 277

INDEX

Duncan, David: murdered, 220
Duncan (Ariz.): 298-299
Dunlap, Three-finger Jack: 247
Dutch Bill: vigilante, 207
Dutton, Reilly: murderer, 219-220
Dyer, Consul: 330-331

EARP-CLANTON FEUD: 242; see O.K. Corral battle
Earp, James: 195
Earp, Morgan: 195-196, 250
Earp, Virgil: 195, 197
Earp, Warren: 195
Earp, Wyatt: 195-196, 200, 202, 205, 231, 253, 305
Earthquake: 154, 157-158, 164
East, James Henry (Jim): 103, 110, 277, 333
Echols, Ed: 24
Eddy, Charles B: 106
Edginton, Edward L: 132
Edwards, L.J.W: 72
Eldridge, Tobe: 72
Elfrida (Ariz.): 281
Elias, Francisco: Gov. of Sonora, 307
Elk Springs (N.M.): 128-129
El Paso (Tex.): 206, 255
El Paso & Southwestern Railroad: 324
Emanuel, A.H: 257
Emory, Lieut: 287
Empire Ranch: 144
English, Allen: attorney, 207, 253
English, Bud: killed, 65
English, Levi: victim of Indians: 65
Erie Cattle Company: 144, 154, 172, 226, 244
Erwin, Allen A: collection, 267, 273
Evans, Jesse: 126

FAIRBANK (Ariz.): 139, 218, 247, 252
Farish, Thomas Edwin: 172
Farrington, G.W: deputy, 218, 229
Fateley, Joe: cowboy, killed, 162
Federal government: 139, 142
Felix (or Felice) River: 128
Fiction writers: 186
Field's Seminary (Calif.): 284
Finney, Arthur "Pegleg": killed, 217, 255-261, 295

Fisher Apartments (Douglas): 331
Fisher, Arthur Jr: 288, 296, 307, 311
Fisher, Arthur Sr: 151, 288, 301-302
Fisher, Edward: 325
Fisher, Gerald: 325
Fisher, Jesse H: deputy sheriff, 151, 218-219, 223, 241, 296, 301-303, 311, 322, 331, 335
Fisher, Mary "Mamie" (Mrs. Jesse): 322-323, 325
Fitzgerald, Minnie Minus: 137, 286
Florence (Ariz.): 135
Fly, Camillus S: photographer, 253, 310
Fly Photo Gallery: 197, 305-306
Forget, Thomas: 249
Forrest Ranch: 171
Fort Worth (Tex.): 81
Forts: Bayard, 137; Ben Ficklin, 119; Bowie, 169, 178; Concho, 102; Ewell, 87, 102, 111; Grant, 123, 303; Huachuca, 179, 206, 217, 225, 236; Jessup, 31, 33; Marion, 179; Sill, 167, 180; Stanton, 101, 126, 129, 138; Stockton, 102; Thomas, 162; Sumner, 101, 107
Fortner, M.D: murdered, 76, 77
Foster, John: 225
Fountain, H.C: 58, 64
Fourr, Uncle Billy: 147, 168
Franklin, A.M: 202
Fraternal organizations: 186
Freeman, Alex: 219
Fremont, John C: 195
French, Jim: 126
French, S.W: 271
Frio Canyon: 59
Frio County (Tex.): 64-65, 79, 85; description, 87; 91, 93, 94, 101
Frio River (Tex.): 65-66, 72, 78
Friotown (Tex.): 32, 64, 66, 67-71, 80-81, 87, 321
Froebel, Julius: 142-143
Fuller-Fortino fracas: 245
Fulton, Maurice G: 24, 127, 129
Fyfe, Walter: cowboy, 170

GABILONDO: Edgardo, Hilario, Josephine, 307
Gabilondo, Rafael: 307, 333
Gabilondo Ranch: 288, 306, 324

356 SOUTHWEST OF JOHN H. SLAUGHTER

Gadsden Hotel (Douglas): 313
Gaines Ferry: 36
Galey, John H: 199; brothers, 199
Galey, Thomas Mellon: 199
Galeyville (Ariz.): 24; description, 200; 301; Militia, 200; *Bulletin*, 200
Galin, John: 225
Gallagher, Barney: killed, 112-116, 127, 224, 313
Gallen, Smith: 216
Gallup-Frazer: saddle makers, 255
Galpin Valley (Montana): 124
Galveston (Tex.): 189
Garcia, Manuel: chore boy, 325-331
Gardner, Thomas: 101
Garrett, Sheriff Pat: 109-111
Garrett, Pauline: 24
Gatewood, Lieut: 177-179
Gebbard Cattle Company: 300-301
General City Business College: 288
George, Joe: outlaw, 188
Geronimo: Apache leader, 263-264, 297
Giddings (Tex.): 78
Gila River: 142, 169
Gilbert, R.M: 113, 127
Gildea, Gus: 113, 126
Gillman, Lloyd L: 256-261, 294-295
Gillman Jewelry Store (Bisbee): 294-295
Gird, Richard (Dick): assayer, 182
Globe (Ariz.): 135, 228, 263
Gobles, Reese: 126
Goldthwaite (Tex.): 85
Goldwater & Castaneda's Store: 207
"Goodbye My Lover": sung by cowboys, 206
Goodfellow, Doctor George E: 157
Goodnight, Charles: 84, 99, 102
Gomez, Gen: 319
Gonzales (Tex.): town, 32
Gonzales County (Tex.): 41
Graham, Jim (cafe bar): 315
Graham, Mary (Mamie): see Fisher
Graham, William (Curly Bill): 200-201, 222, 261
Graham County (Ariz.): 299, 332
Graham party massacre: 105
Grand Canyon: 179
Grand Central Mines (Ariz.): 229

Grant County (N.M.): 257
Gray, Cora: see Cora Henry
Gray, Lou E: deputy, 219
Greeley: killed, 66
Greene, Addie Slaughter: 285-286, 290, 315, 316, 331, 334, 336; see also Addie Slaughter
Greene, Adeline Howell: 286, 334
Greene, John Slaughter: 286, 290, 331, 334
Greene, Doctor William Arnold: 285-286, 290, 315-316, 326, 329, 332, 334-335
Greene, William Arnold (Junior): 286, 290
Greene, William C. (Cananea): 210, 218, 232-233, 276, 304
Grigbaum, John: 333
Grimes, Billy: cowboy, 136
Guadalupe Canyon: 239, 241, 266, 307
Guadalupe County (Tex.): 79
Guadalupe Mountains (Ariz.): 135, 139, 302
Guaymas (Mexico): 138-139, 157, 220
Guffey, James M: 199
Guilding Star Mine: 277
Gulf of California: 138
Gulf of Mexico: 87
Gulf Oil Corporation: 199

HADDEN, Rube: 301
Hagerman estate: 107
Haley, J. Evetts: 102, 248
Hall, Benjamin Franklin "Doc": 239-241
Hall, Caleb (Collins): 126
Hall, Sharlot M: 164
Hallenbeck, Cleve: 141
Hamilton, Patrick: 200
Hamilton (Nev.): 124
Hampe family: 279
Hance, Tom: cowboy, 102
Hancock, Judge James C: 198
Hancock, Louis: shot by Ringo, 203, 205
Hand, Alfred: killed, 301, 305; cabin of, 310
Hankin, John: 335
Hanson, Peter: 261
Hardin, John Wesley: 213
Hardy, Robert: killed, 250

INDEX

Harkness, J.C.B: sheriff, 67, 80
Harkness, J.R.M: sheriff, 72
Harris, Eliza Adeline: first wife of John Slaughter, 87-94, 118-123, 282
Harris, Leasel Bobo: ranger and cattleman, 79, 87, 88, 91-96, 118, 131
Harris, Molly: see Childress
Harrison, Gen. William Henry: 35
Harrison County (Tex.): 38
Hatch, Bob: candidate for sheriff, 196, 211-212, 251
Hayden, Senator Carl: 23
Hayes, Pres. Rutherford B: 126, 195
Hays, Georgia Hiler: 46, 119, 282
Haynie, Justice: 298
Hash-knife cow outfit: 232
Hayhurst, Sam J: Arizona ranger, 248, 262
Hearne, Walter: kills Apache Kid, 266-267
Heath, John: lynched, 207, 242
Heck, N.H: earthquake history, 157
Hennessy, J.B: 216
Henry, Cora Gray: 281, 288, 296, 302, 304, 311, 318, 335
Henry, William R: hide buyer, 166, 288
Hereford (Ariz.): 144
Hermosillo (Mex.): 159, 331
Herring: mining interest, 277
Hermitage Ranch (Ariz.): 188
Hickey, Gus: 175, 264
Higdon, William M: 86
Higginbotham, R.J: 91
Higginbotham: Martha, and Toliver, 92
Hiler, Bill: 83-84, 118-119
Hiler, Jim: Silver City jailor: 265-267
Hiler, Robert (Bob): 154, 315-316
Hill, Joe (Olney): 126, 201, 203, 205
Hillman, Frank E: foreman, 314
Hillman Ranch: 163
Hindes, Caroline: 90
Hinds County (Miss.): 29
Hine, Charles T: 216
Hines murder: 249
Hinnaut, John Battavia: 102, 147-149, 159, 278, 294, 307-308, 317, 322-323
Hinson, Billy: 81
Hogan, Tom: 117
Hogan, William Ransom: 39

Holbrook (Ariz.): 207, 232
Holland, E: 298
Holliday, J.H. (Doc): 195-199, 202, 205
Holmes, Charles: 298
Hood, J.E: sheriff, 267
Hoo-doo War: see Mason County War
Hooker, Henry C: 145, 147, 165
Hooker, Mrs. Harry: 145
Honduras: 248
Horn, John: 222
Horn, Tom: hanged, 176-178, 266
Horsehead Bend: 61
Horsehead Crossing: 101-102
Hospital: 285
Hot Springs (N.M.): 84
Houston, Sam: 61, 88
Houston (Tex.): 189
Howard Wells: 93, 105
Howe, E.G: map maker, 271
Howell, Amazon "Cap": 123-125, 128-129, 146, 198, 221
Howell, Cora Viola: see Cora Viola Slaughter
Howell, Franke: see Stillman
Howell, James (Jimmy): 137, 151, 198, 237, 258-260, 286, 289
Howell, Rachael: 125, 131-132, 158, 279, 283
Howell, Stonewall Jackson: 206, 218, 226-227
Howell, Tommy: Tombstone jailor, 218
Howell Spring (Charleston, Ariz.): 146
Howell's Arroyo (N.M.): 279
Huachuca Mountains (Ariz.): 164, 183-185, 213, 222, 237
Hudspeth, Tom: saloon operator, 272
Hughes, Nick: 200-201, 217
Hughes, William: 329
Hunsaker, Lois: 188
Hunter, J. Marvin: 31, 86
Huston, A: 40
Huston Bayou: 36
Hutchinson, Sam: 74
Hyson, James (Hysaw): 126

IMMACULATE CONCEPTION CHURCH: 232
Indian Bend Ranch: 94
Indian Charley: 196
Indian Hot Springs (Ariz.): 151, 332

Indiana Historical Society: 127
Indians: 101; Comanche troubles in Texas, 37, 41-43, 47, 53, 58-59, 65-67, 82-83, 85, 90-91, 96; Lipan, 53; beef for reservations, 99, 107, 137, 164; in New Mex., 102, 105-106, 137; troubles in Arizona, 118, 135, 147, 153; Mescalero reservation, 125; Apaches, 132, 141, 145, 159, 167-172, 175-180, 182-184, 211, 288, 297-302, 335; Papago, 293 ;see also Apache Kid, Chiricahua, Geronimo, San Carlos
International Land Improvement Co: 271-272
Inyana, Istacio: jailed, 250
Irena, Dona: bandit, 238
Irvin: renegade, 126
Iturbide, Emperor Augustín: 140

JACKSON, Andrew: 61
Jackson, Charles: murdered, 38
Jackson County (Ore.): 181
Jails: 70-71, 241, 270
James, Ed: kills Apache Kid, 266-267
James, John: 266
Jeffords, Capt. Thomas: 169
Jennings, Bob and Bill: cowboys, 81
Jerry's Creek (Tex.): 57
Jesuits: symbols, 139-140
Johan or Johnny Creek (Tex.): 101
Johnny-behind-the-deuce: 205, 207
Johnson, Lieut. Carter: 264
Johnson, Crick-neck: 262
Johnson, David: 261
Johnson, Dick: robber, 227
Johnson, Otto: 191-192
Jones, C.J: 72
Jones, Charles L: 261
Jones, H.E: illegally jailed, 250
Jones, Haskill: 126, 130
Jones, James: 126
Jones, William: 126
Jones, Wynona: 31
Jones family: during Lincoln County War, 24, 130
Jornada del Muerto: 137

KANSAS: shipping center, 64, 73; drives to, 78; places enroute, 81; 83, 164-165

Kansas City (Kan.): 60, 165, 219
Keene, Jim: 266
Keleher, William A: 24, 265
Kelly, George H: 201, 323, 333
Kelton, C.B: 219
Kelton vs. Cochise County: 252
Kemp, H.S: 219
Kengla-Martin Saddlery: 153
Kennedy, Franklin Nashville: see Leslie
Kennedy, Thomas: 189
Kent, William: 265
Kerr, Hal: 264
Ketchum, Black Jack (Tom): 213, 225, 262-263
Ketchum, Sam: 262-263
King, Billy: cowboy killed, 244-245
King, Frank M: author, 115
King, Joseph Manuel: 147, 152
King, Sandy: hanged, 201
Kino, Father Eusebio: 136
Kitchen, Pete: son killed, 172
Kitt, Mrs. George: 23, 204
Kosterlitzky, Col. Emilio: of Border Rurales, 241, 319
Kotulla, Ed: 79
Kreighbaum, Jim: deputy, 219

LA CONIAS RANCH (Tex.): 96
Lagounias pasture: 94
La Grange (Tex.): 43
Lake, Stuart N: author, 196
La More, Vernon: deputy sheriff, 326
Land: 37; Rio Hondo claim, 37; state land office, 37; forgery of certificates, 38; price of, 39; Homestead law, 39; headrights, 40; grants, 64; under Mexican rule, 85-86; patents, 91; General Land Office, 117; Gadsden purchase, 142; court of land claims, 142; soldier's homesteads, 277
Lang, William: cattle buyer, 133
La Parita Creek (Tex.): 58, 64
Lara, Dan de: author, 239
Laredo (Tex.): 78; road to, 88
Larrieu, John: 225
Larrieu, L: 225
La Salle County (Tex.): 72, 80, 86-87, 101
Las Cruces (N.M.): 117

INDEX 359

Las Vegas (N.M.): 106
Lauderdale, R.J: 58, 148
Lavaca, Port of: 45
Lawless, Harden: 81
Lawton, Capt. Henry Ware: soldier, 174, 178, 179, 312, 320
Laxson, Crawford: 50
Laxton, Joe: trail driver, 80, 87
Leahy, Ed: deputy, 326
Lee: Chinese gardener, 319
Lee's Ferry: on Colorado River, 124
Leibson, Art: 267
Leona River: 87, 119
Leona Valley (Tex.): Indian depredations at, 66
Leslie, Buckskin Frank: 188-195, 205
Lewis, A.E: 204
Lewis, Jeff: cowboy, 136
Lewis & Buntzer: 96
Lincoln County (N.M.): 101, 104, 106, 108, 126, 136; War of, 24, 125
Little, Daniel B: 86
Little, John: 81
Livestock quarantine fences: 154, 281
Lockhart (Tex.): 42-46, 60, 71
Lockhart Springs (Tex.): 44
Lockling, Charles: 24, 206-207, 308
Lockwood, Judge Alfred E: 330
Lockwood, Frank C: 200, 289
Loma Vista (Tex.): 66
Long, J. Newton: 86
Longley, Wild Bill: hanged, 77-78, 213
Longwill, Doctor R.H: 120
Lopez, José: wanted for murder, 227-228
Lotritz, Joseph S: 250
Lott, Jesse: 58
Louisiana: 31, 117
Loving, Oliver: trail driver, 101-102
Lowe, Jim: 81, 95-96
Lowther, Tip: constable, 219, 249
Lowther, W.W: murdered, 219, 249
Lucas, Dan: 84
Lucas, George: 84
Lucas, John: 84
Lucero, Cesario: deputy, 239, 243
Lucerio, Tesano: 214-215
Lutley, William: 333
Lyle, Ed: outlaw, 236-238

Lynch, Frank P: constable, 219
Lyons, Ed: 58
Lytle, John L: 73, 93

MAE: Chinese cook: 318-319, 324
Machin, George D: deputy, 219
Macia, Ethel: 280
Macia, J.H: 23
Madero, Francisco I: 275
Magdalena (N.M.): 241
Magdalena River (Ariz.): 136
Mahill (N.M.): 128
Markheim, Art: 261
Marrojo, Librado: horse thief, 241
Martin, J.H: 219
Martin, J.M: 250
Mason, E.J: 190-191
Mason, Sarah Ann: 37
Mason County War (Tex.): 205
Massey, Calvin: wounded, 65
Mathews, H.M: 195
Matthews, Jacob B: 126
Maverick, Capt. Lewis Antonio: 62
Maverick, Mary: 62
Maverick, Samuel H: 62
Maxwell, James: 170
Maytorena, Gen: 275
Mackenzie, Gen. Ranald S: 179
McAffee, Bernard: 72
McClintock, James H: 248, 265
McClure, Jim: cowboy, 170
McConnell, Rev. Joseph: 285
McCormick, Mrs: store keeper, 232
McCormick, Nicholas: killed, 249-250
McCracken Silver Mines (Ariz.): 181
McDaniel, Thomas M: 93
McDonald, Bill: 83
McDonald, J.F: 330
McDonald, Muir A: 72
McGregor, J.C: 204
McKelvey, Nat: 209
McKenzie, Martha Isabelle: 92
McKinney, Frank: 204
McKinney, Joe: 80-81
McLaury (or McLowery), Frank and Tom: 197, 217
McMillan, Sam: 299
McSween, Alexander: 104, 108-109
Meadows, Russell: 275

Medina County (Tex.): 73
Mendibles, Carmen: 225-226
Merril, John S: 208
Merrill, Eliza: killed by Indians, 297-301, 309
Merrill, Horatio H: killed by Indians, 297-301, 309
Mescal Springs: 222
Mesilla *News:* scolds Wallace, 130
Mexico: 300, 301, 316; City, 157; Mexican War, 50, 53, 99, 170; Revolution, see Villa, 275, 322; Border Rurales, 236; officers, 247; sharecroppers, 152; employees, 182; soldiers, 176; Indian campaigns, 178-179; army, 319; trains, 248
Michelana, P: deputy, 219
Middleton, John: 126
Miles, Gen. Nelson A: 177-178, 319-320
Millet (Tex.): 63
Millet, Alonzo A: 101
Mills, W.M: 199
Milton, Jeff: 220, 247-248; wife, 221
Mimbres River: 137
Minshul, Asa: vigilante, 77
Minus, E.M: publisher, 72
Mission Conception Road: 90
Mitchell, Hal: 210
Monk, Edward R: deputy, 218
Monmonier, W.D: deputy, 158, 219
Montezuma Canal (Ariz.): 299
Montgomery, John: runs OK Corral, 242
Moore, Fred: 152, 187; feeds lawless, 188, 262, 264, 276, 281-282, 312, 318; deputy sheriff, 326
Moore, Mustang: killed, town named after, 65
Moore, Nancy: 29
Morenci (Ariz.): 231-232
Moreno, Eduardo: killed, 222
Morgan, James: 204
Morita Draw (Ariz.): 148
Mormon Battalion: 141
Mormon settlement: 297
Morphis, J.M: 41
Morse's Mill (Ariz.): 203
Morton and Baker: in Lincoln County War, 125

Mosher, J.E: butcher, 270
Mossman, Capt. Burton C: of Arizona Rangers, 22, 232, 319
Mud Creek: 57
Mud Springs: 262
Mule Mountains: 171, 182, 221, 271
Muk Hock Ching: 250
Mullin, Robert N: 24, 185
Murchison, Lonnie: 330
Murphy, J.W: 58
Murphy, Lawrence G: 108
Murphy, Owen: 269
Musgrave, Bennett: 90, 93
Musgrave, George (Black Jack): 267
Musgrave, Jim: 81
Musgrove, Calvin: 64
Myers, John Myers: 147, 252, 253

NACO (border town): 233, 247, 255, 276
Nacozari (Mex.): 271
Nash, Bill: 308
Natchitoches: 31, 43
Neagle, Dave: 194
Neatherlin, Doc: saddlemaker, 68, 85
Neatherlin, James Mabry: 59, 95
Nebraska: 164
Neighbors, A.S: 204
Neile, John: 64
Neill Family: Sam, Bob, Ben, Bruce, 81
Nevada: 248
New Mexico: day of the cowman, 99; Cook's Canyon, 100; Hondo River, 100; Bonita River, 100; South Springs, 111; Secretary of State's office, 117; range, 137; Playas Valley, 164; legislature, 212; 217, 226, 262, 276, 279; railroad holdup, 243
New Orleans: 60, 78
New York, University of: 285
Newton, Rev. William C: 71
Nichols, Charles A: 160, 222, 243
Nigger Head Gap (Mex.): 248
Nigger Head Mountain: 255
Nogales (Ariz.): 166, 243, 255
Nolen, O.W: 67, 80
Nooningham, Bess: teacher, 292
Nordleman, Mrs. Jacob: 248
Nueces River: 39, 78, 80, 83, 85, 90, 94, 96

INDEX 361

Nugent: Episcopal minister, 319

OAKDALE (La.): 117
Oakland (Calif.): 147, 284
O'Brien, Eli: 59
Oden, Dean: killed, 65
O'Folliard, Tom: 126
Ogden, James S: 40
Ogden (Utah): 133
OK Corral: 185, 196-198, 210, 217, 219, 242
Oklahoma: 240, 261
Old Bat: see John Battavia Hinnaut
Old Said: trail driver, 102
Olinger, Robert "Bob": 109, 279
Olivan, Antonio: 335
Olmstead, Frederick Law: 41
Olney, Joe: see Joe Hill
Oregon: 133, 136, 138
Oriental Saloon: 239
Outlaws: of Tombstone, 24; in east Texas, 38; Rundles, 66; Dancer, 66; Sam Bass, 75-77; Conchino hangout, 80; Henry Clay Johnson, Wesley Walters, William Dancer, John E. Gardner, Marion McBee, 80; 90, 112; Southern Company robbed, 100; wanted, 126; hiding places, 127; toughs, 133; James gang, 136; renegades, 150; *bandidos,* 159; of Cochise, 186; rustling, 187; principles held, 188-190; stage robbers, 196; stage robbed, 196, 198; Boot Hill, 197-198; Curly Bill gang, 201; cattle thieves, 202; graves, 208; hangouts, 209; American-Mexican, 210; 213-216; gunmen escape, 219; desperados, 220-238; 222-250, 325-331; rewards, 249
Overlock, C.A: 333
Owens, George: train robber, 247
Owens, Jake: 126
Owens, Louis: train robber, 247

PACKARD, Col. B.A: 148, 159-160, 171, 197, 314, 333
Paco, Lorenzo: 219
Padilla, Ricardo: prisoner, 228
Page's Blacksmith Shop (Tombstone): 239

Paley, William: alias Billy the Kid, 226
Panama: 248
Paradise (Ariz.): 290
Pardun, W.W: 218
Parker: thief killed, 267
Parker, James V: 299
Parks, Jim: sheriff, 236
Parks, John: 297, 300
Parks, W.H: 299-300
Patagonia (Ariz.): 236
Pearce (Ariz.): 118, 243-244, 262
Pearsall (Tex.): 46, 63, 87, 95, 149
Pecos Bill: legendary character, 217
Pecos River: 99, 101, 115, 119, 137
Pedregosa Mountains (Ariz.): 139
Peloncilla Mountains: 314
Peñasco River: 123, 125, 128
Pendleton (Tex.): 36
Penitentiary: of Ariz., 270
Perez, Ignacio de: 140
Perez, Pacio: murder suspect, 325-331
Perez, Rafael: fortune hunter, 140
Perryman, W.W: 93
Pershing, John J. "Black Jack": 261, 263, 276
Phelps Dodge mining interests: 271-272
Phoenix (Ariz.): 135, 143, 146, 284
Piedras Negras (Mex.): 290
Pierson, Ballard: 197
Pike, Zebulon: 136
Pilgrim, The: outlaw, 126
Pima (Ariz.): 297, 299-300
Pima County (Ariz.): 135, 146, 184, 205, 218
Pina, Gov. of Sonora: 330-331
Pittman, John and Elizabeth: 57
Placerville (Calif.): 145
Plaster, Uncle Billy: 187
Playas Valley (N.M.): 164
Pleasanton (Tex.): 89, 93, 321
Plum Creek (Tex.): 57
Poe, John W: cattle detective, 127, 131
Pomona (Calif.): 154
Pope, L.M.S: 91
Population: of Arizona, 135
Potter, Andrew Jackson: 71
Potter, Tuck: 172, 187, 283, 336
Powell, Buck: 126
Powell, H.M.T: describes Arizona: 141

Powell, James L: 336
Prescott (Ariz.): 135, 201, 217
Presidio Crossing: 65
Proctor, Charles: 329
Prohibition: 322
Purington, George A: commanding Fort Stanton, 129-130
Putman, J: 299

QUANTRILL, William C: 75
Quincy (Illinois): 288-289

RAGSDALE, R.S: 93
Ragsdale's Battalion: Texas cavalry: 61
Rak family: of Rucker Canyon, Ariz., 279
Rattlesnake Spring (N.M.): 116
Raum, George: saloon, 244
Red River: 39; crossing, 83
Reed, Mrs. Earl, Mrs. Walter: 301
Regulators vs. Moderators: 38-39
Reilly, John J: 193
Rheiner, Dan J: 64
Richards, Alfred: killed, 249
Richardson, Frank: 301
Richardson, J.C: 57
Richardson, John: 116
Riggs, Billy: cowboy, 170
Ringo, John: 24, 195-196, 201-202; coroner's inquest on, 203-207, 213, 250
Rios: Mexican cowboy, 256-261
Rio Grande Baptist Association: 71
Rio Grande River: 67, 78, 119, 137, 162
Rittenberg, William: scalped, 65-66
Ritter, A.J: tax collector, 219
Rivers: outlaw, 126
Roberts, Artie Slaughter: 32, 72, 123, 149
Roberts, Ed: 46, 63, 66, 72, 74, 96
Roberts, James E: 63
Roberts, Jeremiah: 43
Roberts, Joe: trail boss, 83
Roberts, William A: 81, 86
Robles, Guadalupe: bandit, 214; coroner's inquest on, 214-216, 250
Robles, Lola: 296, 306-307
Robinson, Bunk: 172
Robinson, Mrs. Ella: 23
Robinson, N.H: killed, 250

Rock Crossing: 57
Rockbridge County (Va.): 53
Rockman, Ed: deputy, 219
Rocky Arroyo (N.M.): 125
Rodriguez, Florentina: 250
Roe, Richard: 250
Rogan, Edgar Huntley: 44
Rogers, Blanche Anderson: see Anderson
Rogers, Will: humorist, 34; addresses oldtimers, 97
Rohn, Doctor: 320
Roland, Tad: cowboy, 136, 138, 151, 320
Roosevelt, Pres. Theodore: 263
Ross, John F: county attorney, 210, 330, 336
Roswell (N.M.): 99; named for Roswell Smith, 106
Roundup cooks: 152
Roy Hotel: in Douglas, 285
Rucker Canyon (Ariz.): 188
Rundles, John: outlaw, 66
Rush Springs: 57
Russell, Charles Marion: painter, 336
Russian Bill: outlaw, 201
Rustler: defined, 75; song of the, 253-254
Rustling Bob: 126
Rutledge, Ed: 81
Ryan's Ferry Crossing: 36
Rynning, Capt. Thomas H: ranger, 272, 319

SABINAL (Tex.): 81
Sabinal Canyon: 59
Sabine County (Tex.): 38, 40-41
Sabine Pass: 61, river tributaries, 36, 39
Sabine Parish (La.): 31
Sabinetown (Tex.): 36
Sac Hill: 171
Sacramento Mountain (N.M.): 125
Safford (Ariz.): 299
St. Charles County (Mo.): 124
Saint Denis: 65
St. Louis (Mo.): 60, 308; Fair at, 315
St. Matthews Military Academy: 289
Salado, Battle of: 53
Salcido, Pablo: 231-232

INDEX

Salcido, Tomás: killed, 225, 249
Salt Lake City (Utah): 133
Salt River (Ariz.): 142
San Angelo (Tex.): bank, 92
San Antonio (Tex.): 39; mail, 53; road, 64; cattle markets, 65, 67; 78; Edmund's college, 88; Gardner street, 90; Menger Hotel, 90; description, 90-91; River, 90; Pleasanton road, 93; 120, 160, 163, 178
San Antonio Ranch Company: 73
San Bernardino Building: in Douglas, 272
San Bernardino Market: 290
San Bernardino Mission: 139
San Bernardino railroad depot: 328
San Bernardino Ranch: 139, 140-143, 145, 147, 154, 158-159, 161, 164-167, 175-178, 184, 187, 209, 211, 217, 226, 232, 252; cemetery, 255; 256, 259-260, 264-265, 267, 275; illustration, 278; 279, 282-284, 288; school district, 288-289; 290-293, 296, 303, 308, 317, 319-321, 323, 326, 332, 334-336
San Bernardino Valley: 157, 206
San Carlos Indian Reservation: 137, 162, 202, 264, 283, 302
San Diego (Calif.): 137, 264
San Francisco (Calif.): 141, 185, 189, 219, 265, 286
San Francisco Mountains: 135
San Jacinto (Tex.): 88; Battle of, 50
San Juan Batista: 65
San Juan Canyon (N.M.): 267
San Marcos (Tex.): 92
San Mateo (Calif.): 289
San Miguel Creek (Tex.): 94
San Pedro River (Ariz.): 151, 182, 209, 304
San Pedro Valley: 135, 143-144, 200, 229, 261
San Saba Rangers: 63
San Simon Cattle and Canal Company: 144, 177
San Simon Valley: 205, 261-262
Santa Anna, Gen: 32, route taken, 65; capture, 88
Santa Cruz River (Ariz.): 136

Santa Fe (N.M.): 119, 157
Santa Fe Expedition: 43
Santa Fe Railroad: 134, 166
Sanders, G.W: 72
Sanders, R.A: killed, 65
Sanderson, Roy: 143
Sanderson, William G: strikes artesian water, 143
Scheerer, Jake: 24, 144
Schieffelin, Al: 181
Schieffelin, Ed: father of Tombstone, 138; birthplace, 181; Tombstone named, 182; body found, 183; epitaph, 183
Schools: 46, 288, 288-289, 292, 308
Schultz, Henry: robbed, 241
Scow, James: deputy, 218
Scurlock, Josiah G. (Joe): outlaw, 126
Sellers, John: deputy, 219
Selman, John: 126, 213
Seven Rivers (N.M.): 86, 101; cattlemen of, 105; 106, 113; lawless element, 116-117; 123, 127, 279
Shakespeare (N.M.): 201, 203
Shattuck, Enoch A: under-sheriff, 218, 229
Shattuck Denn Mining Corporation: 277
Shearer, W.D: coroner, 214-216
Sheehan, L.M. (Larry): robber, 227
Shelby County (Tex.): 38
Shibell, Charley: sheriff, 205
Short, Luke: customs inspector, 316
Showers, W.J. (Bill): deputy, 219, 229
Sieber, Al: scout, 178, 182-183, 213, 264
Sierra Bonita Ranch: 145; also see Hooker
Sierra Madre Mountains: 175, 179, 264, 266, 300
Silver City (N.M.): 100, 134, 146, 206, 265
Silver Creek (Ariz.): 139, 154, 161, 262, 281
Simmons, "French Tom": 225
Simmons, H.D: deputy, 219
Simonson, Rev. E.W: 332-333
Siringo, Charles: cattle detective, 127, 131
Sivell's Bend: 57
Skeleton Canyon (Ariz.): 177, 187, 266

Slaughter, Addie: 119, 120-123, 137, 159, 219, 282-284; marries, 285; dies, 286; 304, 305, 312; see also Addie Greene

Slaughter, Benjamin (Ben), father of John H: born, 30; married, 31; at San Jacinto, 32; sons born, 32, 33; leaves Mississippi, 32-33; Louisiana stopover, 33; 34-35; Slaughters of south Texas, 34; sees progress, 35; crosses Sabine River, 36; livestock and commodities, 36; land allotted, 40; at Lockhart, 43-44; appearance, 48-49; Texas Mounted Volunteer, 50-51; cronies, 53; Atascosa land, 58; pioneer furnishings of, 59; enlists State troops, 60-61; organizes minute men, 62; brands for each son, 59; philosophy, 63; whiskey to sell, 72; Fortner killed, 76-77; brand of, 72; customs, 73-74; hires cowboy, 79; at La Parita Creek, 79; herd gathered, 78; friends, 81; moves, 83; family marriages, 83-84, 88, 97, 163

Slaughter, Bob: 31

Slaughter, Charles Holmes (Charley) elder brother of John H: born, 32; parents, 31-33; marries, 60; Confederate soldier, 61-62; sells ranch, 64; rock house built, 69; in Frio County, 64; cowboys killed, 66; partnership, 72; sued, 72; San Antonio ranch brands, 73; trail herds, 73; markets livestock, 78; Wyoming-Montana treks, 83; sister marries, 84; children married, 84; disposition, 85; 86; niece is born, 89; land on the Frio, 91; in New Mexico, 100-102; views burned bodies, 105; after Sitting Bull, 105; pony of, 106; at Seven Rivers, 105-106; and Pat Garrett, 109; outlaws visit, 109; canyon named, 116; legislator, 117; in Arizona, 118; near Carlsbad Caverns, 117; dies, 117; defends Mormon settlers, 118; 136; Douglas property, 272

Slaughter, Christopher Columbus ("C. C."): son of George Webb, 34; honored, 37; president of cattle raisers, 97; valley named after, 97

Slaughter, C.C. (Junior): 31

Slaughter, Cora Viola: (see also Cora Viola Howell) 124; sees mate, 124; marries on trail, 132; honeymoon, 133; snow storm experience, 137-138; saved from Indian attack, 138; long life predicted, 139; 146; cousins, 151; 163; Doc Holliday escapade, 198-199; brothers, 218-219; memoirs, 222; cousin murdered, 225; with Lopez the bandit, 227-228; Lyle gang ambush, 236-238; rejects third term of husband, 252; relative killed, 265; politics, 269; real estate, 272; sees Pancho Villa, 275; stocks and bonds, 277; responsibility, 279; sharpshooter husband, 280-281; stepmother, 282; 284; wedding gift, 286; parrot of, 287; 294; takes Robles child, 296; Apache girl presented, 304-306; 307-309; poker parties, 311-312, 315-316; tantrums of rage, 317-318; kinsman marriage, 322-323; a real joke, 324; fatal tragedy, 325-329; husband expires, 332; at funeral, 333; will of, 333-335; death, 336

Slaughter, Eliza Adeline (Harris): 87-94, 118-123; see also Eliza Harris

Slaughter, Francis: early ancestor, 28

Slaughter, Frances Ann (Jones): 28

Slaughter, George: of Roswell, 27

Slaughter, George Webb: 29; son of William, 30; in Texas since 1829, at Alamo, 32, 37; as cattleman, 34, 57; freighter, 35-36; transports Houston library, 36; marries, 37; commemorated at Alamo, 37; land grants of, 39; Baptist minister, 45

Slaughter, Janice: 28

Slaughter, John (early ancestor): 29

Slaughter, John Horton: ancestry, 27, 29-31; born, 33; early to Texas, 40; schooling, 46-47; as cowboy, 56; in Atascosa County, 58; Confederate soldier, 60-62; Texas Ranger, 63; rancher, 73; trail driver, 78-79; cattle holder, 81; courtship and marriage, 88-89; partner with Childress, 93; sued, 94; to Devil's River, 99; to New

INDEX

Mexico, 111; at XIT, 111; kills Gallagher, 112-115; gambler, 118; first wife dies, 120-123; meets Viola Howell, 123-124; as wanted outlaw, 126; arrested, 128-130; second wife, 132; Arizona honeymoon, 133; buys San Bernardino ranch, 138-139; buys second ranch, 143-144; adopts Z brand, 146; quake causes havoc, 154-158; dangerous predicaments, 159-160; opens meat market, 166; Indian trouble, 167-180; relations with Geronimo, 177-180; beef market, 183; unmolested by rowdies, 198; elected sheriff, 211-212; kills outlaws, 214-216; deputies appointed, 218-219; Chacon sends threat, 230-231; house, 245; kills Finney, 256-261; trails Apache Kid, 265-266, 301-303; becomes legislator, 269; defies Pancho Villa, 276; home ranch activities, 278-297; son dies, 281; finds Indian girl, 303-308; tragedy strikes, 308-311; poker parties, 313-316; spat with wife, 317; breaks leg, 317-318; host to generals, 319-320; revisits Texas, 321-322; foreman Fisher killed, 325-331; dies, 332; funeral, 333; will and estate, 334
Slaughter, Minerva Mabry (Mrs. Ben) mother of John H: native of Alabama, 31; marries, 31; sons born, 32-33; to Louisiana via oxcart, 32-33; favors education, 40; among first settlers, 40; as country doctor, 45-46; lives near Friotown, 83
Slaughter, Minnie: see Veal
Slaughter, Nancy: see Tubert
Slaughter, Owen: 30
Slaughter, Rev. Philip: author of *St. Mark's Parish,* 28
Slaughter Ranch Inc: 334
Slaughter, Rebecca Wallen (Mrs. Charles): 60, 272
Slaughter, Reuben: 30
Slaughter, Robert: 27-28
Slaughter, Sallie: 32, 84
Slaughter, Simeon: 30
Slaughter, Solomon: 30

Slaughter, Thomas: 28
Slaughter, W.H: 84
Slaughter, Walter: Revolutionary soldier, 28-29
Slaughter, William: first Slaughter sheriff, 27
Slaughter, William Austin: 28
Slaughter, William James (Billy) eldest brother of John H: born, 32; 52; Confederate soldier, 61-62; sheriff of Atascosa, 63; buys ranch at Millet, 63; trail drive to Kansas, 64; cowboys killed, 66; as Mason, 67; restores public building, 68-71; his brand, 72; records ranch brands, 73; foreman found dead, 76; markets cattle, 78; hires Harkness, 80; description of, 85; daughters of, 86; cowhand marries, 87; properties, 100-101; 111; saves brother's life, 114; nephew named for, 118; trail drive out of Texas, 123
Slaughter, Willie: 90, 118, 154, 219, 228, 282-283; dies, 284; 286, 288, 331, 333
Slawson, S.W: 271
Slinkart, Burt: 266
Sloan, Eleanor B: 23
Sloan, Richard E: 145, 229-230
Sloan, Ross: of Skeleton Canyon, 146
Smith, Alfred: of Turkey Creek, 204
Smith, Beaver: 110
Smith, Benjamin F: of Turkey Creek, 203-204
Smith, Charlie: 225
Smith, Joseph: dies of gunshot, 250
Smith, Mark: attorney, 207
Smith, Rosa Anna: 204
Smith, W.W: 204
Smith, Walter: 83
Smissen, M.Z: 84
Socorro County (N.M.): 226
Soldier's Holes (Ariz.): 143, 218
Solomonville (Ariz.): 232, 236, 297-300
Solomonville *Bulletin:* 297
Song: cowboy, 206
Sonnichsen, C.L: 246, 248
Sonora (Mex.): 139, 159, 164, 175, 187, 225, 241, 243, 247, 264, 275, 277, 307
Soto, Jose: 229

Soto, Juan: desperado, 228-229
Southern Hotel: 48-49
Southern Pacific Railroad: 90, 166, 178, 208
Sowell, A.J: 58
Spalding, Oliver L. (Junior): 179
Spaniards: ponies of, 55; vaqueros, 56
Spanish-American War: 179
Speakes, Robert: 126
Speed, Jim and Steve: cattlemen, 79
Spindles, George: 313-314
Spohr, Mrs. H.H: 248
Stanfield, John E: 95
Stayton, Capt. John W: 58, 61; chief justice, 61
Stein's Pass: 226, 262
Stephens, George D: foreman, 24, 146, 160, 265, 267, 323, 335-336
Stephens, Nancy: 335
Sterling City (Tex.): 84
Sterling Creek: 119
Stevens, "Little Bob": gambler, 267
Stew, of cowboy: 56, 152
Stewart, William M: of Nevada, 208-209
Stidham, Ben: tried for rustling, 80
Stiles, Billy: outlaw, 232-236, 242, 246-247
Stillman, Mrs. Franke Howell: 295
Stillman, Horace C: 333
Stillman, Jack: 290
Stilwell, Cap: outlaw, 236
Stilwell, Frank: murdered, 196
Stilwell, W.H: district attorney, 222
Storms (weather): 47; cause stampedes, 74-75
Stowe, Edith: school teacher, 269-270, 285-286, 289, 290, 308, 325-326, 334
Strauss, H.B: 261
Sulphur Springs Valley (Ariz.): 108, 135, 137-138, 143, 157, 161, 170, 208, 241, 261, 282, 290
Summit Station (Ariz.): 147
Swain, John: trail driver, 136-137; tracker, 149-150
Sycamore Springs (Ariz.): 185

TACK, Mary: 187
Taft, Tim: 333

Taiban (N.M.): stinking springs, 110
Taiopa Mine: 139
Taylor, Hugh A: bronk peeler, 48-49, 85, 143, 160, 163; deputy, 219
Taylor, Isaac Milton: wagon boss, 86-87, 102; snake killer, 116
Taylor, Jack: train robber, 242-243
Taylor, T.U: 78
Terrell, Joe: ranch foreman, 298-299
Tex Spring (Ariz.): in Texas Canyon, 176
Texas: history, 24; independence, 32; Republic, 33, 41, 60, 74; admitted to union, 35; invaded, 50; wild cattle, 60; legislature, 61; state troops, 62; minute men, 63; early families, 65; crowded rangelands, 99; panhandle, 111; 151, 163, 187, 205, 217; Rangers, 221; 262, 272, 284, 321
Tewksbury-Graham feud: 207-208
Thomas, Allison: 219
Thomas, E.B: 58
Thomas, George: 305-306
Tilden, Ridjely: 216
Tobin: killed in Texas, 127
Toluca (Mex.): 157
Tom, Capt. John Files: Ranger-Indian fighter, 61
Tom Green County (Tex.): 262
Tombstone (Ariz.): mining camp, 138; road, 147; 157; growth, 183; description, 183-186; incorporated, 184; justice in, 187; recollections of, 187; old cemetery, 206; 209-210; distances from, 217; 219, 226-227, 231-232, 240-243, 253, 280-281, 284, 289, 305, 323, 333, 336; Tombstone canyon, 171
Tombstone *Daily Prospector:* 189, 218, 220-221, 225, 229-230, 241, 245, 249, 251-252, 254, 277, 303, 307, 320
Tombstone *Epitaph:* 165, 185, 196, 199, 208, 211, 221, 241, 248, 252, 277, 305-306
Tonto Basin (Ariz.): 264; War, 207
Torres Ranch: on Pecos, 102
Trail drivers: association of, 36, 81-83, 97; methods, 81-82
Travis, William B: defender of Alamo, 32, 37, 88

INDEX 367

Treasure: buried, 140-141
Treaty of Guadalupe Hidalgo: 141
Tubert, Nancy Slaughter: 77, 80, 84, 89, 108, 180, 262, 267, 272, 276
Tucson (Ariz.): 119-120, 135; Meyers Street, 152; 160, 204, 206, 221, 242, 267, 289, 296, 331, 335
Tula Ranch (south Tex.): 94
Tularosa: (N.M.): 131
Tunstall, John H: 128
Turkey Creek (Ariz.): 170
Turner, Marion: 126, 130
Tyler, Pres. John: 35

U.S. CAVALRY: 168, 174-175, 179; troops, 275-276; seventh, 303
U.S. Customs: line riders, 161-162, 176, 316
U.S. Department of Interior: 277
U.S. Marshal's office: 26
Utah: 297, 299
Uvalde (Tex.): 59, 71

VAIL BROTHERS RANCH: 144; company, 225
Van Nuys (Calif.): 294
Varela, Raphael: 225
Vasquez, Fernando: prisoner, 228
Vaughn, John: cattleman, 225
Veal, Minnie Slaughter: 29
Venezuela: 248
Victorio: Apache leader, 132, 138
Vigilante Committee: 77
Vilbiss, Tom: 64
Villa, Albino: prisoner, 228
Villa, Pancho: 275-276, 287, 320
Votaw, Billy: 85; cowman, 96; marries a Slaughter, 96
Votaw, Mary: 84

WACO (Tex.): 39
Waite, Fred: 126
Waldren, Calvin and Jennie: 68
Wallace, Bigfoot: 50; sketch, 53; 65, 89
Wallace, Jim: shoots Curly Bill, 201
Wallace, Lewis (Lew): governor, 109, 115; *Ben Hur,* 126; appointed, 126; letter from Slaughter, 128-129; orders arrest, 129; chided by press, 130

Wallen, Rebecca: 60; see also Rebecca Slaughter
Walters, Lorenzo D: 200
War of 1812: 29
Ward, Frederick: teamster, 204
Washington County (Ky.): 61
Washington Territory: 165
Water: 143, 147, 156-157
Watkins, Gladys: 290
Watkins, Mae: 289, 290, 293, 335
Watkins, Margaret: 335
Watkins, William E: 289-290
Watson, Douglas S: 142
Watters, J.L.T: 298-299
Webb, Walter P: 221
Wells Fargo Express: 238
Wharton, Clarence R: 58
Wheeler, Grant: outlaw, 189
Whetstone Mountains (Ariz.): 135, 164, 215-216, 220, 243
Whipple, W: 297, 299
Whitaker, Bill: cowboy, 102
White, Grace Miller: 102
White, Jim: finds caverns, 117
White, Thomas: 204
Whitewater (Ariz.): 264
Whitlock Mountains (Ariz.): 300-301; cienega, 300; ranch, 300-301
Whitney, A.M: 226
Wickenburg (Ariz.): 182
Widdowsen, A.M: 202
Wight, Arthur: sheriff, 299-300
Wilder, Lieut: 176
Wilkerson, L.V: 219
Willcox (Ariz.): 151, 191, 208; shipping center, 230, 232, 243, 245, 246, 317
Willcox, George: 81
Williams, Ben: police chief, 265-266
Williams, Dan: killed, 65
Williams, John S: 216
Williams, Judge Starr: 255, 257-261
Williams, Juanita H: 141
Williams, Henry W: 336
Williams, Marion L: rancher, 255, buys Slaughter ranch, 255, 334
Willis, Doctor G.C: 191
Wilson, Charles: 227
Windom, Lee: 298

Windom, Tom: 298
Winsor, Mulford: 23
Winters, James: killed, 65
Withers, Gus: 47
Wittig, Ed A: 261
Wolf, James: 207, 221
Woll, Gen. Adrian: 43
Wood, H.M: 333
Woodman, W.W: deputy, 219
Woods, Henry: 290
Woods, John: 299
Woods, Curtis: 335
Woods, Steele: 151, 290, 312, 322
Woodward, Charles B: 86
Woodward, Caven: attacked by Indians, 67; trail driver, 73, 80
Woolsey, King: 169
World War I: 296
Writ of habeas corpus: 330

YOAS, Bravo Juan: outlaw, 247
Yoast, John: 203
Youngman: indicted, 241
Yuma Prison (Ariz.): 189, 226, 228, 230, 248, 264, 270

ZABRISKIE: lawyer, 204, 206
Zavala County (Tex.): 80